CHILDREN'S BRITANNICA

CHILDREN'S BRITANNICA

Volume 13
Nitrogen to Philistines

Encyclopædia Britannica, Inc.

AUCKLAND / CHICAGO / GENEVA / LONDON / MADRID / MANILA
PARIS / ROME / SEOUL / SYDNEY / TOKYO / TORONTO

First edition 1960
Second edition 1969
Third edition 1973
Fourth edition 1988

© 1988, 1989, 1990, 1991, 1992, 1993, 1994, Encyclopædia Britannica, Inc.

International Standard Book Number: 0-85229-239-2
Library of Congress Catalog Card Number: 93-72368

Printed in U.S.A.

NITROGEN is a gas. It has no color, smell or taste, and will neither burn by itself nor help other substances to burn. Although it seems so lifeless, nitrogen plays a vital part in the lives of all living things. Nitrogen gas makes up rather more than three-quarters of the air we breathe, most of the rest being oxygen. When combined with other substances nitrogen forms compounds. These compounds may be nitro-compounds, nitrates, ammonia or ammonium salts, or the proteins, nucleic acids, and other organic compounds found in living things (see PROTEIN).

People and animals cannot obtain the nitrogen they need simply by breathing in the air containing it, nor can plants take in nitrogen through their leaves in the way they take in carbon dioxide. What happens is that plants get their nitrogen from the soil in the form of nitrates and use it in the production of proteins and other nitrogen-containing organic compounds. Animals eat the plants and convert the nitrogen compounds into substances required for their own growth, and renewal or repair. Animals cannot store excess nitrogen compounds, so these are broken down and expelled from the body in the animal's waste matter, or droppings. Farmers collect the droppings in a manure heap, which is spread over the land to give the nitrogen back to the soil. If the plants are not eaten, they die and rot, and bacteria and fungi change the nitrogen-containing compounds in them back into nitrates once again (see BACTERIA; FUNGI). Thus nitrogen from the soil passes through plants and animals, and back to the soil again. This is called the "nitrogen cycle".

There are some losses in the nitrogen cycle. The greatest loss is caused by returning only a part of the treated human waste matter to the land. In a country such as the United Kingdom, for example, the annual total of nitrogen in sewage sludge may be as high as 40,000 tonnes (44,000 US tons), but only about 40 per cent is returned to the land. There are also considerable losses from leaching (washing out) of nitrates from the soil as a result of heavy rain.

Some of the losses are made up by the action of certain bacteria found in leguminous plants such as beans, peas, clover, and alfalfa (see LEGUMINOUS PLANTS). These bacteria live in swellings called nodules on the roots of the plants. The bacteria take nitrogen from the air in the soil and change it into nitrates, which are taken up by the plants. This is called "nitrogen fixation". More important, the bacteria produce more nitrates than the plants need and thus enrich the soil. So farmers sometimes grow clover or another leguminous crop and plow it into the soil. This is called "green manuring". More often they spread the soil with natural manures (dung, leaf-mold or seaweed) or artifical ones (nitrates or ammonium compounds). (See FERTILIZER; SOIL.) A certain amount of nitrogen is added to the soil when high-energy bolts of lightning force atmospheric nitrogen and oxygen to combine forming simple compounds that dissolve in rainwater and thus fall to the ground.

For many years artificial fertilizers containing nitrogen were obtained from sodium nitrate. Ammonium sulfate, obtained as a by-product, or extra, in the manufacture of coal gas, was also used. Then the German chemist Fritz Haber found a way of making ammonia from the nitrogen in the air. Nitrogen obtained from liquid air (see AIR) is mixed with hydrogen gas. The mixture is then compressed and heated and passed over an iron catalyst that helps the two gases to combine into ammonia (see CATALYST). The resulting ammonia can be used to make nitric acid, and also nitrogen compounds, which are used as fertilizers. (See AMMONIA.)

NIZHNY NOVGOROD (formerly Gorky) is a major transportation and industrial center in western Russia about 400 kilometers (250 miles) east of Moscow. The city has grown up where the Volga and Oka rivers meet, and three important railroads now serve it. It is the capital of the Gorky *oblast* (region).

Nizhny Novgorod is one of the leading industrial cities in Russia. Motor vehicles, agricultural equipment, river steamers, machinery, wood products, and a wide range of consumer goods are manufactured there. The wood-products industries depend on great forests near the city.

Nizhny Novgorod has three quite different sections. The old city stands on the right side of the River Volga, about 120 meters (400 feet) above the river. In the old city are a 16th-century kremlin (fortress) and watchtower, and modern government buildings. At the base of the hills, on the right banks of both the Volga and the Oka, is the modern city center. The city's shopping center and commercial institutions are located there. Across the Oka lies the new, industrial part of the city, with factories, a harbor, and warehouses. A great bridge connects the industrial part with the older part of the city. The city area is well served by a network of railroads. The main streets are wide and well paved. There is a university which gives special training in medicine, agriculture, and engineering.

Nizhny Novgorod was founded in 1221 by local princes, who built a fort on one of the hills that is now part of the old city. Historically it is best remembered for the great trade fairs that were held there between 1817 and 1917. They were the largest and most important in Russia. The city's name was changed in 1932 to Gorky, in honor of the Russian novelist Maxim Gorky, who was born there in 1868 (see GORKY, MAKSIM). The name was changed back to Nizhny Novgorod in 1991. The population of Nizhny Novgorod is 1,445,000 (1991), making it the fourth largest city in Russia.

NOAH, whose story is told in the Book of Genesis (chapters five to nine), in the Old Testament of the Bible, was the son of Lamech and tenth in descent from Adam.

The story tells how God became sorry that he had created people because they had become so wicked. He therefore decided to destroy the Earth with a great flood. However, Noah was a good man and God did not wish to destroy him, so he told Noah to build a large ship called an ark and to take into it his wife, his sons Shem, Ham, and Japheth with their wives and at least two of every kind of beast, bird, and insect.

Then came the great flood (see FLOOD, THE)

Sonia Halliday Photographs

Noah loads two of every species of animal into the ark. From a 17th-century stained glass window.

and the ark floated away. As the water subsided, the ark came to rest on Mount Ararat (near what is now the eastern border of Turkey). Noah opened the window and let out a dove but it returned, finding no dry land on which to alight. After seven days he sent it out again and in the evening it returned, carrying in its beak an olive leaf. After waiting another seven days he sent it out a third time and, as it did not return, Noah knew that it had found dry land. God then told Noah to leave the ark and to take with him his wife and family, and the animals. God promised that he would never again destroy the Earth by a flood and to remind people of this promise he set his bow (a rainbow) in the clouds.

NOBEL PRIZES are six prizes that can be awarded to people of any country who are considered to have done the best work in the fields of physics, chemistry, physiology or medicine, literature, and economics, and for the cause of peace. The prizes are paid for out of the income from money left by Alfred Nobel (1833–96), the Swedish scientist who invented dynamite.

Everyone who wins a Nobel Prize receives a gold medal, a diploma stating what they have done to win the prize, and a sum of money. Prizes in the same subject may be divided among two or three people or they may not be awarded at all if no outstanding work has been done.

The awards are made on the recommendations of four learned societies. Three of them are Swedish: they are the Royal Swedish Academy of Sciences, which awards the prizes for physics, chemistry, and economics; the Royal Caroline Medico-Chirurgical Institute, which awards the prize for physiology or medicine; and the Swedish Academy, which awards the prize for literature. The fourth body is the Norwegian Nobel Committee, which awards the peace prize. Presentation of the prizes takes place in Stockholm, except for the peace prize, which is presented in Oslo.

Some Famous Prizewinners

Many famous people have been Nobel prizewinners. The physics prize has been awarded to such well-known people as Pierre and Marie Curie, the discoverers of radium (1903); Guglielmo Marconi, inventor of radio (1909); Max Planck, who discovered that energy only exists in particular amounts, called quanta (1918); Albert Einstein, who evolved the theory of relativity (1921); and Niels Bohr, a Danish physicist, for his work on the structure of the atom (1922). More recently the prize has been awarded to the West German Klaus von Kitzing for discovering an exact method for measuring electrical resistance (1985); and to the Canadian Richard Taylor and the Americans Jerome Friedman and Henry Kendall, for their work on quarks, the particles that make up protons, neutrons and electrons (1990).

Winners of the prize for chemistry include Lord Rutherford for his work on radioactivity (1908) and Marie Curie, who received her second Nobel prize in 1911. More recently, the prize has been won by the American scientists Willard Libby for developing radiocarbon dating (1960) and Elias Corey for his work in synthesizing chemical compounds (1990).

Among famous physiologists and doctors who have gained prizes are the Canadian Sir Frederick Banting for the discovery of the drug insulin (1923); Sir Alexander Fleming and Ernst Chain, both of Britain, with the Australian Lord Florey, for discovering penicillin (1945); the American James Watson and Britons Francis Crick and Maurice Wilkins for discovering the molecular structure of DNA (1962); and fellow Americans Michael Bishop and Harold Varmus for their study of cancer-causing genes (1989).

The prize for literature has been awarded to the following, among others: the English writer Rudyard Kipling (1907); the Indian poet Rabindranath Tagore (1913); the Irish poet W.B. Yeats (1923) and dramatist George Bernard Shaw (1925); the German novelist Thomas Mann (1929); the Italian dramatist Luigi Pirandello (1934); the British poet T.S. Eliot (1948), who was born in America; the English philosopher Bertrand Russell (1950); the English statesman and historian Winston Churchill (1953); the American novelist Ernest Hemingway (1954); the French novelist Albert Camus (1957); the Russians Boris Pasternak (1958) and Alexander Solzhenitsyn (1970); and the Nigerian novelist and playwright Wole Soyinka (1986).

The prize for furthering the cause of peace has been won by societies such as the International Red Cross, Amnesty International, and the United Nations peace-keeping forces. It has been awarded to statesmen such as the Americans Theodore Roosevelt (1906) and Woodrow Wilson (1919); Austen Chamberlain of Britain (1925); the Canadian Lester Pearson (1957), and Willy Brandt of West Germany (1971). It was awarded to the German missiondoctor Albert Schweitzer (1952); American civil rights leader Martin Luther King, Jr. (1964); Russian scientist and dissident Andrey Sakarov (1975); Mother Teresa of Calcutta (1979); Lech Walesa of Poland (1983); and Soviet president Mikhail Gorbachev (1990).

The economics prize was first awarded in 1969, to the Norwegian Ragnar Frisch and Dutchman Jan Tinbergen. In 1976 it was awarded to the American economist Milton

Sonia Halliday Photographs

San hunters return with their kill. Once all the San were nomadic hunter-gatherers, although today most herd cattle.

Friedman, and Robert Solow, also American, received it in 1987.

NOMAD. Nomads are groups of people who move around from place to place with their possessions, instead of building permanent houses and settling in one place. The term *nomad* is from the Greek word meaning "to pasture". "Nomad" originally referred only to pastoral people, that is people who kept livestock and who moved around in search of grazing land for their animals. However, "nomad" now covers all groups of people who move around, whether they have livestock or not.

Nomads can be broadly grouped into hunter-gatherers and pastoral nomads.

Hunter-Gatherers

Hunter-gatherers are people who wander about in small groups (of between about 30 and 100 people) within an area they know quite well, collecting food – usually roots and vegetables – and hunting small animals, and, in some cases, fishing. About 12,000 years ago, all the Earth's inhabitants lived by hunting and gathering, but today there are only a few full-time hunter-gatherers left. They all inhabit parts of the world where it is difficult to cultivate crops or raise animals for food. In most cases, the men do the hunting and the women gather the food. Within the territory in which they move, they know where waterholes are located, and where edible plants can be found. Hunter-gatherer groups today include the Pygmy, Hadza, and San (Bushmen) of Africa; some groups of American Indians and Australian Aborigines; and several isolated communities in the Philippines and Malaysia.

Pastoral Nomads

Traditionally, pastoral people moved with all their belongings and their livestock in fairly large groups. There are many more pastoral nomadic people in the world today than there are hunter-gatherers, although they, too, have decreased in numbers. Not many pastoral people are still truly nomadic, and some spend the greater part of their lives in settled communities.

Some pastoral nomads, or pastoralists, live for most of the year in one area, where they may also do some cultivating, or obtain part of their food from agricultural neighbors in exhange for animal produce. They move elsewhere for short periods in order to find suitable grazing ground for their animals. These are regular seasonal migrants. Other pastoralists move about in a more irregular fashion, depending on the availability of adequate pasture for their herds. Like the hunter-gatherers, pastoralists know where there is likely to be good grazing land, where there are wild crops growing, and where there is water. Pastoral groups include the Bedouin of the Arabian deserts, the Fulani of West Africa, and the Masai of Kenya.

For thousands of years pastoral nomads were able to move about freely. Over time they were able to control vast tracts of land in Asia and Africa, and they dominated and sometimes displaced the earlier settlers. Also, since domestic animals could be used as transportation, many pastoralists traveled great distances, and were involved in trade. However, the pastoral life-style was threatened when countries with fixed borders were created.

Since they were no longer able to move away from an area during times of drought, many pastoralists fell victim to famine. In Africa during the severe drought years of the 1970s and 1980s, for example, pastoralists were more vulnerable to starvation than ever before.

NORFOLK is one of the largest counties in England. It lies in the east, surrounded by the North Sea on its curving north and east coasts. On the northwest is the county of Lincolnshire; on the west is Cambridgeshire; and on the south is Suffolk. The county has an area of 5,368 square kilometers (2,073 square miles) and a population of 736,700 (1991).

Much of Norfolk is low-lying, with some areas below sea-level, but there are gentle hills in the west and north, and steep, crumbling cliffs along parts of the coast.

Dr. Alan Beaumont

Hickling Broad, the largest of the Norfolk Broads, is known for its rare plants, butterflies, and migrant birds.

Dr. Alan Beaumont

The Broads, or lakes, area of Norfolk is a popular vacation spot for boaters. This is Ranworth Broad.

Norfolk has five distinct areas: Fenland, Broadland, Breckland, the coastal marshes, and central Norfolk. The Fenland is a large, flat area of rich soil in the west. It was once marsh, but the water has been drained away and it is now among the best areas of farmland in Britain. In eastern Norfolk is Broadland, named after the many "broads" or lakes in the valleys of the rivers Bure, Yare, and Waveney.

The broads are flooded peat cuttings, dug chiefly during the Middle Ages and now popular for boating vacations. Breckland, in the southwest, is named after its brecks, or large fields. On the north coast are large salt marshes washed by high tides and protected from the sea by sand dunes and pebble beaches. In central Norfolk the soil is mainly clay. This area was once largely forest, and still has many trees, but is now fertile farmland. The main rivers of Norfolk are the Yare and the Great Ouse.

Towns and Industries

The largest town in Norfolk is Norwich, the county town. It is the center of government and industry, and the site of the University of East Anglia. Its Norman cathedral was part of a Benedictine monastery and its Norman castle is well preserved. Great Yarmouth and King's Lynn, both ports, are two other fairly large towns. Great Yarmouth is on the east coast, by the River Yare, and has become a center for North Sea oil and gas exploration. It is also famous as a tourist resort. King's Lynn, a market town, is on the River Ouse in the west of the county, close to the large inlet of sea called the Wash. The town is an important market for west Norfolk and has many old buildings, including two medieval guildhalls and two magnificent churches. East Dereham, almost in the center of Norfolk; Swaffham to the west; and Diss, on the border of Norfolk and Suffolk, are also market towns.

In Broadland, many small places such as Wroxham, Potter Heigham, Acle, and Reedham are centers for yachting vacations, and the broads are also famous for fishing and for observing wildfowl. Along the north coast are several vacation resorts, including Cromer, Sheringham, Hunstanton, and Wells-next-the-Sea.

Norfolk is otherwise mainly a farming county, growing barley, wheat, and oats on the uplands, and potatoes, celery, soft fruits, apples, and flowers in the fens. Sugar beet is an important crop. Cattle are fattened on the marshes of east Norfolk and some sheep can still be seen on the uplands of the west.

History

At Grimes Graves are flint mines dug during the Stone Age, and on the county's heathlands are round barrows showing where Bronze Age people buried their dead. During the 1st century AD, Norfolk was the home of a people called the Iceni. When the Romans tried to seize their kingdom, the queen, Boudicca (or Boadicea), led an uprising which nearly destroyed Roman government in Britain (see BOUDICCA). Norfolk later formed part of the Anglo-Saxon kingdom of East Anglia and in the Middle Ages, more people lived in Norfolk than in any other part of England. Rich farmers and wool merchants built the great churches that can be seen today in many small villages. Great monasteries were also founded, and thousands of pilgrims visited the famous shrine of Our Lady of Walsingham.

Famous people of the county include Thomas Coke (Coke of Norfolk) who did much to improve agriculture in the 18th century. Sir Robert Walpole, England's first prime minister, was born in 1676 at Houghton near Walsingham, and Elizabeth Fry, the prison reformer, at Norwich in 1780.

NORMANDY is a region of north central France. It is divided into the *départements* (local government areas) of Manche, Calvados, Seine-Maritime, Eure, and Orne. In the 10th century the region was settled by Vikings from Norway and Denmark. They became known as Normans, and made the region (which became known as Normandy) into a powerful dukedom, and adopted Christianity and the French language and customs. Their dukes later became the kings of England, who finally lost Normandy to France in 1450.

J. R. Karrach

The Gothic cathedral at Bayeux, Normandy. The town is also home to the famous Bayeux Tapestry.

Many Normans are farmers, growing grain and fruit, especially apples, on their fertile lands, and breeding cattle and horses. The coastal plain of Calvados produces a famous apple brandy bearing its name, and it is also an important dairy farming district producing the cheese called Camembert. Along the coast there are many fishing villages as well as attractive seaside resorts such as Trouville and Deauville. Iron is mined near Caen and there are manufacturing and shipbuilding industries, as well as textile factories making cotton, woolen, and linen goods in Rouen and several other towns.

The chief towns of Normandy are Rouen on the River Seine, Caen on the River Orne (and a major port), and two great seaports at Cherbourg and Le Havre. The typical Norman town is a busy market center where the farmers from the surrounding country areas sell their produce.

In World War II the beaches of Normandy between St. Vaast and the mouth of the Orne were chosen by the Allied forces fighting Hitler for their invasion of Europe in June 1944. Bayeux was the first town in France to be liberated (see WORLD WAR II). In the fighting tremendous damage was caused in Caen, Lisieux, Falaise, and several other Norman towns.

NORSE LEGENDS. Few nations have possessed a greater gift of story-telling than the Norsemen, the ancestors of the people who today live in the Scandinavian countries of Denmark, Sweden, Norway, and Iceland. There are Norse tales of outlaws and heroes, of ghosts and dragons, of sea-kings and peasant farmers, of love and adventure; but perhaps the most interesting of all are the legends of the gods who used to be worshipped in Scandinavia.

The same gods, under slightly different names, were once worshipped by many other peoples, including the ancestors of the English and German nations, but here only scattered traces of the mythology remain. In Scandinavia, especially in the remote island of Iceland, Christianity was not established until the year 1100, or even later, by which time the legends had taken a firm hold on people's minds. The fullest and clearest picture of the Norse gods is given in two Icelandic collections of tales called the *Edda*.

The Gods of the Norsemen

The Norsemen thought of their gods as like human beings but larger than life. They ate and slept, they were born and they died, they felt love and hate, fear and wonder, they could

Michael Holford

This picture stone, dating from the 8th century, shows a warrior in Valhalla, the paradise of slain heroes.

be surprised by treachery or overcome in battle.

Foremost among them were the Aesir-gods who lived in a mysterious dwelling-place in the heavens called Asgard. Of these the chief was Odin, All-Father of gods and people, lord of the sky, and ruler of the dead, who received in his great hall Valhalla the spirits of warriors slain in battle. He bestowed the gift of song on poets and was skilled in all magic. Odin was pictured as an old white-bearded man in a cloak which changed its color like the sky. He had only one eye, for he had sacrificed the other as the price of a drink from the god Mimir's well of wisdom. At Odin's feet crouched two wolves, on his shoulders perched the two ravens Thought and Memory, and his eight-legged steed Sleipnir ran swifter than the wind. His wife was the queenly Frigg, goddess of the fruitful earth, but several tales told of Odin's love affairs with other goddesses or with human women.

Of Odin's many sons the most powerful was Thor (Thursday is "Thor's-day"), with his red beard and magic belt of strength. In his iron-gloved hands he wielded the mighty hammer Mjolnir whose strokes flashed in the lightning, while the rolling thunder was the sound of his chariot-wheels. He was the champion of gods and people against the evil race of the giants and many were his fights and adventures in Giantland. Thor's wife was the golden-haired Sif, goddess of harvest and the family. Third among the chief gods was the war-god Tyr, who protected men in battle. His name survives in our word Tuesday.

Michael Holford

Odin watches as his son Balder descends into the underworld in the arms of a prophetess. This painting, by the 18th-century artist Fuseli, illustrates the poem "The Descent of Odin" by Thomas Gray.

An important but rather puzzling figure was Odin's brother Loki. He began as a fire-god, but in the *Edda* was usually a mischief-maker, half-ally, half-enemy, feared for his cunning and disliked for his ill-nature, though his quick wit sometimes made him a useful companion. He could change his shape at will, appearing sometimes as an animal, sometimes as a human being. He had three monstrous children—Hel, Queen of the underworld, the terrible wolf Fenrir who was bound in chains by the gods (although not before he had bitten off Tyr's right hand), and the Midgard serpent, who was believed to lie coiled round the world in the depths of the sea which he lashed into storms with his tail.

Loki's worst deed was to cause the death of Odin's son Balder, the beloved young god of the sunshine. His mother Frigg made every creature promise not to harm him, but she overlooked the mistletoe, which Loki then formed into a dart by which Balder was killed. All creation mourned him and the angry gods chained Loki in torment to a rock till the end of time.

Other, less important, gods were the wise Mimir, Heimdall the sentinel, Njord the sea-god, Idun goddess of youth, and the singer Bragi. There were also Njord's two children Frey, the lord of life, and Freya, the goddess of love. Day and night, sun and moon, fire and wind, dawn and twilight, mist and snow, all had their own god or goddess. There were frost- and mountain-giants, cave-dwelling dwarfs and elf-smiths, trolls who rode the house-tops at night, and spirits who howled in the wind.

The Creation and the World's End

Like nearly every nation, the Norsemen had a story of the creation of the world. In the beginning of things all was emptiness and confusion. First the gods were created and then the world was shaped from the body of a huge giant. The arch of heaven was his skull, which rested on the shoulders of four strong dwarfs at the world's corners. The Earth, called Midgard, was flat and washed on all sides by the ocean in which lay the Midgard serpent. It was supported by the great ash-tree Yggdrasil, whose topmost branches touched Asgard, while its roots in the underworld were watered by Mimir's well and by the fountain of the three Norns, or Fates. The human race sprang from two beings, Ask and Embla, who were fashioned by the gods from logs of wood.

There was also a story of the end of the world—Ragnarok, the Twilight of the Gods. Then Loki and the wolf Fenrir would free themselves, the giants would attack Asgard, the Ship of Death would break loose, the Midgard serpent would rise from the sea, and the mountains would tremble. A last great battle would be waged between the gods and their enemies, in which all would perish alike, slaying and being slain, and the world with all the people would be swallowed up by fire.

Then, however, a new age would dawn; Balder would return and a second Earth would rise bright from the ashes of the old.

See also MYTH AND LEGEND.

NORTH AMERICA is the northernmost of the two continents of the western hemisphere. It is connected with South America by a narrow strip of land called the Isthmus of Panama. North America is third in size and fourth in population among the continents. It has an area of 24,229,883 square kilometers (9,355,182 square miles) and a population of 376,347,000 people. Its population density of about 15.5 persons per square kilometer (40 persons per square mile) is low compared with Asia and Europe.

On the continent are Canada and the United States (not including Hawaii). Even though Mexico and the Central American countries are often called Central America, they are part of the North American continent. (See CENTRAL AMERICA.) The West Indies, St. Pierre and Miquelon, and Greenland are also a part of the North American region.

Only Asia has as many different types of climate as North America. Climates range from the bitter cold tundra along the Arctic coast of Canada to the hot, wet tropical rainforests found in Central America.

Alaska and northwestern Canada have short, cool summers, long, cold winters, and little rain. Northeastern United States and southeastern Canada have warm summers, cold winters, and moderate rainfall. The Labrador current and the Gulf Stream have an important effect on the climate in this area. Southeastern United States is warm and humid (see ATLANTIC OCEAN; GULF STREAM).

From California to Alaska the mountainous coastal belt receives moderate rainfall brought by winds from the Pacific Ocean. Higher up the slopes there is heavier rainfall. The air from the Pacific is dry after crossing the mountains. Thus, a large region east of the Sierra Nevada and Cascade ranges receives little rainfall.

Much of Mexico is hot and dry. The Pacific Coast from central Mexico into Panama has hot summers, warm winters, and most rainfall during the summer. The Atlantic Coast has hot weather and heavy rainfall the whole year round.

Mountains

Mountain belts along the east and west sides of North America surround a great central plain. In the eastern part of the continent are the Laurentian and the Appalachian Mountains. The Appalachians, a chain of

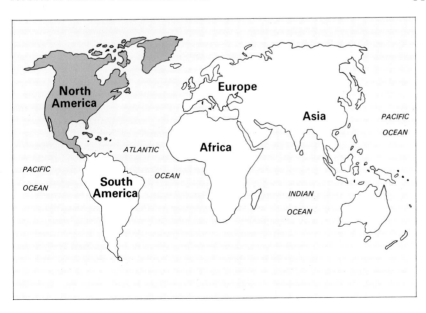

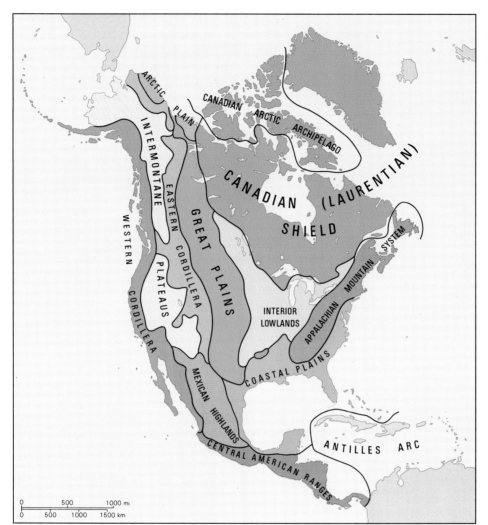

This map outlines the major geographic regions of the North American continent.

old, worn-down mountains, run southwards from the Gulf of St. Lawrence in Canada to central Alabama. Their highest peak, Mount Mitchell, rises to over 2,000 meters (6,600 feet) above sea-level (see APPALACHIAN MOUNTAINS).

On the west, inland from the Pacific Coast, are mountain ranges that extend from Alaska through Canada, the United States, Mexico, and Central America. This chain, the Western Cordillera, includes the Alaska Range with the continent's highest peak, Mount McKinley, over 6,188 meters (20,300 feet); the Coast Mountains of British Columbia; the Cascade and Sierra Nevada ranges; the mountains of Lower California; and the

Sierra Madre Occidental of Mexico. (See BAJA CALIFORNIA; SIERRA NEVADA.)

Further inland are the Rocky Mountains, the world's second longest mountain chain. They make up the Eastern Cordillera and the Mexican Highlands. They run from Mexico, where they join the Sierra Madre Oriental, through New Mexico, Colorado, Wyoming, and Montana into Canada and northern Alaska. (See ROCKY MOUNTAINS.)

Between the two mountain belts lie the interior (intermontane) plateaus of the Highland Region. They include the Great Basin and the Columbia and Colorado plateaus in the United States and the interior plateau of Mexico.

Lawrence R. Lowry—Rapho/Photo Researchers

Northern New England view looking across the Connecticut River valley, towards the low mountains of Vermont. This is part of the Appalachian landscape.

Plains

Between the Appalachians and the Atlantic Ocean is a low plain. This coastal plain extends along most of the continent's east coast. It is widest in southeastern United States, along the Gulf of Mexico.

Between the Rocky Mountains and the Appalachians is the great Interior Lowland. The lowlands extend from the Gulf of Mexico north to the Arctic shore of Canada. There is an eastward extension, higher and more rugged, across northeastern Canada to Labrador. It is known as the Laurentian Upland. Within this area are thousands of lakes formed by the glaciers that covered the northern half of the continent during the Ice Age (see LAURENTIAN MOUNTAINS; CANADIAN SHIELD). The famous wheat-growing region called the Great Plains forms the western part of the Interior Lowland.

Waterways

The Great Lakes are connected to the Atlantic Ocean by the St. Lawrence River. The lakes are the largest body of fresh water in the world

and, with the St. Lawrence Seaway, make up the greatest inland waterway. The Seaway permits ocean-going ships to penetrate as far inland as Chicago and Duluth (see ST. LAWRENCE RIVER AND SEAWAY).

The continent's large rivers include the Mackenzie, flowing into the Arctic Ocean; the Yukon, flowing to the Bering Sea through Canada and Alaska; the Nelson-Saskatchewan system, flowing into Hudson Bay; and the Mississippi-Missouri-Ohio system, flowing to the Gulf of Mexico. All of these, as well as the Hudson and Mohawk rivers of New York, were waterways used by the early settlers.

Many great seaports have grown around the fine harbors on the Atlantic, Pacific, and Gulf of Mexico coasts. The Atlantic Coast faces the industrial countries of Europe. The Pacific Coast faces eastern Asia, from which it receives both manufactured goods and raw materials. Through the Gulf of Mexico pass North American manufactured goods in exchange for the raw materials of South America. (See MEXICO, GULF OF.) Among the port cities are: Baltimore, Maryland; New York City; Boston, Massachusetts; Halifax, Nova Scotia; San Francisco, Califor-

ZEFA

Mount Rainier, part of the Sierra Nevada, provides a majestic backdrop to the alpine vegetation.

Freshfield Glacier runs through Banff National Park in the Rocky Mountains—part of the Eastern Cordillera of North America.

George Hunter/Publix

Alpha Photo Associates, Inc.

nia; Seattle, Washington State; Vancouver, British Columbia; and Houston, Texas. (There are separate articles on all these cities.)

Other great seaports reached by river are Montreal and Quebec, on the St. Lawrence in Canada; New Orleans, Louisiana, on the Mississippi; and Portland, Oregon, on the Columbia River. Hudson Bay opens into the frozen Arctic Sea, so it is of little use to ocean shipping (see HUDSON BAY).

Resources

North America has rich mineral, timber, and waterpower resources. Large deposits of coal lie in eastern and central United States. Iron ore is found in the Great Lakes region and Labrador. Copper, zinc, lead, and other metals are chiefly in southeastern Canada and west central United States. There are gold and silver in the mountainous regions. Petroleum resources are mainly in south-central United States and Alaska, western Canada, and eastern Mexico.

The mountainous eastern and western parts of the continent contain large thickly forested areas. Large forests of Douglas fir, pine, and spruce trees along the Pacific Coast in Alaska,

Cypress trees growing in a Florida swamp forest. The trees are hung with Spanish moss.

Canada, and northern United States provide much of North America's timber. There is also a valuable pine belt along the Gulf Coast in the United States, and tropical hardwood forests are found in Mexico and Central America.

Esther Henderson—Rapho/Photo Researchers
The rugged Pacific coastline of the western United States. This is Big Sur in California.

Animals native to North America include: Rocky Mountain sheep and goats, puma, bison (buffalo), muskrats, raccoons, opossums, rabbits, porcupines, and squirrels. Deer and bear still survive in wilderness areas, while the prairie dog, rabbit, and coyote have adapted to areas mainly inhabited by man. The original animals also include caribou, elk, moose, and many types of small furbearing animals in the northern lands. Alligators, snakes, wild pigs, colorful birds, and even monkeys and jaguars live in the warmer southern regions.

Agriculture

The Indians of North America grew many plants that are still important: corn, beans, squash, white potatoes, yams, tomatoes, pineapples, chili peppers, and cacao beans (from which chocolate and cocoa are made).

Present-day crops are grown where climate, soils, and water are best suited to them. Wheat fields cover the north-central United States and south-central Canada. The dairy and hay belt stretches from Minnesota east to the New England states. The corn and soybean belt is in the middle western United States; and the cotton belt (now mostly mixed crops and livestock) is in southeastern United States. Citrus fruits (oranges and lemons) are grown in subtropical Florida, south Texas, and southern California. There are wheat and fruit districts in Washington and Oregon. Further south, in Central America, bananas, cacao beans, and coffee are grown.

Industry

Since about 1870 manufacturing has been more important than agriculture as a way of making a living in the United States. It has also become increasingly important in Canada. In the rest of North America, most people depend on agriculture for a living. During the first half of the 20th century the United States became the leading manufacturing nation of the world. More than one-third of all the people who work in manufacturing plants in the United States make machinery and process foods.

Most of the factories of North America are in the east north-central part of the continent. In the United States the chief manufacturing belt extends from Boston, Massachusetts, and Baltimore, Maryland, on the east, to St. Louis, Missouri, and Minneapolis, Minnesota, on the west. This area makes up only about 10 per cent of the area of the United States, yet it has more than 70 per cent of all the factory workers. New York, Chicago, Detroit, and Philadelphia are the chief industrial centers.

The second most important manufacturing belt in the United States extends along the South Atlantic Coast from Virginia to northern Alabama. In Canada manufacturing industries are not as widespread as in the United States, but they have grown rapidly since World War II. Most of Canada's factories are along the Great Lakes and in the St. Lawrence River Valley. Wood and paper, iron and steel, and food and textile products are the chief industries. Ontario and Quebec are the leading industrial provinces. Montreal, Toronto, Hamilton,

Windsor, Winnipeg, and Vancouver are the chief manufacturing cities.

The People

The earliest known people of North America were Indians and Eskimos. They probably migrated to North America from Asia by way of Alaska, over a long period of time. They spread to the east and south throughout North America. The Eskimos and many of the Indian tribes lived in primitive ways, using stone weapons and tools. Many were wandering hunters in the plains and forests. (See ESKIMO; INDIANS, AMERICAN.)

The Indians of Mexico and Central America had an advanced civilization, with fine buildings, art, and systems of law and government. The greatest of the ancient Indian peoples, the Mayas, Toltecs, and Aztecs, built beautiful stone temples and palaces. (See AZTECS; MAYA.)

In the southwestern United States, farming Indian tribes lived in terraced houses called *pueblos* made of *adobe* (mud) bricks. Some of their descendants still live similarly.

The present population of North America is mostly of European descent. Settlers came to the United States and Canada chiefly from the countries of northern Europe and Italy, while those of Central America came chiefly from Spain. There are many black people who are descendants of Africans brought to North America as slaves, and also people of Chinese and Japanese descent.

Migration to North America has continued during the past 150 years although it has been decreasing. In the early years most settlers made their homes on the lowlands bordering the Atlantic Ocean. However, some people, chiefly Spanish, had settled along the Pacific Coast and established missions in Mexico and southwestern United States. Movement to the West Coast was rapid after the discovery of gold in California in 1848. Today, people are still moving westwards for other reasons.

English is the most widely spoken language. French is also spoken in Canada and on some of the islands of the West Indies. In Mexico, Central America, and parts of the West Indies, Spanish is the chief language.

The continent's greatest density of population is along the eastern seaboard of the United States, the Great Lakes region, and the St. Lawrence Valley. In Mexico, it is most dense around Mexico City. More than 80 per cent of the people of the United States and 75 per cent of Canada's population live in the eastern part of the continent.

After 1900 the population in North America began shifting from the farms to the cities. At each census the proportion of farmers is smaller – in fact, about 73 per cent of the population of the United States now live in urban areas.

FACTS ABOUT NORTH AMERICA

AREA: 24,229,883 square kilometers (9,355,182 square miles).

POPULATION (estimated): 432,232,000 (1992).

NATURAL RESOURCES: Grain, sugar (cane and beet), coffee, fruit, cocoa, timber, cotton, tobacco, furs; gold, silver, copper, nickel, iron ore, aluminum, zinc, cobalt, lead, mercury, petroleum, uranium.

FEATURES OF SPECIAL INTEREST: The highest mountain is Mt. McKinley at 6,194 meters (20,320 feet). The largest lake (second largest in the world) is Superior, between Canada and the United States at 82,412 square kilometers (31,800 square miles). The longest river (third longest in the world) is the Mississippi-Missouri in the United States at 6,212 kilometers (3,860 miles). Greenland, which is considered part of North America, is the largest island in the world at 2,175,000 square kilometers (840,000 square miles).

The largest grouping of people in all of North America is in the New York City area. This population center stretches northeastward to Boston and southwestward to Philadelphia. The area has many good harbors and a fine system of waterways connecting these harbors with interior of the continent.

Canada's nearness to the United States has held back its growth. The United States' warmer climate and good resources attracted more immigrants.

The works of man have added to the wonders of the continent. The Panama Canal is a world waterway linking the Atlantic and the Pacific oceans. Huge bridges span the Golden Gate between San Francisco Bay and the

Pacific Ocean and the Straits of Mackinac between Lakes Michigan and Huron. Dams, such as Hoover Dam on the Colorado River and Grand Coulee Dam on the Columbia River, conserve water for electric power and irrigation.

NORTHAMPTONSHIRE is a county in the east of the English Midlands. It is bordered by six counties: Leicestershire to the north; Warwickshire to the west; Oxfordshire to the southwest; Buckinghamshire to the south; and Bedfordshire and Cambridgeshire to the east. Northamptonshire has an area of 2,367 square kilometers (914 square miles) and a population of 578,800.

The largest river of Northamptonshire is the Nene. The valley of the Nene is divided into three parts. In the northeast is a wooded district which once formed the three baili-wicks, or districts, of Rockingham Forest. Huge areas of the county were given over to royal hunting forests from the 12th to the 14th centuries and although much of the woodland has since disappeared, parts, for example Geddington, remain. Bordering the forest area and extending to near the county's southern boundary is a belt of industrial towns, including Wellingborough, Kettering, and Northampton, the county town. West of the industrial belt is the main farming district. The fertile soil of the Nene and Ise river valleys provide the county's chief arable lands and higher ground is mostly pasture. This area is also famous as hunting country.

Other rivers of Northamptonshire include the Welland, which forms half the northern boundary of the county as it flows beside the steep slopes of the Northamptonshire uplands. The Cherwell flows along the Oxford-shire border. The Avon, Leam, and Ouse are other rivers of the county, which is also crossed by the Grand Union Canal.

Industries and Towns

In modern times, Northamptonshire has seen changes in its industries, and a rapid growth in its population. Corby was made a new town

ZEFA

The Waterways Museum, at Stoke Bruerne, near Towcester, lies on the Grand Union Canal.

in 1950 to provide extra houses and amenities for a growing population, and Northampton expanded greatly in the 1970s. New busi-nesses have moved to the county, and these help to provide work for newcomers.

Northamptonshire is famous for its tradi-tional industry of shoemaking. Although the number of workers and factories has steadily declined in recent years, the county still produces many of the shoes made in Britain, including high quality and special-ized types of footwear. In the county town of Northampton itself, more people are now employed in light manufacturing, cosmetics, and electronics than in shoemaking. Kettering and Wellingborough are two other manu-facturing towns with a range of activities including plastics, printing, clothing, and book-binding. Corby's steelworks, built in 1933 to manufacture steel from the local ironstone, closed in 1979 and ironstone mining stopped.

Except where mining or quarrying have destroyed the soil, or where there are towns or woodlands, all the land in Northamptonshire is farmed. Rich grassy pastures cover most of the hilly uplands of the northwest. Here beef cattle, sheep, and pigs are kept, and the crops are mostly grown as foodstuffs for the animals in winter.

The rich meadows of the river valleys, particularly the Welland, are used for fatten-ing cattle, and dairy farming is carried on over much of the county. Wheat, potatoes, and other crops are grown in the Ise and Nene valleys.

History

In prehistoric times, forts were built on Hunsbury Hill near Northampton, and trackways spread across the countryside. One of these, the Banbury Lane, extends from Hunsbury to Banbury in Oxfordshire. The remains of about 25 Roman villas have been found in the county.

Northamptonshire itself dates from the time of the Danish occupation of England, being the region that was ruled from the military center of Northampton in the 9th century. At the time of the Domesday Book survey in 1086, Northamptonshire was divided into 28 hundreds, or divisions of a hundred households each (see DOMESDAY BOOK). After the Norman Conquest (1066), several castles were built, of which Northampton Castle was once an important fortress controlling the English Midlands. It fell into disrepair, however, and the ruins were finally cleared in 1875. Parts of other castles at Rockingham, close to the Rockingham forest; and at Barnwell, near Oundle, still exist.

An important battle in the Wars of the Roses (see ROSES, WARS OF THE), took place in the meadows just outside Northampton in 1460. Close to the village of Naseby, not far from Market Harborough in Leicestershire, the Battle of Naseby was fought in 1645 between the forces of King Charles I and Oliver Cromwell. The king was defeated and imprisoned for a time at Holdenby House near Northampton.

Fotheringhay, north of Oundle, has connections with Mary, Queen of Scots, who was executed in 1587 in Fotheringhay Castle (which no longer exists). The family of George Washington, first President of the United States, originated at Sulgrave Manor, built by Lawrence Washington in 1560.

From Elizabethan times onwards, a number of great landowners built magnificent houses on their estates, and some of these can still be seen: Easton Neston near Towcester; Boughton House near Kettering; and Castle Ashby to the east of Northampton. Althorp House has

been the home of the Spencer family since 1508 and is the family home of the Princess of Wales.

NORTH ATLANTIC TREATY ORGANIZATION see NATO.

NORTH CAROLINA had, by 1980, become the 10th largest state in the United States by population. It is one of the most heavily industrialized states in the Union, with a larger percentage of its people working in manufacturing than such leading industrial states as Illinois, Michigan, and Ohio. Yet North Carolina is a very rural state. None of its cities are very large. Charlotte had about 315,000 people in 1980 and Raleigh—the capital—had only about 150,000.

One reason for maintaining its rural qualities is the nature of its industries. North Carolina is the chief tobacco producing state in the Union. Four of the major tobacco companies have their headquarters there. Hence tobacco farming is very extensive. Its other two chief industries, textiles and furniture, also depend on the soil: farming for cotton and the forests for the timber industry.

The high level of industrialization, however, has not raised the living standard of the population, as has been the case in the northern states. The level of unionization is the lowest of any state, and wages are consequently quite low. This fact has led to the relocating of plants within the state, providing more jobs. But the tobacco and textile industries have both been in trouble in recent years. Tobacco use has dropped appreciably among Americans, to the lowest level in this century. And textile production has been harmed by a great increase in foreign imports.

The Land

North Carolina is located in the southeastern part of the United States. It is bordered on the north by Virginia, on the west by Tennessee, and on the south by Georgia and South Carolina. On the east is the Atlantic Ocean. In extent from east to west, North Carolina is the longest state east of the Mississippi. The distance is 809 kilometers (503 miles). From

ZEFA

The Great Smoky Mountains form a distant backcloth to the wooded hills around Lake Fontana.

north to south the greatest distance is 303 kilometers (188 miles).

The surface of the state slopes downwards from west to east. Along the Tennessee boundary are the Appalachian Mountains, with some peaks more than 1,829 meters (6,000 feet) high. The Great Smoky Mountains of North Carolina are the highest in the eastern half of the nation. To the east the land slopes down to an elevation of between 152 and 304 meters (500 to 1,000 feet) in the Piedmont Plateau region. On the eastern edge of the Coastal Plain the average elevation is less than 6 meters (20 feet) above sea-level.

North Carolina is composed of three regions: the Coastal Plain, the Piedmont Plateau, and the Mountain Region. The largest region is the Coastal Plain. It comprises about 45 per cent of the state. Off the Atlantic coast a long chain of islands, the Outer Banks, extends from Virginia to South Carolina. Three capes, Cape Hatteras, Cape Lookout, and Cape Fear, jut into the ocean in an area known as the "graveyard of the Atlantic", because of all the ships that have gone down in the treacherous waters.

The plain itself extends westwards from 193 to 225 kilometers (120 to 140 miles) to the plateau. Most of its soil is rich, level, and sandy. About two-thirds of the land is covered with forest. The inner coastline is deeply indented by Albemarle Sound in the north and Pamlico Sound on the central coast inside the Outer Banks. Much of the coastal area is low and swampy. It includes the great Dismal Swamp in the northeast, and the Whiteoak, Angola, Holly Shelter, and Green swamps stretching south.

The Piedmont Plateau is in the center of the state and is the second largest region. It begins at the base of the Blue Ridge Mountains and extends eastwards to the start of the coastal plain. About half the plateau is timbered. Within the Piedmont are the major cities of North Carolina, as well as the state's industrial heartland. In the southeast, where the plateau merges with the Coastal Plain, is the Sandhills region, with its winter resorts and summer peach crops.

The Mountain region covers about 15,539 square kilometers (6,000 square miles), about one-quarter the size of the Coastal Plain. Its major ranges are the Great Smokies and the Blue Ridge. It is a high and cool resort country. Two-thirds of the mountains are covered with hardwood forests. The valleys are rich farmland, and pastures exist at slightly higher elevations. Mount Mitchell, at 2,037 meters (6,684 feet), is the highest peak in the Appalachian Range.

North Carolina has a very pleasant climate, ranging from subtropical in the southeast to temperate in the northwest. The state is protected from severe cold by the western mountain barrier. In the east, the climate is tempered by the Gulf Stream, which approaches to within 19 kilometers (12 miles) of Cape Hatteras. The growing season can be as long as 295 days along the coast, and it is at least 240 days throughout the Coastal Plain. In the western mountain region it ranges from 160 to 195 days a year. Rainfall is adequate throughout the state.

The People

The most numerous of pre-European settlers were Cherokee and Tuscarora Indians. After 1713, the Tuscarora moved north into New

York State. The Cherokees readily adapted to the ways of the white settlers, but during the 1830s most of them were forcibly removed to Oklahoma, then known as Indian Territory, to allow whites to settle their land. Descendants of the Cherokees who escaped the removal still live in the state.

The majority of Europeans who settled in North Carolina were Scots and Scotch-Irish. Germans also arrived from Pennsylvania. Today there are few foreign-born residents. Blacks number about 22 per cent of the population.

The Economy

There are about 150,000 farms in North Carolina, a number exceeded only by Texas and Iowa. Farm size is generally small, however. The average is only 40.5 hectares (100 acres). The large number of small farms is accounted for by many industrial workers who farm in their spare time. The chief crop is tobacco.

North Carolina Department of Conservation and Development

Tobacco is the state's chief crop and bright-leaf tobacco ripening in fields is a familiar sight.

North Carolina raises about two-fifths of the nation's output. Cotton is raised in the Piedmont and on the Coastal Plain. Peanut production is second only to that of Georgia. Dairying and the production of beef cattle are increasing. Truck farming supplies food-processing-and-packaging firms. Other crops include hay, oats, soybeans, fruits, and sweet potatoes. Tree nurseries grow millions of seedlings for reforestation.

The waters of the Atlantic provide the basis for a profitable fish and seafood industry. The most valuable catches are menhaden, sea trout, swordfish, flounder, crabs, oysters, shrimps, and clams.

The state has one of the largest deposits of phosphates. Other mineral reserves include kaolin, mica, feldspar, granite, copper, limestone, marble, marl, olivine, talc, sand, gravel, and shale.

North Carolina ranks 10th in the nation in annual industrial output. The traditional leading industries, since the late 19th century, have been textiles, tobacco, and furniture making. In the making of textiles North Carolina ranks first in the United States. The primary products are cotton and synthetic fibers, yarns, threads, and knitted goods. There is a sizable clothing industry as well. The second largest industry is tobacco products, in the manufacture of which it also leads the nation. The state is also first in the manufacture of wooden household furniture.

In the late 1950s and early 1960s, the Research Triangle Park was created near Durham, Raleigh, and Chapel Hill. By the early 1980s more than 40 companies and government agencies had research facilities and plants for the manufacture of high-technology goods located there. The advantage of the area is easy access to the state's three major institutions of higher learning, Duke University, the University of North Carolina, and North Carolina State University.

The rapid industrialization of North Carolina has been fostered in large part by the development of hydroelectric power. In the western region four large dams supply power for the Tennessee Valley Authority. The state ranks seventh in the United States in the harnessing of its water power.

Education

A public, state-supported, school system was not founded until 1933. Today schooling is available to all from grade school to high school.

Vocational education is strongly emphasized in the state. There are about 40 technical institutes and more than a dozen community col-

North Carolina Department of Conservation and Development

Tryon Palace in New Bern was built in 1770 for Governor Tryon. It became North Carolina's first statehouse.

leges offering technical and vocational training.

North Carolina University, the first state university in the nation, opened in 1795. The system has 16 campuses around the state. Duke University, at Durham, is the largest private college and one of the best institutions of higher learning in the nation.

History

Roanoke Island, inside the Outer Banks near Albemarle Sound, is the site of the first attempt at English colonization in the United States. The ill-fated colony was the result of an exploring expedition set out by Sir Walter Raleigh in 1584. In 1585 a group of colonists arrived. Conflicts with the Indians caused them to return to England. In 1587 a party was sent over with John White as governor. His granddaughter, Virginia Dare, was born there on 18 August. She was the first child of English parents to be born in America. By 1591 the whole colony had disappeared, and its fate has remained a mystery.

The first permanent settlement was made by Virginians near Albemarle Sound in 1653. Ten years later King Charles II granted the Carolina region to a group of proprietors. North and South Carolina became separate provinces in 1730. Boundaries between the two were agreed upon in 1735, but there was no survey taken until 1815.

North Carolina's early growth was slow. Virginia imposed restrictions on shipping its already abundant tobacco crop. Settlers quarreled with absentee proprietors, and in 1677 and 1708 there were rebellions. There was war with the Tuscarora Indians from 1711 until 1713. Coastal pirates harassed shipping.

After Charles II issued his land grant, the colony began to prosper. The population rose rapidly, and settlement spread westwards. A large slave population maintained an economy based on rice, tobacco, and pine tar (naval stores).

When the American Revolution began, North Carolina found itself involved in a civil war. Loyalists fought rebels, and the Indians in the west attacked both. When the war began, the residents of Mecklenberg County met at Charlotte and drew up a declaration of independence on 20 May 1775 the first such declaration in the colonies.

North Carolina's economy continued to prosper until the state was caught up in the slavery conflict prior to the American Civil War. Unlike South Carolina, which was very much pro-slavery, North Carolina was reluctant to secede (withdraw) from the Union. It did not do so until Fort Sumter had fallen to Confederate forces in April 1861. (See CIVIL WAR, AMERICAN.)

North Carolina was readmitted to the Union on 4 July 1868. Its postwar government was run by the Republican Party. Democrats regained control in 1876. The state's modern industrial development began after the American Civil War. By World War I, manufacturing had overtaken agriculture as the most important part of the economy.

FACTS ABOUT NORTH CAROLINA

AREA: 136,412 square kilometers (52,669 square miles).
POPULATION: 6,530,000 (1988).
CAPITAL: Raleigh, 149,771.
CITIES: Charlotte, 314,447; Greensboro, 155,642; Winston-Salem, 131,885; Durham, 100,831.
HIGHEST PEAK: Mount Mitchell, 2,037 meters (6,684 feet).
PRODUCTS.
  Agriculture: Tobacco, corn, peanuts, sweet potatoes, oats, soybeans; dairy products, beef cattle, chickens, pigs.
  Minerals: Sand and gravel, phosphate rock, feldspar, kaolin, talc, mica.
  Manufacturing: Cotton and synthetic fibers, knitted goods, cigarettes and tobacco, timber, furniture, paper products, electrical equipment, chemicals, processed food.
STATE EMBLEMS. Flower: Dogwood. Tree: Pine. Bird: Cardinal.
JOINED THE UNION: North Carolina was the 12th state to ratify the US Constitution, in 1789.

NORTH DAKOTA lies at the heart of the North American continent. The stone marking the geographical center of the continent is located near the small town of Rugby. North Dakota is the most agricultural state in the United States, and it has the least manufacturing. This northern Great Plains state is second only to Kansas in wheat production, and in durum wheat it leads the nation.

Only after 1951, when oil was discovered at Tioga in the Williston Basin, did the state find another source of income apart from the produce of its farms. Also in the western part of the state are rich deposits of coal.

The overwhelming emphasis on farming means, of course, that North Dakota is a non-urban state. Its largest city, Fargo, had only slightly more than 60,000 residents in 1980; and its capital, Bismarck, had fewer than 50,000. The state's rural components are strikingly different. The region from Minnesota to the Missouri River is eastern farming country, while from the river to Montana, the state is western ranch land.

North Dakota is a state of family-owned farms. Corporate farming, in which the farms are owned by commercial companies, has been outlawed unless the corporate owners are families. The reason for this law stems from the early part of the 20th century. Tired of exploitation by outside banks, railroads, and grain companies, a political movement called the Nonpartisan League (NPL) took over the state government in 1917. It created a state bank (the only one in the United States), state mills and grain elevators, state insurance programs, and a state workmen's compensation bureau. These measures helped save family farming during the crisis years of the Great Depression and the devastating drought (the Dust Bowl) of the 1930s. They have helped preserve agricultural prosperity in North Dakota.

The Land

North Dakota is bounded on the north by the Canadian provinces of Manitoba and Saskatchewan, on the west by Montana, and on the south by South Dakota. Along the eastern border runs the Red River of the North, separating the state from Minnesota. Except for the river border, North Dakota would be a perfect rectangle. It is 563 kilometers (350 miles) east to west and 338 kilometers (210 miles) north to south.

The state has three natural regions: Red River Valley, Glacial Drift Prairie, and Missouri Plateau. Of the three, the Red River Valley is the smallest. Only 16 kilometers (10 miles) wide in the south, it widens to 64 kilometers (40 miles) at the Canadian border. The fertile black soil of the valley makes it ideal for growing wheat, sugar beet, oats, soybeans, and other crops.

The Glacial Drift Prairie has the appearance of a mis-shapen funnel. Only about 193 kilometers (120 miles) wide at the South Dakota border, it broadens in width to encompass all of the center and much of the western part of the state at the Canadian border. The average elevation is from 396 to 488 meters (1,300–1,600 feet). The region

The area of badlands in the Theodore Roosevelt National Memorial Park, central North Dakota.

takes its name from the drift left by glaciers during the last Ice Age.

The Missouri Plateau in the west rises about 122 meters (400 feet) above the prairie. Its rolling surface is dotted with flat-topped hills, called buttes, which rise 90 to 120 meters (300–400 feet) above the surrounding plains. This is an arid region. Vegetation is relatively sparse. The Missouri River flows across the plateau in a near diagonal direction, from Montana into South Dakota. In the southwest corner of the plateau are the Badlands, so called because pioneers found them difficult to cross. White Butte, at 1,069 meters (3,506 feet) the highest point in the state, is in the Badlands.

North Dakota has the most continental of climates, ranging from very hot to very cold. It has no mountains and few trees to break the relentless winds, and the sun beats down almost without respite in the summers. Average annual precipitation ranges little, from only 500 millimeters (20 inches) in the east to 360 millimeters (14 inches) in the west. The longest growing season, in the south, is only 135 days. In the northeast and north-central parts it is 110 days.

The People

The original inhabitants of the state were Indians of the Mandan, Hidatsa, Arikara, Cheyenne, Sioux, Chippewa, and Assninboin tribes. Today the state still has a population of more than 20,000 Indians.

In no other state did such a large proportion of settlers come directly from Europe. The earliest immigrants were Russians, Germans, and Norwegians. The black population is very small, numbering only about 2,500 in 1980.

The Economy

North Dakota has about 50,000 farms averaging in size nearly 364 hectares (900 acres). Ninety per cent of the land is cropland or pasture. Because farming is highly mechanized it is not labor-intensive. Thus only about one-fifth of the state's workers are employed on farms. The major crop is wheat. Hard spring wheat and durum are especially suited to the climate and soil. North Dakota is the chief flax-growing state, as well as the leading barley and rye producer. After wheat, cattle are the second most valuable farm product. Sheep, pigs, and chickens are also raised. Other crops include soybeans, sugar beet, oats, potatoes, and hay.

Lignite (brown coal) was once the most valuable mineral. It was mostly made into small briquettes that yielded such by-products as gas, oil, and tar. Since the petroleum discoveries of 1951, oil has surpassed coal in

Agriculture far exceeds manufacturing in North Dakota's economy. Wheat is the chief crop.

economic value. There are about 4,330 producing wells in some 650 oilfields. A refinery at Mandan can process more than 50,000 barrels of crude oil per day.

Apart from mineral production, the most valuable component of manufacturing is food processing. This includes flour, meal, meat, bakery goods, dairy products, and beet sugar. The city of Fargo has iron foundries, farm machinery manufacture, and meat packing.

Education

The present system of free public education was established during territorial days, before Dakota was a state. Between 1959 and 1981 there was extensive consolidation of school districts and many schools were shut. Therefore many pupils now have great distances to travel to school every morning.

The largest state-supported institutions of higher learning are the University of North Dakota, at Grand Forks, and North Dakota State University, at Fargo.

History

The first known European visitor to North Dakota was Pierre Gaultier de Varennes, Sieur de La Vérendrye, who arrived from Canada in 1738. Other Canadians soon arrived to trap furs.

The territory came to the United States as part of the Louisiana Purchase of 1803, and soon afterwards the Lewis and Clark expedition made its way up the Missouri River. They built Fort Mandan in the winter of 1804–5. The Indian woman, Sakakawea, who guided them westwards, was from North Dakota (see LEWIS AND CLARK EXPEDITION). The first white settlement was made at Pembina in 1812 by a group of Icelanders who had originally come to Canada.

Fur trappers were gradually replaced by farmers and ranchers, and steamboats came up the Missouri River from the south. Military posts were set up to protect settlers from the Indians. The coming of the railroads brought in thousands of new settlers, and the rail companies actively promoted emigration from Europe. The vast acreages owned by the railroads along their rights of way were sold to farmers at low rates.

North Dakota Economic Development Commission

Garrison Dam on the Missouri River is one of the world's largest rolled-earth-fill dams. It provides flood control, electric power, irrigation, and recreation.

Cattle ranching arrived in the western part of the state after the American Civil War.

FACTS ABOUT NORTH DAKOTA

AREA: 183,117 square kilometers (70,702 square miles)
POPULATION: 660,000 (1988).
CAPITAL: Bismarck, 44,485.
CITIES: Fargo, 61,383; Grand Forks, 43,765; Minot, 32,843; Jamestown, 16,280; Dickinson, 15,924; Mandan, 15,513.
HIGHEST PEAK: White Butte, 1,069 meters (3,506 feet).
PRODUCTS.
   Agriculture: Wheat, durum, barley, flaxseed, sunflowers, rye, oats, sugar-beet, potatoes, soybeans; cattle, sheep.
   Minerals: Petroleum, natural gas, lignite.
   Manufacturing: Food processing, agricultural and electrical equipment.
STATE EMBLEMS. Flower: Wild prairie rose. Tree: American elm. Bird: Western meadowlark.
JOINED THE UNION: North Dakota became the 39th state in 1889.

The Dakota Territory was organized in 1861. The territory was divided in 1887, and North and South Dakota were both admitted to the Union in 1889.

Poor agricultural practices removed the thick mats of grass which held moisture in the soil and protected the land from winds. When the great drought of the 1930s occurred, high winds blew much of the topsoil away. Since then, energetic conservation policies reduced the danger of drought.

NORTHERN AND SOUTHERN LIGHTS.

The northern and southern lights are dazzling displays of colored lights which can sometimes be seen in the sky at night. They flicker across the skies in the form of luminous arcs and may be constantly in motion. At times, brilliant rays of light spread upwards in the shape of a fan, and they may flash here and there like giant searchlights or move up and down in a way which has led to their being called the Merry Dancers in Scotland. Far to the north and to the south of the equator, the lights often look like vast fiery draperies hanging from the sky, while colored flames play up and down the moving folds.

NHPA/ANT

The southern lights, seen from Wilkes Land, Antarctica, move across the sky at incredible speed, creating a beautiful shawl-like effect.

Science Photo Library

Ghostly northern lights hover above this brightly lit house in Fairbanks, Alaska.

Scientists call these displays of light the *aurora*. The northern lights, which are those seen in the northern hemisphere, are called *aurora borealis*, and the southern lights, which are those seen in the southern hemisphere, are called *aurora australis*. *Borealis* and *australis* are Latin words meaning "northern" and "southern".

In the northern hemisphere the aurora is seen at its best round the Hudson Bay region in Canada, in northern Scotland, and in northern Norway and Sweden. However, the aurora is sometimes seen as far south as Mexico. In the southern hemisphere the aurora is best observed in Antarctica.

Displays of aurora are caused by gigantic eruptions, called flares, which take place on the Sun (see SUN). During a flare, millions of small, electrically charged particles, electrons and protons, are sent out by the Sun. Traveling at about 1,600 kilometers (1,000 miles) a second, the particles reach the Earth about 24 hours after they leave the Sun. They are caught by the Earth's magnetic field and move down very quickly through the air. As they travel down, they collide with the atoms and molecules of the air. These collisions produce light, and it is this light that is seen as a display of aurora. The Earth's magnetism works in such a way that it is easier for the particles to come down far away from the equator than near to it, which is why the aurora is seen more often at places far from the equator.

NORTHERN IRELAND see IRELAND, NORTHERN.

NORTHERN TERRITORY.

The northern part of central Australia is called the Northern Territory and covers an area of 1,346,200 square kilometers (519,800 square miles). It has a low, flat coastline from which the ground rises gradually to the great plateau, or tableland, which covers most of the central and western parts of the continent. The only mountains are the Macdonnell Ranges rising to about 1,500 meters (4,920 feet) almost in the middle of Australia (see MACDONNELL RANGES). The chief rivers are the Victoria, Daly, and Adelaide flowing northwest into the Timor Sea and the Roper River flowing east-

Hutchison Library

The Todd River rises in the Macdonnell Ranges north of Alice Springs and only flows after heavy rains.

wards into the Gulf of Carpentaria. In some dry seasons these rivers shrink to little more than chains of water-holes.

Most of the soil of the Northern Territory is poor and there is much desert, especially in the west. However, there is a large area of valuable pasture land in the north. Here it is warm all the year round, with a hot wet summer from November to April. In the south, at Alice Springs, the climate is continental – that is, it tends to extremes, with very hot summers and frequent night frosts in winter.

Because of the poor soil and lack of rain, much of the Territory is covered with tropical grass and scrubby bushes, although there are trees, palms, and flowering plants in the coastal region. Almost everywhere there are giant ant-hills scattered over the land. There are some marsupials (mammals which carry their young in pouches) such as kangaroos and opossums, and in the rivers and swamps live many crocodiles. There are also water buffaloes, introduced in the 19th century from Timor, an island some distance to the northwest.

People, Towns, and Economy

The vast distances and the lack of fertile land have hindered the development of the Northern Territory, which is thinly populated. About one-fifth of the people are the native Aborigines (see ABORIGINALS, AUSTRALIAN). In 1976 a law was passed which granted certain

areas of land to the Aborigines. It is expected that eventually Aboriginal groups will legally own about one-quarter of the total land area of the Northern Territory.

There are only two fair-sized towns in the Territory: Darwin (on which there is a separate article), and Alice Springs. Darwin, on the northwest coast, has a splendid land-locked harbor and is the starting point of the railroad and of the road to South Australia. This railroad ends at Birdum and the road, known as the Stuart Highway, continues southwards to Alice Springs, which is linked by rail with Adelaide on the south coast of the continent. The rail and road link make Alice Springs a major freight center for cattle. The town attracts much tourism, being in the center of Australia. Alice Springs is also the area headquarters for the Flying Doctor Service and the School of the Air (teaching children in remote settlements by radio). Its population is about 20,000. Another good road, the Barkly Highway, joins Tennant Creek in the center of the Territory with the rail terminus of Mount Isa in Queensland.

Promotion Australia

Alice Springs seen from Anzac Hill, looking south towards Heavitree Gap in the Macdonnell Ranges.

The most important rural occupation in the Northern Territory is cattle raising. There are more than a million cattle and they are kept on vast unfenced stretches called stations, the biggest of which are larger than some small countries. Cattle are now usually transported by truck to the railways, instead of being driven hundreds of kilometers into Queensland, as they were in the past. Sheep are pastured in the Alice Springs district. A little land is irrigated for growing fruit and vegetables and raising dairy cattle near Darwin and Alice Springs. Peanuts and fruits such as pineapples and bananas are also grown. Vessels at Darwin collect oysters from whose shells mother-of-pearl is obtained.

Promotion Australia

Workers at the open-cut Ranger uranium mine survey this vast mined area in the Northern Territory.

Mining is the region's chief activity. Bauxite is exported from Gove Peninsula, where there is also a large aluminum plant. At Groote Eylandt is a manganese plant, and copper mines have been established at Tennant Creek. Gold is also mined here. Tungsten, used to make hard steel, is mined at Hatches Creek and uranium, used to produce nuclear energy, is mined at Rum Jungle, south of Darwin.

Air services play a big part in the life of the Northern Territory. Mail and passengers are flown to the widely scattered settlements, which rely on radio sets for communication. With these they can call the "flying doctor" when medical help is needed. Children who live too far from the towns or settlements to be able to attend school learn by correspondence courses (lessons sent by mail) and by taking part in the "School of the Air". This is a two-way school: not only are lessons broadcast, but children from all over the Northern Territory can ask questions and receive answers by radio.

History

Northern Australia was discovered by the Dutch in the 17th century (see TASMAN, ABEL JANSZOON) and its coast was mapped early in the 19th century by Lieutenant Philip King. Several attempts were made to establish settlements on the coast between 1824 and 1849, but they all failed and the Northern Territory was finally settled by "squatters" from South Australia in search of grazing land. It was taken under the control of South Australia in 1863. Herds of beef cattle were moved into the Territory from Queensland and the pioneers began their long struggle with drought, disease, and lack of money.

There were many setbacks and South Australia was quite willing to hand over control of the Territory to the Australian Commonwealth (that is, the central government of Australia) in 1911. After that, the Commonwealth government looked after affairs in the Northern Territory. During World War II, the Japanese made bombing attacks on Darwin. In 1978 self-government was introduced. The Northern Territory will eventually become a full state.

The Northern Territory has one representative in the Australian House of Representatives, and two Senators in the Senate. The population of the Territory is 150,300 (1987), of whom approximately 20 per cent are Aborigines.

NORTH SEA. Between the east coast of Great Britain and the continent of Europe is the North Sea. To the south it is joined to the Atlantic Ocean by the narrow Strait of Dover and the English Channel. To the east it joins the Baltic Sea through the straits known as Skagerrak and Kattegat. The North Sea is generally shallow, especially in the south. Its basin is really part of the great plain of north Europe, flooded by the Atlantic when the land sank at the end of the Ice Age. It is part of what is called the continental shelf. The Goodwin Sands, which are partly uncovered at low tides, were once low hills on land joined to the county of Kent in southeast England. The Dogger Bank off north England was once a low plateau, or tableland, on the surface of the plain but is now a fishing ground. (*Dogger* is the Dutch word for "cod fisherman".)

The North Sea has rich fisheries and its shallowness makes trawling for bottom-feeding fish easy. (Trawling is explained in the article FISHERY.) Shoals of herring frequent the surface waters in summer and autumn. However, there is danger from over-fishing, and from time to time bans are imposed on the fishing of certain species, particularly herring, to allow stocks to build up.

The shallowness of the water also means that tides come in and go out a long way, especially on the British side. This has helped the growth of ports on the river estuaries.

Beneath the North Sea are natural gas and oil reserves which are exploited by the surrounding countries. (See the article PETROLEUM.) Before the 1950s drilling for oil was done on land. But then it became possible to extract oil from the land beneath shallow bodies of water – that is, the continental shelves surrounding countries. The North Sea was one of the first offshore areas to be explored. The Brent and Forties fields (off the coast of Scotland) are two of the largest offshore oilfields in the world (see also UNITED KINGDOM).

The North Sea is also an important trade route and on its coasts are some of Europe's major ports, including Rotterdam. The North Sea receives the waters of rivers such as the Rhine, Scheldt, and Elbe in Europe, and the Humber and Thames in Great Britain. The basins of these rivers are among the most thickly populated and heavily industrialized regions in the world.

NORTHUMBERLAND is the most northerly county of England and one of the largest in area, though its population is small. Its northern borders are with Scotland and it has the North Sea to the east. To the west is Cumbria, while to the south are Durham and the Tyneside region, centered on the city of Newcastle upon Tyne (see NEWCASTLE UPON TYNE and TYNE AND WEAR). Northumberland

has an area of 5,032 square kilometers (1,943 square miles) and a population of 307,000.

The county can be divided into four distinct areas. In the east is the coastal plain. The ports of Northumberland, including Blyth and Amble, are all to be found here, and so are fishing villages and beaches. Off the coast lie the Farne Islands and Lindisfarne, or Holy Island.

At its southeastern corner the coastal plain is overlapped by the Northumberland and Durham coalfield.

The Tyne flows into the sea as one river, but in the west of Northumberland it is two rivers, the North Tyne and the South Tyne, which join near Hexham. The range of hills known as the Pennine Chain runs from north to south along the border with Cumbria.

North of the North Tyne are the Northumberland Fells, a region of vales and hills, narrow glens, and gentle wooded slopes extending to the Cheviot Hills on the northwestern border with Scotland. Through this upland area flow the rivers Till, Coquet, Aln, Wansbeck, and Rede, and on the Scottish border is the Tweed.

The Great Whin Sill, a sheet of basalt formed by volcanoes long ago, stretches across the county from Bamburgh on the east coast to the west end of the Tyne Valley. Part of this are the Farne Islands, a group of islets, rocks, and reefs lying off the coast. The

Eric Kay

The ancient remains of the Priory stand on Holy Island, or Lindisfarne, which was the center for the spread of Christianity throughout Northumberland.

Eric Kay

Rolling fields lead towards the rounded Cheviot Hills in the Alnwick district of Northumberland.

largest island is called Inner Farne or House, and the islands next in size are Staple, Brownsman, North and South Wamses, Longstone, and Big Harcar. The Farne Islands are a sanctuary, or refuge, for seabirds and seals.

About half of Northumberland is hill and moorland country and large areas in the north and west such as Kielder, Wark, and Redesdale have been planted with trees by the Forestry Commission. Kielder also has the largest artificial lake in Europe. Much of the county's hill and moorland country lies within the 1,000-square kilometer (400-square mile) Northumberland National Park.

Chillingham Castle near Wooler has a park in which are kept a herd of pure white cattle. They are the last remaining descendants in England of the wild cattle that wandered through the forests of Britain in ancient times.

Towns and Industries

One of the most interesting towns in Northumberland is Berwick upon Tweed on the border. In the past it was regarded as belonging to neither England nor Scotland. It stood on the point where the east coast road crossed the Tweed, and in the constant warfare between England and Scotland was continually being burned and besieged.

Blyth, which is on the coast at the mouth of the River Blyth, became one of the most important coal shipping ports in England and also an exporter of grain. Both Blyth and the new town of Cramlington have modern light industries with several pharmaceutical factories.

Overlooking the River Aln in Alnwick is Alnwick Castle, home of the Dukes of Northumberland. Morpeth, the center of local government, stands in the pleasant valley of the Wansbeck. The industries of the Morpeth area include pharmaceuticals and mining, while fruit and flowers are grown in truck farms there.

Coal has been mined in Northumberland since Roman times. Much of it is mined by open-cut methods. Since the 19th century new industries such as engineering and the manufacture of soaps, chemicals, and drugs have grown up.

Northumberland farmers graze sheep on the moors and uplands. Herds of beef and dairy cattle are kept, and there are fields of wheat, barley, and oats on many lowland farms.

History

Weapons of Stone Age people who lived in Northumberland in prehistoric times have been found in the band of well-drained limestone country between Alnwick in the northeast and Hexham in the southwest. The later Iron Age people built hill forts in the Cheviots.

In Northumberland there are stretches of Hadrian's Wall, the barrier built in the 2nd century by the Romans to keep out the Picts of Scotland. (See HADRIAN'S WALL.)

In Anglo-Saxon times Northumberland was part of the kingdom of Northumbria, which in the 7th century extended from the River Humber between Lincolnshire and Yorkshire to the Firth of Forth in Scotland. Several founders of the early English church lived in Northumberland. St. Aidan founded a monastery on Lindisfarne (Holy Island) in the 7th century and St. Cuthbert later lived and died there.

From the days of the Norman kings until the 17th century, when James VI, King of Scotland, became James I, King of England, Northumberland was frequently a battlefield.

At Flodden field, not far from the River Till, James IV of Scotland was killed in battle with the English in 1513. This was one of Scotland's greatest disasters.

Among Northumberland's famous sons are the railroad engineer George Stephenson (1781–1848), the landscape architect Lancelot "Capability" Brown (1716–83), and a number of famous English soccer players including the brothers Jack and Bobby Charlton.

NORTHWEST PASSAGE.

The Northwest Passage is a sea route between the Atlantic and Pacific oceans. This historic sea channel lies 800 kilometers (500 miles) north of the Arctic Circle, and less than 1,900 kilometers (1,200 miles) from the North Pole. It is made up of a series of channels stretching some 1,450 kilometers (900 miles) east to west from Greenland and through Canada's Arctic Islands. The landscape is bleak, there are many icebergs, and the weather is bitterly cold. Many famous early explorers including Cartier, Cabot, Drake, and Cook hoped to find a short trade route to India. (There are separate articles on these men; see also POLAR EXPLORATION.) They failed, however, because the narrow channels between the islands were frozen almost all year.

While searching for a Northwest Passage, explorers charted most of the Canadian Arctic waters. Among the most important explorers were John Davis, who in 1585–87 reached Davis Strait; William Baffin, who discovered Baffin Bay; and Henry Hudson, whose voyages from 1609 to 1611 explored Hudson Strait and Hudson Bay (see HUDSON, HENRY). Sir John Franklin passed through Barrow Strait to King William Island in 1845, but after three winters his entire party perished (see FRANKLIN, SIR JOHN). In searching for the Franklin party, other men pushed further west. In 1851–52 R. J. McClure walked over frozen McClure Strait and thus proved that the Northwest Passage existed.

Only a few times in history has the passage been crossed. In 1903–06 Roald Amundsen

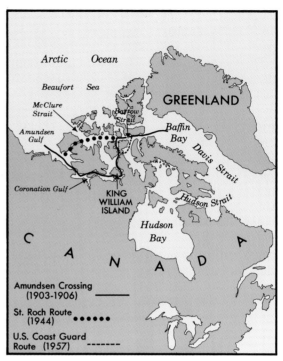

Map showing the Northwest Passage and some of the routes taken across it.

of Norway made the first crossing. He went from Baffin Bay by way of Barrow Strait to King William Island, and then through Coronation Gulf and Amundsen Gulf to Alaska. The next trips were made by the Canadian ships *St. Roch* and *Labrador*. In 1957 the United States Coast Guard charted a new deep-water route from Beaufort Sea to Baffin Bay. The route goes through Amundsen and Coronation gulfs to and around King William Island, and through James Ross, Franklin, and Bellot straits. Canada claims the passage as part of Canadian territory, while some countries claim it is in international waters.

NORTHWEST TERRITORIES.

North of the Canadian prairie provinces of Alberta, Saskatchewan, and Manitoba, and east of the Yukon Territory is a vast region of almost 3,293,000 square kilometers (1,271,442 square miles) occupying more than one-third of Canada's total area. This is the Northwest Territories. It includes the islands north of the

Canadian mainland which are known as the Arctic Archipelago. They form the largest group of islands in the world.

The greater part of the area is a low-lying glaciated shield (a region of old, hard rocks that have been worn down by masses of ice over millions of years). The shield slopes inwards to a saucer-shaped depression which forms Hudson Bay. The Mackenzie Mountains rise along the western boundary of the Territories and there are other lofty mountains on the easternmost shores of the Arctic Archipelago. The Mackenzie district is an area rich in minerals and covered with forests of poplar, spruce, birch, and jackpine. Two of the world's largest lakes, the Great Slave and the Great Bear, are linked to the Arctic Ocean by Canada's longest river, the Mackenzie (see MACKENZIE RIVER).

In the northeast is the tundra, a region of rock and muskeg (sphagnum bog) that is rich in wildlife. There are thousands of lakes. In winter it is hard-packed with snow but in summer the lower parts are carpeted with such flowers as mountain avens, crocuses, lupins, anemones, and arctic poppies. Even in summer, however, less than a meter below the surface the soil is permanently frozen. This

B. & C. Alexander

Snowmobiles make ideal transportation. This Eskimo boy is using his for shopping at Pond Inlet.

is the case through the northern third of the Territories.

The climate in the Territories cannot be judged from how far north or south a place is. The temperature at the mouth of the Mackenzie River, where it flows into the Arctic Ocean, is about the same as in Churchill on Hudson Bay, 960 kilometers (600 miles) further from the North Pole. Around Great Slave Lake, where many of the people live, the winters are severe but in summer the temperature often rises above 27°C (80°F).

Animals include muskrats, foxes, wolves, martens, weasels, and mink, which are trapped for their fur by native Eskimos, and Indians. There are a few lynxes and beavers. Vast numbers of geese, ducks, gulls, and other birds migrate northwards each spring to nest and can be seen gathering on the cliffs of the Arctic Archipelago. Ptarmigans, snowy owls, and hawks are common in the lowland areas and in the more southerly districts of the Territories there are American robins, warblers, sparrows, and snow buntings.

The key problem of the north is transportation. The early explorers used the Mackenzie River and it still remains the chief route for bringing in heavy supplies during the four months in the year when it is free of ice. Air travel, however, has opened up the vast region and there are many airstrips.

The search for minerals has gone forward rapidly. They are now the most valuable

ZEFA

Barren arctic wastes of Baffin Bay, by Cape Dorset.

An eskimo settlement at Lake Harbour on Baffin Island, Northwest Territories. Snow has melted from the land, but the sea is still ice covered.

Canadian High Commission.

resource of the Northwest Territories. Zinc and lead are particularly important. Gold is produced in Yellowknife and on the Snare River, copper is extracted on the Coppermine River and there is iron ore on Baffin Island, and oil in the Beaufort Sea.

The Eskimos were the first people to live in this land while the Vikings were the first Europeans to discover the eastern shores of the territory. Martin Frobisher claimed Baffin Island for England in 1577. In 1670, England granted the Hudson's Bay Company control over the area drained by all rivers emptying into Hudson Bay and the Arctic Ocean (see HUDSON'S BAY COMPANY). This land was placed under control of the Canadian government in 1860 and given its present name.

In 1967, the Canadian Government declared Yellowknife the capital, and administration passed to a Commissioner and a 22-member elected council. The Territories are represented in the Canadian Parliament by two elected representatives in the House of Commons.

The population is 54,000 (1990).

NORWAY is a country which occupies the northern and western parts of the Scandinavian peninsula. It also owns a number of outlying islands. These are Svalbard, a group of islands far north in the Arctic Ocean, Bear Island in the Barents Sea, and Jan Mayen, an island in the Greenland Sea. Queen Maud Land, a large area of the Antarctic continent, also belongs to Norway. Norway is the sixth largest country in Europe, but it is so mountainous that it only has a small population. Norway's neighbors are Sweden, Finland, and Russia.

Most of the Norwegian frontier with Sweden consists of a mountain range called Kjølen, meaning "the keel", for the Scandinavian peninsula is like a huge boat upside down with the keel sticking up in the middle. Where Norway broadens out towards the south there is a mass of high mountains and tablelands, including the highest peaks in the country: Galdhøpiggen and Glittertind, both over 2,440 meters (8,000 feet). These peaks are in the Jotunheim Mountains, the "home of the giant".

The most striking features of the Norwegian scenery are the fiords, which are long narrow arms of the sea, usually very deep, running inland between mountainous cliffs. Sognefiord, which stretches from the coast almost to Jotunheimen, is about 180 kilometers (112 miles) long with a greatest depth of 1,305 meters (4,280 feet). Fiords are glaciated valleys flooded by the sea.

The whole of the long coastline of Norway is fringed with islands. These are of great importance to small vessels fishing or traveling between the villages on the fiords as they can use the leads (narrow passages) between the islands and the mainland without being exposed to the open sea. The islands number about 150,000. Best known are the Lofoten Islands, lying north of the Arctic Circle.

The highlands of Norway contain many large icefields and glaciers. The Jostedalsbreen, to the north of Bergen, is the largest icefield in Europe, excluding Iceland. The rivers in the far north of the country are broad and slow enough to be used for water transportation, but most Norwegian rivers are too rapid for this and some tumble over steep waterfalls. The rivers are sometimes used for floating timber down from the forests or, more importantly, for providing hydroelectric power. The chief lowland in Norway lies along the south coast and includes the lower Glomma Valley and the land around Oslo.

ZEFA

The Romsdal fiord lies just north of Ålesund.

This is the most fertile and thickly peopled part of the country.

Although gales and winter snowstorms are common on the west coast of Norway, the climate there is mild for somewhere so far north, and the ports are not ice-bound in winter. This mildness is due to the easterly drift of warm air and water across the Atlantic. (See GULF STREAM.) Inland, the winters are severe with heavy falls of snow. Northern Norway is called the "land of the midnight sun". At North Cape the sun does not set in summer for more than two months, nor does it rise above the horizon in winter for more than two months. Even as far south as Trondheim there is practically no night during June.

Although Norway is a somewhat barren country, its valleys are bright with wild flowers in summer and there are large forests of spruce and pine. On the higher ground birches and rowan grow among juniper bushes and the mountain tablelands are covered with moss and lichen. Blueberries and cranberries are plentiful and the yellow cloudberry grows in the swampy parts.

Norwegian wild animals include foxes, deer, hares, wild reindeer, and elk (found in the

Eric Kay

Mount Steindalsnosi, 1,981 meters (6,500 feet), stands above the high pasture land of Sygnefell.

eastern forests). Bears and lynxes are rare, wolves more so. The lemming is noted for its remarkable migrations (see LEMMING). Herds of reindeer kept by the Lapps feed on the moss in Finnmark. (See LAPLAND.)

The People

Most Norwegians are of Nordic stock – that is, tall, with fair hair and blue eyes. (Between 60 and 70 per cent of people have blue eyes.) Living in southwestern Norway are settlers from the Baltic and the Mediterranean. There are also some 25,000 Lapps, a dark-haired people, short in stature, who were Norway's original inhabitants. Only a few still follow their ancient way of life as herders of reindeer.

The Norwegian language has two forms. One form, close to Danish, is called *bokmaal* (that is, "book language") and used to be Norway's official language. The other *nynorsk* ("new Norwegian") is based on Old Norse and country dialects. For most children *bokmaal* is the main language used at school. Efforts are being made to bring the two forms closer together.

Children must attend a comprehensive school, which is free, between the ages of 7 and 16. They can then take vocational or higher education courses if they wish. There are universities in Oslo, Bergen, Tromsø and Trondheim, and many colleges. Adults can also attend "folk high schools", which are residential colleges without entry requirements or examinations.

FACTS ABOUT NORWAY

AREA: 323,878 square kilometers (125,050 square miles).
POPULATION: 4,246,000 (1990).
GOVERNMENT: Constitutional monarchy.
CAPITAL: Oslo, 455,632.
GEOGRAPHY: A long, narrow mountainous country, partly within the Arctic Circle. Nearly all the coast has cliffs and is shielded from the open sea by a fringe of about 150,000 islands. Long arms of the sea called fiords stretch far into the heart of the country.
CITIES: Bergen, 211,214; Trondheim, 136,629; Stavanger, 97,093; Baerum (part of Oslo's built-up area) 88,752.
ECONOMY: Products and exports.
  Agriculture: Barley, oats, potatoes, sheep, cattle, pigs, wood, fish.
  Mining: Iron ore, titanium, zinc, copper.
  Manufacturing: Machinery and electrical and transportation equipment, paper products, food products, chemical products, wood and wood products.
  Exports: Crude petroleum, natural gas, iron and steel, machinery and transportation equipment, fish and fish products.
EDUCATION: Children must attend school between the ages of 7 and 16.

Most Norwegians (over 90 per cent of the population) belong to the Protestant (Lutheran) Church. Norway has a constitutional monarchy. The Norwegian parliament, called the *Storting*, is elected every four years. Norway has an excellent welfare system provided by the state. There are good pensions for the old and disabled, unemployment benefits, child allowances, and medical treatment for everyone.

Norwegians excel at skiing – downhill and cross-country – ski-jumping, and other winter sports, and the children learn to ski almost as soon as they can walk. Sailing, tennis, and football (a summer game in Norway) are also popular.

Over 70 per cent of the people live in towns. Most densely populated are the areas around Oslo and the coastline facing Denmark. Oslo, the capital, has a population of nearly half a million. (See OSLO.) The next largest city is the port of Bergen, on the west coast, ringed by seven mountains. In the Middle Ages it was a Hanseatic port (see HANSEATIC LEAGUE). Other important towns are Trondheim, the old capital, and Stavanger. In the countryside most

Bergen is centered on the city's deep-water harbor. The city has been an important port since the days of the Hanseatic merchants, in the 14th century.

ZEFA

houses are wooden, and some wooden churches built in the 12th century are still standing.

Industry, Agriculture, and Fisheries

In the 1970s oil fields such as the Ekofisk field in the Norwegian sector of the North Sea began to yield large amounts of oil and natural gas. Most of this is exported, providing about 20 per cent of all Norwegian exports. The only coalfield is in Spitsbergen, but iron ore is mined near the Russian border and elsewhere. Other minerals include sulfur and copper and also ilmenite, from which titanium is produced. The abundant supply of electricity from water power makes it worthwhile to bring metallic ores (rocks and earth) from overseas for smelting (extracting the metal). Aluminum and iron alloys are the chief products of this industry, and Norway is an important exporter of these. Other industries are the manufacture of nitrogen fertilizers, the cutting of timber for pulp and paper, and engineering, including ship and oil platform building.

Farming in Norway now employs fewer people than industry. The chief crops are hay and root crops for animal feed, barley, oats, and potatoes. Wheat production is rising but most of Norway's grain is still obtained from other countries. Blue foxes, silver foxes, and minks are bred for their fur.

Norwegian fisheries are very large and the chief catches are cod, capelin, and brisling.

However, the fish population is falling because of over-fishing. Herring have almost disappeared from Norway's coastal waters. Some of the catch is made into animal feed or fish oil, or dried, salted or canned and sent abroad. In the spring and summer seals

Courtesy, Norway Travel Association

This road in western Norway forms a zigzag pattern with its sharp hairpin bends.

are hunted in the Arctic. Norway was formerly one of the world's leading whaling nations. (See WHALING.)

Transportation

Although the building of roads and railroads is difficult in such a mountainous and snowy country as Norway, there are many good roads, and the railroad network covers 4,258 kilometers, 58 per cent of it electrified.

For Norway, however, the sea is the main highway, and many small steamers and motor vessels ply up and down the coasts and into the fiords. Besides this coastal shipping, Norway has one of the largest merchant fleets in the world. Half the ships are oil tankers and most of them earn money for Norway by carrying goods between other countries. Inland air traffic is well developed and is very important for sparsely populated areas. Norway has joined with Denmark and Sweden to form the Scandinavian Airlines System (SAS) with services from Oslo, Bergen, and Stavanger.

History

The Lapps came to Norway at least 10,000 years ago, probably from central Asia. In the 8th century the Scandinavian Vikings began to raid and seize large parts of northern Europe, pushing the Lapps further north. Some Vikings settled in Ireland, Iceland, and Greenland. Some even reached the coast of North America. The Vikings were most active before the arrival of Christianity (see NORSE LEGENDS; VIKINGS).

In AD 872 Norway was united under Harald Haarfager (Fairhair), who had promised not to have his hair cut until he had conquered his enemies. Shortly after the year 1000 the country was converted to Christianity by King Olav, later Norway's national saint. By the 13th century the Norwegian kings ruled over part of Scotland (Caithness), the Hebrides, the islands of Shetland, Orkney, the Faeroe Islands, Iceland and Greenland, as well as their own country. In 1349 the plague called the Black Death raged through Norway killing two thirds of the population. In 1397 Norway, Sweden and Denmark were united. Sweden

withdrew from the union in 1523 but Norway remained and in 1536 was declared part of Denmark. Following Denmark's lead Norway accepted Lutheranism, which remains the state church. After the Napoleonic wars, Denmark gave up its claim to Norway and in 1814 the country was forced into a union with Sweden, but had first succeeded in establishing its own parliament and its own laws and constitution. A strong national movement grew during the 19th century, leading to complete Norwegian independence in 1905. A Danish prince was elected king and was crowned Haakon VII. His grandson, Harald, is the present king of Norway.

Norway remained neutral in World War I, but in World War II Germany invaded Norway and the king and government took refuge in Britain. The Germans set up a government under the Norwegian Vidkun Quisling – whose name came to be used in many countries to mean a traitor – but the people did all they could to oppose German rule. Fishing boats sailed so often from Norway to the Shetland Isles with refugees and secret agents that it became known as the "Shetland bus".

After the war Norway joined the North Atlantic Treaty Organization (NATO) and the United Nations.

Art, Music, Literature, and Explorers

A great deal of Norwegian folk art dates from the time Norway was part of Denmark, and took the form of weaving, knitting, wood carving, and metal work. Some districts also have a rich folk-music and folk-tale tradition. During the period of nationalism in the 19th century many Norwegian artists found inspiration in these traditions.

The folk-music tradition is preserved in the compositions of Edvard Grieg (1843–1907), Johan Svendsen (1840–1911), and those of the violinist Ole Bull (1810–80). Early Norwegian literature consists largely of the ancient Norse sagas (see SAGA), which were written mainly by Norwegian settlers in Iceland.

Later writers include the playwright Henrik Ibsen (1828–1906), the poet, novelist, and

Philip Gendreau

This fine old wooden church stands at Borgund.

playwright Bjørnstjerne Bjørnson (1832–1910), and the novelists Knut Hamsun (1859–1952), Sigrid Undset (1882–1949), and Tarjei Vesaas (1897–1970).

Among Norwegian artists, Edvard Munch (1863–1944) was a leading painter of the Expressionist school, and the sculptor Gustav Vigeland (1869–1943) filled the Frogner park in Oslo with large figures of men, women, and children.

There are separate articles on the Arctic and Antarctic explorers Roald Amundsen and Fridtjof Nansen. Other famous Norwegian explorers include the Vikings Eric the Red and Leif Eriksson (on whom there are separate articles), and the present-day traveler Thor Heyerdahl (see HEYERDAHL, THOR). Weather forecasting owes much to the work of the Norwegian scientist Vilhelm Bjerknes and his son Jacob.

NOSE. The nose does several important things besides enabling its owner to enjoy the delicious smell of dinner cooking in the oven. It is one of the links between the outside air and the blood which carries oxygen to all parts of the body.

The air which is breathed in is filtered in the nose before it reaches the lungs, for the nose has a very efficient and important air-conditioning system. Just inside the nostrils are hairs which filter off the larger bits of dust and grit that are breathed in. Then the air passes over some curled folds called the turbinate bones. Each nostril has three. They are covered with a sticky membrane, or lining, which gives off moisture and is called a mucous membrane. The inside of the nose is covered with this mucous membrane and dust particles stick to it. The membrane is covered with cilia, which are like tiny hairs. The cilia are constantly waving backwards and forwards and their movements sweep dust particles and germs back again towards the nostrils, and outside when a person sneezes or blows the nose. The many small blood vessels in the nose keep the air warm, and so before it reaches the lungs it is both warmed and filtered and moistened.

Odors are detected by two small areas with many nerve cells right at the top of the nose, called the olfactory epithelium. These are almost outgrowths of the brain, which lies just above. Humans can detect nearly 3,000 different odors. It is thought the "smell molecules" floating in the air fit into "detectors" in the olfactory epithelium, like a key fits into a lock.

Lastly, the nose has some effect on the tone of the voice, which alters, for example, if the nose is blocked by a cold or if the nostrils are held closed by the fingers.

See also SENSES.

NOTTINGHAMSHIRE is a county in the north Midlands of England. Its northern border is with South Yorkshire and Humberside. To the east is Lincolnshire. Leicestershire is to the south and Derbyshire to the west. Nottinghamshire has an area of 2,164 square kilometers (836 square miles) and a population of 1,000,100 (1984).

Its main river is the Trent, which flows through the county from south to north.

Although Nottinghamshire is not close to the sea, the waters of the Trent rise and fall with the tides for nearly half its course through the county. Along the river are a number of large power plants, which use its water for cooling purposes.

There are four different areas of Nottinghamshire. In the middle, from the county town of Nottingham almost to the Yorkshire border, are the remains of Sherwood Forest. In the Middle Ages Sherwood was far larger and, it is said, the English folk hero Robin Hood lived and hunted there. (See ROBIN HOOD.) Most of the forest was cut down in the 17th and 18th centuries and the wood burned to provide charcoal for forging iron, but many oaks can still be seen.

Much of Sherwood, which was a royal forest, belonged to the great abbey churches, and after they were closed by Henry VIII in the 16th century, the estates passed to noble families, such as the dukes of Newcastle. In the 19th century this area became known as the Dukeries. Some of the great houses and parks can still be seen.

The second area is to the west of Sherwood Forest, along the Derbyshire border. Here coal seams are found near the surface and all around are pitheads and huge heaps of mine waste.

The third area, the broad Trent valley, has fertile soil with orchards and truck farms. Roses, and many other flowers, are grown.

The fourth area is south of the Trent, towards the Leicestershire border. It is high and windy, and is sometimes called the Nottinghamshire Wolds. The highest points are Cresswell Crags.

Towns and Industries

Nottingham is much the largest town in the county. Its name means "the home of caves", for the city is built on a great sandstone ridge with many caves. "The Trip to Jerusalem" is claimed to be the oldest inn in England and has rooms cut into the rock.

Nottingham's busy industrial life began in the reign of Elizabeth I, when the making of stockings on frames, instead of by hand, was begun. Today Nottingham is a center of the clothing trade and is known for its lace. It also has important pharmaceutical, manufacturing, and tobacco industries, and a cycle factory. There is a university in Nottingham. The city also has an old fair, the Goose Fair, held at the beginning of October.

Southwell, northeast of Nottingham, is a town with a cathedral dating from the 13th century. Newark-on-Trent has a castle that was ruined in the English Civil War, a fine church, and several Roman remains. King John died at Newark in 1216. It has been a great malting and brewing center since the Middle Ages.

Mansfield, on the edge of Sherwood Forest, and Worksop, near the Dukeries, are both industrial towns where brewing and mining take place, as well as other industries. East Retford, in the north of the county, is a market town.

Much of Nottinghamshire is farmland where crops are grown and many dairy cattle and sheep are kept. Stilton cheese is made in the county. Nottinghamshire is, however, more famous for its mining and industries. The coalfield has some of the most modern mines in Britain; coal has been mined there since the 13th century. Canals were cut to carry coal by ship from the mines to the Trent and then down to the sea. They also carried

ZEFA

Nottingham Castle, first built by William the Conqueror, now houses a museum and art gallery. Note the caves in the rock on which it is built.

Barnaby's

The modern city center of Nottingham seen from the castle grounds.

iron and other heavy goods; some canals are still navigable.

History

After the Norman Conquest in 1066 a castle was built at Nottingham. King John, Edward IV, Henry VII, and Henry VIII all eventually occupied this castle. Henry VII set out from it in 1487 to win the battle of Stoke a few miles away against Lambert Simnel, who claimed the throne of England. The castle was pulled down by order of Oliver Cromwell, and the first Duke of Newcastle built another there in the 17th century. In 1831, however, it was burned down during riots over the Reform Bill, which sought to increase the number of people allowed to vote at parliamentary elections (see PARLIAMENT). The castle was rebuilt and is now a museum.

Nottinghamshire was industrialized from the 16th century, when landowners such as Sir Francis Willoughby gained wealth from coal mines. He built Wollaton Hall, a mansion close to Nottingham, which is now a museum.

Among famous people who were born in the county are the churchman Thomas Cranmer (1489–1556); General William Booth (1829–1912), founder of the Salvation Army; and the novelist D. H. Lawrence (1885–1930).

NOUN. In grammar, all the words in a language are divided into a number of different groups according to what kinds of words they are. Nouns form one of these groups, and they are "naming-words", words which name persons or places or things. *Michael, Elizabeth, president, storekeeper, England, Australia, Paris, tree, dog, chimney, sky*—all these words are nouns.

Nouns themselves are divided into two main types, called common and proper. Proper nouns are words that name particular things or people, picking them out from among all other similar things or people; for example, *Everest, Glasgow, Baltic Sea, John Smith* are all proper nouns. Everest is the name of one particular mountain, Glasgow of one particular town, and so on. Proper nouns begin with a capital letter, and if there are two or more words in the name each word usually begins with a capital, as in *Panama Canal* or *Niagara Falls*. All other nouns are common nouns, words which are the names for things in general rather than for particular examples; such words are *cat, field, table, river, mountain*.

Most nouns, of course, are common nouns, and among them are two special kinds besides all the ordinary ones. These are collective nouns and abstract nouns. Collective nouns name groups of things or people taken together, such as *herd, flock, committee, people, army*. Abstract nouns are names of qualities or ideas which we cannot touch or see or hear as we can the ordinary objects around us; examples are *bravery, justice, fear, speed*.

Singular and Plural Nouns

A noun which names one person or thing such as *book* is described as being in the singular number. When it names more than one, *books*, it is in the plural number. Most nouns make the plural by adding *s* or *es* to the singular: *toy, toys; church, churches; glass, glasses*. Nouns ending in *o* usually form the plural by adding *es* to the singular: *hero, heroes; tomato, tomatoes*. There are a few exceptions to this, such as *piano, pianos*.

Nouns ending in *y* when the *y* comes after a consonant change the *y* to *i* and add *es* to form the plural: *lady, ladies*. Nouns ending in *ey* simply add *s: monkey, monkeys*. Some nouns ending in *f* or *fe* form the plural by changing *f* to *v* and adding *es: knife, knives; wharf, wharves*.

Some nouns, however, do not follow the usual rules in forming the plural, but instead they change vowels in the middle of the word: *man, men; woman, women; goose, geese; mouse, mice. Children* used to have two plural endings, *er* and *en*, and the form *childer* is still sometimes used in country speech. Another word with a plural ending in *en* is *ox, oxen*. A few names like *deer* and *sheep* are the same whether they are singular or plural.

Nouns that are made up of several words joined together – called compound nouns – make their plural by adding the plural ending to the chief word; thus *mother-in-law* changes to *mothers-in-law*, not *mother-in-laws*.

Gender and Case

In some languages nouns have special endings or changes not only to show the difference between singular and plural, as in English, but also to show what is called their gender. In French there are two genders – a noun is either masculine or feminine; in Danish the two genders are called common or neuter; in Latin there are masculine, feminine, and neuter genders. These genders are important because they make a difference to other words being used with the noun. In modern English, nouns do not have genders of this kind (though pronouns do) and the only nouns that are masculine or feminine are ones that refer to something male or female. For example, *boy, bull, gander, actor* are masculine, *girl, cow, goose, actress* are feminine. A few nouns such as *child* and *person*, which may be either masculine or feminine, are sometimes said to be of the common gender. All other nouns in English are of the neuter gender.

The only other change in the spelling of English nouns besides the change from singular to plural occurs when a noun is in what is called the possessive case; that is, when it is showing ownership of something. An example is *Mary's doll*, which means "the doll that Mary owns" or "the doll that belongs to Mary". Other examples are *my father's house, Tom's bicycle*.

The spelling of the possessive form of nouns sometimes causes trouble, so it is a good idea to learn the rules.

1. The possessive singular of any noun is formed by adding *'s: clock, a clock's hands; sailor, a sailor's cap; Burns, Burns's poetry*. (Proper names of more than one syllable and ending in *s*, however, sometimes have only an apostrophe added, as *Moses, Moses'*.)

2. Plural nouns ending in *s* form the possessive by adding the apostrophe only: *boys, boys'*.

3. Plural nouns not ending in *s* form the possessive by adding *'s: men, men's; children, children's*.

In English, nouns have two other cases but these are not shown by any change in spelling. The first is called the nominative case. A noun which is the subject of a verb or a noun which comes after the verb "to be" is said to be in the nominative case. The second case is called the accusative or objective case. A noun which is the direct object of a verb or a noun which follows a preposition is said to be in the accusative or objective case.

See also PRONOUN.

NOVA SCOTIA is one of the Atlantic Provinces of Canada. It has two main parts, the peninsula and Cape Breton Island, which are separated from each other by the Strait of Canso. The peninsula is connected to the mainland by the Isthmus of Chignecto, a narrow strip of land 27 kilometers (17 miles) wide. New Brunswick and the Bay of Fundy lie to the west and north of the provinces; Prince Edward Island in the Gulf of St. Lawrence lies north of the peninsula; and the Atlantic Ocean is to the east and south. The length of the province is about 595 kilometers (370 miles) and its width varies from about

80 to 170 kilometers (50 to 105 miles). No point of the province is more than 96 kilometers (60 miles) from the sea. The area is 52,840 square kilometers (20,402 square miles) which makes Nova Scotia the second smallest of Canada's ten provinces; Prince Edward Island is the smallest.

Nova Scotia has many small lakes and rivers. The largest lake, Bras d'Or Lake in Cape Breton, is unusual since it connects with the Atlantic Ocean to form an inland sea. Other lakes are Lake Ainslie, in northern Cape Breton, and Lake Rossignol, in the western part of the province. Among the important rivers are the Annapolis, Medway, Mersey, Shubenacadie, and Lahave.

The Atlantic coastline is rocky and provides excellent harbors for the many fishing vessels of the province. The western shore of the peninsula looks towards the mainland across the Bay of Fundy, which has a greater rise and fall of tide than any other place. The difference between high and low water levels at the head of the bay can reach 15 meters (50 feet). This coast is protected from Atlantic gales by a low mountain backbone running the length of the peninsula. The fertile valley of the Annapolis River, parallel to the shore, is called the garden of Nova Scotia.

Climate and Peoples

Nova Scotia's climate is moderate. The province is in the paths of the prevailing westerly winds that bring the harsh weather of North America, but the nearness of the sea has a warming effect. Summers are pleasant, especially on the seacoast where cool daytime breezes blow in. Fogs are common on the southern and eastern coasts.

Most of the people live along the seacoast, but there are inland settlements wherever there are fertile valleys. The density of population is the second highest in Canada. More than half of the people live in towns and cities.

About three-quarters of Nova Scotians have English, Scottish, or Irish ancestry. There is also a sizable French and German population. Descendants of the Micmac Indians, earliest of all the province's inhabitants, now number only several thousand.

Economy

Nova Scotia is known for its fruit, especially apples, grown in orchards around the Annapolis valley, but dairy farming is the chief form of agriculture. About ten percent of the land is suitable for farming. Most of it is in the Annapolis Valley. Besides dairying, there are poultry and mixed farming (crops and animals). The fisheries are very important and lobsters, cod, mackerel, herring, and haddock make up most of the catch. Much of the province is covered with forest – mainly spruce, balsam, fir, hemlock, birch, maple, and pine – and the network of small lakes and rivers is a great help in bringing logs to the sawmills. Some of the timber is made into wood pulp for newsprint (paper).

More than one-third of Canada's coal comes from Nova Scotia, the chief coalfields being around Sydney in Cape Breton Island. There are large iron and steel mills at Sydney and New Glasgow, using iron ore obtained from Newfoundland and coal and limestone mined in Nova Scotia. Competition from other parts of the world is making Nova Scotia's steel industry unprofitable and it requires large amounts of government funds to survive. Much gypsum, a substance used for making plaster and building-blocks, is also mined.

Halifax, with its large ice-free harbor, is the capital and chief port of Nova Scotia (see HALIFAX). Other important towns are Sydney, which also has an excellent harbor, and the mining and manufacturing center of Glace Bay. Many tourists visit the province for fishing and other sports or to enjoy the scenery.

History

Nova Scotia was first settled in 1604 by the French, who called it Acadia (see ACADIA). In 1621, however, King James I of England

Crab pots are stacked ready for fishing at this waterfront along Cheticamp, Nova Scotia.

Barnaby's

granted the land to Sir William Alexander under the name Nova Scotia, which means "new Scotland". For nearly a century the French and British colonists fought for control, until in 1713 the Treaty of Utrecht recognized the peninsula as British. More British colonists arrived and in 1755 about 3,000 French settlers were driven from Nova Scotia to other American colonies.

For the hundred years following 1750 Nova Scotia grew rapidly. Halifax, founded in 1749, became a garrison and naval city as well as the capital of the colony. Thousands of American colonists loyal to Britain settled in Nova Scotia after the American Revolution. At that time Cape Breton became a separate colony, and it was not reunited with Nova Scotia until 1820. During the first half of the 19th century thousands of Scottish and Irish people moved to the colony. Trade and shipping boomed. Products of the fisheries, forests, farms, and later of the mines were carried over the seas—often on ships built in Nova Scotia's shipyards.

During these prosperous years some great changes in government took place. An elected assembly was granted in 1758, the first in what is now Canada. But real power remained with the governor and his council.

In 1848, Nova Scotia became the first Canadian province to obtain self-government. The main leader in the movement for self-government was newspaper publisher Joseph Howe, one of Nova Scotia's most

Courtesy, Government of Canada

Citadel Clock is a familiar landmark in Halifax, a city of historic sites and modern skyscrapers.

famous men. The province was also the first to have a university, a printing-press, and a newspaper.

The American and Canadian nickname for a Nova Scotian is "bluenose". The population of the province is about 879,600 (1985).

NOVEL. A novel is a book-length tale of fiction, usually written in prose. A novel has characters, settings, and actions that represent real life in the past, present, or future. These are presented in a series of events, called the plot, that tell a story. The length of novels varies a good deal. Novels may have several thousand pages, or they may be as short as a hundred. Tales of fewer than a hundred pages are usually called short stories.

Although fiction is the invention of a writer, many novels are based upon real people or events, and most give a feeling of truth. Often an author selects a real town and country as a background for fictional characters and actions. The characters, their lives, the events, and the surroundings of a novel, however, may all be created by the writer. A person who writes novels is usually called a novelist.

The many events of a novel's plot are organized in a more complicated way than in a story or a fable. In a fable, the reader's interest normally comes from following the mere sequence of events. In Aesop's *Fables*, for example, the reader is just waiting to see what will happen next to the fox or the wolf. In a novel, on the other hand, the reader is as interested in the causes and effects of what happens as in the events themselves. The novelist wants the reader to understand why a character did a certain thing, or why a certain thing happened as a result of somebody's character.

We can understand the novel better by comparing it with its earliest ancestors, notably the romance. The romance has many things in common with the legend and the fable. It deals with events and experiences that could not really happen, and it treats those events in a general way, without giving the reader much detail about the world in which the characters live, and without giving the reader much information about the minds of the characters. *Daphnis and Chloe*, for instance, is an interesting love story. It takes place in an idealized countryside, which has little to do with the actual world that existed in Greece when it was written by Longus in the 2nd century. *Daphnis and Chloe* is called a pastoral romance. This kind of fiction was popular in ancient Greece and Rome, and in Europe during the 16th century.

Another kind of romance, called the chivalric romance, was popular in the Middle Ages. One famous example is Sir Thomas Malory's *Morte d'Arthur*, written in England in the 15th century. This series of stories presents the adventures of knights with dragons, sorcerers, and enchanted castles, without much reference to the characters' thoughts or ideas.

Another form of early prose fiction that was popular in the 16th century was the picaresque novel. The word *picaresque* comes from the Spanish word *picaro*, which means rogue. The picaresque novel deals with the adventures of a main character who is the opposite of the knightly hero of the chivalric romances—he is a rascal, although often a likable one, and through him the reader experiences the ridiculous or ugly side of life. One famous example of the picaresque novel is the Scottish novelist Tobias Smollett's *Roderick Random*.

Great novelists have sometimes used the forms of the romance and the picaresque novel for different purposes. An example is *Don Quixote*, written in the early 17th century by the Spanish novelist Miguel de Cervantes Saavedra. In *Don Quixote* the author makes fun of the romances of chivalry and presents his two main characters in a series of adventures similar to those which a picaresque hero encounters. *Don Quixote* is one of the greatest works of fiction ever written.

Classification

The kinds of novel can be classified according to their subject, or to the way in which they are told. J. D. Salinger's *The Catcher in the Rye*, for instance, is a novel of character, because its chief aim is to give a full picture of its hero. A historical novel deals with past times, as Charles Dickens's *A Tale of Two Cities* dealt with the French Revolution. As for classifying novels according to the way they are told, there are two main methods. Where everything is concentrated in a few important scenes, which are given in full, rather like a play, the novel is called dramatic, or scenic: Henry James's *Portrait of A Lady* is one example. The panoramic novel gives the reader a large view of life going on in many different places at many different times: William Makepeace Thackeray's *Vanity Fair*, which covers the whole lives of many characters, in many parts of England and Europe, is panoramic in method.

History

The novel has become a highly developed and distinct literary form in many countries. The separate national LITERATURE articles you will find in the encyclopedia describe the development of the novel in many different languages and cultures. The following history describes the development of the novel in the United Kingdom (the English novel) and in America. Many of the novelists mentioned also have separate articles. Consult the Index volume.

The English Novel

Prose fiction in English was written during the 16th and 17th centuries. In the early 18th century, however, the English novel came much closer to its modern form with Daniel Defoe. His *Robinson Crusoe* (1719) and *Moll Flanders* (1722) were written in the form of autobiographical memoirs. In them Defoe made his fiction appear to be literally true, and portrayed characters who were ordinary people mainly engaged in making their living. Samuel Richardson, writing two decades after Defoe, has been called the father of the English novel. In *Clarissa* (1748), his masterpiece, Richardson gives a picture of the inner social and psychological struggle of his young heroine. Richardson's contemporary, Henry Fielding, is the first great English comic novelist.

Sir Walter Scott was one of the most prolific and influential novelists of the early 19th century. His *Waverley* (1814) is the first of a long series of historical novels. Jane Austen, writing at the same time as Sir Walter Scott, used the comic aspects of familiar domestic life to make people think more seriously about social and moral values.

" *To whom I have related the affair* "
Mary Evans Picture Library

The pompous Mr. Collins addresses his Bennett hosts, a scene from Jane Austen's *Pride and Prejudice*. Her novels were comedies of manners making gentle fun of society.

The novels of the Victorian period often reflected the social changes produced by the Industrial Revolution and attacked the sufferings that resulted. Charles Dickens was a reformer in everything he wrote, but he was also a great comic novelist. Dickens is the greatest as well as the most popular novelist of the Victorian Age. The finest individual novel of that period, however, is probably *Middlemarch* (1872) by George Eliot (Mary Ann Evans). In it she shows a whole community being changed by the Industrial Revolution.

Later in the 19th century George Meredith and Thomas Hardy, were prominent. Meredith's novels, such as *The Egoist* (1879), present the mind of an individual character in the setting of a larger social problem. Thomas Hardy deals with isolated individuals whose destinies are rendered tragic by related circumstances.

The American Novel

The American novel did not come into its own until the 19th century. When it did, it reflected the fact that America was a relatively new country with a growing population spread out

Huck Finn is one of the best-loved boys in fiction. His adventures on the Mississippi River have been relived by generations of readers. This picture is by E. W. Kemble and was drawn in 1884 for the first edition of *The Adventures of Huckleberry Finn.*

Bettmann Archive

over many distant and often isolated regions. It lacked the history, tradition, and shared customs of an older and smaller country such as Britain. The great American novelists of the 19th century wrote more of the experiences and thoughts of isolated individuals.

James Fenimore Cooper is best known for his "Leather-Stocking Tales," a series of five novels dealing with the adventures of Natty Bumppo, the lonely seeker of a truer way of life which endlessly eludes him. Nathaniel Hawthorne also deals with characters who seek truth beyond the established attitudes and ideas of their society. *Moby-Dick* (1851) is perhaps the greatest American novel of the 19th century. In it Herman Melville dramatized the plight of Ahab, the sea captain driven to destruction by his search for a great white whale.

The most influential novel of the 19th century was Harriet Beecher Stowe's *Uncle Tom's Cabin* (1852). This novel, dealing with the horrors of black slave life in the South, did much to arouse opposition to slavery.

Like Cooper, Hawthorne, and Melville, Mark Twain (Samuel L. Clemens) wrote about characters who look for the meaning of life outside the customs of the community into which they were born. Unlike those authors he was primarily a humorous writer.

Towards the end of the 19th century, two American novelists, William Dean Howells and Henry James, came closer to the English pattern of the novel and showed characters acting within established societies. Howells' *The Rise of Silas Lapham* (1885) is a study of the attempt of a self-made manufacturer of paint to push his family into the fashionable society of Boston. James's novels show Americans confronting European culture.

In the 20th century, there was much less difference between British and American societies. The Industrial Revolution had transformed both countries; and, later, World War I made the United States part of the international world. As a result, modern American novelists tended to share the same pessimism about progress and the peaceful solution of world problems as did British writers. See the sections on the 20th century in AMERICAN LITERATURE and ENGLISH LITERATURE.

There is no limit to the possible forms and subjects of the novel. Its history will go on as long as novelists can both entertain us and increase our understanding of ourselves.

See also CHILDREN'S LITERATURE.

NOVOSIBIRSK is Russian for "New Siberia", and it is the largest city in Siberia. It is the administrative center of Novosibirsk *oblast* (administrative region) and a major transportation, industrial, and scientific center. The city lies over 2,400 kilometers (1,500 miles) east of Moscow.

Camera Press

The Novosibirsk Opera and Ballet Theater helps to make the city the cultural center of Siberia.

Novosibirsk has been called the "Chicago of Siberia". The city was founded in 1893 at the point where the Trans-Siberian Railroad crossed the Ob River. It grew as a transshipment point between rail and water. The modern city contains a variety of industries, but it is most important as a producer of metals and heavy machinery. Its tin smelter is the largest in Russia. Consumer products include furniture, shoes, clothing, and foods. Much of its power comes from a hydroelectric dam on the Ob. The river is also navigable. The rail line carries much freight and many passengers, and there are also two airports.

Novosibirsk is developing rapidly as the cultural center of Siberia. It contains an impressive theater for opera and ballet, a botanical garden, an art gallery, and museums. It is also notable for its educational institutions, including the Novosibirsk State University founded in 1959. The city has its own symphony orchestra. The population is 1,446,300 (1991), making it the third largest city in Russia.

NUCLEAR ENERGY is the energy released in a nuclear reaction – that is, a reaction involving changes within the nucleus, or central portion, of an atom. For information on the relevant chemical and physical issues with which nuclear energy is concerned see ATOM; CHEMISTRY; ELECTRON; ELEMENTARY PARTICLES; MOLECULE; NEUTRON; PROTON; RADIOACTIVITY.

A normal chemical reaction involves only some of the outermost electrons of the reacting atoms – the atoms themselves remain unchanged but combine with other kinds of atoms to produce molecules. During chemical reactions some of the chemical energy that lies in the arrangement of the atoms may be released as heat, for example, in the burning of fuels such as wood, coal, and oil. A nuclear reaction involves the nucleus, the very heart of the atom, composed of protons and neutrons, and some of the mass of the atom is converted into energy. A nuclear reaction releases several million times more energy than a chemical reaction and, unlike a chemical reaction, involves a change in which one element is turned into another.

Nuclear Fission

Nuclear reactions are of two types. One involves *fission*, in which the nucleus is broken apart; the other involves *fusion*, in which the nuclei of light atoms are forced together to form a heavier one.

In nuclear fission, the nucleus is split into

Neutron

Proton

How a chain reaction works. A neutron is cannoned into a heavy nucleus of a fissile atom. The heavy atom splits into two lighter ones, releasing great energy and more neutrons to continue the reaction.

several particles by collision with a free neutron. The mass of all the particles concerned is less than the mass of the original "target" atom plus the colliding neutron. The difference appears in the form of energy. This fact was first recognized in 1905 by Albert Einstein who set out the formula $E = mc^2$. In this formula, E, the energy released, equals m, the mass lost, multiplied by c^2, the speed of light squared. As the factor c is very large, the energy released by even small losses of mass is enormous.

An element whose atomic nucleus can be split by fission is called *fissile*. The only naturally occurring fissile element is uranium, on which there is a separate article. In 1938, two Germans, Otto Hahn and Fritz Strassmann, succeeded in splitting the large uranium atom by bombarding it with neutrons. Two other Germans, Lise Meitner and Otto Frisch, showed that the uranium nucleus split into two fragments, and a group of French scientists then found that when fission occurred, not only were two lighter elements and a lot of

radiation produced, but also more free neutrons. It was clear that these neutrons could in turn also cause fission in surrounding uranium atoms, producing yet more neutrons and developing a "chain reaction" which might spread throughout the uranium atoms resulting in the release of enormous amounts of energy.

The energy released by fission appears in the high speed given to the particles, and as they collide with atoms in the surrounding material they are slowed down and the energy of motion is turned into heat which can be extracted. The heat can be harnessed to produce steam and drive turbines for the production of electricity (see ELECTRIC POWER); or else it can be given off in a huge destructive explosion, as in an atomic bomb or nuclear warhead.

The Fission of Uranium

Uranium appears in nature as a mixture of two main forms (isotopes). The term *isotope* is explained in the articles on ATOM and

NEUTRON. More than 99 per cent of uranium is uranium-238 (U-238) and less than 1 per cent is uranium-235 (U-235), the number in each case being the mass number (the combined number of protons and neutrons in the nucleus). Thus U-238 has three extra neutrons in the nucleus and so the two forms have different physical properties. Only U-235 atoms are fissile; atoms of U-238 are *fertile*—that is, they do not themselves readily undergo fission, but can absorb high-speed neutrons to produce an atom of the heavier element plutonium-239. This isotope of plutonium is fissile. Both uranium and plutonium are used as fuel in nuclear reactors.

The Nuclear Reactor

As already explained, the fission of uranium atoms by free neutrons produces more neutrons and leads on to further fission and a chain reaction. The smallest piece of uranium in which a chain reaction will build up is called the *critical mass*. If two pieces of uranium that are both smaller than the critical mass are brought together, forming a lump that is larger than the critical mass, the result is an enormous explosion. This is how an atomic bomb is made.

It is possible, however, to control a chain reaction in a nuclear reactor. The first such reactor was built by the Italian-born American physicist Enrico Fermi in the squash court of the University of Chicago in 1942. Here a self-sustaining chain reaction was made artificially for the first time. The *atomic pile* (the structure in which the reaction was generated) was made of graphite, a very pure form of carbon, in which were inserted rods of uranium metal enclosed in thin cans of aluminium. Neutrons escaping from one rod were slowed down, or "moderated", in the graphite by colliding with the carbon atoms and re-entered another rod to produce further fission. Although materials have changed, the basic principles for controlling a nuclear chain reaction remain roughly the same as those employed by Fermi in 1942.

Nuclear Power Plants

A nuclear power plant is basically not unlike an ordinary coal-burning power plant. Heat boils water, producing steam which spins a turbine and the turbine generates electricity. In a nuclear power plant, the heat needed is released by splitting atoms in a reactor.

Types of Reactor. The first reactors to produce a usable amount of power were built in the 1950s at Calder Hall in Great Britain. They were built mainly to make plutonium for military purposes and to gain experience in nuclear power; they began to generate electricity in 1956. The moderator (as in Fermi's pile) was graphite, and the fuel was metallic natural uranium canned in a magnesium alloy and cooled by carbon dioxide under pressure. The carbon dioxide gas was circulated over the fuel thereby conducting away the heat produced by the reaction, and then through heat exchangers, where steam was raised to drive turbo-alternators producing electricity. This was known as a "magnox" type of reactor; other reactors of similar design were built, and a second generation of *Advanced Gas-Cooled Reactors* (AGRs) followed.

In the United States, researchers concentrated in the early 1950s on building a reactor small enough to power a submarine. The American authorities had a lot of enriched uranium (that is, uranium in which the U-235 content had been increased) and chose ordinary water as a moderator. This is more efficient than graphite at slowing down neutrons, although it is also a neutron absorber, thus cutting down the number of neutrons available for keeping the chain reaction going. When they had developed their submarine power unit, the American researchers turned their attention to building a similar type of reactor suitable for making electricity cheaply. Two main types were designed: the *Pressurized Water Reactor* (PWR) and the *Boiling Water Reactor* (BWR).

In the PWR, the fuel is uranium dioxide artificially enriched to about 3 per cent U-235 and canned in a special alloy. The moderator and coolant is ordinary water, pumped through the reactor and then through a heat exchanger

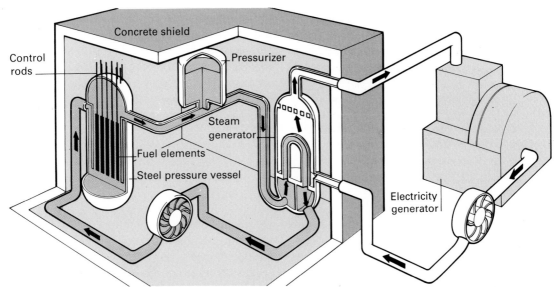

In the Pressurized Water Reactor water at high pressure is both moderator and coolant. It takes heat from the reactor core and is kept under pressure until converted into steam to drive a generator.

where it is turned into steam for the turbines in a second water circuit. In the BWR, the nuclear part of the reactor is similar, but there is no second water system, and steam from the reactor cooling circuit goes straight to the turbines. Most countries with nuclear power programs have chosen either PWR or BWR reactors of various designs.

Inside a Reactor. In a modern nuclear reactor, uranium is sealed into rods, grouped in clusters known as fuel elements. The rods are arranged so that a liquid or gas coolant can flow to remove the heat. "Control" rods of a material (such as boron) which will readily absorb neutrons and so stop the chain reactions are arranged to be raised or lowered in channels between the fuel elements. In this way, the power output can be controlled. The whole assembly of fuel elements and control rods is embedded in a moderator of graphite, water, or heavy water (water rich in the hydrogen isotope deuterium). The reactor vessel is surrounded by a very thick shield of concrete or steel to contain the radioactivity created in the fission process.

"Fast" Reactors. Each uranium fission reaction releases two or three neutrons, but only one is needed to keep the chain of fission reactions going, so there are many "spare" neu-

trons. Some escape to be absorbed in the reactor shielding, in the moderator, and in non-fissionable U-238. The remainder are "mopped up" by the control rods.

As explained earlier, the neutrons absorbed in U-238 eventually produce fissile plutonium-239. Plutonium is not waste but a fuel of greater potential value than U-235. Some of it undergoes fission in thermal (heat-producing) reactors, but the remainder is separated out when the spent fuel is reprocessed. It can be made into fresh fuel rods and used in a "fast" reactor. In this kind of reactor there is no moderator and the neutrons therefore are not slowed down. However, plutonium is a very hazardous material, and great care must be taken when handling it.

Fast reactors can produce 50 to 60 times as much energy from the same amount of uranium as the conventional thermal reactor. As well as burning the plutonium produced as a by-product from thermal nuclear reactors, fast reactors also convert the non-fissionable U-238 (which thermal reactors cannot "burn") into more plutonium fuel, and are therefore also known as *fast-breeder reactors*.

France built the first full-size commercial fast reactor, called the Super Phenix, at Creys-Malville in the southwest of the country. This reactor uses liquid sodium as a coolant. Prototype breeder reactors are also generating electric power in Britain.

Safety

When nuclear fission occurs, a range of radioactive particles are produced. These particles *decay* (break up) and release radiation that can cause death through the destruction of body tissues, can cause cancers, and can produce genetic defects in future generations (see RADIATION; RADIOACTIVITY). Nuclear reactors are designed and built to make as small as possible the risk of both exposure to radiation for the workers in the plant and escape of radiation into the atmosphere. However, radiation leaks have occurred. Leaks from the Sellafield plant in Cumbria, northern England, have since the 1950s caused serious radioactive pollution of the Irish Sea.

More serious in the short term were the much-publicized reactor accidents in the United States and the former Soviet Union. In 1979, at the Three Mile Island reactor at Harrisburg, Pennsylvania, in the United States, there was a partial meltdown (destruction through over-heating) of the reactor core and a release of radioactive gases into the atmosphere. Worse still was the explosion in a reactor at Chernobyl, near Kiev in Ukraine in April 1986. A huge cloud of radioactive particles escaped from the damaged reactor and rapidly swept across Europe for a distance of 2,000 kilometers (1,200 miles). Thirty-one people were reported to have died as a result of the Chernobyl incident, and some 200,000 were evacuated from their homes. It is feared that more victims from radiation-induced diseases are likely in the coming years. Another immediate effect of the incident was that land and water in many areas, both in Ukraine and in other countries, were contaminated by the fallout of radioactive particles from the atmosphere.

Nuclear Waste. After a few years in the reactor, spent fuel has to be replaced with fresh fuel. Used fuel rods from a nuclear reactor consist of about 97 per cent unburned uranium, 2 per cent waste products, and about 1 per cent plutonium. The fuel is kept under water for a few years to allow some of the fission products to decay. Then, still highly radioactive, it is moved to a reprocessing plant, where the uranium can be recovered and the plutonium separated out, leaving the remaining waste fission products to be disposed of.

Most radioactive wastes are stored as liquids in multi-walled tanks. But they can also be "fixed" in a kind of glassy substance, which can be buried underground. Because of their extremely slow decay, many waste products remain dangerously radioactive for thousands of years and thus have to be stored under guard against terrorists or criminals for all that time.

Not all by-products of nuclear reaction are hazardous, however. Some of the radioactive isotopes produced inside nuclear reactors have useful applications in industry, medicine, and many fields of scientific research.

Nuclear Fusion

Today's nuclear reactors use the energy released by fission (the splitting of heavy atoms). But it is possible to obtain nuclear energy by *fusion* – the joining together of the nuclei of light atoms. Nuclear fusion is the process that powers the Sun and other stars, and is the basis of the hydrogen bomb. A fusion power plant must recreate these processes under safe, controlled conditions.

The reaction most likely to prove successful is that between two of the isotopes of hydrogen – deuterium and tritium (see ATOM). Deuterium and tritium are fused together to form helium and a neutron, and in doing so release enormous amounts of energy. Sea water contains virtually unlimited reserves of deuterium, and tritium can be made from the light element lithium, which is also plentiful.

Unfortunatley, fusion is more difficult to achieve than fission. Basically, this is because the reaction is between two nuclei, which repel each other because they both carry a positive electrical charge as a result of the protons they contain. To overcome this natural barrier, the nuclei must approach one another at high speed. One method of achieving this is to heat

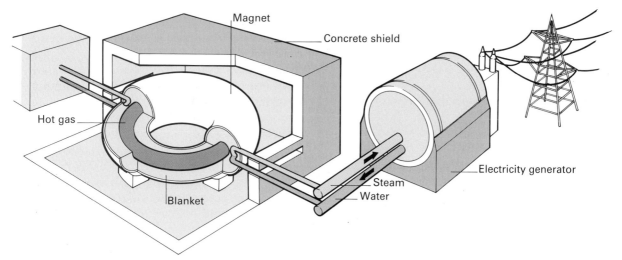

The fusion reaction occurs in a hot gas, or plasma, inside a magnetic bottle lined with a lithium blanket to capture neutrons. The heat produced inside the blanket is conducted away to make steam for powering an electricity generator.

the fuel in the form of a gas. If a gas is heated to a high enough temperature (in the region of several million degrees centigrade), the electrons in the atoms of the gas effectively reach "escape velocity" and fly away from their nuclei. Thus an electrically neutral gas is transformed into a collection of fast-moving charged particles called a plasma (see MATTER). The hotter the plasma, the faster the nuclei are moving.

The amount of plasma is very small, having a density of less than one hundred-thousandth that of normal air. If the plasma at this temperature and density were to come into contact with its container, the walls of the container would melt, the plasma would cool down, and the reaction would stop. The problem then is to keep the hot plasma away from the walls of the container.

This can be done by using magnetic fields. Being made up of electrically charged particles, the plasma can be influenced by both electrical and magnetic forces. Thus a magnetic field can "bottle up" a plasma in a confined space. To achieve this, the gas is put into a tire-shaped vacuum vessel known technically as a torus, enclosed in a series of magnetic coils. An electric current is passed through the gas and heats it and at the same time produces a magnetic field. This field, combined with the external magnets, keeps

the reacting mixture away from the inside walls of the torus.

Because of the problems of containing a plasma, scientists are looking for alternative methods of nuclear fusion. One method under study is *laser fusion*, in which powerful laser beams are fired at small pellets of fusion material (deuterium or tritium).

Fusion research has been going on since the 1950s. One of the most advanced fusion research projects is the European program, which is supervised by Euratom (the European Atomic Energy Community). The center of this program is the JET (Joint European Torus) device at Culham, in Oxfordshire, England.

The amount of energy produced by a nuclear fusion reaction is far greater than the amount of energy that can be produced from fission. If fusion can be achieved safely, then fusion reactors of the future will need very little fuel and will produce very little waste.

NULLARBOR PLAIN is a vast, dry, flat and featureless plain covering an area of 260,000 square kilometers (100,000 square miles) in southern Australia. It runs north from the Great Australian Bight (a giant bay on the south coast) 400 kilometers (250 miles) to the Great Victorian Desert. From Ooldea in South

Promotion Australia

The Indian-Pacific train crosses the Nullarbor Plain, providing a pickaback service for motorists.

Australia it stretches 650 kilometers (400 miles) into Western Australia. Where the plain meets the coastline in South Australia, it falls in a sheer drop of up to 90 meters (300 feet) to the Indian Ocean.

The Nullarbor Plain gets its name from *nullus arbor*, the Latin for "no tree", and what vegetation there is consists of bushes, grasses, and some flowers if there is winter rain. Rainfall is so low, however, less than 250 millimeters (10 inches) every year, that such flowers are rare. Wildlife includes wombats, owls, and bustards.

The plain has no surface water, but there are some underground caverns with water. One cavern, Koonolda Cave, was discovered to have Aboriginal paintings dating back 18,000 years (roughly the same age as the cave paintings discovered in France and Spain—see CAVE DWELLER; ABORIGINALS, AUSTRALIAN). A mummified carcass of the extinct thylacine, or Tasmanian "tiger", was also discovered there.

The Trans-Australian Railway from Sydney to Freemantle crosses the Nullarbor parallel to the coast, 160 kilometers (100 miles) inland. One 479-kilometer (297-mile) section is dead straight, making it the longest stretch of straight railroad track in the world. The engineer on this line has to set a switch every 30 seconds to keep from losing concentration. Running nearer the coast is the Eyre Highway, named after a British explorer and

administrator who crossed the plain in 1841. There are a few sheep ranches and railroad workshops around the plain, and the largest settlement, Eucla, has several hundred inhabitants. To the north is the nuclear-weapons testing site at Maralinga.

NUMBAT. One of the shyest of Australia's smaller mammals is the numbat (*Myrmecobius fasciatus*). This alert, neat-looking creature is about 40 centimeters (16 inches) long, of which half is tail. It looks like a combination of squirrel, small badger, and large mouse. It has reddish-brown fur, a long quivering whiskery nose, beady black eyes, squirrel-like perky ears, white and black stripes on its cheeks like a badger, and a fluffy tail which it holds up like a squirrel.

The numbat also has white and dark stripes across its back, which have given it the name "banded anteater". But it eats hardly any ants—at least, not true ants. It lives almost entirely on termites (see TERMITE). During daylight the numbat snuffles about in the undergrowth, smelling for a termites' nest. On finding one it digs up the termites with its strong claws, flicks out its long sticky tongue, licks them up speedily and swallows them with the help of its 50 or so small, peg-like teeth.

Numbats are marsupials (pouched mammals), although in the course of evolution they have lost their pouches. Their close relatives

NHPA/ANT

Nine-month-old numbats. This marsupial is now found only in the southwest of Western Australia, in dry eucalyptus forests.

are the marsupial cats (see MARSUPIAL). Four baby numbats, tiny and hairless, are born to a female in the autumn. They grip their mother's nipples with their mouths and her fur with their front feet. After about three or four months the mother leaves them in their nest in a burrow while she goes out to feed. By late summer the young venture out to feed for themselves.

Numbats live in scattered woodland in Western Australia and perhaps in South Australia. Each numbat feeds in its own territory of about 150 hectares (370 acres). These rare animals are preyed on by foxes and wild dogs, and their woods have been cut down for farmland. At one time naturalists feared they would die out for ever. However, nature reserves have been set aside specially for their protection.

NUMBER. Numbers are what we use when we wish to count a set of things or express the value of something. When we write numbers down we use symbols called *numerals* or *digits*. You can read more on how numbers are used for *calculation* (working things out) in the articles ARITHMETIC, ADDITION, SUBTRACTION, MULTIPLICATION, DIVISION, DECIMALS, AND FRACTIONS.

This article is concerned with what mathematicians used to call *number theory*, the study of numbers and the relations between them. Although numbers are probably the most useful and practical aids in mathematics, mathematicians right from earliest times have been interested not only in the ways in which numbers can be used in calculations but also in numbers for their own sake and the way they behave. Records of number puzzles go back to Babylonian times almost 2,000 years before Christ.

Sets of Numbers

One of the most fascinating things about numbers is the way that some of them can form patterns or series. You can read in MATHEMATICS about *square* numbers and their relationship to *odd* numbers. There are also *triangular* numbers.

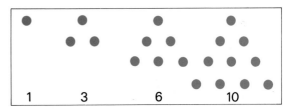

You can see how these are built up. If you look at the rows of dots you can see why we can write:

$$1=1$$
$$3=1+2$$
$$6=1+2+3$$
$$10=1+2+3+4$$

and this shows how we can calculate the rest of the triangular numbers: 1, 3, 6, 10, 15, 21, 28, 36, 45, 55, and so on.

If we add *pairs* of triangular numbers,

$$1+3=4$$
$$3+6=9$$
$$10+15=25$$
$$15+21=36$$

then we get the square numbers. The following diagram explains this curious connection.

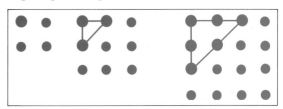

Diagrams are not always helpful, however. These look like triangular numbers,

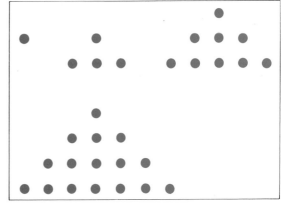

but if you count the dots, they are in fact square numbers! (If you look at the rows of dots, you will see the relation to *odd* numbers mentioned above.)

Natural numbers (ordinary whole numbers) can also be added in pairs,

$$1+2=3$$
$$2+3=5$$
$$3+4=7$$
$$4+5=9$$

and the sums are the *odd* numbers. This is because we are adding consecutive natural numbers (those which come after one another). Since two consecutive natural numbers must be one even and one odd, and

odd+even=odd

then the result must be an odd number.

If we add together three consecutive natural numbers,

$$1+2+3=\ 6$$
$$2+3+4=\ 9$$
$$3+4+5=12$$
$$4+5+6=15$$

we always get multiples of 3, that is, numbers exactly divisible by 3. Can you explain why? This diagram may help.

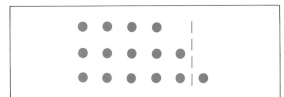

What do you think will happen if you add four consecutive natural numbers? Or five? Do you think any number can be written as the sum of consecutive natural numbers? What about 4, for example?

Number sequences often throw up fascinating questions like these. We shall leave you to solve the ones above and shall pose a few more in the course of this article.

One especially interesting set of numbers is the *Fibonacci sequence*, named after Leonardo Fibonacci of Pisa, the Italian mathematician who invented it in the 13th century. This is how the sequence starts:

$$1, 1, 2, 3, 5, 8, 13, 21, 34, \ldots$$

Each number after the second is the sum of the previous two numbers.

The numbers in the Fibonacci sequence have many interesting features. You will see, if you write out more of them, that every third number is even, every fourth number is a multiple of 3, and every fifth number is a multiple of five. This series has other fascinating features that you can find out for yourself.

Take any Fibonacci number (say 8) and square it (64); multiply together the numbers either side ($5\times13=65$). Does this procedure always work this way?

If you do the same exercise with the natural numbers the result is not quite the same. Square 8, and it becomes 64. Multiply together the numbers either side: $7\times9=63$. Does this always happen? What happens with odd numbers?

Prime Numbers

Prime numbers (or *primes*) are numbers that have just two divisors (see DIVISION), 1 and the number itself. So the following numbers are prime:

$$2 \text{ (divisors: 1, 2)}$$
$$17 \text{ (divisors: 1, 17)}$$
$$347 \text{ (divisors: 1,347)}$$

But these numbers are not prime:

$$1 \text{ (divisors: 1)}$$
$$6 \text{ (divisors: 1, 2, 3, 6)}$$
$$1001 \text{ (divisors: 1, 7, 11, 13, 77, 91, 143, 1001)}$$

The reason for 1 not being a prime is that it has only one divisor, but a divisor that can be repeated an indefinite number of times. All numbers can be written as a *product* (multiplication) of prime factors. For instance,

$$6=2\times3$$
$$1001=7\times11\times13$$
$$210=2\times3\times5\times7$$

The interesting thing is that however you group these prime factors, they always give the same results. For example,

$$18=2\times9=2\times(3\times3).$$
$$\text{or } 18=3\times6=3\times(2\times3).$$

Now, if 1 were a prime factor, then we could write

$$18=2\times3\times3\times1=2\times3\times3\times1\times1$$
$$=2\times3\times3\times1\times1\times1$$

and so on, including as many ones as we like. It is easier to say that 1 is not a prime.

Primes are probably the most awkward numbers there are, because they do not conform to rules like other sets of numbers do. They are about the only numbers which appear irregularly. If we look at successive sets of 10 numbers we can see this.

Between 0 and 10: 2, 3, 5, 7
Between 10 and 20: 11, 13, 17, 19
Between 20 and 30: 23, 29
Between 30 and 40: 31, 37
Between 40 and 50: 41, 43, 47.

This gives 15 primes between 0 and 50, but there are only 10 between 50 and 100, 10 between 100 and 150, and 11 between 150 and 200. Sometimes we get a run of 10 numbers without any primes; for instance, there are no primes between 320 and 330. And there are no primes between 1130 and 1150, or between 1330 and 1360.

Sometimes primes *almost* come in patterns. If we start writing numbers in rows of 6, we see that, after the first row, all the primes come in the first or in the fifth column.

1	2	3	4	5	6
7	8	9	10	11	12
13	14	15	16	17	18
19	20	21	22	23	24
25	26	27	28	29	30

Obviously the second, fourth, and sixth columns contain even numbers, and the third column multiples of 3; so after 2 and 3 all the primes *must* come in the other columns, but not *all* the numbers in the other columns are prime.

Since primes never correspond to a pattern, attempts to find a formula for them have always failed. Some look promising to start with. Consider the formula

$$n^2+n+11$$

and substitute different values of n, starting at 1.

n	1	2	3	4	5	6	7	8	9	10	11
n^2+n+11	13	17	23	31	41	53	67	83	101	121	143

All of these are prime, except 121 and 143. Such formulas are called "prime-rich" formulas, because at least they give a large number of primes. One of the best was discovered by the 18th-century Swiss mathematician Leonhard Euler:

$$n^2+n+41.$$

This starts off with 39 primes, but for $n=40$ we get 1681, which is 41×41.

There are an infinite number of primes, a fact proved centuries ago by the Greek mathematician Euclid. However, even though high-speed computers have been used to look for them, larger primes are difficult to find. Primes are important in the construction of secret codes, because a number which is the product of two large primes is very difficult to factorize. To find how difficult, try using a calculator to find the two prime factors of 189911.

Repeating Decimals

Repeating decimals are explained in DECIMALS, and some more examples are given in MATHEMATICS. Here we mention one or two other interesting things about them.

One thing to decide is which fractions repeat and which do not. The following do not, for instance:

$\frac{1}{2}=0.5$	$\frac{1}{10}=0.1$
$\frac{1}{4}=0.25$	$\frac{1}{16}=0.0625$
$\frac{1}{5}=0.2$	$\frac{1}{20}=0.05$
$\frac{1}{8}=0.125$	$\frac{1}{25}=0.04$

If we look at $\frac{1}{16}$ we can see why. 0.0625 is $\frac{625}{10000}$, and this cancels down to $\frac{1}{16}$. This is possible because 16 is a divisor of 10,000. If you check the other fractions above you will see that the denominator (the bottom number) of each divides in to 10, or 100, or 1000, or some other power of 10. If it does not, then the decimal will be a repeating one.

The next thing to look at is the *periods* of the repeating decimals. The period is the number of digits that repeat, as in these examples:

$$1/7 = 0.\dot{1}4285\dot{7}$$
$$1/13 = 0.\dot{0}7692\dot{3}$$

The periods of $1/7$ and $1/13$ are 6, because 6 digits repeat. (Remember that the dots over the top show the first and last digits of the group that repeats.)

The sevenths are interesting because they always give the same sequence of repeating digits, starting at a different point in the sequence:

$$1/7 = 0.\dot{1}4285\dot{7} \qquad 4/7 = 0.\dot{5}7142\dot{8}$$
$$2/7 = 0.\dot{2}8571\dot{4} \qquad 5/7 = 0.\dot{7}1428\dot{5}$$
$$3/7 = 0.\dot{4}2857\dot{1} \qquad 6/7 = 0.\dot{8}5714\dot{2}$$

This works out fairly conveniently, because there are 6 different fractions to work out, from $1/7$ to $6/7$, and 6 different digits to start the recurring sequence. Something similar happens with the thirteenths, but we will not be able to make all of them from $1/13$ to $12/13$ from the 6-digit sequence. Use a calculator to find out what happens.

There are other fractions which have a period of 6, but in a different way. For example:

$$1/14 = 0.0\dot{7}1428\dot{5} \qquad 1/28 = 0.03\dot{5}71428\dot{}$$
$$1/21 = 0.\dot{0}4761\dot{9} \qquad 1/35 = 0.0\dot{2}85714\dot{}$$

You will notice that the denominators above are all multiples of 7, and that some of the sequences are the same as the one for sevenths. This will suggest a way of exploring to find out more about these. Do you think something similar will happen with denominators which are multiples of 13?

The shortest possible period is obviously 1. You may already know that

$$1/3 = 0.333333 \ldots = 0.\dot{3}.$$

Which fraction do you think gives

0.111111 . . . ? To give yourself a clue, remember that $1/3 = 3/9$. What other fractions have a period of 1?

If we want to investigate this generally, then we can work out lots of different fractions to see what periods we can get. An interesting one given in MATHEMATICS is $1/61$, which has a period of 60. You can also find that $1/17$ has a period of 16, $1/19$ has 18, $1/23$ has 22, and $1/29$ has 28. As you may have already seen, 17, 19, 23, and 29, as well as 61, are all primes.

Unfortunately, as we might expect, no rule applied to primes works all the time! And in fact, $1/31$ has a period not of 30, but of 15. Still, 15 is half of 30; maybe that will help. The next prime denominators have periods as follows:

DENOMINATOR	37	41	43	47	53	59	67
PERIOD	3	5	21	46	13	58	33

Would you like to suggest a rule now?

One of the difficulties about this investigation is doing the calculations. Most calculators only display 7 digits after the decimal point, so you will have to think of a way of obtaining the rest. If you have a computer available at school, then your teacher may be able to help you write a suitable program.

Magic Squares

This diagram shows the simplest magic square. It was known to the ancient Chinese, and according to legend a Chinese emperor found it inscribed on the shell of a tortoise. It was often used as a charm.

8	3	4
1	5	9
6	7	2

Its properties are simple. It contains the numbers from 1 to 9, and if you add up any row, column, or diagonal you always get the same total.

Furthermore, if you try to arrange the nine numbers in the square in a different way, the result will be the same as this one, but perhaps turned round or turned over.

To find out what the "magic" total has to be we can work as follows. The total of all the numbers is 1+2+3+ ...+9. One way to add these together is to arrange another set underneath:

$$1+2+3+4+5+6+7+8+9$$
$$9+8+7+6+5+4+3+2+1$$

If we now add each *vertical* pair, each pair adds to 10; there are 9 pairs, which gives 90 altogether. But this is two lots of numbers, so we divide by 2 and get 45. But this was all the numbers from 1 to 9. If we share them among three rows, each to total the same, then each row must be 45÷3=15.

The above magic square is said to be of *order* 3, because it has 3 numbers in each row. We can make larger magic squares. See if you can complete this magic square of order 4. You will have to decide what the magic total is. Remember the diagonals.

1	8	13	
14	11		
15	10		

Then see if you can find some different magic squares of order 4; or some of order 5; or more.

NUN

NUN. A nun is a woman who withdraws from the world in order to devote her life to God. Nuns live together in organized communities in buildings usually known as convents. When the first communities of monks were organized in the Egyptian deserts by St. Pachomius in the 4th century, communities of nuns were formed at the same time

Barnaby's

Poor Clares, of the order founded by St. Clare and St. Francis of Assisi, are encouraged to develop artistic skills.

and followed the same Rule. (A religious Rule consists of a number of rules which lay down how the members of an order are to live and work.) St. Pachomius, St. Basil, and St. Benedict founded monasteries and wrote Rules, and all three had sisters who became nuns and lived under similar Rules. In the 5th and 6th centuries, St. Augustine of Hippo and St. Caesarius of Arles also gave a Rule to nuns. (See AUGUSTINE OF HIPPO, SAINT.)

When in the 8th century St. Boniface was sent to convert the Germans to Christianity, he asked English nuns, including St. Walburga and St. Lioba, to accompany him. So far all nuns had followed the Rules of the monks. When the orders of friars—the Franciscans, the Dominicans, and the Augustinians—were founded in the 13th century they, too, had nuns who lived according to the same Rules as the men. St. Francis of Assisi (on whom there is an article) and St. Clare jointly founded the first community of Franciscan nuns now known as Poor Clares. The Carmelite nuns were founded in 1452 and St. Teresa of Avila reformed the Spanish branch of the Carmelites in the 16th century.

Until the 17th century girls who were educated usually received their education in convents, where the nuns taught them reading, writing, needlework, and the preparation of simple medicines.

We know something of how nuns lived in the late Middle Ages from the account books kept by the Augustinian nuns of the convent of Grace Dieu in Leicestershire, England, from 1414 to 1418. Dame Petronilla gives an exact account of the animals they kept, the rents their tenants paid, the amount spent on hospitality to guests and on the needs of the poor. The nuns spun their own wool and

Barnaby's

African nuns at the Nyangara Roman Catholic mission in Namibia, southwest Africa.

Courtesy, Acoustifone Corporation

Teaching is among the many vocations to which modern nuns may devote their lives.

flax to make their clothes, and spent many hours reciting divine services and assisting at Mass.

Until the 17th century all nuns were enclosed; that is, they were not allowed to leave the grounds of their convent without special permission and for good reasons—to go on a pilgrimage (journey to a holy place), for example, or because they were ill. Then in France in 1633 St. Vincent de Paul and St. Louise de Marillac founded the Sisters of Charity. Their work was among the poor and the sick, and they therefore had to leave their convents and go out into the world. (Such an order is known as an active order.) Since then many active orders have been founded in the Roman Catholic Church and several in the Anglican Communion (see ANGLICAN COMMUNION). Their members teach, work in hospitals, orphanages and prisons, visit the poor, the sick and the handicapped, and do missionary work. In the 20th century new organizations have been started in the

Roman Catholic Church for women who do not wear a religious dress or live in a convent, but who take vows and live under a Rule.

Nuns, like monks and friars, go through a period of probation before being admitted to full membership of an order. First they are postulants, then novices— and must spend at least a year in this grade—and then at a solemn ceremony they take the vows of poverty, chastity, and obedience (see MONK AND FRIAR) and are accepted as full members of the order.

The head of a community of nuns is called an abbess, prioress, or Mother Superior and is usually elected by the community.

NURSERY RHYME. The very first poetry most of us ever hear is usually a nursery rhyme. It may not be very good poetry, but it is lively and has rhythm, which all young children love, and it is easy to remember. By nursery rhymes we are first carried out of our everyday world into the land of imagination, where all sorts of curious and romantic things happen; and because nursery rhymes are pleasant, jingling arrangements of simple words, they sound like music even when they are said and not sung. Many of the best-known ones are old and have been repeated to children for hundreds of years.

Kinds of Nursery Rhyme

Rhymes have been used for centuries to quieten babies when they are restless, to make them laugh, and to encourage them to talk. Almost as soon as babies are born they hear words strung together in a musical way. They are rocked to sleep with "Hush-a-bye baby on the tree top" or "Bye, baby bunting". Soon they learn to clap their hands to "Pat-a-cake, pat-a-cake, baker's man". They laugh happily as someone pulls their toes and says, "This little pig went to market". They ride on a foot or a knee to verses that jog, trot, and gallop. Long before they understand the words, they say rhymes themselves as they skip, roll, climb, hop, or ride a hobbyhorse.

Small children chant rhymes for such ring games as "Farmer in the Dell" and "Ring a Ring o' Roses". Many games begin by choosing one person to chase the others. A leader may use a counting-out rhyme to decide which girl or boy will be "It".

Many rhymes are based on ancient methods of counting. More than 2,000 counting-out rhymes have been recorded throughout the world.

J. R. Karrach

"This little piggy went to market" is a popular counting rhyme in many English-speaking countries.

Hundreds of rhymes belong to games of skipping rope and bouncing balls. Nearly everyone knows verses that start "Last night and the night before, twenty-four robbers came to my door", or "One, two, three O'Leary", or "Mother, Mother, I am sick". Words are changed sometimes. For example, "Butterfly, butterfly, touch the ground" may become "Teddy bear, Teddy bear, touch the ground".

Teasing rhymes are very old: "Johnny's mad and I am glad and I know what will please him". Tongue-twisters are always tempting: "Peter Piper picked a peck of pickled pepper".

Riddles are an important group of nursery rhymes that once were used only by grown-ups. Nursery rhymes are even used in everyday converation: "Early to bed, early to rise", "If wishes were horses beggars would ride", "Hold up your head, turn out your toes", and "Rain, rain, go away, come again another day".

Many rhymes are used by girls to tell what kind of man they'll marry: "Tinker, tailor, soldier, sailor", or "Strawberry, apple, my jam tart, tell me the name of your sweetheart: A . . . B . . . C . . . D . . .".

Origin of Nursery Rhymes

Many rhymes known today have grown out of festivals, ceremonies, and rites used hundreds of years ago in Europe and the British Isles. Some have been made to explain the wonders of the world, the change from day to night, and the rising of ocean tides. Some repeat old chants for controlling rain, storms, droughts, and floods. "London Bridge Is Falling Down" is said to date back to ancient days when a human sacrifice was made to keep a bridge from falling, burning, or being washed away.

Rhymes may come from games that are centuries old. "Knick Knack Paddy Whack, give a dog a bone" comes from a game of knucklebones, which started in Japan. It traveled to ancient Rome and was carried all over Europe by Roman soldiers.

Rhymes sometimes come from street cries. In the days when peddlers sold their wares from house to house, they called out their services in rhymes such as "Hot pease, hot, hot, hot," or "Hot cross buns . . . one a penny, two a penny".

Rhymed stories and songs, printed on long sheets of paper called broadsides, were sold from door to door by persons called hawkers. The rhyme "Frog went a-courting, he did ride" was sold in 1549. The nonsense tale of "Three Jovial Welshmen" began as a song in 1632. Hawkers, or chapmen, also sold small paper-backed leaflets, or chapbooks. "Three Blinde Mice", for example, was printed in 1609.

Some rhymes were learned from traveling actors who gave plays in the streets. Schoolboy actors used the verse "Thirty days hath September" in 1602. Many rhymes have come from traditional Christmas celebrations. Two of them are "Dame, get up and bake your pies", and "The Twelve Days of Christmas".

Rhymed verses took the place of newspaper cartoons in the 17th century. Anyone could spread gossip and criticism about rulers, bishops, or ladies in high society if verses were used. How could a person be arrested for printing the verses about Bo-Peep? Even if, as most people thought, Bo-Peep referred to Mary Queen of Scots? Jack Sprat might have been King Charles I. Simple Simon is said to refer to King James I. Queen Elizabeth I is said to be the lady who rode a cockhorse to Banbury Cross. The Little Jack Horner who "Sat in a corner, Eating his Christmas pie" is said to have been the ancestor of the family of Horners of Mells in the English county of Somerset, who was Steward to the Abbot of Glastonbury in the reign of Henry VIII. The story goes that the abbot gave the title-deeds of several manors to the king (such deeds were documents giving the person who owned them the right to possess the property) and sent them to him, not in a box, but in a huge Christmas pie. This pie John Horner took to London, and on his way he opened it and "pulled out a plum" or, in other words, took one of the title-deeds for himself. This rhyme started life as a popular verse which was sung in London's streets to mock the dishonest steward.

"Jack and Jill" takes us still further back in time, right out of history to the far off world of ancient myths and legends. All of us have known since we were babies that Jack and Jill went up the hill to fetch a pail of water. What is not so well known is that originally they and their pail stood for the sea-tides that are drawn up by the moon's power and afterwards fall back again. There is an old Scandinavian legend about two children called Hjuki and Bil who were caught up to the moon while they were drawing water from a well, and these were probably the ancestors of Jack and Jill. In Sweden people still say that if you look at the moon you will see Hjuki and Bil with their pail between them.

About half of the 800 rhymes commonly known today are 200 or more years old. About 300 rhymes have been found to have been in print before 1800, and about 70 were in print popular rhymes including "Bah, Bah, black sheep". *Mother Goose's Melody or Sonnets for the Cradle* was published in London in 1780.

Since no one knew exactly where popular rhymes had come from, publishers made up author's names for their books. They might say "These rhymes were composed by Peter Puzzlewit". Other author's names they made up were Jacky Nory, Nurse Lovechild, Tommy Thumb, and Gammer Gurton.

Books began to use more rhymes in the 19th century. In 1810 *Gammer Gurton's Garland* had 136 rhymes. *Mother Goose's Quarto or Melodies Complete*, printed in Boston, Massachusetts, in 1824, had 180 different rhymes. Today, Mother Goose books sometimes have 800 or more, and there are hun-

Mary Evans Picture Library

In the rhyme about Jack and Jill, "Jack fell down and broke his crown and Jill came tumbling after".

before 1700. In 1606 a man reporting a murder trial in London wrote that children in the streets were singing "Cock-a-doodle-doo! My dame has lost her shoe". The riddle "Two legs sat upon three legs" was mentioned in a 7th-century scroll.

Nursery Rhyme Books

In 1697 a French book called *Histoires ou contes du temps passé* ("Histories or Stories of Past Times") appeared. It had eight old fairy tales that were rewritten by Charles Perrault. A picture showed an old woman spinning and telling stories to several children and a cat. A card in the picture said "Tales of My Mother Goose". This book was translated into English in 1729 as *Mother Goose's Tales*.

The earliest complete nursery rhyme book was printed in London in 1744 with the title *Tommy Thumb's Pretty Song Book*. It had 39

Mansell Collection

A popular British nursery rhyme from a collection engraved in the later 19th century.

dreds of books of Mother Goose or nursery rhymes in all sizes and shapes, illustrated in many styles. Illustrations add to the nonsense, humor, beauty, and enjoyment of nursery rhymes.

See also CHILDREN'S LITERATURE.

NURSERY SCHOOL AND KINDERGARTEN.
Nursery school is a school for children aged between two and five years. It provides organized programs of play activities and simple instruction, often through play, for children who are too young to begin formal schooling. Nursery school may be followed by kindergarten, which caters for children of five or over, although in some countries a child will go directly from nursery to primary, or elementary, school at the age of five. In this case the first year of primary school is run rather like a kindergarten, with limited emphasis on "work". In some countries, nursery schools are funded by the state, but most nursery education is organized by religious institutions, research centers, and child welfare groups, and usually only available free to needy children. Nursery school and kindergarten both fall into the category of "preschool education".

ZEFA

Chinese children wearing masks perform in a play at their kindergarten in Beijing.

Nursery School Program

Children usually attend nursery school for at least 2½ hours a day. In some cases they may spend a longer time there, and may eat a meal and have a rest in the course of the day. The children are divided into small groups, in charge of a teacher trained in early childhood education and child development. The children's activities are supervised, and all materials are carefully selected to suit young children.

Barnaby's

Most nursery schools provide equipment for sand play, an absorbing activity for many young children.

Not all children go to nursery school, but for those who do, this is often the first time in their lives that they are separated from their mothers or guardians for several hours in the day and are in close contact with a group of other children of their own age. At nursery school children learn basic social skills, such as how to get along with others, how to play together and to co-operate.

In a nursery-school day some activities are structured, such as listening to music, learning a song or dance, or going out on a nature walk. Other activities are less structured, such as playing in a sandpile, climbing on a frame, doing a puzzle, or sitting quietly and looking at a book. Basic nursery-school equipment includes building blocks, paints and paper, modeling material, sand and water, dolls' house, dressing-up boxes, puzzles, and simple counting equipment such as rods or an abacus (see ABACUS).

The classroom should be light and airy, and there should be areas set aside for the various activities. There should also be an outdoor play area, with sandpile, climbing frame, or jungle gym. Equipment must be just the right size for small children, and be easy to move about. Most nursery schools encourage parents to take an active interest and to help their children in the transition from home to school life.

History of Pre-school Education

In 18th-century rural France and early 19th-century Britain and Italy, there were some schools for educating very young children. But these were organized like ordinary schools. There was too little play and too much emphasis on formal learning. The first person to change this was the German educator, Friedrich Froebel, who founded the first *kindergarten* (meaning "garden of children") in 1841. Like plants in a garden, children, said Froebel, had to be carefully nurtured so that they would grow up strong and healthy. The best way of teaching was through play. Froebel opposed all formal instruction. His ideas caught on, and by the late 19th century, there were kindergartens in a number of European countries and in the United States, where German immigrants introduced the first kindergarten to Watertown, Wisconsin in 1856.

Another famous name in pre-school education is Maria Montessori, an Italian doctor, who opened a children's house in Rome in 1907 (see MONTESSORI, MARIA). She was against organizing children and felt that they should be allowed to learn for themselves and should choose what to learn, and when, rather than be told by teachers. Teachers would be around to provide suitable educational materials and to show the children how to use them. Both Froebel and Montessori had a lasting influence on the style of nursery-school education all over the world.

Nearly everywhere kindergartens predated nursery schools. The first American nursery school was established by wives of the teaching staff at the University of Chicago in 1915, almost 60 years after the first kindergarten. (Nearly all of the early nursery schools were funded by and located at universities, colleges, and research centres, where they provided a living laboratory for students of child development.) Later, during the 1930s depression, federally-subsidized nursery schooling was

Raymond Levin

This Montessori classroom is light and spacious, and is filled with carefully designed equipment.

provided as part of a programme to find work for unemployed teachers when jobs were difficult to find.

Nowadays, government-supported nursery schools exist in many countries for children from deprived backgrounds, or with mental or physical handicaps. An example is the Head Start pre-school programme in the United States, funded by the federal government, which serves almost 500,000 such children. Universal state-funded nursery education, however, is still rare, except in the East European Communist countries, where it is available for all. Yet, more and more children in industrialized nations attend nursery school. This is partly because there are so many more working mothers than there used to be. In the United States, for example, 60 per cent of 5-year-olds and 40 per cent of 4-year-olds go to nursery school.

NURSING is an occupation in which scientific and practical skills are used to care for the sick, the disabled, the mentally ill, the elderly and the very young, and also in the area of

Barnaby's

A nurse at a rural health-centre in Ghana chats with pregnant women waiting for their check-ups.

public health. Nursing is an ancient service, but as a profession it is comparatively new. During the Middle Ages, religious orders untrained but devoted to nursing, developed, and they opened hospitals throughout Europe. But it was not until the 19th century that nursing began to be established as a profession.

The founder of modern nursing was the Englishwoman, Florence Nightingale. In 1854 she took a small band of women from England to the battle fronts of the Crimean War. These women tended a hospital there. In 1860, on her return to England, Florence Nightingale founded the first ever nursing school, in London, attached to St. Thomas's Hospital. The methods of training that Miss Nightingale worked out have been copied by nursing schools all over the world.

In the United States, the first nursing school was established at Bellevue Hospital in New York City in 1873. Since that time, hundreds of schools have been set up in the country to prepare both registered nurses and licensed practical nurses. Canada's first nursing school was founded at St. Catharines, Ontario, in 1874, and in Australia, the first training schools started in the 1860s.

Nursing has come a long way since then. The modern nurse is expected to use initiative and imagination. As well as undergoing a period of training in hospital, the nurse also learns to work in the community, and in co-operation with medical colleagues such as doctors, radiographers, physiotherapists, and dieticians. (For more about the work of a hospital nurse, see under HOSPITAL.)

In many parts of the world, and especially in poorer countries, where hospitals are few, trained nurses spend much of their time preventing disease as well as nursing the sick. Massive programmes of health education and disease prevention are carried out by the World Health Organization (WHO), an international organization run by the United Nations, which employs large numbers of trained nurses. They teach the local population how to care for the sick and how to prevent sickness.

Today, nurses are being trained for positions of greater responsibility and authority than they held in the past. They are taking over some of the functions which were previously performed by doctors. As medical technology has become more advanced, nurses have had to be taught to work with complicated equipment. Highly skilled nurses in emergency wards or intensive-care units have to monitor complex instruments. Educational levels of nursing are consequently also rising. Another recent emphasis

Richard & Sally Greenhill

Like specialist doctors, nurses are becoming specialists in areas such as geriatrics, or care for the old.

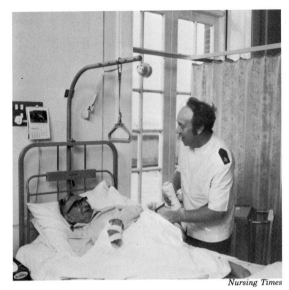

Nursing Times

Nurses are not always female. This male nurse takes care of an elderly patient in an English hospital.

in training is specialized geriatric nursing (care for the elderly) and the nursing of terminally ill patients, many of whom are looked after in hospices (hospitals for those with incurable illnesses).

Training

Most training of nurses takes place within the hospital setting, combines practical work with classes, and leads to a nursing diploma. But starting in the United States in 1909, and now offered in other countries, too, is nursing training in a college or university, leading to a degree in nursing.

To become a professional nurse in the United States an individual must be at least 17 years old and a high-school graduate. There are three types of training courses: a four-year college programme, with a major in nursing, leading to a bachelor's degree; a three-year hospital school programme leading to a diploma in nursing; and a two-year junior or community college programme leading to an associate degree. A graduate of any of these programmes may take state examinations to obtain a licence to work as a registered nurse (RN). Practical nursing is usually a one-year course either in a hospital or a vocational school. A graduate is required to take a state

examination to obtain a licence as a licensed practical nurse (LPN).

In Great Britain, most nurses successfully complete a three-year training course. The usual entry age for training is 18, and the student nurse must have a good school background. The Registered General Nurse (RGN) is trained to nurse the sick and injured, and deals with everything that might affect the patient's recovery. Most training takes place in hospital. Registered Mental Nurses (RMN) receive training in the care and treatment of mental illness, and in the work of special units dealing with psychiatric care, drug addiction, and mentally ill children. A Registered Nurse for the Mentally Handicapped (RNMH) is trained to look after people with different kinds of mental handicap, in residential homes, within the community, or attending special schools. Some British universities and polytechnics offer a nursing degree programme, which combines practical training with university courses.

Promotion Australia

A nurse in Australia's Northern Territory spends much of her time instructing Aboriginal mothers in infant care.

In Canada most nurses train in hospitals. There are 142 diploma schools throughout the country, 25 universities offering undergraduate degrees in nursing, and 8 universities which provide graduate-level training of nurses.

In Australia most nurses do a three-year hospital training course. Some states, in addition, have degree programmes for registered nurses.

After training, the nurse may go on to

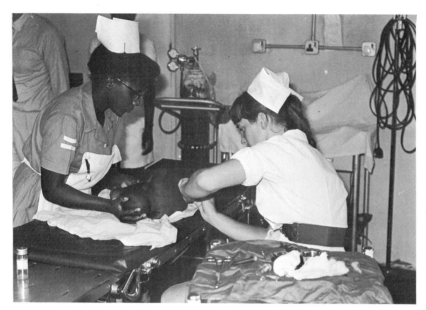

At work in a mission hospital in Maua, Kenya. Because there are few hospitals locally, these nurses have a very heavy workload.

Barnaby's

specialize in a particular field, such as midwifery (the care of pregnant women and new babies).

Preventing Sickness

Nurses have an important job to do in helping to prevent sickness. Prevention of sickness can best be taught outside hospital; it should be taught to the patient and to the potential patient in the home or in the place of work. The nurse may become a health visitor (who often works with the family doctor) or an occupational health nurse (who is a trained nurse employed in people's work places). In either case, she (or he) must take a further course of study, in order to learn more skills. She must learn how to detect signs of ill health and how to prevent sickness by health education. As an occupational health nurse she must learn about the dangers of a variety of forms of employment and teach people to avoid these dangers.

Nursing skills are needed all over the world. Nurses go to developing countries to teach health rules, care for children, and start nursing schools. Nurses also travel to countries where there are wars or natural disasters, helping the wounded, the sick, and the homeless. Often this means working in difficult and dangerous conditions. Trainee nurses from developing countries often go to study in countries which have advanced schools of nursing. When they are qualified, most of them take their much-needed skills back to their own countries.

See also MEDICINE and NIGHTINGALE, FLORENCE.

NUT. Nuts are a class of fruit consisting of one seed enclosed in a wooden shell called a pericarp which does not open completely when ripe. Many nuts can be eaten. They are a useful part of the diet in many countries, as they contain energy-giving substances. They may be eaten fresh, roasted, or prepared in various other ways.

Most nuts contain oils which may be used in making perfumes, varnishes, and soaps. The candlenut, or kukui, which grows in Hawaii, has so much oil in its seed that the nut can be lighted and used as a candle.

Nuts are found in all but very cold climates and generally grow on trees, although some grow on bushes. The tall and splendid coconut palm (*Cocos nucifera*) is perhaps the king of nut-bearing trees. It grows from 12 to 30 metres (40–100 feet) high, and one tree may bear more than 150 nuts in a year. Young coconuts contain a liquid known as milk. Some coconuts are sold in the shops to be eaten, but many more are dried and become known as copra, which is pressed for its oil.

European and American Nuts

In Europe walnuts, almonds, sweet or Spanish chestnuts, and hazelnuts are the most important nuts grown to be eaten by people. Beech nuts and acorns (the nuts of oak trees) fall to the ground in great quantities in many woods of northern Europe and North America, but they are too coarse to be eaten by people, so they are fed to pigs.

The English walnut (*Juglans regia*) is a very tasty nut with a brittle shell. Large quantities are grown, particularly in the United States (notably in California and Oregon), China, and Turkey.

Almonds (*Prunus amygdalus*) are flat white nuts covered by a bitter skin which is removed before eating. When surrounded by shells they resemble the stones of large plums. In its turn, the shell has a tough green covering which later becomes dry and splits open. Almonds are grown mainly in the United States (notably in California), Spain, China, and Italy, and, to a lesser extent, in Iran, Greece, Tunisia, Turkey, Pakistan, and Syria.

The sweet or Spanish chestnut (*Castanea sativa*) is closely related to the horse chestnut or buckeye, but is larger and sweeter. It does not contain the bitter and poisonous substances that make horse chestnuts unpleasant.

The American sweet chestnut (*Castanea dentata*) has practically disappeared. The trees were killed by a serious bark disease known as the Oriental chestnut blight, which later spread to the Mediterranean region. To replace the lost sweet chestnut, the blight-resisting Chinese chestnut (*Castanea mollissima*) was planted in some parts of the United States, particularly in the southeast. The nuts are very like those of the Spanish chestnut.

Hazelnuts or filberts (*Corylus avellana*) grow on low trees or bushes which are grown mainly in Turkey, Italy, the United States (particularly in Washington and Oregon), Spain, and Greece.

Hickory nuts are grown in North America. There are several kinds of hickory nut. The pecan (*Carya illinoensis*), which has a thinner, smoother shell than the ordinary hickory nut, is cultivated in Texas, Oklahoma, Georgia, and other southern states. Hickory nuts are related to the walnut.

The pistachio nut tree (*Pistacia vera*), which grows wild in the Middle East, China, and Mexico, is cultivated in parts of southern Europe and in California. Pistachio nuts are small and white with thin, wrinkled, reddish skins.

Tung nuts grow on two species of tung trees

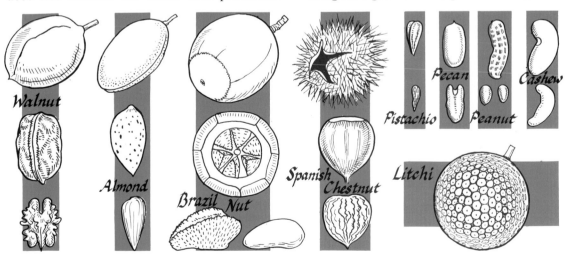

Each kernel is shown with its shell and green covering (if it has one). Lychees contain a tasty pulp.

(*Aleurites fordii* and *Aleurites montana*) native to China. They are also grown in other countries with a warm temperate climate, particularly Argentina and Paraguay. The nuts are a source of industrial oil for paints and varnishes.

Many species of pine nuts (for example, *Pinus pinea* in southern Europe and Asia Minor and *Pinus monophylla* in the western United States) are prized for their flavor and food value.

Tropical Nuts

The best-known tropical nut is the peanut (*Arachis hypogaea*), also called the monkey-nut and the peanut. Peanuts are eaten all over the world. They are grown in Africa, India, China, and the southern United States. They may have been given the name monkey-nuts because monkeys are so fond of them. In many parts of Africa monkeys and baboons have to be scared away from newly sown plots and from crops nearly ready for harvest. The name peanut was given because they grow on low bushy plants and the flower stems bend down, thrusting the developing fruits into the ground, where they ripen.

Most of the world crop of peanuts is made into peanut oil, used in cooking and making margarine, and peanut meal, used to feed animals.

Brazil nuts (*Bertholletia excelsa*) have rough, angular shells that are difficult to split. They are really hard-shelled seeds, many being produced in the same fruit.

The cashew or acajon (*Anacardium occidentale*) is grown in Brazil, India, and other tropical regions for its small, kidney-shaped nuts. From the nuts, an oil may be obtained that is used for cooking. A gum resembling gum arabic comes from the stem of the cashew.

The lychee (or litchi) nut (*Litchi chinensis*) of China, India, and the Philippines, eaten fresh, canned, or dried, is a thin-shelled nut with a seed covered with pulp.

Betel or areca nuts are the fruit of the betel palm (*Areca catechu*) and are grown in many tropical countries, particularly India, Sri Lanka, Thailand, and Malaysia. They are gathered before they are quite ripe, boiled and dried. The people of the countries where they grow chew them wrapped in leaves, and their lips and gums become dyed bright red.

There are separate articles on many of the nuts mentioned in this article.

NUTHATCH is the name for about 20 species (kinds) of stumpy little birds about 15 centimeters (6 inches) long that can run down tree-trunks head first. They have a short, square tail and a fairly long, pointed bill.

Nuthatches can run down tree trunks head first. When feeding, a nuthatch will often wedge a nut into a crack in the bark and pound it open with its strong bill.

Nuthatches are constantly calling, and have several different notes, including a ringing call, repeated several times, which is their song. They are seldom seen on the ground, but spend a good deal of time running up and down tree-trunks in search of insects. They are also very fond of nuts. When one finds a nut that needs cracking, it wedges it in a crack in the trunk of a tree and hammers at it with its beak, using the whole force of its body to do so.

The nests are usually made in holes in trees or walls. The bird plasters mud around the hole until it is the exact size it wants. Inside, the nest is made of flakes of bark or dried leaves. The eggs are white, spotted with reddish-brown.

The upper parts of the European nuthatch

(*Sitta europaea*) are grey-blue in colour, its under parts are buff and it has chestnut sides. The throat is white and there is a black stripe on each side of the face, above the white. The cock and hen are alike. There are four North American species; most are bluish above and white or reddish below. One of the most widespread is the red-breasted nuthatch (*Sitta canadensis*).

NUTMEG is a well known spice used, after being grated, to flavour food. It comes from the kernel of the fruit of a tropical tree, *Myristica fragrans*. The common cultivated nutmeg tree grows to a height of about 20 metres (65 feet). After growing for eight years it begins to bear fruit and does so for 25 years. The flowers are pale yellow and ripe fruits are on the tree at all seasons.

The fruit is about the size and shape of a small pear, and when ripe it is golden-yellow in colour. It splits open, showing a red fleshy part called the mace, which covers the nut-like seed. Inside this seed is the portion of the nutmeg that is grated.

The mace is separated from the seed, dried and used as a spice, although its flavour is different from that of grated nutmeg. Another way of using the mace is to preserve it in syrup as a sweetmeat. After the nuts are separated from the mace they are dried in ovens until the kernels rattle. The shells are then removed.

Oil of mace is a fatty yellow oil obtained from the ground kernel, not the mace. It is also called nutmeg butter. Nutmeg balsam is a product of mace and other substances.

Most nutmegs come from the Moluccas in Indonesia, the West Indies, and Brazil. Other species, or kinds, of the common nutmeg tree produce similar nuts but they are not as good. Trees of other families, such as the Brazilian nutmeg (*Cryptocarya moschata*), clove nutmeg (*Ravensara aromatica*), Peruvian nutmeg (*Laurelia aromatica*), and the Jamaican nutmeg (*Monodora myristica*) produce nutmeg-like fruits.

NUTRITION is the process by which plants and animals take in and use food. Food is needed to keep the body running smoothly. It provides energy for work and play, for breathing, and for the heart's beating. The building material for muscles, bones, and blood comes from food. You cannot have a healthy body without healthy eating and drinking. Not enough of some foods, or too much of others, can lead to illness. Experts on nutrition are called nutritionists.

The food and drink you take in are called your *diet*. (This word is sometimes used in another way, to mean eating less food than normal in order to lose weight, as in "going on a diet".) A person's diet is so important because growth and health depend on it. Dieticians are people with knowledge of special diets (dietetics), such as those used for sick people in hospital.

We should never forget that across the world 40 million people die each year from starvation and the diseases it brings. Fifteen million of them are babies and young children. For the millions more who suffer from malnutrition (not enough of the right foods), healthy eating is out of the question. It is hard enough just to stay alive.

A Balanced Diet

The body needs many different nutrients. These are various substances necessary to provide energy and the materials for growth, body-building, and body maintenance. Every day millions of cells in the body die and must be replaced by new ones.

Not all foods contain all nutrients. So it is not just the quantity of food eaten that is important, but also the variety. People who

The flowers, fruit, and kernel of a nutmeg tree.

have enough food available may still become ill because they are eating too much of one kind of food and not enough of another.

To stay healthy, we need to eat a balanced diet. This means a diet containing the right proportions of the main nutrients: carbohydrates, proteins, fats, fibre, minerals, vitamins, and fluids. Many foods are a mixture of these basic nutrients. A balanced diet also contains enough energy (in the form of food) to power the chemical reactions of living.

Energy and Food

Even when asleep the body needs energy. The more active a person is, the more energy the body uses. The energy comes from the chemical "burning" of carbohydrates, fats, proteins, and certain other substances such as alcohol.

The energy values of different foods can be measured by burning them in a special small oven called a calorimeter. Energy in food is often measured in calories. One kilocalorie, usually written as kcal or Calorie (with a capital C), is the amount of energy required to raise the temperature of one kilogram of water by 1° Celsius. In fact the Calorie is a unit of heat, not energy. In the modern system of measurements, energy is measured in joules. (1 Calorie equals 4.2 kilojoules.) You can find the calorie content of almost any food by looking in a slimming magazine or book.

An adult needs, on average, a little under 3,000 Calories a day. A manual worker would need 4,000 or more, because of the energy used up in physical activity. Children, who are growing and also very active, need extra Calories as well. As people become older they need fewer Calories, partly because they are physically less active and partly because some of their body tissues become chemically less active.

Calorie-counting is all very well; but there is one sure way for a fully grown person to know if he or she is taking in enough energy, and that is regular weighing. If you are putting on weight, it means you are taking in too much energy. The excess is being converted to fat for storage in your body. If you are getting lighter, you are not getting enough energy and your body is using some of its fat stores to make up for the lack.

Carbohydrates

Most energy in the diet comes from carbohydrates. They are made of the elements carbon, hydrogen, and oxygen and come in the form of sugars and starches. Glucose is a sugar carbohydrate and the one the body uses as its basic energy source. It is found in the blood and stored in the liver as glycogen. However, we rarely eat glucose as such. Most foods rich in carbohydrate contain complicated sugars and starches which must first be broken down into glucose during the process of digestion (see DIGESTION).

Some carbohydrate foods have been treated during manufacture to such an extent that they contain only carbohydrates, that is, pure energy and no body-building materials. These are called refined carbohydrates and include sugar, treacle, syrup, and jam.

Other carbohydrates are less processed during their manufacture. In addition to providing energy they contain other nutrients. They include bread, wholegrain breakfast cereals, peas, beans, potatoes, and fruit.

Proteins

Proteins are large molecules made from smaller building-blocks named amino acids (see PROTEIN). They contain carbon, hydrogen, oxygen, and nitrogen, and some have sulphur and phosphorus. Some amino acids can be made in the body from their elements. Others cannot and must be present in the diet. These are the essential amino acids. In general, animal foods such as meat and fish provide a better balance of amino acids. However, by combining vegetable foods carefully, a good balance of proteins can be eaten.

Proteins are the true "body-builders". Much of your body, including your bones, muscles, nerves, and skin, is largely protein. As you eat proteins in food they are broken down into their amino acid building-blocks, absorbed into your body, and then these are reassembled into the proteins of your own tissues. Animal foods rich in protein include eggs, meat, fish, cheese, and milk; protein-rich plant foods include bread, potatoes, nuts, peas, beans, and lentils.

Fats

Fats are also made of carbon, hydrogen, and oxygen. They fall into two main groups. One group comes from animals and includes butter, lard, fatty meat, cream, cheese, and eggs. The other group contains fats from plants such as corn oil, sunflower oil, safflower oil, and nuts.

Fats are a vital part of the balanced diet, but too much fat can be harmful. There has been much research into whether eating too much of certain fats increases the risk of heart disease. It does seem likely that this is so. To avoid heart disease, most doctors now advise that you should avoid too much fat, and especially animal fat.

Fibre

Fibre or "roughage" is not strictly a nutrient since it is indigestible and so not absorbed by the body. But it does add "bulk" to the diet and enable the intestines to grip the food as it passes through. Constipation and certain diseases of the intestine are made more likely by a diet low in fibre.

In prehistoric times, human beings probably ate a high-fibre diet, and this is the kind of food our digestive systems are designed for. Eating too much modern, highly processed food is unnatural. High-fibre natural foods such as wholegrain cereals (especially bran) and breads, vegetables, and fruit are the basis of many slimming diets. The fibre makes you feel full and satisfied, yet it is not absorbed by the body and so you do not put on weight. As with all aspects of nutrition, however, fibre needs to be part of a balanced diet.

Minerals

Minerals are elements that the body needs for healthy functioning. One is calcium, required for strong bones and teeth. It is present in milk and milk products. Iron is another, needed for healthy red blood cells and to prevent anaemia. It is found in red meat (particularly liver), eggs, pulses (lentils, chickpeas, and so on), and green, leafy vegetables. Required in smaller amounts are copper, zinc, manganese, and iodine. Fluoride helps prevent tooth decay (see TEETH).

There are many other minerals, but provided you eat a good variety of foods as part of your balanced diet, you are unlikely to miss them.

Vitamins

These substances are also vital for health and are described in a separate article, VITAMIN.

Fluids

Water is essential for life. Two-thirds of the weight of your body is water and it is constantly being lost in urine, sweat, and breathed-out air. Water in the diet comes in many forms: as drinks such as tea, coffee, milk, fruit juices, lemonade, beer, and so on. A large proportion also comes from the foods we eat. A green salad might be nine-tenths water. In addition, water is formed in the body during the chemical reactions which "burn" carbohydrates, proteins, and fats to release energy.

Healthy Eating

Mealtimes are an important part of the day. Food should be carefully prepared and attractive to look at when served, so that we are encouraged to eat it.

Experts have devised many schemes and plans for working out a balanced diet. Some are quite complicated and difficult to follow. But the most important point is variety. Always try to have new foods, foreign foods, strange foods, fresh and raw fruits and vegetables, meals without meat, pastas or rice instead of potatoes, and anything else that takes your fancy.

Most of us in the industrialized countries eat too much processed, factory-made foods and animal fats, and fats generally. Yet the occasional hamburger or prepacked and frozen TV-dinner does no harm. By eating a little of a lot of foods, you are more likely to receive all the nutrients you need to keep you fit and healthy.

NYERERE, Julius (born 1922), led Tanganyika's struggle for independence and became the first president of Tanzania. His attractive personality embodied a determination to secure improvements in the political and social status of all Africans. He played a leading part in the foundation and work of the Organization of African Unity (OAU).

BBC Hulton Picture Library

Julius Nyerere, president of Tanzania (a union of Tanganyika and Zanzibar) from its formation in 1964.

Nyerere was born at Butiama in Tanganyika, the son of a chief. He was educated at Makerere College, in Uganda. After a period teaching in Catholic schools he went to study at Edinburgh University, Scotland, obtaining a degree in liberal arts in 1952. By then Tanganyika was under the trusteeship of the United Nations but was still administered by Britain. Nyerere worked for complete independence and formed in 1954 the Tanganyika African National Union (TANU).

He twice travelled to the United Nations in New York to put the case for immediate independence. He resigned his seat on Tanganyika's Legislative Council in protest at the slow progress of reforms. In general, however, he preferred persuasion to confrontation and built up a good relationship with the governor Sir Richard Turnbull. His party gained in influence and power until in 1960 Tanganyika became self-governing. A year later Nyerere became the prime minister of an independent country. In 1964 he became president of the newly formed Tanzania, a union of Tanganyika and Zanzibar. He remained president until his retirement in 1985.

As a founder of the OAU in 1963, Nyerere constantly urged political and economic action against the racial policies of South Africa. But he also strongly opposed Idi Amin's cruel regime in Uganda, especially when Amin expelled all Asians in 1978. The intervention of the Tanzanian army in 1979 helped to bring about Amin's overthrow.

NYLON. So many articles of everyday use are now made of nylon that people do not always realize that it was not manufactured until 1938, nine years after its discovery.

Silk is the loveliest of all textile materials but it is also the most expensive. Because of this, scientists tried for about 300 years to make a cheap imitation of it, redoubling their efforts after 1900. Their first great success came in 1929 when a team of organic chemists led by Dr. Wallace H. Carothers, an American chemist, invented nylon. Before that, many useful kinds of rayon, or artificial silk, had been made but nothing that was as strong and useful as natural silk.

In all their work scientists were helped by knowing how the silk-worm makes silk thread. It does so by squeezing a treacly solution through two tiny holes in its head. The solution hardens as it comes out of the holes and the two fine threads of silk are coated with gum which sticks them together. (See SILK.)

Scientists decided that they would have to make imitation silk by forcing a treacly liquid through tiny holes. What should the liquid be?

It would have to be something that would harden as soon as it came out of the holes. Obviously what was needed was something that melts when heated and sets solid as soon as it is cooled. Nylon does this, and nylon fibres are made from melted nylon. Before Carothers had actually made any nylon he was fairly certain that it *could* be made into fibres. This was because he knew why cotton and wool, as well as silk, are such excellent fibres for making textile materials.

If you take a length of knitting yarn and untwist it, you will be able to pull out single wool fibres. Some of them will be about 10 centimetres (4 inches) long, but they are so fine that you will be quite unable to measure their thickness. This can be done only by using a microscope—which would show that they are about 0.025 millimetre (0.001 inch) thick. Thus they are about 4,000 times as long as they are thick. Silk filaments (very long fibres are called filaments) are far longer and much finer than wool fibres and the proportion of length to thickness is enormous. The reason why textile fibres are so much longer than they are thick is that they are built up from molecules which themselves are very long and thin. These chain-like molecules are called polymers, and there are about 10,000 of them in the width of a silk filament. (See MOLECULE; POLYMER.) They lie along the length of the filament, and silk is strong because the chains cling to one another firmly.

Before he could make fibres like silk, Carothers had to plan suitable polymers and then make them. It was too difficult to make any exactly like those of silk filaments, but he managed to make some which were very similar. This is how he set about it. He built up the long chains by joining short links together. He used two kinds of link, both made from benzene (see BENZENE). The benzene is oxidized (see OXYGEN) to make one kind of link, and this kind of link is treated with ammonia to make the other. Let us imagine that one kind of link has a hook at each end and that the other kind has an eye at each end. The links can join together to

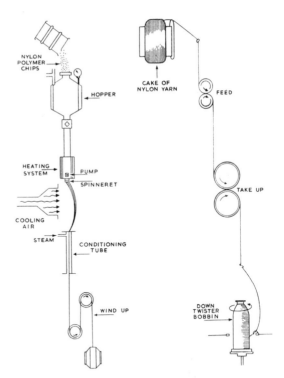

Unstretched nylon yarn   Stretched nylon yarn "cold drawing"

make a chain. Each chain of nylon has 200 or more links along its length. The first kind of nylon was made from only one kind of link, which had a hook at one end and an eye at the other, but it was found to be cheaper to use the two different kinds of links.

After the nylon has been made, it is melted and forced through a slit to form a ribbon of nylon. The ribbon is cooled suddenly in water and is then broken into small pieces called chips. Nylon filaments are made from the chips. The chips are melted and forced through the tiny holes of a metal jet, called a spinneret. If a thread with 15 filaments is required, a spinneret with 15 holes in it is used. As soon as it enters the air the melted nylon sets solid, and the 15 filaments are wound on to a bobbin as one thread.

However, the nylon thread is still not ready for knitting or weaving because it must first be stretched. Stretching is necessary because, until this is done, the chain-like molecules are scattered higgledy-piggledy in the filaments. When the thread is stretched, they are made to arrange themselves along the length of the filaments. As soon as this happens they cling together very firmly sideways and make the thread strong. Stretching is easily done by passing the thread between two pairs of rollers. The process is called "cold-drawing" because the thread is drawn out, or stretched, while it is cold.

Besides being strong and hard-wearing, nylon yarn can be stretched about one-fifth of its length without breaking. Because of this it has taken the place of silk in the making of parachutes and is often used for such things as tow-ropes for gliders. Its uses vary from those just mentioned to the making of ladies' stockings, of shirts, and of all kinds of underwear. Nylon absorbs much less water than cotton or wool, so nylon garments dry much more quickly than those made of cotton or wool. The nylon filaments can also be cut up into short lengths, called staple fibre, and can then be mixed with other fibres such as wool and cotton. Yarn made from a mixture of wool and nylon staple fibre is very hard-wearing and so is used to make men's socks. Ordinary woollen socks can have nylon thread knitted into the heels and toes to strengthen them. Nylon fibres are also often woven into carpets, and used to make ropes, fishing nets, and bristles for brushes.

Because nylon absorbs so little water it is

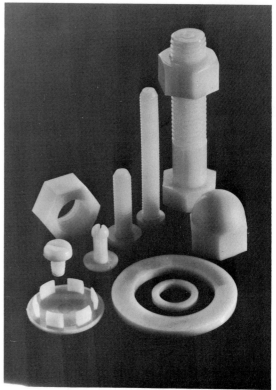

Courtesy, Nylon and Alloys Ltd.

These screws, washers, nuts, and bolts are made of nylon. They will not corrode or rust, and are not affected by fungus, most acids, or other chemicals.

Shell Photo Service

Polypropylene is a nylon fibre used for inexpensive carpets. It is very hard-wearing and can be made in traditional patterns in a variety of colours.

easily electrified by rubbing and then attracts dust particles from the air. Thus nylon soils very easily. One of the reasons for mixing other fibres with it is to overcome this trouble. However, there is another difficulty. Nylon tends to be weakened in sunlight, and scientists are now busy trying to solve this problem.

In the form of a solid plastic, nylon is used for making gear wheels and bearings for items such as foodmixers and childrens' toys, for curtain hooks, and many other articles in common use. When used to manufacture articles such as these, nylon is forced into specially designed moulds, a process known as injection moulding. Nylon flows well when liquid and can fill complicated moulds easily. Nylon not only is one of the toughest and most hard-wearing plastics but also is not attacked by chemicals and will tolerate high temperatures. It also has a very low coefficient of friction which makes it an ideal material where a high degree of wear is expected (see FRICTION).

OAK. The oak belongs to a family which includes the sweet chestnut and beech and is of the genus, or group, *Quercus*.

There are over 450 species of oak spread over the north temperate zone, with about 60 North American species. They have simple leaves with lobed or toothed edges.

Many plants called "oak" are not *Quercus* species. These include African oak, Australian oak, and poison oak.

Male and female flowers grow on the same oak, the males being clusters of catkins. Wind carries pollen from them to the female flowers, which later form the acorns. The flowers come out at the same time as the wavy-edged leaves. The bark of young oaks is smooth, but with the passing years it becomes thick and furrowed. It is hard to realize while looking at a magnificent oak, well over 30 metres (100 feet) tall and measuring 4 metres (13 feet) or more round the trunk, that it has grown from a single acorn.

It is said that oak trees can live 2,000 years. Before the time of Christ men worshipped oak trees, and the Druid priests of Britain and Gaul offered sacrifices under them. The Greek god Zeus is said to have instructed his worshippers under the old oak of Dodona in the mountains of Epirus. The Romans valued the wood of the oak and built their ships with it. It is extremely strong and has for centuries been used in the building of houses, ships, wheel spokes, ladder rungs, and many other things. It is also a source of charcoal and in olden days its bark was much in demand for tanning leather.

OASIS. A fertile area in a desert is called an oasis. Rivers around the desert edge often disappear underground but flow on over solid rock under the sands. If this water comes to the surface or can be reached by sinking wells then it can be used to grow crops in the fertile desert soil. Date palm trees are the most commonly cultivated crop on oases. Citrus fruits, figs, apricots, and peaches, and simple vegetables such as onions and carrots are also grown. On larger oases cereal crops such as wheat, barley, and millet may be raised. If the springs and wells are numerous the oasis may support a city; others have only a handful of huts. Oases are stopping places for desert caravans and the oasis towns thus become trading centres, such as Murzuk in Libya and Buraida in Saudi Arabia.

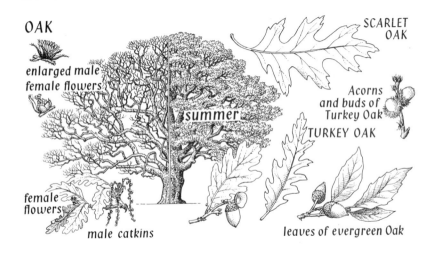

OAK
enlarged male female flowers
SCARLET OAK
summer
Acorns and buds of Turkey Oak
TURKEY OAK
female flowers
male catkins
leaves of evergreen Oak

The English oak, shown here, is also grown in other parts of the world. Scarlet, Turkey, and evergreen oaks are among the numerous other species of this impressive tree.

Aerofilms

An oasis is usually identified by its tall, feathery date palms. Other crops are also grown.

OATES, Titus (1649–1705).

Titus Oates was a religious fanatic who stirred up violent anti-Catholic feelings and fabricated the Popish Plot against King Charles II. Born at Oakham, now in Leicestershire, he was expelled from the Merchant Taylors' School, London, from Cambridge University, from the royal navy, and from two religious colleges.

In 1677 he pretended that he wished to become a Roman Catholic and it was then that he went to study in Spain. His purpose was to discover information about the Catholics which he could use for his own benefit. (This was a time when Catholics were under great suspicion in England, and Oates made the most of it.) Expelled from the Spanish college, he went to a French one, was expelled, and returned to England. Together with a man named Israel Tonge he invented details of a Catholic plot, known as the Popish Plot, to murder Charles II and to massacre Protestants. The king himself disbelieved this tale. Oates deposited a written account with a magistrate named Sir Edmund Godfrey, who was then mysteriously murdered.

This made people believe the story and a wave of fear and anti-Catholic fury swept through London: more than 35 Catholics, probably entirely innocent, were executed on Oates's accusations and many more were imprisoned. He became the hero of the day and was given a pension and a bodyguard.

Gradually the panic died down. Inconsistencies were found in his story and in 1685 he was found guilty of perjury (that is, of telling lies while under oath to tell the truth) and was sentenced to flogging and imprisonment. Released shortly after the Revolution of 1688, when James II was deposed, Oates died in obscurity in 1705.

OATS,

the edible starchy grain of the oat plant (*Avena sativa*), are a cereal crop, grown mainly as food for animals, although they can also be eaten by people. A field of oats can easily be recognized by the way in which the grains appear on graceful nodding stems in clusters called panicles. These stems each carry two or three grains partly enclosed in two tiny papery leaves. Each grain consists of a nourishing kernel closely covered by two husks.

There are many different varieties of oats. Some have white grains, others black, yellow, red or grey. Some have long stems and others short. Plant breeders have developed varieties suited to different soils and climates. For example, red oats are grown in warm, moist climates.

Oats probably came in the first place from mild parts of eastern Europe and from western Asia. They were grown in England in the 13th century and in Germany long before that. Today they are grown in much larger quantities than either barley or rye. They like a cool, moist climate, and so flourish in northern parts such as Western Europe, Scandinavia, the Soviet Union, and North America. They are also grown in New Zealand and Australia. In a dry climate they tend to have long thin grains with thick husks.

The United States and the Soviet Union are the countries that produce most oats, but smaller, northern countries, such as Scotland, Sweden, and Finland, make great use of oats, which are generally a more satisfactory crop in those countries than wheat or rye. Sometimes oats are used as green fodder before they ripen, or are made into hay.

People eat oats in the form of oatmeal, made from the kernels of the grain and commonly used in porridge, oatcakes, and scones. These took the place of bread made from wheat or rye when those grains were expensive. But even in northern countries oats are now more important for feeding-stuffs than for bread.

The flowering part of the oat plant bears many branches of florets that each produce a single seed.

In most oat-growing areas the crop is sown in spring, usually on fields where hay or pasture was grown the summer before. Winter oats are not sown as far north as winter wheat because they cannot survive frosts and snow so well. Oats are harvested by combine harvesters, which cut and thresh the crop, or by reaper-binders, which cut and tie it into sheaves. Ten or twelve sheaves are stood together in what are known as stooks or shocks to dry and ripen further before being stacked and threshed.

Like barley, oats often serve as a nurse crop, which means that seeds of grasses and clovers are sown soon after oat seeds in spring. As the grass and clover seedlings grow, they are protected by the oat seedlings

from the sun or wind. (See also CEREAL.)

OBOE FAMILY. The oboe is a woodwind instrument that developed from a raucous medieval instrument called the *shawm*. It was first used in France at the end of the 17th century. Its name comes from the French *hautbois*, meaning high, or loud, wood, and was in English originally spelled hautboy. The different notes are obtained by covering fingerholes and operating keys. The tone of the oboe is sharper, or more piercing, than that of the flute and the clarinet, and it is often sad and dreamy, as in the solo passage for the oboe in the second act of Tchaikovsky's *Swan Lake* ballet. But it can also be cheerful and bright, as is shown by the music for two oboes in "The Arrival of the Queen of Sheba" from Handel's oratorio *Solomon*.

The oboe is usually made of African blackwood or of rosewood. Sound is produced by blowing through two pieces of cane, called a double reed, fixed to the top of the instrument. The bore, or hollow space inside the tube of the instrument, is in the shape of a long cone, and the bottom opens out like a bell. The range of the oboe is from middle C on the piano to two octaves above.

The instruments called oboe d'amore and cor anglais are larger forms of the oboe and therefore sound deeper or lower in pitch. The origin of their names, which mean "oboe of love" and "English horn", is not known. The oboe d'amore is used in the music of Johann Sebastian Bach, and the cor anglais may be heard in the *Symphony* of César Franck and the *New World* symphony of Anton Dvorak. Sometimes a deep bass oboe is used. This is called a heckelphone and it was first heard in Richard Strauss's opera *Salome*.

The lowest, or bass, instruments of the oboe family are the bassoon and the contrabassoon. The bassoon consists of a tube nearly 2.5 metres (over 8 feet) long. Since it is impractical to play an instrument of such length in the ordinary way, the tube is bent double. A small piece of hollow metal bent into the shape of a crook is fitted into one end of the wooden tube, and the reed is set into the end of this crook-

Fritz Curzon, The Albion Ensemble, Quadriuium

Left: The oboe (far right) and the bassoon (second from left) are often used in wind quintets alongside the horn, flute, and clarinet. **Right:** The oboe compared with its larger relative the cor anglais, or English horn. The mouthpiece of the cor anglais is extended and curved to make it easier to play.

like attachment. The bassoon has a wide range of notes. The lower ones have often been used by composers for humorous compositions; the higher ones can often be sweet in quality and have led to the instrument's being used in more serious works. A brief high passage for bassoon forms the introduction to Stravinsky's ballet *The Rite of Spring*.

The contrabassoon is the "double bass" of the oboe family, sounding about an octave lower than the ordinary bassoon. Both the bassoon and contrabassoon are developments of an earlier instrument known in England as a curtal. The bassoon came into use during the 17th century.

OB RIVER, a great river of Russia, is one of the longest rivers in Asia. It is formed by the joining of the Biya and the Katun rivers. From the junction of these two rivers to its mouth on a bay of the Arctic Ocean, the Ob flows 3,650 kilometers (2,268 miles). Small cargo boats can sail the entire length of the river when it is not frozen over. The headwaters of the Biya and Katun rivers are far south in the Altai Mountains of central Asia. With its largest tributary, the Black Irtysh,

it forms a river 5,411 kilometers (3,362 miles) long. Its basin covers some 2,990,000 square kilometers (1,154,000 square miles).

The Ob flows generally northwest for about 645 kilometers (400 miles), past Novosibirsk, an important center for science and technology (see NOVOSIBIRSK). Near this city is a rich agricultural region of grain and livestock production. The Trans-Siberian Railroad crosses the Ob River at Novosibirsk.

North of Novosibirsk the Ob enters an area of swampy coniferous forest called taiga. It flows generally northwest for more than 2,735 kilometers (1,700 miles) through this region of western Siberia. There is almost no agriculture and few towns or cities; however, forestry is important. The timber is floated down the river in great floating rafts to the Arctic Ocean and then to ports in northwestern Russia.

Near the settlement of Khanty-Mansiysk the Ob is joined by the Black Irtysh. The Ob empties into the Gulf of Ob, a deep inlet of the Arctic Ocean. In the last 1,130 kilometers (700 miles) the river divides into many separate channels as it makes its way through the taiga.

The Ob is a wide river. At Barnaul it is about 2.5 kilometers (1.5 miles) wide. Near the mouth it is more than 19 kilometers (12 miles) wide. The winters along the Ob are very cold, and the entire river is frozen for about six months a year, from the end of November. The central part of the course of the Ob has great floods. The upper or southern part of the river thaws out in the spring, long before the lower or northern part is free of ice. The ice near the river's mouth blocks the flood water and it spreads over wide areas.

OBSERVATORY is a building equipped with special instruments to study the universe (an astronomical observatory), weather (a meteorological observatory), or other natural phenomena. This article deals with astronomical observatories.

Thousands of years ago, astronomers had to make all their observations with the naked eye. They had only very simple astronomical instruments, such as rods with sighting-marks attached to them for fixing the directions of stars, and sundials and water clocks for telling the time.

Later on, more complicated instruments were invented. There was an observatory at Alexandria in Egypt from about the 3rd century BC, and the Greek astronomers there may have used instruments called astrolabes for measuring the angles between the directions of different stars. This observatory existed for over 800 years.

Other early observatories included one at Baghdad, built in about AD 820 by the Caliph of Baghdad; one at Maragheh in northwest Persia, founded in 1259 by Hulagu Khan; and another at Samarkand in central Asia, begun in about 1420 by the Persian prince Ulugh Beg.

The last great observatory built before the invention of the telescope was that of Tycho Brahe, the Danish astronomer (see BRAHE, TYCHO). It was erected in 1576 on the little island of Hven. Although it is no longer standing, drawings and plans made in Tycho's time show how wonderful and complete it was as a scientific center. The telescope, invented in

BBC Hulton Picture Library

The Royal Observatory, Greenwich, was set up in 1675. Sir Christopher Wren designed the main building.

about 1608, was first used for astronomical observation by Galileo in Italy in 1609 (see GALILEO GALILEI). It enabled Galileo and others to make many remarkable discoveries.

To encourage astronomy in France, King Louis XIV founded a national observatory in Paris, which was completed in 1672. Three years later, King Charles II of England set up the Royal Observatory in Greenwich Park, near London. Its main purpose was to aid navigation at sea by preparing a new star catalogue with which mariners could plot the position of the Moon accurately against the background of stars. This was vital for working out longitude at sea (see LATITUDE AND LONGITUDE). After the end of World War II the Royal Observatory was moved to Herstmonceux Castle, in Sussex, away from the lights and smoke of London, and renamed the Royal Greenwich Observatory. It moved again in 1990, to Cambridge. The original observatory buildings at Greenwich still stand, and are part of the National Maritime Museum.

After the founding of these two famous observatories, many others were built throughout the world. The first observatory in the United States was built by David Rittenhouse at Philadelphia in 1783. Another American observatory was founded at the University of North Carolina, at Chapel Hill, in 1831. The Royal Observatory at the Cape of

Siding Spring Observatory photographed from the air. The dome of the 1.2-meter (47.2-inch) Schmidt telescope is nearest the camera and that of the 3.9-meter (153-inch) Anglo-Australian telescope is in the background.

Royal Observatory, Edinburgh

Good Hope, in southern Africa, was completed in 1829. Australia's first state-run observatory was set up at Melbourne in 1853.

Most observatories today belong to governments, or to universities or scientific institutions. Very few large ones are privately owned. Yet this has not always been the case. Sir William Herschel, who discovered the planet Uranus in 1781, later had his own observatory at Slough, near Windsor, England. And an Irish nobleman, William Parsons, Third Earl of Rosse, not only built his own observatory at Birr in central Ireland in about 1825, but in 1845 installed a telescope with a mirror 1.8 meters (72 inches) across, larger than any other in use at that time.

Today there are major observatories all over the world. Those in the United States include Kitt Peak, in Arizona, Mauna Kea, in Hawaii, and Palomar, in California. For many years the 5-meter (200-inch) Hale Telescope at Palomar was the largest in the world. Some countries, such as the United Kingdom, have observatories in other countries, where conditions for astronomy are more favorable. In the southern hemisphere, for example, the United Kingdom and Australia jointly own the 3.9-meter (153-inch) Anglo-Australian Telescope at Siding Spring in Australia.

The best location for an observatory is a place where the sky is usually clear, well away from the lights and smoke of cities. A moun-

tain top is ideal, since the air is thin and there is less movement of the atmosphere, which hampers observations at lower levels. One

Jay M. Pasachoff, Special Astrophysical Observatory

The building housing the 6-meter (236-inch) telescope of Russia's Special Astrophysical Observatory in the Caucasus. Note the telescope, which is visible through the slit, and the people standing on top of the dome.

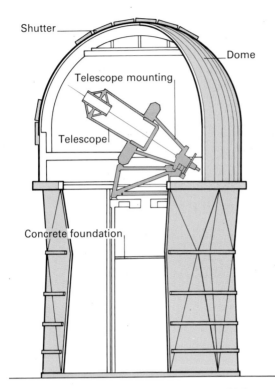

Shutter

Dome

Telescope mounting

Telescope

Concrete foundation

A modern observatory building: the 19-story high building housing the 4-meter (158-inch) Mayall Telescope of Kitt Peak National Observatory.

modern mountain-top observatory is the Roque de los Muchachos Observatory, 2,400 meters (7,900 feet) above sea-level on La Palma in the Canary Islands. There, observers from Britain, Spain, Denmark, and Sweden can work under superb conditions. The largest telescope there is the 4.2-meter (165-inch) William Herschel Telescope which came into use there in 1987.

A building housing a telescope has two parts. The lower part is fixed to the ground, but the roof, which is dome-shaped, can rotate so that the telescope can see out, no matter to which part of the sky it is pointing.

Nowadays astronomers hardly ever use large telescopes for looking at the sky by eye. Instead they take photographs with special cameras fitted to their telescopes, and measure the spectrum of light from the stars with an instrument called a spectrograph. Other instruments are used to amplify (enlarge) the image, which may be displayed on a television

screen. Computers can be used to guide the telescope and to process information.

Astronomers have programs of observation arranged for months in advance, and have to take turns in using the large telescopes. When the moon is full or nearly full, the sky gets so bright that seeing or photographing faint objects becomes difficult.

Many observatories specialize in certain types of work. For example, the Big Bear Solar Observatory in California specializes in observation of the Sun. Some observatories, such as the one at Mauna Kea, Hawaii, have infrared detection equipment. Others are equipped with radio telescopes (see RADIO ASTRONOMY). Observations are also made in space, from specially designed satellites. The Hubble Space Telescope, which was launched into Earth orbit in 1990, contains a 2.4-meter (94-inch) telescope – larger than many on Earth.

See also TELESCOPE.

OCCUPATIONAL DISEASES are diseases
that are linked to hazards at work. Most jobs are relatively safe. A few, such as deep-sea diving or driving a racing car, have a high risk of accidents. There are also jobs that put workers in danger from a particular illness or disease (as distinct from an accident).

The list of occupational diseases and the jobs that cause them is extremely long. As medical research continues, it gets longer. Today, one question doctors ask new patients is: "What is your job?" A person's occupation can hold the key to diagnosing an illness.

Dust Diseases
Diseases of the throat and lungs were among the earliest occupational diseases discovered, in the 17th century. People who work in dusty places breathe in floating particles. The lungs can cope with a certain amount of dust, which is coughed up. But exposure day after day, year after year, makes them slowly clog up, and this can lead to infections such as pneumonia, bronchitis, and tuberculosis.

Depending on the exact type of dust, the particles themselves can cause disease. One of the

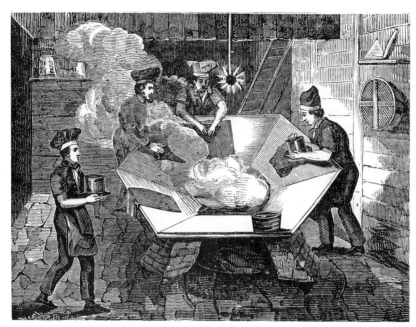

A 19th-century illustration of *The Hatmaker's Hattery*. The felt used to make top hats was painted with mercury nitrate. As they handled the felt, and then licked their fingers to smooth down the felt, the hatmakers swallowed mercury. In this way, many of them were afflicted with mercury poisoning.

Mansell Collection

best-known is "coal-miner's lung" or pneumoconiosis. The affected person becomes wheezy and breathless and coughs a lot. Workers with asbestos are at risk of a similar disease called asbestosis. In this case the breathed-in asbestos particles can also cause lung cancer many years later.

There are several other dust diseases such as silicosis, which affects quarriers, stone masons, and others who work with rocks; and "farmer's lung" which is due to breathing in the spores of a fungus that grows in mouldy hay or grain. Similar to farmer's lung is "bird-fancier's lung", where the cause is the dust inhaled from dried bird-droppings. Strictly speaking, unless your job involves caring for birds, this is not usually an occupational disease!

Some people get occupational asthma. Their lungs become sensitive to substances in the air at work, and they get attacks of wheezing and breathlessness (see ALLERGY). Among the causes are substances in paints, biological detergents, printers' inks, furniture foam, solder, platinum ores, and epoxy glues.

Skin Diseases

Some factory processes use substances that can burn the skin or produce skin rashes. Often the worker is not affected at first, but after a time he or she becomes more sensitive and the merest touch of the substance causes the rash. This may happen in the paint, dye, chemical, and cosmetic industries. The rash is called contact eczema (or contact dermatitis). Often a metal such as nickel is to blame.

Heavy Metal Poisoning

Some workers who handle chemicals containing heavy metals such as lead and mercury are at risk of disease. The body absorbs these metals through the skin, or as a vapour through the lungs, but it does not get rid of them and so they build up. Lead poisoning affects workers in the ship-building, smelting, and paint-making trades. Mercury poisoning comes from the refining of mercury itself or its use in making scientific instruments such as thermometers.

Both these metals affect the brain and nerves, causing weakness and loss of co-ordination and mental powers. To make top hats, old-time hatters (hatmakers) used felt painted with mercury nitrate. As they handled the felt and licked their fingers to smooth it out, they swallowed mercury. The resulting mercury poisoning led to the saying "as mad as a hatter".

Cancers and Leukaemia

It is known that exposure to radiation can cause cancer or leukaemia. Workers in the nuclear industry are given protective clothing and have regular checks to see if they have absorbed too much radiactivity. If your dentist takes an X-ray of your teeth, he or she will probably hide round the corner or wear a protective apron. The small amount of radiation from one X-ray carries virtually no danger to you, but a dentist who takes many X-rays every day is much more at risk. (See CANCER; LEUKAEMIA.)

Some cancers are linked to exposure to the chemicals benzene, cadmium, and aniline (used in dyes). Skin cancer is much more likely after handling tar and pitch or the salts of chromium used in chrome-plating.

Other Occupational Diseases

There are many other occupational diseases. Noise from loud machinery or aircraft may produce deafness. The hammering of a pneumatic drill can cause loss of feeling and blood circulation in the hands and fingers. And there is a large group of problems caused by repetitive movements of a part of the body: typist's finger, sewer's thumb, and even housemaid's knee.

Anyone who is worried about risks at work should contact his or her own doctor, the company or factory doctor, or an organization dealing with safety at the workplace.

Prevention is Better

If the risks associated with a particular occupation are known, then workers can use precautions to guard against disease: air-filtering masks, special gloves, protective clothing, airtight compartments for gases, darkened goggles for their eyes, and so on. In most countries the employers must provide such safety equipment to bring the risks down to a "reasonable level".

This is not always so simple. In poorer parts of the world, people may not know of the risks, or they cannot afford protective equipment, or they are prepared to put up with the dangers in order to earn a wage. Also, the link between disease and job may not be discovered for

Courtesy, MSA (Britain) Limited

Workers in radiation detection and decontamination must wear radiation suits for protection.

many years. Once someone has developed an occupational disease it is usually too late for a cure.

OCCUPATIONAL THERAPY. Anyone who has been in hospital for a time will know how boring it can be. Occupational therapy is both a way of "occupying" someone's time while ill and a kind of treatment (therapy). It can help many people, but particularly those with long-term illness or disability. It is a fairly new profession, developed during and after World War I (1914–18). While the war-wounded people were recovering in hospital, some were given jobs such as making uniforms, to help the war effort. It was soon noticed that those who stayed busy and active (as far as their illness allowed) and who had an interest recovered more quickly than those who were bored and miserable.

Occupational therapy can involve doing

almost anything, within reason. The occupational therapist (as the expert is called) first finds out about the person's interests and abilities, and assesses the effects of the illness and any handicaps. The therapist and patient together choose an activity – learning to paint or draw, carpentry, gardening, computer programming, for example. In more serious cases the person may need the therapist's help simply to learn to get dressed, have a bath, or cook meals.

Occupational therapy does not only combat boredom but also is a positive part of the overall treatment. Often it involves being active, since this helps the person to become fit again. It helps disabled people and those who have been in bed for a long time to regain their co-ordination, strength, and muscle control. In this area it overlaps with a similar form of treatment, physiotherapy (see PHYSIOTHERAPY).

To some extent, occupational therapy also overlaps with industrial and vocational training. Some people can no longer carry on their original job after their illness or injury. Occupational therapy can help to retrain them for a new trade. And what starts as a pastime can soon grow into a new business.

For people with mental problems occupational therapy is often most valuable. While recovering from mental illness, many people feel as though they have failed in some way. Learning a new skill and finding an absorbing interest can boost their confidence and help to speed their recovery. (See MENTAL ILLNESS.)

OCEAN AND OCEANOGRAPHY. Oceans

and seas cover about 70 per cent of the Earth's surface. Most of this area is taken up by five great oceans, the Atlantic, Pacific, and Indian oceans (on which there are separate articles), the Arctic which surrounds the North Pole, and Antarctic (or Southern) ocean which surrounds the continent of Antarctica. The Antarctic is not always seen as an ocean in its own right but regarded as the southernmost portions of the Atlantic, Indian, and Pacific Oceans. Parts of the deep oceans have been called seas, such as the Arabian Sea and the

Sargasso Sea. Other seas are just as deep, at least 2,000 meters (6,500 feet), but are separate from the oceans and are surrounded by land, such as the Mediterranean Sea, the Black Sea, and the Red Sea. Shallow seas, less than 200 meters (650 feet), such as the North Sea and the Baltic Sea, represent the flooded edges of the continents. The plants and animals of the ocean are described in MARINE LIFE.

Oceanography is the study of the oceans and seas. The first scientific expeditions to study the sea were carried out in the 19th century. Today scientists on research ships from many countries, and remote-sensing satellites in orbit, are constantly studying the oceans.

The Bottom of the Sea

Scientists make maps of the shape of the sea floor with an instrument called an echosounder. This instrument emits a "ping" in the water and times how long the sound takes to travel from the surface to the bottom of the sea (where it is reflected) and back again. The depth of the sea is calculated from the travel time and from the speed of sound in the water (1,500 meters or almost 5,000 feet per second). In fact an echo-sounder does this calculation automatically and makes a new measurement every few seconds. A development of this device, called a side-scan sonar, can produce realistic pictures looking remarkably like photographs of the seabed.

The maps show that in the deep water beyond the flat-bottomed shallow seas of the continental shelves there are great ocean basins containing flat plains, high ridges, and deep valleys. The plains of these deep ocean basins have become flat from the gradual addition of small grains of sand and finer particles of rock which were originally carried into the sea by the rivers of the continents. The ridges under the sea run in a meandering line through all the oceans of the world, and are formed by layer upon layer of lava, which has been erupted from just a few long narrow cracks in the sea floor. Due to a soft region some tens of kilometers below the seabed the layers of lava can move sideways away from

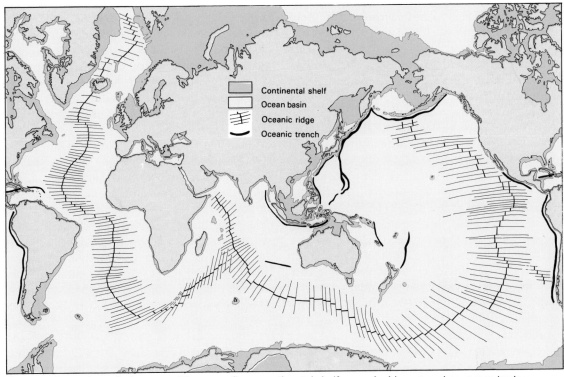

The map shows the main features of the ocean floor: continental shelf; oceanic ridges; trenches; ocean basins.

the narrow cracks when new lava is erupted. These lava layers form the ocean floors. Eventually, after the layers of lava have moved hundreds or thousands of kilometers horizontally they sink below the Earth's crust. This happens in the deep trenches, such as the Marianas Trench in the northwest Pacific Ocean which contains the deepest known point on Earth, 11,034 meters (36,200 feet) below sea-level. (See EARTH; PACIFIC OCEAN.)

The Sea Water

Sea water differs from fresh water in being salty. For millions of years the rivers of the continents have been carrying soil and rock particles into the seas and oceans. Many of these particles eventually fall to the bottom of the sea and become part of the sediments that collect there, but some of the particles can dissolve in water. These substances never reach the sea floor but stay dissolved in the sea for ever. Ordinary salt is the most common natural substance which dissolves in water and therefore the sea has a salty taste. Because

the salt in the sea stays dissolved for ever, the sea is getting slowly more and more salty every year. Besides salt there are also very small quantities of other substances in the sea, some of which are valuable metals such as gold, nickel, and magnesium.

In most places there are about 35 grams of solid matter dissolved in every 1,000 grams of sea water. In some regions of heavy rainfall or where large rivers run into the sea, the saltiness is less, as for instance in the Baltic Sea, especially in the Gulf of Bothnia. There are no big rivers flowing into the Red Sea and because the heat of the sun evaporates the water (see EVAPORATION) leaving the salt behind there may be more than 40 grams of solid matter dissolved in every 1,000 grams of Red Sea water. However, these places are the exception and it was shown as long ago as 1819 that all samples of sea water from all parts of the world contain the same dissolved substances in the same proportion. This means that the waters of the oceans and seas are well mixed. The degree of saltiness of the oceans, the salinity, can be measured by oceanographers and plotted on charts.

The surface temperature of the sea varies from about −2°C (28°F) in the polar regions to about 29°C (84°F) near the equator. The temperature at which water freezes decreases as the saltiness of the water increases. The temperature at the bottom of the deep oceans is everywhere above freezing point, although it is very near it in parts of the Arctic and Antarctic Oceans. Although the sea surface surrounding the North Pole is frozen the ice is mostly less than 15 meters (50 feet) thick, so that submarines are able to pass over the North Pole underneath the ice. The Baltic and other landlocked northern seas freeze readily because of their low salt content. In the tropics the temperature of the sea falls very rapidly below a depth of some 60 meters (200 feet) and at about 750 meters (2,460 feet) is only 4°C (39°F). Water temperature can also be plotted and recorded on charts.

A liter of sea water weighs about 1,030 grams (1 cubic foot weighs 64.3 pounds). This means that there is a pressure of 103 grams per square centimeter at a depth of 1 meter and consequently 103 kilograms, or 1.03 tonnes, per square centimeter at a depth of 1 kilometer (1.18 US tons per square inch at a depth of 1 mile). Such large pressures make it very difficult to design submarines which can reach the ocean floor.

The color of the sea ranges from a deep blue in the open oceans to greenish-brown or even yellow near the shore. The deep blue color is an indication of purity and usually means that the water is not only free from mud but also contains only a few of the tiny plants and animals called plankton. These can cause water to appear brown, green, or even red, as in the Red Sea. The color of the Yellow Sea off the coast of China is caused by the many particles of clay washed down into it by the rivers. Clear sea water allows green and blue light to pass through it more readily than other colors. Therefore everything looks bluey-green to a diver or underwater swimmer. The colors we see in underwater photography are due to the white camera lights used by the underwater photographer. The general appearance of a large area of sea surface often depends on the color of the sky. For example, the Mediterranean Sea looks gray and dull under heavy clouds, but sparkling blue under a bright sunny blue sky.

The Surface of the Sea

When the wind blows over the sea from the same direction for several hours waves are produced (see WAVE). The longer the wind blows the bigger the waves become. Waves continue to travel across the ocean long after the wind has stopped blowing. As the waves travel further and further they become smoother and the distance between successive waves increases; finally the waves die away or break when they approach the coast. Waves from a big storm in the Antarctic have been detected in Alaska, over 12,000 kilometers (7,500 miles) away.

The sea surface also moves up and down due to the tides (see TIDES), which are caused by the pull of the Moon and Sun on the oceans as the Earth revolves. This vertical movement is greatest in confined bays and estuaries. The greatest known tide is 15 meters (50 feet) and occurs in Nova Scotia, Canada, in the Bay of Fundy. A tide of 13 meters (43 feet) is found at the head of the Bristol Channel, England. In the open ocean the tides are probably less than 1 meter (3.28 feet).

Currents at the surface of the ocean are caused by prevailing winds which blow in the same direction, on average, all the year round. When the prevailing wind blows away from a coast, cold water rich in nutrients may be drawn up from below. The nutrients support vast quantities of marine life, and areas off Peru and southeast Arabia, for example, abound in fish. The currents are as steady as the winds which produce them. Other currents also exist within the ocean below the sea surface. They are produced by masses of water whose movements are controlled by their saltiness and temperature (see CURRENTS, OCEAN).

Careful study of the oceans is necessary because they are important to mankind – from the points of view of weather, transportation, and food sources. Any changes in oceanic conditions may herald a change in climate or in fish supplies, and an early warning of these is useful to all countries.

OCEANIA see PACIFIC ISLANDS.

OCELOT. One of the most beautiful members of the cat family is the ocelot (*Felis pardalis*), which gets its common name from a Mexican word *tlalocelotl*, meaning field-tiger. It is among the smaller of the wild cats, growing up to 130 centimeters (51 inches) long, excluding the tail.

Frank Lane Picture Agency

The coat markings of the ocelot camouflage it in the dappled light of the tropical forest.

Ocelots live in forests and dense scrub from Texas in the United States southwards to northern Argentina in South America.

The coat color varies from pale gray and yellow to a deep warm brown blotched with large brown, black-bordered spots, with black streaks around the head and neck. The patterned coat blends in well against the dappled light filtering through the forest trees. The ocelot is an agile climber, and hunts mainly at night, preying on small mammals, birds, and reptiles.

The ocelot is endangered because it has been hunted for its fur. To protect this animal from becoming extinct, the trading of ocelot pelts (skins) is against the law in many countries.

O'CONNELL, Daniel (1775–1847). A great 19th-century Irish leader, Daniel O'Connell was born on 6 August 1775, near Cahirciveen in County Kerry. He was educated in County Cork and at Catholic schools in France. After studying law in London he started work in the Irish law courts in 1798 and soon won fame by his skill in examining witnesses and public speaking.

At that time Catholics did not have the same rights as Protestants and were not allowed to become members of parliament unless they took an oath against the Catholic religion. O'Connell organized a movement to demand that Catholics should be given the same rights as Protestants. His first campaign, around 1815, was stopped by the government, but later he started the Catholic Association, which began again the agitation for rights for the Catholics.

In 1828 he was elected member of parliament for County Clare, though he could not sit in parliament unless he took the oath against the Catholic religion. Parliament was then forced to pass the Catholic Emancipation (freedom) Act in 1829, which gave Catholics most of the same rights as Protestants. For this achievement O'Connell became known as "the Liberator".

However, O'Connell was still dissatisfied with the way in which Ireland was governed. Since the Act of Union with England (passed in 1800), Ireland had not had a parliament of its own in Dublin but had sent 100 members to the parliament in Westminster, London. O'Connell believed that Ireland could never be justly governed or prosperous until it had its own parliament in Dublin, and he therefore demanded that the Act of Union should be repealed, or done away with.

After taking his seat in the Westminster parliament in 1829, he fought the government for further Irish reforms. In 1840 he founded the Repeal Association to try to bring these about. It held enormous meetings in all parts of the country and the government became so alarmed that in 1843 it prohibited a great meeting that had been planned to take place at Clontarf, near Dublin. O'Connell was arrested, and convicted of creating discontent and disloyalty, but the sentence was afterwards canceled by the House of Lords.

By this time O'Connell was an old man and his health was failing. His more active followers, the Young Ireland movement, took over the leadership and demanded more defiant action. They believed that Irish independence could be won only by fighting, whereas O'Connell had always believed in peaceful agitation and had condemned policies that might produce bloodshed.

Many monuments to him exist in the cities of Ireland, but the most famous is his statue in O'Connell Street, Dublin.

OCTOPUS. The name of the octopus comes from a Greek word meaning "eight-footed", and this is because its foot is divided into eight tentacles, rather like long, flexible arms. Each arm has rows of suckers on the underside, and with these it holds very tightly to anything it catches.

The octopus is a kind of mollusk (see MOLLUSK) called a cephalopod, and so is related to the squid. Like the squid, its bag-like body is covered with skin. In the back part of the body is a funnel-siphon, through which it shoots out a stream of water with such force that the octopus is propelled backwards at high speed. In this way it can escape from an enemy, such as a large fish, which approaches the octopus too quickly to give it a chance of crawling away over the rocks or hiding in a hole or crevice.

The octopus also has a way of screening its escape by squirting out a cloud of black, inky fluid from a sac in the lower part of its body. The fluid darkens the water and baffles the pursuer, who cannot see where the octopus has gone.

When it is lying quietly at the bottom of a shallow pool, the octopus spreads out its tentacles on the ground. If a crab comes by, the octopus whips out its tentacles, seizes the prey and draws it into its beak-like mouth. As well as crabs, it catches lobsters and other mollusks.

The octopus has been credited with considerable intelligence. The female is a devoted mother. Each of her eggs is enclosed in a capsule, or case, which attaches itself to some object in the water. There are always a number of them close together, and the mother watches over them faithfully. She changes the water in which they lie by squirting more water over them by means of her funnel-siphon. Like the adult, the young octopus can change color rapidly, turning from dull red to gray, yellow, brown or blue-green, according to its surroundings. This it does by varying the pigment, or coloring substance, in its skin.

Octopuses often live among crevices in rocks. The octopus swims by jet propulsion, forcing water out through its siphon and shooting backwards at high speed.

There are about 150 species, or kinds, of octopus, and they are found in all the seas of the world, although there are only a very few in Arctic and Antarctic waters. The common octopus (*Octopus vulgaris*) measures up to 1.8 meters (6 feet) across its tentacles. The giant octopus of the Pacific (*Octopus apollyon*) sometimes has arms up to 9 meters (30 feet) long.

Many stories have been told of the dangers of swimming in seas where octopuses live, but in fact most are harmless. However, the bite of the brightly marked blue-ringed octopus (*Hapalochaena lunulata*) is deadly. This octopus lives in Pacific and Australian waters. Its poison paralyzes the nervous system and can kill a person within a couple of hours.

In some countries, including Greece, Italy, and China, octopuses are caught for food. The flesh may be stewed or dried and pickled.

ODE. The first meaning of the word "ode" was a chant or poem meant to be sung and accompanied by music and dance. Gradually the idea of musical accompaniment disappeared, however, and an ode came to be a particular kind of lyric poem, usually solemn and stately in feeling and written in a dignified and elaborate style (see LYRIC). Odes are often written as though they were addressing someone or something. For example, William Collins, an English poet of the 18th century, wrote an "Ode to Evening".

One of the first poets to compose odes was an ancient Greek named Pindar. He wrote odes in honor of the winners of athletic competitions and other heroic subjects, and centuries later many English poets admired him and tried to follow his way of writing. Other odes of classical times were those written by the Roman poet Horace.

An English poet who imitated the style of Pindar's odes was John Dryden (1631–1700). One of his poems is an ode called "Alexander's Feast, or the Power of Music". Another writer of Pindaric odes, as they are called, was Thomas Gray in the 18th century.

Some of the best-loved odes are the simpler and more natural ones by poets of the early 19th century such as William Wordsworth, John Keats, and Percy Bysshe Shelley. They include Wordsworth's ode "Intimations of Immortality from Recollections of Early Childhood"; Keats's "Ode to a Nightingale"; and Shelley's "Ode to the West Wind". Here is how another of Shelley's odes, "To a Skylark", begins:

> Hail to thee, blithe Spirit!
>   Bird thou never wert,
> That from Heaven, or near it,
>   Pourest thy full heart
> In profuse strains of unpremeditated art.
>
> Higher still and higher
>   From the earth thou springest
> Like a cloud of fire;
>   The blue deep thou wingest,
> And singing still dost soar, and soaring ever singest.

ODER RIVER. Across the North European Plain, from the western Carpathian Mountains to the Baltic Sea flows the Oder. The length of its course is some 850 kilometers (530 miles). It is the second largest river in Poland (after the Wisla) and empties into the Baltic. It rises in The Czech Republic and receives many rapid tributaries from the mountains. These tributaries cause much flooding of the main river in spring and early summer. The mud they carry makes the valley fertile but hinders navigation by settling in the channel. Navigation is normally possible for 710 kilometers (442 miles). On entering Poland the Oder (in Polish, Odra) turns northeast and flows in a wide valley through the Silesian plain, which centers round Wroclaw (formerly Breslau). This is the most important part of the river basin, with a rich coalfield, steelworks, woolen mills, and crops of wheat and rye.

The lower Oder and its tributary the Neisse form the boundary between Poland and Germany. The Warta, much the largest tributary of the Oder, flows through the heart of Poland. The Oder enters the Baltic through a wide shallow estuary at the head of which is Szczecin (formerly Stettin). Seagoing ships can reach Szczecin and barge traffic can reach the rivers Elbe and Wisla (Vistula) through canals linking them with the Oder. The Oder-Havel Canal (formerly the Hohenzollern Canal) links Berlin, on the Havel, and the port of Szczecin.

ODYSSEY. The *Odyssey* is one of two great epic poems traditionally thought to have been composed by the ancient Greek poet Homer. (See EPIC; HOMER.) Its name comes from the Greek name of its hero, Odysseus, who in Latin and English is often called Ulysses. Homer's other poem is the *Iliad* (described in a separate article), and both the *Iliad* and the *Odyssey* belong to the series of legends, or stories, told by the Greeks about the war between the Greeks and the Trojans.

In this war the armies of the Greek princes besieged the city of Troy for ten years before they could capture and destroy it. The events that Homer described in the *Iliad* happened in the tenth year of the siege, but the story of the *Odyssey* came later, when the Greek heroes were all returning to their homes after the long war was over. There were many stories of returns like this, but Homer's tale of the homecoming of Odysseus became the most famous because it was full of hardship and adventure and because Homer told it so well.

Odysseus' home, where his wife Penelope and his son Telemachus were waiting for him, was on the island of Ithaca off the west coast of the Greek mainland. To get there from the northwest coast of Asia Minor (now Turkey) where Troy stood would take perhaps two or three weeks in the type of little ship that the Greeks had in those days, sailing the whole way in sight of land as they always did. It took Odysseus ten years, however, and the *Odyssey* is chiefly the story of the adventures that delayed him on the way. Homer started the story not at the beginning of the legend, but at a moment quite near the end, when Odysseus was detained on an island by the sea-nymph Calypso, who had kept him there for several years.

At the beginning of the poem, there was a meeting of the gods in heaven, where they decided that Odysseus should be allowed at long last to return home after all his wanderings. The gods were continually interfering in human affairs, not always very reasonably. While some of them favoured Odysseus, others hated him and wanted to do him harm. His chief enemy was Poseidon, the god of the sea, and that was why he was always being shipwrecked or driven off his course. Even when the gods decided that Odysseus must be allowed to go home, Poseidon had not finished with him.

Odysseus' chief ally, on the other hand, was the goddess Athena. After the meeting she went straight to Ithaca to give advice to Odysseus' son Telemachus. Telemachus and Penelope were in difficulties because a large gathering of neighbouring chieftains had settled in Odysseus' home, telling Penelope that her husband was dead and that she must choose a new husband from among them. Penelope put them off by insisting that she must finish weaving a shroud for Odysseus' aged father before she decided. She worked at the weaving every day, but every night she pulled it to pieces so that it should never be finished. It was a great relief when Athena came (disguised as an old friend of Odysseus) to suggest that Telemachus should set out to seek news of his father: for this journey, on which Athena went with Telemachus, helped to postpone the decision still further. The suitors for Penelope were furious and plotted to murder Telemachus on his return.

Journeying through Greece, Telemachus learned at last from Menelaus, king of Sparta (whose wife Helen had been the cause of the Trojan War), that Odysseus was alive on Calypso's island; and meanwhile the gods had ordered Calypso to set him free. With Calypso's help Odysseus built a boat and set sail, but once again Poseidon's hatred brought disaster. The sea-god caused the boat to be wrecked and Odysseus only just managed to escape alive to the shores of the island of Scheria. Luckily for him he was found and helped by Nausicaa, the king's daughter, who fell in love with him and begged him to stay. She took him to her father's palace and there, to King Alcinous and his court, he told the story of all the wearisome adventures of his journey that had at last brought him to their shores.

The Adventures

Odysseus told how after the Trojan War he embarked on his ship to return to Ithaca, but before long the winds blew him off his course to the land of the Lotus-eaters. There some of his sailors ate the fruit of the lotus, which made them forget their journey and their friends, and it was only after dragging them away by force that Odysseus was able to set sail again. Their next landing was on the island of the Cyclopes, one-eyed giants. Six of Odysseus' men were killed and eaten there by the terrible Polyphemus, but Odysseus finally managed to make the monster drunk and then put out his eye.

After a narrow escape from Polyphemus' cave, the ships sailed on to visit the god of the winds, who gave Odysseus all the winds that might hinder him on his homeward course tied up in a bag. After ten days they were actually in sight of Ithaca, but then, when Odysseus was sleeping, the crew were overcome by curiosity and opened the bag to see what was inside. Out rushed the winds and in a moment a great tempest began to drive the ships away from their homeland. Most of the sailors were never to see it again, for not long afterwards, in the land of the Laistrygonian cannibals, all perished except the crew of Odysseus' ship and Odysseus himself.

The single ship, full of sorrowing and despairing men, next came to an island called Aeaea, ruled by the goddess Circe. She was an enchantress who turned her victims into animals. After some of the ship's company had accepted her invitation to feast in her palace, she changed them into pigs. However, Odysseus, with the aid of a magic herb given him by the god Hermes, came to their rescue and Circe was persuaded to free them from their enchantment. For a year the Greeks stayed on in Circe's palace, but at last their desire to reach Ithaca became strong once more, and again they set sail—not for Ithaca yet but for the underworld of the dead where Odysseus

Michael Holford

A scene from the *Odyssey* depicted on a 5th-century Greek vase. As Odysseus' ship passes the island of the Sirens, whose lovely song lures men to death, he stops his crew's ears with wax while he himself is tied to the mast and alone hears the Sirens' music.

sought the advice of the ghost of the wise prophet Teiresias. Teiresias warned him of further perils to come on his journey and told him how to deal with them.

Adventures, in fact, followed one after another, but through all of them Odysseus himself remained safe. He escaped from the dangerous magic of the Sirens—enchantresses with beautiful voices whose singing lured men to a dreadful death—and managed to steer a course through the strait guarded by the monster Scylla on the one side and the whirlpool Charybdis on the other. On the coasts of Sicily, Odysseus' companions disobeyed his orders not to kill any of the herds of cattle and sheep they found there, and because of this deed—for the animals belonged to the sun god Apollo—a great storm arose when the ship set sail. With one stroke of lightning all its crew were hurled overboard and drowned. Odysseus alone survived, and after nine days drifting on the open sea was washed up on the isle of Ogygia, the home of Calypso.

The Homecoming

King Alcinous, was so moved by this tale of difficulties and disasters that he gave Odysseus a ship to enable him to return home, and sent men from among his own people to sail it.

This time Odysseus reached Ithaca safely and the friendly sailors laid him gently on the sands, fast asleep. When he awoke, he was warned by Athena about Penelope's suitors and the plot to kill Telemachus. To disguise him, she made Odysseus look like a beggar and brought back Telemachus secretly to help him. Only Telemachus and one faithful servant were allowed to know who he was and they all took refuge in the servant's cottage while Odysseus made a plan of action. In his own palace, the suitors for Penelope's hand treated him with contempt, taking him for a beggar.

Penelope offered at last to marry whichever of them could pass the test of stringing Odysseus' bow and shooting an arrow through 12 axeheads in a row. Of course all the suitors failed and only Odysseus, still disguised as a beggar, easily succeeded. Then he cast off his disguise and with the help of Telemachus and Athena killed all the suitors. Penelope herself was the last to recognize him but when she did, Odysseus' long troubles were over. He was home.

OEDIPUS. The story of Oedipus, son of Laius and Jocasta, king and queen of Thebes, is one of the saddest of all the tales told by the ancient Greeks. Laius had been warned by the god Apollo that he would be killed by his own son, so when the child was born he pierced its feet with a spike and left it on a hillside to die. The baby was found by a herdsman and taken to Corinth where he was adopted by King Polybus and given the name of Oedipus, which means Swollen Foot.

One day, when Oedipus had grown up, someone made fun of him about his unknown birth, and though he begged Polybus to tell him the truth the king refused to answer. Oedipus then set off to Delphi to consult the oracle, the place where human beings might obtain answers to their questions from Apollo (see ORACLE). There he was told that he would kill his father and marry his mother. In great distress he decided never to return to Corinth and wandered to Thebes, meeting Laius by chance on the way and killing him in a quarrel without even realizing

that he was a king. Thus the first part of the oracle's prophecy was fulfilled.

When he came to Thebes, Oedipus found that the city was threatened by the Sphinx, a monster half lion and half woman which killed all passers-by who could not answer its riddle. This was: "What animal goes on four feet in the morning, on two at noon, and on three in the evening?" Oedipus answered: "Man is the animal, because as a child he crawls on hands and knees, as a man he walks upright and in old age he helps himself with a stick." At this correct answer the Sphinx promptly killed itself. The grateful Thebans made Oedipus king of their country and gave him Jocasta, the widow of their former king, Laius, for his wife. Thus he married his mother and the second part of the oracle's warning had come true.

Jocasta and Oedipus, not knowing that they were really mother and son, lived happily together and had four children. Years later a mysterious plague broke out in Thebes and a messenger was sent to the oracle to ask what could be done to save the townspeople from death. The oracle replied that the murderer of Laius must be punished. In all the questioning that followed, Oedipus finally discovered the truth about his parents and all he had done. In horror Jocasta killed herself and Oedipus put out his own eyes. Accompanied only by his daughter, Antigone, he wandered through the land as a blind beggar until at last he found rest at Colonus, a village near Athens.

O'HIGGINS, Bernardo (1778–1842), is sometimes called "The Father of the Chilean Nation". Much of his life was spent fighting to free Chile from Spanish rule.

His unusual combination of Irish and Spanish names was the result of his being the son of an Irishman who was governor of Chile. He was born in Chillan, and at the age of 17 was sent to England to complete his education. One of his professors there was Francisco Miranda, a Venezuelan who devoted his life to freeing the Spanish colonies. His influence inspired O'Higgins in his fight for Chilean independence.

BBC Hulton Picture Library

Bernardo O'Higgins became president of Chile after leading the country to independence in 1818.

After his father's death in 1801, O'Higgins returned to South America. In September 1810 Chile began its fight for freedom. O'Higgins became commander of the revolutionary army. Unfortunately the different leaders could not agree, and there was a threat of civil war. The revolutionary army was defeated at Rancagua in 1814. The Spaniards reconquered the colony and drove the leaders of the rebellion into exile.

O'Higgins, with thousands of Chileans, went to Mendoza, Argentina, across the Andes. There José de San Martín was training an army to fight the Spaniards in Chile and Peru. O'Higgins joined them and soon rose to the rank of general. In 1817 San Martín led his troops across dangerous passes of the Andes. He defeated the surprised Spaniards at Chacabuco and entered the capital city of Santiago. There O'Higgins was chosen to head the new government. In January 1818 he declared the complete independence of Chile.

As the leader of his nation, O'Higgins brought about many changes. He set up schools, libraries, and strong police forces. He soon became unpopular, however, because he was too strict and because he was changing things too fast. In January 1823 he was asked to resign and did so for the good of his country. He then went to Peru as an exile and lived there with his mother and sister. In 1839 Chile restored his military rank and honours. Illness prevented his return and he stayed in Peru until his death.

OHIO lies in the heartland of the huge industrial belt that stretches from the iron mines of northern Minnesota to the coal mines of West Virginia. The basis of its economy has for many decades been "smokestack industries"—steel, rubber, motor vehicle assembly and parts. Ohio is one of the most heavily industrialized states in the Union, as well as one of the most built-up. Unlike such states as New York, Illinois, or Wisconsin that have one major city, Ohio has seven cities with populations exceeding 100,000: Cleveland, Columbus (the state capital), Cincinnati, Toledo, Akron, Dayton, and Youngstown. Canton and Parma both have more than 90,000 people, and Lorain exceeds 75,000. There are, in addition, about 150 cities with populations of more than 10,000. Although only 35th among the states in geographical area, Ohio is 6th in population.

Ohio has long prided itself on its industrial base, but by the late 1980s the old smokestack industries were in trouble nationally. There was high unemployment, owing in large part to foreign competition. And the newer high-technology industries had established themselves elsewhere.

Economic comeback is possible, as Cleveland has demonstrated. In the late 1970s Cleveland became the first city that could not pay its debts since the Great Depression. Since 1979 it has, under capable business leadership, undergone a major turnaround. Means have been found to refinance its debts and to rebuild seriously deteriorated streets, bridges, water systems, and sewers. Whether such a comeback could occur in the state as a whole depended on Ohio's political leadership

Cincinnati became a river port after the first steamboat arrived in 1814 on its downriver journey from Pittsburgh. It is now home port for two restored "stern-wheelers".

ZEFA

and on co-operation from the many unions, and public interest and business groups.

Ohio has long provided national leadership in proportion to its economic strength. It has given eight presidents: William Henry Harrison, Ulysses S. Grant, Rutherford B. Hayes, James A. Garfield, Benjamin Harrison, William McKinley, William Howard Taft, and Warren G. Harding. Among the many other individuals from Ohio to gain national fame are the authors Sherwood Anderson, Langston Hughes, and James Thurber; astronauts John Glenn and Neil Armstrong; inventors Thomas Alva Edison and the Wright Brothers; actors Clark Gable, and Dorothy and Lillian Gish; soldiers such as Colonel George Armstrong Custer, and General William Sherman; historian Arthur M. Schlesinger, Jr.; lawyer Clarence Darrow; immunologist Albert Sabin; golfer Jack Nicklaus; Olympic gold medallist Jesse Owens; pilot Eddie Rickenbacker; and oil millionaire John D. Rockefeller.

The Land

Ohio is the easternmost of the North Central states. It is bordered on the east by Pennsylvania, on the north by Lake Erie and Michigan, and on the west by Indiana. The Ohio River forms a southern border of 702 kilometres (436 miles), separating the state from West Virginia and Kentucky. Ohio extends

362 kilometres (225 miles) east to west and 346 kilometres (215 miles) north to south.

During the Ice Age, glaciers turned most of Ohio into a relatively level plain. Today, Ohio has three natural regions: the Allegheny Plateau, the Interior Plains, and the Lake Plains. The Allegheny Plateau covers most of eastern Ohio, except for a narrow stretch of land along Lake Erie. It is a hilly area ranging in elevation from 274 metres (900 feet) to 427 metres (1,400 feet). Here are the largest lakes, the greatest extent of the state's forests, and the richest deposits of coal.

The Interior Plains, which cover western Ohio, are an eastern extension of the prairies that cover so much of the Midwest. The highest point in the state is located in these plains: Campbell Hill, at 472 metres (1,550 feet). The lowest point, 131 metres (433 feet), is at the southern end of the plains along the Ohio River.

The Lake Plains extend from Pennsylvania to Indiana in the northern part of Ohio. In the east, along the shores of Lake Erie, the plains are only 8 to 16 kilometres (5 to 10 miles) wide. Midway across the state they begin to widen until they reach a depth of 80 kilometres (50 miles) along the Indiana border.

Ohio's inland location gives it a continental climate, with hot summers and cool (but not excessively cold) winters. Rainfall varies from 760 millimetres (30 inches) in the north to

1,120 millimeters (44 inches) in the southeast. Snowfall is quite heavy in the north because of prevailing winds off Lake Erie. The growing season ranges from 140 days in the northeast to 180 days in the southwest.

The People

When European explorers and fur trappers arrived in the Ohio region in the 18th century they found numerous Indian tribes. Among them were the Miami, Shawnee, Ottawa, Huron, and Delaware. Some of the most intense frontier rivalry between colonists and Indians took place in Ohio. It was not until 1794 that the power of the Indian confederation was broken, when General Anthony Wayne defeated a British-Indian alliance at the Battle of Fallen Timbers. But the last tribal lands were not released until 1842.

Today's Ohio has as varied a population as any state in the Union. The earliest settlers came from eastern states. Many were veterans of the American Revolution who had received land grants from the government. During the 19th century, immigrants came from every part of Europe, from Scandinavia in the north to Italy in the south. From the 1870s onwards, as industry was expanding, there came Germans, Irish, French, Welsh, Scots, Bohemians, Poles, Jews, Hungarians, Russians, and many more to create one of America's great melting-pot states.

By 1843 Ohio, which was a free state, had a black population of 25,000. By 1870 it had risen to 62,000, mostly in southern Ohio where Wilberforce University had been established. This is one of the first black educational institutions in the United States. Black immigration from the South increased markedly during the two World Wars as industries boomed and needed workers. By 1980 blacks made up about 8 per cent of the state's population.

The Economy

In 1850 Ohio ranked first among the states in agricultural production. Today, despite its large industrial base, 60 per cent of the land is still used for farming. There are 100,000 farms, of which about 17,000 are dairy farms. The main field crops are corn, soybeans, hay, wheat, and oats. In addition to these grains, Ohio produces potatoes, vegetables, grapes, and other fruit. Grape production made Ohio one of the first wine-producing states in the 19th century. Some tobacco is grown in the south, near the Ohio River. Like other corn belt states, Ohio produces pigs, cattle, sheep, and poultry.

Ohio's mineral wealth is extensive. Coal has been the most profitable mineral, and most of it is taken from six eastern counties bordering West Virginia, another coal-rich state. There are, however, usable coal deposits in 32 counties. Most of the state's electrical energy comes from coal-fueled plants. Limestone and sand-

Howard Oberlin

An Amish farm scene in eastern Ohio. Members of this religious sect do not use modern farm machinery, but are expert farmers nevertheless.

stone quarries produce stone used for building. Rich clay deposits have made Ohio a leader in the manufacture of pottery, firebrick, and tile. The state is fourth in sand and gravel production among the states.

About one-fifth of Ohio is covered with forest, chiefly red oak, white oak, and hard maple. These form the basis of a substantial hardwood industry.

Ohio has been a producer of oil and natural gas since 1860. Production declined after 1900, but new deposits were discovered in the 1960s, and the industry revived. By 1980 there were about 38,000 oil- and natural-gas-producing wells.

Ohio ranks third among the states in manufacturing. There are about 15,500 manufacturing establishments. Transportation equipment is the largest industry. Ohio produces more bus and truck bodies, truck trailers, and similar equipment than any other state. Primary metals is the second largest industry. Ohio ranks second in production of non-electrical machinery and is a leader in manufacturing electrical machinery and rubber. Food processing and chemicals are also significant industrial components.

Much of Ohio's industry is situated according to what it produces. Cincinnati, for instance, leads the world in the production of machine tools, soaps and detergents, and playing cards. Dayton is the major producer of cash registers, plastics, and putty. Akron is the center of the rubber industry. The Youngstown area is a major metals producer. Canton specializes in bank vaults, roller bearings, and vacuum cleaners. Wright-Patterson Air Force Base near Dayton is a flight-testing and research center. Mound Laboratory for atomic research is also near Dayton. Toledo is in the forefront of glass manufacture, and has one of the largest coal shipping ports in the world.

Education

The first school west of the Alleghenies was opened at Schoenbrunn, Ohio, in 1773. It closed four years later when the town was abandoned. The system of free public schools was not founded until 1825. State supported colleges and universities include Ohio State University, at Columbus, long famous for its football teams; and Kent State University, at Kent.

There are several excellent private colleges and universities. Of these, Oberlin College has one of the most interesting histories. It was the first coeducational college in the United States, and the first college to admit black students. Founded in 1833, it became a haven for the anti-slavery movement, and a hiding place or "station" on the "Underground Railroad". This was a network of routes organized by anti-slavery northerners to help slaves escape to freedom in the North or Canada.

History

Remains of ancient civilizations have been found in Ohio, dating from 5,000 to 7,000 years ago. Of later cultures, the Hopewell Indians, who died out about AD 400, represented the highest development. Their burial mounds, which contained well-crafted artifacts when they were discovered, are now a tourist attraction.

The French explorer La Salle may have crossed Ohio in 1669. France claimed the territory in 1773 but founded no towns. The first settlement was founded by Moravians at Schoenbrunn in 1772, but it lasted only a few years. The first permanent settlement was in 1788 at the mouth of the Muskingum River. Called Marietta, it was settled mainly by Revolutionary War veterans. Cincinnati was founded later that year. After the American Revolution Ohio belonged to the United States.

In 1787 Congress passed the Northwest Ordinance which created the Northwest Territory. The ordinance provided that no fewer than three, and not more than five, states should eventually be created from this territory. By 1799 the population had grown sufficiently to justify a territorial legislature being set up at Cincinnati. Ohio became the first state carved out of the Northwest Territory, when it was admitted to the Union in 1803.

Soon after statehood a program of internal transportation improvement was begun. The first steamboat on Lake Erie reached

Cleveland and Sandusky in 1818. The Ohio and Erie Canal was opened in 1832, and the National Pike reached Columbus by 1833. It was later extended across Indiana to Vandalia, Illinois. The first railroad was built in 1836.

Boundary disputes with Michigan unsettled the first decades of statehood. The controversy resulted in the Toledo War of 1835. Michigan troops were poised against the Ohio militia, but violence was avoided when President Jackson settled the dispute in favor of Ohio, and Congress gave Michigan Upper Peninsula in return.

Barnaby's

Furnace works and ore docks along the Cuyahoga River, near Cleveland.

By 1850, Ohio was the third most populous state, with a population of nearly 2 million. The basis of its industrial growth was built between 1850 and 1880, when the value of manufacturing grew to more than twice that of agriculture. A great stimulus to economic growth was the American Civil War. After the war this growth continued, and the industrial area in the northeastern part of the state developed rapidly. The opening of the St. Lawrence Seaway in 1959 made possible the development of Toledo, Cleveland, and other Lake Erie ports as inland seaports for ocean-going vessels.

During the 1960s, Ohio was caught up in the racial strife that emerged from the Civil Rights Movement and in the protests against the Vietnam War (on which there are separate articles). Race riots took place in Cleveland in the summer of 1966, as they did in many other American cities. Within two years, however, Cleveland had a black mayor, Carl B. Stokes. The state became the focus of national attention in 1970 when four students at Kent State University were shot and killed by national guardsmen during anti-war protests.

By the 1980s, Ohio had become part of what has been called the Rust Belt, an area of declining industries in the northeastern section of the United States. Foreign competition in steel, motor vehicles, and other products undercut the profitability of many Ohio firms. Many jobs were lost to the Sun Belt, where warmer climates and lower wages prompted many American companies to relocate.

FACTS ABOUT OHIO

AREA: 115,998 square kilometers (44,787 square miles).
POPULATION: 10,847,115 (1990).
CAPITAL: Columbus, 632,910.
CITIES: Cleveland, 505,616; Cincinnati, 364,040; Toledo, 332,943; Akron, 223,019; Dayton, 182,044; Youngstown, 95,732; Canton, 84,161.
HIGHEST POINT: Campbell Hill, 472 meters (1,550 feet).
PRODUCTS
    Agriculture: Corn, wheat, oats, soybeans, hay, potatoes, grapes, tobacco, maple syrup, cattle, pigs, sheep, poultry.
    Minerals: Coal, petroleum, natural gas, stone, clay, sand and gravel.
    Manufacturing: Electrical and non-electrical machinery and tools, transportation equipment, steel and steel products, processed food, car parts, rubber and rubber equipment, paper.
STATE EMBLEMS: Flower: scarlet carnation. Tree: buckeye. Bird: cardinal.
JOINED THE UNION: Ohio became the 17th state in 1803.

OHIO RIVER flows 1,579 kilometers (981 miles) through east-central United States. It forms the state boundaries between Ohio and West Virginia; Ohio and Kentucky; Indiana and Kentucky; and Illinois and Kentucky. The Ohio River is a tributary of the Mississippi, and more water flows from it into the Mississippi than from any other tributary. Two headstreams, the Allegheny and Monongahela, join at Pittsburgh to form the Ohio which flows generally west and south, reaching the Mississippi at Cairo. The Ohio's longest tributary, the Tennessee, rises in the Appalachian Mountains. The Ohio is navigable, and falls only 130 meters (429 feet) along its course.

The Gallipolis Dam on the Ohio River stands about midway along the southern border of Ohio. This immense roller dam improves navigation and helps control floods. The view looks south across the Ohio River to the rolling hills of West Virginia.

Ohio Development Department

Robert La Salle is believed to have been the first European to see the river, in 1669. The French reached the Ohio from the north, at an early date, and built Fort Duquesne on the site of an American Indian village. The British took this in 1758 and renamed it Fort Pitt, which afterwards became Pittsburgh. Later, farmers began to cultivate the valley and the Ohio became a highway for pioneers settling in the lower valley.

The largest city on the Ohio is Pittsburgh, the great iron and steel center on the Pennsylvania coalfield (see PITTSBURGH). Lower down is Cincinnati with a big meat-packing industry. Much of the meat is pork, for many pigs are fattened on the great crops of corn from the Ohio valley. Below this is Louisville, where the water power of the Ohio rapids is used to make electricity. A canal bypasses the rapids and the river can be used by steamers and barges from Pittsburgh to its junction with the Mississippi. The barges carry coal, oil, steel, and manufactured articles. (See also MISSISSIPPI AND MISSOURI RIVERS.)

OIL is a greasy liquid that does not mix with water, and most oils float on top of water. Because it is viscous (that is, it clings and flows fairly slowly), oil is especially useful for lubricating machinery. (This use of oil is explained in the article FRICTION.)

There are three kinds of oil: mineral oils, fatty oils, and volatile or essential oils. Mineral oils come from the Earth's crust and are distilled from petroleum. (See PETROLEUM.) They are also distilled from oil-bearing shales.

Fatty oils come from both animals and vegetables and have long been used by man. Traces of animal fats have been found in ancient Egyptian tombs, and vegetable oils were used by the Greeks and Romans for cleaning and anointing their bodies. Oils that come from the bodies of sea creatures such as whales are used for treating leather, while those from fish livers (cod and halibut) are medicines.

All fatty oils – liquid or solid, animal or vegetable – belong to one family of chemicals called glycerides which are compounds of glycerin and fatty acids.

Some fatty oils harden when thin films are exposed to the air. These are known as drying oils, but most fatty oils do not behave like this and are classed as non-drying oils. The drying oils such as linseed oil (see FLAX) and tung oil, which is made from the seeds of a tree growing in China (*Aleurites fordii*), are used to make paint and varnish. The most common non-drying oils are those found in food: lard (pork fat), beef and mutton fat (tallow), butter-fat (in milk), olive, peanut, and sunflower seed flowers are needed to produce a small amount of essential oils. Almost 500,000 roses are needed to produce 0.5 kilogram (1 pound) of rose oil. (See PERFUME.) Bay oil is used in toiletries.

Some substances, nutmeg is one of them, contain both a fatty oil—nutmeg butter—and an essential oil.

OKAPI. The okapi (*Okapia johnstoni*) is one of the shyest animals in the world. It hides so well that scientists did not discover one until the 20th century.

Sir Harry Johnston, an English explorer, heard about a strange animal in the Congo valley in Africa. He went there about 1897 hoping to discover this new animal. The natives gave him pieces of a skin and showed him tracks in the soft mud, but he never saw the animal. On another trip to Africa in 1900, Johnston succeeded in capturing a live okapi. The animal was given the scientific name *Okapia johnstoni* after the native name "okapi".

Ann Ronan

A mill used in 19th-century France for pressing seeds, such as mustard, sesame, and sunflower. The oil is squeezed out and flows into the tub below.

oil. Margarine (see MARGARINE) is made from vegetable and animal oil, while the soap-making industry uses large quantities of palm oil, palm-kernel and coconut oil, and tallow. Some castor oil is still used as a lubricant and some is used in medicine.

The volatile or essential oils are not glycerides, and they belong to quite different chemical groups. They give the scents and flavors to flowers and fruit, and may come from the rind (for example, lemon oil), from the seed (caraway oil), or even from the bark (cinnamon). They are obtained either by pressing or by using a liquid known as a solvent, which dissolves the oil but not the fruit. The solvent is then boiled away leaving the oil behind (see DISTILLATION).

Many essential oils are used in perfumes. Common among these are attar of roses, lavender oil, jasmine oil, and geranium oil. The cost of some of them is very high since so many

C. A. W. Guggisberg/Bruce Coleman

The okapi's coloration, with striped legs and hindquarters, disguises it in the equatorial rain forest.

Okapis are members of the giraffe family. They are about 1.5 meters (5 feet) tall at the shoulders. Their neck and legs are shorter than a giraffe's. The tongue is long and can grip bunches of leaves and also grasses which form its main food. Only the males have horns, which are short and covered with skin except for small polished tips.

Okapis are found only in the dense forests of the Congo region of Equatorial Africa. Their coloring is very striking with red foreheads, yellowish-white cheeks, and purplish backs.

Their upper legs are white with black stripes, and their lower legs are yellowish-white. They stand perfectly still when enemies are around. Their strange color pattern makes them almost impossible to see against the forest background. An okapi travels alone or with one other okapi.

OKLAHOMA is a state in the south-central part of the United States. On 22 April 1889, the Indian Territory (as it was then called) in the southwestern part of the United States was opened up for settlement by whites. Thousands of people lined up early to begin the race into the new land as soon as word was given. Many were in covered wagons. Others were on horseback, and some were on foot. As soon as the announcement was made at midday, one of the greatest and most frenzied land rushes in American history was under way. Some whites, however, had sneaked into Indian Territory early and staked land claims illegally. Since they got there earlier, they were called "sooners", and when the Indian Territory became Oklahoma, it was called the Sooner State.

ZEFA

An old-fashioned trolley bus stands out in front of these modern skyscrapers in Oklahoma City.

These land-hungry homesteaders had entered certain "unassigned lands" within Indian Territory in what is now central Oklahoma. In May 1890, this area became the Oklahoma Territory. After 16 years the rest of the territory was opened to white settlement and attached to these lands.

Oklahoma's colorful past has been celebrated in fiction. John Steinbeck's novel *Grapes of Wrath* (1939) recounted the sad years of the Dust Bowl, when the land suffered terrible drought, and many "Okies" left their state to seek a better living in California. In 1943 Richard Rodgers and Oscar Hammerstein brought to the Broadway stage their very successful musical comedy *Oklahoma!*, which made the state's name a household word. The sometimes larger-than-life image of Oklahoma was also the basis for much of the humor of actor and comedian Will Rogers, who was probably the state's most famous son.

Like Kansas to the north, Oklahoma is a wheat state; and like Texas to the south, it is a cattle state. But more than anything else, Oklahoma is an oil state. Tulsa calls itself the "Oil Capital of the World", and Oklahoma City, the capital, competes with it for population and prosperity. Oil made the state rich before petroleum was drilled in Texas; and it made the state poor when Texas started outproducing it. It became rich again when oil prices were drastically increased in the 1970s; and poverty once again showed its face when an oil glut led to an enormous price drop in the mid-1980s. For the foreseeable future Oklahoma will probably follow the fortunes of oil.

The Land

Oklahoma is bounded on the north by Kansas and a part of Colorado. To the west its panhandle meets New Mexico. (A panhandle is a strip of land stretching out from the main region like the handle of a pan.) To the south is Texas, although the Red River of the South flows along much of the Texas border. To the east is Arkansas and a small stretch of Missouri. From east to west along its northern border the state is 756 kilometers (470 miles) long. From north to south it is 330 kilometers (205 miles). The panhandle itself is only 55 kilometers (34 miles) wide.

Oklahoma is primarily a plains state, and its surface rises gradually as one goes west. It has five natural regions. The Gulf Coastal Plain occupies a portion of the Red River

Valley in the southeastern corner. This area is part of the fertile lowlands that stretch south to the Gulf of Mexico. Here the Red River descends to the lowest point in the state, 91 meters (300 feet) above sea-level.

Just to the north of the Gulf plain are the Ouachita Mountains. These highlands are a series of parallel ridges covered with forests of oak and pine. To the north of the mountains is the Ozark Plateau, which extends into the state from Missouri and Oklahoma.

Largest of the regions are the Central Plains, which cover most of Oklahoma up to the panhandle. The region is a rolling grass-land that rises from 152 meters (500 feet) in the east to 610 meters (2,000 feet) in the west. In the southern part of the Central Plains are the Wichita Mountains and the Arbuckle Mountains.

The Great Plains section of Oklahoma takes in the whole panhandle and a small area east of it. In the far northwest corner is Black Mesa, the highest point in the state, at 1,517 meters (4,978 feet).

Oklahoma has a generally warm and dry climate, except for the Red River Valley region, where it is humid and subtropical. Most of the rainfall occurs in the southeast, an average of 1,420 millimeters (56 inches) per year. In the far west the annual rainfall may be as little as 400 millimeters (16 inches) each year. The growing season ranges from 220 days in the southeast to 170 days in the panhandle.

The People

The original inhabitants of Oklahoma were Plains Indians, members of the Caddo, Wichita, Pawnee, Osage, Comanche, Cheyenne, and Arapaho tribes. The Apache and Kiowa arrived later in the 19th century. In the 1830s the "Five Civilized Tribes" from the East (Cherakee, Choctaw, Chickasaw, Creek, and Seminole) were forced to move to what was then intended to be a permanent Indian Territory.

After the Territory was opened to settlement in 1889, homesteaders came from every ethnic group then in the United States. There were even a number of settlers from China. By the 1980s Oklahomans represented a fairly typical Midwestern society.

The Economy

Since homesteading days agriculture has played a major role in the state's economy. There are today more than 85,000 farms. In order of income, livestock ranks first, followed by grains, dairy products, cotton, other field crops, and general produce. The biggest cash crop is winter wheat, which grows chiefly in the prairies of the north and west. Cotton grows in the humid southeast, often called "Little Dixie", because of its similarity to the cotton states to the east. Oklahoma is the leading producer of mung beans (a bean often used for forage), and it is among the top states in production of broomcorn (used in brooms and brushes), and sorghum. Other field crops are hay, peanuts, barley, soybeans, and corn.

Mac McGalliard

Cattle being loaded for market. Cattle make up the state's most valuable agricultural product.

Manufacturing industries include food processing, non-electrical machinery, coal products, refined petroleum (oil), glass and metal products, and transportation equipment. The state has about 1,740,210 hectares (4,300,000 acres) of forest divided almost equally between

A great expanse of wheat farms in western Oklahoma.

Courtesy, Standard Oil Company (New Jersey)

softwoods and hardwoods. A pulp and paper industry was started in the 1970s.

It is mineral production, especially oil and natural gas, that accounts for the bulk of Oklahoma's income. The state ranks fourth nationally in mineral production. The first oil well began producing on 15 April 1897 near Bartlesville.

Education

The first school law was enacted by the Cherokee in 1832. In 1890 the territorial legislature provided for public schools. The largest of the state institutions of higher education is the University of Oklahoma at Norman, considered one of the finest universities in the United States.

History

What is now Oklahoma was claimed by Spain in the early 16th century and by France late in the 18th century. The area came to the United States as part of the Louisiana Purchase of 1803 (see UNITED STATES OF AMERICA, HISTORY OF). In 1828 Congress created the Indian Territory and required all whites to leave. By 1880 there were more than 80 tribes living within Indian Territory.

During the American Civil War many tribes sided with the Confederacy. Afterwards, the federal government forced them to give up the western half of their lands. These were made available to tribes from the western plains.

Pressure from whites seeking land and from the railroads wanting to build across the territory finally forced opening the area to settlement in 1889. An Indian attempt in 1905 to establish a state called Sequoyah was refused by the government. In 1906 delegates met to frame a state constitution. Congress accepted it, and Oklahoma was admitted as the 46th state in 1907.

The growth of agriculture and drilling of oil wells kept the state prosperous until about 1930. Then competition from Texas oil, followed by the Dust Bowl disaster, tumbled Oklahoma into economic depression. Prosperity returned with the onset of World War II. New farming methods, including extensive irrigation, promoted better and more pro-

Courtesy, Oklahoma City Chamber of Commerce

The land rush of 1889 when Congress opened part of the Oklahoma territory to settlement.

ductive agriculture. Significant attempts have been made to encourage new industries and outside investment. Computer, aerospace, and metal-producing industries added to the state's income.

FACTS ABOUT OKLAHOMA

AREA: 181,185 square kilometers (69,956 square miles).
POPULATION: 3,260,000 (1988).
CAPITAL: Oklahoma City, 445,300 (1986).
CITIES: Tulsa, 373,000; Lawton, 82,700; Norman, 78,300; Enid, 50,300; Midwest City, 53,700; Broken Arrow, 52,000; Edmond, 51,200.
HIGHEST PEAK: Black Mesa, 1,517 meters (4,978 feet).
PRODUCTS.
  Agriculture: Cattle, wheat, rye, pecans, peanuts, cotton, sorghum.
  Minerals: Petroleum, natural gas, coal, limestone, sand and gravel, gypsum, granite.
  Manufacturing: Machinery, metal products, processed food.
STATE EMBLEMS. Flower: Mistletoe. Tree: Redbud. Bird: Scissor-tailed flycatcher.
JOINED THE UNION: Oklahoma became the 46th state in 1907.

OKRA is a plant of the mallow family (see MALLOW). Its pods are an ingredient in various soups and stews. They can also be cooked and served cold in salads. Sometimes they are

J. Horace McFarland

The long pods of the okra plant are often used in soups and stews, but are also eaten as a vegetable.

pickled. In the southern United States the pods are known as "gumbos" and used to make a famous spicy dish of the same name. Another common name is "lady's fingers", from their long, delicate shape. Only the tender, unripe pods are good to eat. They have a mild flavor and a thick, sticky juice.

Okra (*Hibiscus esculentus*), an annual plant that grows to about 2.5 meters (8 feet) tall, is native to Africa but is grown in many temperate and tropical regions. Okra has yellow flowers with red centers. Its leaves usually have several deep indentations similar to those of maple leaves. The pods, 8 to 30 centimeters (3 to 12 inches) long when mature, are green to whitish and contain many small, round seeds. The plant may continue to bear pods throughout the growing season, especially if all harvestable pods are picked daily.

In some countries the pods are sliced and dried for winter use, but canning and freezing have largely replaced this method of preservation in the United States. Fibers from the stem of the okra plant may be made into cloth and twine. Okra was introduced into Europe in the 13th century. The plant is easily raised in ordinary garden soil, in warm frost-free conditions.

OLD AGE. In all societies, a section of the population is labeled as "old". What is different from place to place is the age at which people are considered old, and the way old people are regarded. In modern industrialized societies old age begins at 65 or 70; in contrast, in the 19th century old age began at 55. In many poor countries, where people's life expectations are much lower, someone as young as 40 may be an old person.

In some societies elderly people are thought of as wise and experienced, and they may even be the leaders of the community. But in Western societies, the elderly are sometimes disregarded. Having reached a certain age, somewhere between 60 and 70, they may be expected to retire from their jobs, even if they are still able to work efficiently. Gradually their ties with the community are loosened, and in many cases they live in communities made up entirely of old people.

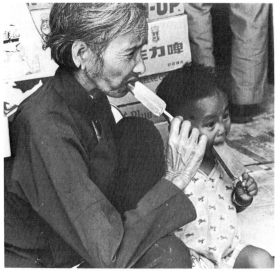

Barnaby's

In most societies, old people play an active role in caring for their grandchildren.

Today in industrialized societies, because of the enormous strides in medical science in the past 40 years, improved diet, and better social conditions, many people live much longer than in any previous generation. For example, in the United States, the proportion of people over the age of 60 rose from 4 per cent of the population in the early 1900s to more than 16 per cent in the late 1980s. There is an even higher proportion of old people in the United Kingdom: in 1990 more than 20 per cent of the population was over 60. The rapid aging of the populations of all the industrialized countries is due not only to people living longer, but also to a sharp decline from the 1970s onwards in the number of babies being born. Women tend to live longer than men, so that in 1985 for every 100 women over the age of 70, there were only 63 men. It is also true that the better-off members of the society can expect to live longer than the poorer, since they are generally better fed and have superior medical care.

In the late 1980s economists began expressing alarm about the burden that caring for the old would place on the shrinking working population. They warned that for every worker paying tax, there would be more and more elderly people needing pensions.

The Aging Process

The actual process of growing old, or aging, proceeds at different rates in different people. Some old people are still active, working, involved in various recreations, and have few of the mental and physical disabilities that are associated with age. Others are not so fortunate. They may suffer from various chronic illnesses, including arthritis, heart disease, rheumatism, diabetes, high blood pressure, and atherosclerosis, which is the thickening of the interior coating of the arteries. In an aging body there is a loss of calcium from the bone, which leads to greater fragility; the body stiffens, the reflexes become slower, the skin less elastic; the hair thins; some shrinkage occurs; the loss of nerve cells results in hearing loss, poorer eyesight, and other sensory afflictions. Older people are less capable of performing tasks that they used to perform and are also likely to suffer from a decline in memory, and thus perform less well in a variety of mental tasks. People who have lived active lives and been quite independent may have to be looked after like small children. This is why old age is sometimes referred to as "second childhood".

Format Photographers

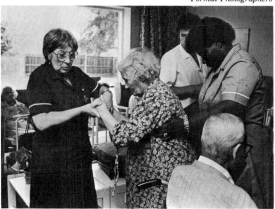

In modern Western societies, many old people are cared for in old people's homes.

The elderly also have social problems. They have to learn to deal with illness, dependence on others, loneliness, and, often, a reduced income. They have to find new ways of filling their time once they have stopped working; and to learn how to survive on their own after they are widowed – a problem more often faced by women than men – and how to cope with the fact that they may no longer feel needed.

In industrialized societies most older people live apart from their children and grandchildren, and they cannot always depend on their children to care for them. These societies are very mobile, for people often leave the place where they were born and move to a distant part of the country, or even go abroad. Then ties with their families tend to loosen. Many old people thus live alone, or in institutions for the aged, or in retirement villages. By contrast, in most parts of southern Europe, the Far East, India, and in practically all of Africa, most elderly people are taken care of in the homes of their grown-up children.

OLEANDER is an evergreen shrub cultivated for its showy flowers and handsome foliage. It belongs to the dogbane family. In warm regions it grows outdoors all year. In cooler regions it makes a fine house and greenhouse plant.

The common oleander, *Nerium oleander*, native to the Mediterranean region, grows to 6 meters (20 feet) tall. Its thick, lance-shaped

ARDEA

The oleander is a poisonous flowering shrub that comes from the Mediterranean region.

leaves, up to 25 centimeters (10 inches) long, are grouped in threes or fours along the stem. Except in double-flowered varieties the red, white, pink, or purple blossoms have five petals. The large, attractive blossoms form clusters at the branch tips. Narrow seed pods contain many fuzzy seeds. Similar to the common oleander is the vanilla-scented sweet oleander, *Nerium indicum*, native to southern Asia.

All parts of the plant are poisonous. So is the smoke from burning oleander wood and honey from oleander nectar. One leaf of oleander can kill the cow or horse that eats it.

OLIVE. Gray-green olive trees are a familiar sight in the countries of the Mediterranean. About 35 species, or kinds, are known and most of those are grown by farmers. They are evergreen trees of the family Oleaceae. They have small white flowers and egg-shaped fruits which are purplish-black when ripe. The hard, light-colored wood of the olive tree makes beautiful furniture.

Olive trees have been cultivated for thousands of years. The Egyptians grew them in very early times, and they are often mentioned in the Bible. The olive tree is associated with Greece. It was sacred to Athena, the goddess of peace and victory, and so olive wreaths were worn as a sign of victory. Men seeking peace carried olive branches, and today the phrase to hold out the olive branch means to show a wish to make peace.

Olive-growing spread rapidly through Greece, and olives were taken to southern Italy by the Greeks who settled there. Today the chief olive-growing countries are Spain, southern Italy, Greece, and southern California. Olive trees need deep, fertile soils and a mild climate free from frost. Young olive trees are usually grown from the cuttings of old ones. They begin to bear fruit when they are 5 years old and are at their best for fruit-bearing at 15 to 20 years old. They range in height from 3 to 12 meters (10 to 40 feet).

Most of the world's olive crop is grown for the valuable oil in the fruit. Olives are crushed between steel or stone rollers and the oil from the pulp is squeezed out by a press. This first

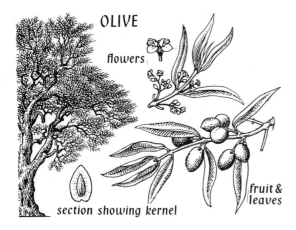

OLIVE

flowers

fruit & leaves

section showing kernel

cold pressing produces a greenish colored oil with a fruity taste. It is the most expensive kind of olive oil. Afterwards the olives are heated and pressed again and this gives a harsher-tasting oil with a golden color, which is less expensive. Oil from the kernels is made into soap and skin cream, or used for oiling machinery.

Olives for eating are carefully picked by hand. Green olives are the ones picked before they are ripe and then pickled in brine. Black olives are ripe fruit that have been preserved in oil with salt and pepper.

OLIVIER, Laurence (1907–89). The British actor and director Laurence Olivier was thought by many to be the greatest theatrical figure of the 20th century. His stage career encompassed tragedy and comedy, Shakespeare and modern drama. In the cinema he was both a popular actor and a highly accomplished director. He was made director of the National Theatre Company in London in 1962. And in 1970 he became the first-ever theatrical peer: Baron Olivier of Brighton.

Laurence Olivier was born in the Surrey town of Dorking where his father, of French Huguenot origin, was the local curate. Even as a small boy his genius for acting was apparent. At the age of 10 he made his public debut playing Brutus in a production of Shakespeare's *Julius Caesar*. His performance was seen by the famous actress Ellen Terry who wrote in her diary: "The small boy who played Brutus is already a great actor."

After many stage appearances as a child, Olivier enrolled in the Central School of Dramatic Art in London, then began his professional career with the Birmingham Repertory. He was soon in demand, both in London's West End and Hollywood, because of his dashing good looks and fiery athleticism. But his early career was not all success. In 1932 he was turned down by the Swedish film star Greta Garbo as her leading man in the film *Queen Christina*. ("Not tall enough," she said.) And in his first major Shakespearian role as Romeo in 1935 he was attacked by the critics for his verse-speaking. ("Mr. Olivier plays Romeo as if he were riding a motorbike," wrote one.) In this production Olivier alternated nightly between playing Romeo and Romeo's rival, Mercutio.

But he went on to triumph in every field. In 1937 he joined London's Old Vic theater where he became a great classical actor, capable of moving easily from high tragedy to period comedy. After a series of films in the United States, including *Wuthering Heights* and *Rebecca*, he returned to England to serve in the British navy during World War II.

In 1944 he became co-director of the Old Vic with the actor and producer Ralph Richardson. Together they were responsible for some of the company's greatest productions, including *Richard III* and *Oedipus Rex*, in which Olivier played the title roles. In 1946 he was knighted for his services to the theater. During the postwar years Olivier produced, directed, and starred in popular film versions of *Henry V*, (for which he received an Academy Award in 1949), *Hamlet*, *Richard III*, and *Othello* (1965). On the stage his most notable successes were in *Antony and Cleopatra* and John Osborne's *The Entertainer* (1957).

Olivier was the inevitable choice to become the first director of Britain's new National Theatre (from 1962 to 1973). He appeared in many of its productions, including *Othello* and Eugene O'Neill's *Long Day's Journey into Night*. In later life he continued his career in films and appeared in many television dramas.

Olivier was married three times. His most celebrated marriage was to the actress Vivien

Leigh. The marriage ended in 1960 and Olivier married Joan Plowright in the following year.

OLYMPIC GAMES. The Olympic Games are considered the world's foremost sporting competition for athletes and sports teams. They are the modern version of the contests held by the ancient Greeks at Olympia. Olympia lies about 15 kilometers (9 miles) east of the town of Pyrgos in the western Peloponnese in Greece. Every four years from 776BC athletes, poets, artists, and sculptors met to take part in a great festival at the temple of Zeus in Olympia in honor of the god (see ZEUS). The artists and writers held exhibitions of their work or gave recitals and the athletes held a race over a distance of 175 meters (191 yards). Later the festival, which took place during the full moon period of midsummer, lasted for five days and became an expression of the Greek idea that a man's body should be just as fit and healthy as his mind.

On the first day of the festival the competitors took the Olympic oath and there were processions and sacrifices in honor of Zeus. The Olympic Games themselves began on the second day and lasted until the end of the fourth. There were running races, wrestling, boxing, horse racing, and the pentathlon, which was a competition in the five events of running, jumping, throwing the discus and the javelin, and wrestling. Other events were chariot racing and the pancration, a combination of wrestling

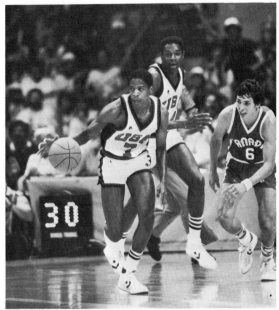

Colorsport

Basketball has been an Olympic sport since 1936. Here Canada and the United States compete at the 1984 Games.

and boxing. There were contests for both boys and men, who had to be freeborn Greeks, not slaves. The fifth day was given up to processions, prize-giving, and feasting. So important did these festivals become that the Greeks measured time by the four-year interval between them – called an "Olympiad".

In AD393 the games were abolished by the Roman emperor Theodosius and forgotten for nearly 1,500 years. Then a Frenchman, Baron Pierre de Coubertin (1863–1937), considered the father of the modern Olympics, suggested that the Olympic Games should be revived. He believed that the glory of ancient Greece was partly due to its athletics festivals. In 1894 he held a meeting in Paris of the representatives of athletics associations from nine different countries and they decided to hold the Olympic Games again. Greece was given the honor of restarting the Games and built a marble stadium in Athens, where the Games were held in 1896.

Since then, the Games have been held in Paris (France) in 1900; St. Louis (United States), 1904; London (Britain), 1908; Stockholm (Sweden), 1912; Antwerp (Belgium),

Allsport

Opening ceremonies in the stadium, purpose-built for the 1984 Olympic Games in Los Angeles, US.

U.P.I.   *AP/Wide World*

Left: Nadia Comaneci of Romania, a spectacular performer, helped to popularize gymnastics. **Center**: In 1968 Norma Enriqueta Basilio of Mexico became the first woman to light the Olympic Fire. **Right**: In 1984 Carl Lewis (US) won four gold medals for track and field, equaling Jesse Owens' 1936 record.

1920; Paris (France), 1924; Amsterdam (Netherlands), 1928; Los Angeles (United States), 1932; Berlin (Germany), 1936; London (Britain), 1948; Helsinki (Finland), 1952; Melbourne (Australia), 1956; Rome (Italy), 1960; Tokyo (Japan), 1964; Mexico City (Mexico), 1968; Munich (West Germany), 1972; Montreal (Canada), 1976; Moscow (USSR), 1980; Los Angeles (United States), 1984; Seoul (South Korea), 1988.

The International Olympic Committee has a membership of 70 countries. It makes the rules and regulations that govern the Games. This committee selects the site for each Olympic Games. The Games are always awarded to a city, never to a country. This is done in an attempt to keep politics out of the Games. Each Olympic Games lasts about two weeks. Every participating country is limited to three entries in individual events (four in the winter games). Competitors must be citizens of the country they represent, and each must sign a statement that he or she is an amateur. There is no age limit. Medals are awarded for individual events. A gold medal goes to the winner of each competition, silver to the competitor in second place, and bronze to the competitor in third place.

The Games start with an elaborate and impressive opening ceremony. The highlight is the arrival of a runner with a lighted torch which has been carried all the way from Olympia in Greece by a chain of runners. The Olympic oath, which is read out to the assembled athletes by a competitor from the host team, is as follows: "In the name of all competitors I promise that we will take part in

Allsport

The West German four-man bobsled team at the 1988 Winter Olympics in Calgary.

Olympic medalists receive their awards. Britain's Daley Thompson (center) won the decathlon at the 1984 Games.

Allsport

these Olympic Games, respecting and abiding by the rules which govern them, in the true spirit of sportsmanship, for the glory of sport and the honor of our teams."

Sadly the Olympic Games have over the years become a focus for international rivalry and disputes. In the Munich Olympics of 1972, Israeli athletes were murdered by Arab terrorists. The 1980 Olympics held in Moscow were boycotted (unattended) by many countries in reaction to the 1979 Soviet invasion of Afghanistan. More than 60 countries withheld their teams. In retaliation to this, the USSR and most of its allies in Eastern Europe and elsewhere did not participate in the 1984 Games held in Los Angeles.

The 1988 Games were the first in 16 years in which there were no major political disputes, but drug taking was a focus of attention. Ben Johnson, winner of the 100-meter sprint, was disqualified after it was found that he had been taking steroids.

Not all sports are included in the Olympics. The following sports usually are: athletics, archery, basketball, boxing, canoeing, cycling, fencing, football (association), gymnastics, handball, hockey, modern pentathlon, riding, rowing, shooting, swimming and diving, volleyball, water polo, weight lifting, judo, wrestling, and yachting. Other sports recently included have been tennis, windsurfing and synchronized swimming.

The Olympic winter games were begun in 1924 and include various forms of skiing, ski-jumping, skating, ice hockey, bobsled, and tobogganning. Gold, silver, and bronze medals are awarded in these events too.

OMAN is a country on the southeastern coast of the Arabian Peninsula. It is situated on the Persian Gulf. Most of Oman is rocky and sandy. The coastal plains of al-Batinah in the northwest and Dhofar in the southwest are the only fertile, populated regions. The Al-Hajar mountain range in the northeast separates al-Batinah from the vast gravel desert that covers almost three-quarters of the country. The climate is dry and very hot. On the coastal plains cattle are raised and vegetables, dates, sugarcane, pomegranates, and limes are grown.

Oman has been an important trade center since ancient times when Omanis shipped frankincense to the Middle East and the Mediterranean. In the 1960s oil was discovered in Oman. With profits from oil exports, much development took place, especially in Muscat, the capital. A drop in the world price of petroleum in the late 1980s brought a slower rate of growth,

but Oman remained a prosperous country.

Oman is ruled by a monarch (called the Sultan). There is no consitution, political parties, or legislature. The country is strictly Islamic. The population includes Arabs, Indians, Pakistanis, and black Africans, as well as Europeans working in the oil industry.

FACTS ABOUT OMAN

AREA: 300,000 square kilometers (120,000 square miles).
POPULATION: 1,500,000 (1986).
GOVERNMENT: Monarchy with appointed council.
CAPITAL: Muscat, 500,000 (1989).
GEOGRAPHY: Mostly desert, with fertile coastal plains and many oases. Al-Hajar mountain chain in northeast.
CITIES: Sur, Barka, Sohar, Salalah.
EXPORTS: Petroleum, fish, copper, fruit and vegetables.
EDUCATION: Education is not compulsory, but the government has increased the number of primary schools.

OMAR KHAYYAM (1048–1122) was a Persian poet, mathematician, and astronomer. He is best known for his four-line poems (*rubais* or quatrains) that were translated into English in the middle of the 19th century by the English poet Edward FitzGerald. FitzGerald called his translation *The Rubaiyat of Omar Khayyam.*

Omar Khayyam was born in the ancient Persian town of Nishapur (the modern Neyshabur, in Iran). His name *Khayyam* means "tentmaker", and it is probable that this was the trade followed by his father. Omar received a good education in science and philosophy, and traveled to Samarkand, where he wrote a book on algebra that formed the basis of his future scientific reputation. Malik Shah, the ruler of Persia at that time, invited him to his capital at Isfahan to help in reforming the calendar and in building an astronomical observatory. After Malik Shah died in 1092, Omar went on a pilgrimage to Mecca and then returned to Nishapur, where he devoted his remaining years to study, teaching, and service to the court.

Omar Khayyam was better known in his own day as a writer on science, mathematics and medicine. Not until after FitzGerald's English version of 1859 did his poetry become popular.

FitzGerald's *Rubaiyat* was not an accurate translation of Omar's poems, but the meaning and feeling were the same. The verses praise the pleasures of nature, love, and wine, and declare the poet's sadness for the uncertainty of human life.

Omar's original verses were each a separate thought, but FitzGerald wove the verses together so that they resemble a connected poem. Revised editions came out in 1868, 1872, and 1879.

O'NEILL, Eugene (1888–1953) was one of the most outstanding American playwrights. He won the Nobel Prize for Literature in 1936, and was also four times winner of the Pulitzer Prize. (See NOBEL PRIZES and PULITZER, JOSEPH.)

O'Neill was born in New York City, the son of the famous actor James O'Neill. He left college after a year. While he was young he went on a gold prospecting trip to Honduras, shipped as a seaman for Buenos Aires, and worked his way to South Africa.

After he developed tuberculosis he began to write plays. Out of his experiences with family conflicts and living among society's outcasts came the background for many of his plots and characters. Most of his plays are tragic. His Pulitzer prize-winning plays are *Beyond the Horizon* (1920), *Anna Christie* (1922), *Strange Interlude* (1928), and *Long Day's Journey into Night* (1956). Other highly regarded plays of his include *Desire Under the Elms* (1925) and *Mourning Becomes Electra* (1931), which were influenced by Greek tragedies; and *The Iceman Cometh* (1946), a play concerned with the ways that people cling to hopes for a better life.

O'Neill distinguished himself not only as a playwright. He was also a founder of the Theater Guild, and for a time a director of the Provincetown Players.

ONION is a bulbous, biennial plant that is widely used for food – either raw or cooked – and for seasoning food. The many onion species differ in size, shape, and color. When dried, their round or oval bulbs keep well and travel well. Their hollow green leafstalks can be used as a salad.

J. Horace McFarland

The onion belongs to the lily family. It has been cultivated since prehistoric times.

The onion (*Allium cepa*), a member of the lily family, is a native of Asia. It has been used as food from earliest times. Like its relatives, garlic, chives, leek, and shallot, it contains an oil which gives it its sharp odor and brings tears to the eyes of a person peeling onions. Its tiny white flowers are found in clusters at the top of the tall flower stalks.

Growing of Onions

The onion is a cool-weather crop and is grown during the winter in mild climates. In cooler places it is started as early in the spring as possible. The soil must always be rich, well-sunned, and cultivated. Usually the seed is sown in the open, without transplanting. For an early crop, for green bunching onions, or for home gardens, sets, or seedlings, are often used instead of seed. These are small bulbs grown the season before by sowing the seed thickly. Sets from 12 to 18 millimeters ($\frac{1}{2}$ to $\frac{3}{4}$ inch) in diameter are the best size for planting. Shallow cultivation and careful weeding are necessary.

It is also necessary to keep a careful watch for the two most common diseases of onions. One of these is onion smut, which attacks the seedlings. The other, onion mildew, blights the full grown leaves.

Most onions are gathered when the hollow stalks wilt down. The bulbs are pulled up and allowed to dry in the sun for several days. Then the tops are cut off and the onions are packed in coarse sacks or loose crates. They are usually dried still further in cool, airy storerooms before marketing.

Onion Varieties

Onion sets which have grown too large for planting are often used for pickling, but a small variety known as pearl onions are also specially grown for this.

Spanish onions are large and may be yellow or red. They have a mild flavor and may be eaten raw. Italian onions are red and flatter in shape. They are also mild. Globe-shaped onions may be white or yellow and have a stronger flavor.

Onions in History

Onions were known in ancient times in China, India, and the Middle East. The name probably comes from the Latin word *unus*, meaning "one", for the Egyptians used the spherical shaped onion as a symbol of the universe. The Romans took the onion to Britain, and in North America, Indians found wild onions growing, which they used to flavor their food.

ONTARIO is the second largest of Canada's provinces. It lies in central Canada and is bounded on the east by Quebec, on the west by Manitoba, and on the north by the cold waters of James Bay and Hudson Bay. Some 1,600 kilometers (1,000 miles) to the south lies the United States. The greatest part of the boundary between Ontario and the United States runs along the upper St. Lawrence River and through the middle of Lakes Ontario, Erie, Huron, and Superior. (There are separate articles on these lakes, and also on GREAT LAKES.) Point Pelee on Lake Erie is Ontario's most southerly point. It is in the same latitude as northern California. In fact, 25 US states, either in whole or in part, lie further north than this point. The name Ontario comes from the local Indian word meaning "beautiful lake".

The province can be divided into two parts, one north and the other south of a line running roughly eastwards from Georgian Bay on Lake Huron to the upper Ottawa River. The southern part (sometimes called Old Ontario) is much the smaller of the two, but it contains far more people and has more fertile soil. It is made up of a wide lowland south of Ottawa and of the Lake Peninsula surrounded by

Courtesy, Government of Canada

The Algonquin Provincial Park, established in 1893, is an outstanding recreational area.

Lakes Huron, Erie, and Ontario. Most of the Lake Peninsula consists of rolling hills and fields from which much of the forests have been cleared to make good farming land. Overlapping into northern Ontario is the Algonquin Park, a hilly area with forests and lakes which are very popular for camping and canoeing. Northern Ontario, except for a low-lying shelf around Hudson Bay, is a vast hummocky tableland forested with spruce and balsam and dotted with countless lakes. There are large areas of bare rock. The region is not suited to farming but its richness lies in forestry, minerals, and water power. The highest point, Ogidaki Mountain, is 665 meters (2,182 feet).

Ontario has many lakes set in fine woodland scenery. Beauty spots shared by Ontario with the United States are the Niagara Falls (see NIAGARA FALLS) and the Thousand Islands at the entrance to the St. Lawrence River. A road bridge 13 kilometers (8 miles) long crosses these islands to link Canada with the United States.

Climate and People

Generally the winters in Ontario are long and severe with heavy snowfall, and the summers delightfully sunny. The Great Lakes never freeze completely and their comparative warmth causes the winters in the Lake Peninsula to be milder than those elsewhere in the province, with more rain and less snow. Similarly, in the far north, the waters of the Hudson Bay tend to make winters less severe than along the higher ground north of the Great Lakes.

The people of British origin make up the largest percentage of the population. The second largest group is the French. Other important groups are the German, Italian, Portuguese, West and East Indian, and Chinese. Many of the thousands of Indians still live in reservations provided by the government.

Industry and Agriculture

Most of the people of Ontario live in the southern part of the Lake Peninsula. Here are most of the farms and factories, as well as Toronto, the capital of the province (see TORONTO), the great industrial city of Hamilton—sometimes called "steel city" (see HAMILTON)—and the manufacturing city of London. At the tip of the peninsula are Windsor, which lies across the river from Detroit, and Sarnia, to which petroleum (oil) is brought by a pipeline from Alberta and thence to Toronto, a total distance of 3,106 kilometers (1,930 miles). Ottawa, the capital of all Canada, is near the eastern tip of the province (see OTTAWA).

Although Ontario has no coal, it is near enough to the United States to obtain coal easily from there. This fact and its abundant supplies of electricity from water power and

Popperfoto

Popperfoto

The free-flowing falls of Kakabeka on the River Kaministikwia in summer (left) take on impressive ice formations in winter (right). Kakabeka ("high falls" in Indian) are 47 m (154 ft) high, and located near the twin cities of Fort William and Port Arthur in the Thunder Bay district.

nuclear power have made Ontario into Canada's leading industrial province. Its factories make goods of practically every description. Motor vehicles, furniture, textiles, farm implements, and aircraft are among the leading manufacturing industries.

Ontario has large supplies of minerals, including half the world's nickel and the largest deposits of uranium in the western world. The nickel mines are at Sudbury, and copper is also mined there. Gold is mined near Timmins and Kirkland Lake 200 kilometers (125 miles) north of Sudbury. Other metals mined are silver, platinum, zinc, and iron. The largest uranium mining area is half way between Sudbury and Sault Ste. Marie, at Blind River.

The climate and soil of southern Ontario provide favorable conditions for agriculture. Many of the farms are large mixed farms (crops and animals), their main products being cattle, pigs, dairy produce, grain, poultry, eggs, fruit, and vegetables. Some of the best farm land is in the Lake Peninsula, especially near the lake shores, where peaches, grapes, and tobacco are grown. In the northern part of the province, between the Quebec border and Hearst, the railroad passes over a wide belt of clay which was once the bed of a vast lake. Despite the short growing season, this belt is farmed to supply dairy produce and potatoes to the mining and lumber (timber) camps. Only just over three per cent of the population make their living by farming.

The lumber industry—the felling of trees for timber, fuel, and wood pulp—is also important in Ontario. The forests in the southern part of the province have been greatly reduced by felling, but much white pine, spruce, and birch still remains. The northern forests supply spruce and poplar for making wood pulp and newsprint (paper). A constant watch for forest fires is kept.

Quentin Bell

The CN Tower in Toronto, the world's tallest, dwarfs the skyscrapers of this modern city.

The Lake Peninsula has a network of roads and railroads. Ontario is crossed by the Trans-Canada Highway, and by railroads linking it with the United States and with the rest of Canada. Heavy and bulky cargoes can be carried by ships using the Great Lakes, and the St. Lawrence Seaway allows large ships from all parts of the world to reach Ontario's ports on those lakes. (See ST. LAWRENCE RIVER AND SEAWAY.)

Ontario has a lieutenant-governor as head of the province's government. The government is run by a cabinet which is responsible to a legislature (parliament) elected for five years by men and women of the province. Ontario, like other provinces, sends members to the Canadian parliament at Ottawa. Children between the ages of 6 and 16 must attend school. The public schools are free and every important town has secondary schools. Further education is available at universities in Toronto, Kingston, London, Hamilton, Ottawa, Windsor, Waterloo, Sudbury, Guelph, St. Catherine's, Thunder Bay, and Peterborough.

History

Before European explorers arrived in the 17th century, Ontario had been the home of several Indian tribes, including the Crees, Algonkin, and Iroquian. The first European to explore Ontario was the Frenchman Samuel de Champlain, on whom there is a separate article. He went up the Ottawa River in 1613 and reached Lake Huron in 1615. The French, including the French explorer La Salle, established missions and trading posts on the shores of the Great Lakes but made few other settlements. The northern part of the province was probably first sighted by Henry Hudson. Ontario was still a wilderness when, together with other French possessions in Canada, it was handed over to Great Britain in 1763.

In 1783, after the American War of Independence thousands of people who remained loyal to Great Britain left the United States and settled in Ontario. In 1791 this region (Ontario) was separated from Quebec and called Upper Canada. The first governor, John Simcoe, established the first capital at Newark (now Niagara), but this was thought to be too near the United States and was soon changed to York (now Toronto). Simcoe also oversaw the building of many roads, and the division of the province into counties. In 1812

the Americans invaded the province and burned York, but were defeated by the colonists and British troops. After peace in 1814 many settlers came from Europe, and by 1837 the population was 350,000.

In 1840 Upper and Lower Canada (Quebec) were joined by the Act of Union. This union lasted until 1867 when the Dominion of Canada was created (see CANADIAN HISTORY). Upper Canada then changed its name to Ontario and, with Quebec, New Brunswick, and Nova Scotia, joined the new confederation. One of the men chiefly responsible for this was John Macdonald (on whom there is a separate article).

The building of railroads opened up the prairie provinces to the west and at the same time encouraged the development of industry in Ontario. As a result, Ontario changed gradually from an agricultural area to an industrial area.

The population of Ontario is about 9,047,000 (1985).

ONTARIO, LAKE, is the smallest of the Great Lakes of North America with an area of about 19,000 square kilometers (7,340 square miles). It is bounded by the province of Ontario (Canada) in the north, and by New York State (US) in the south. Its longest point is about 310 kilometers (193 miles), and its widest about 85 kilometers (53 miles). Its surface is about 75 meters (245 feet) above sea-level, and its greatest depth is 244 meters (802 feet), so that the bottom is more than 152 meters (500 feet) below the level of the sea.

Lake Ontario is about 100 meters (325 feet) lower than Lake Erie, from which it receives most of its water through the Niagara River. The drop of 100 meters (325 feet) occurs in Niagara Falls and in rapids above and below them in the Niagara River. No other large rivers empty into Lake Ontario. The lake's outlet is the St. Lawrence River at the northeast, through which all the Great Lakes' waters flow to the sea. At the entrance to the St. Lawrence River are the Thousand Islands.

The principal cities on Lake Ontario are

Lake Ontario is the smallest of the Great Lakes, and the most easterly. There are thousands of other lakes throughout the province.

National Film Board

Toronto, Hamilton, and Kingston in Ontario, and Rochester and Oswego in New York state.

The principal freight moved on Lake Ontario is coal, iron ore, timber, wood pulp, and wheat. Coal is shipped from Pennsylvania to Hamilton for the steel mills, and to Toronto and elsewhere. Iron ore comes from the Lake Superior region in large lake vessels and passes through the Welland Canal, where eight locks take care of the difference in level in linking Lakes Erie and Ontario. The St. Lawrence Seaway makes it possible for large ships from overseas to reach Lake Ontario and the other Great Lakes. However, the harbors are ice-bound from mid-December to mid-April.

There are also separate articles on HAMILTON; NIAGARA FALLS; ONTARIO; ST. LAWRENCE RIVER AND SEAWAY; TORONTO; and the other Great Lakes.)

ONYX is a semi-precious stone that belongs to the agate group of the chalcedonies (see AGATE). Chalcedony includes many stones used by jewelers, such as agate, bloodstone, and cornelian. Onyx can be distinguished from the other chalcedonies because it is striped with alternate bands of black and white. When the bands are brown or red the stone is called sardonyx.

Because of its unusual coloring, onyx has been made into jewelry and small ornaments such as vases since very early times. It is often used for carved jewelry. There are two kinds of carved jewels, and they are named according to the way in which the carving is done. When the carved designs are raised above the surface they are called *cameos* and when they are cut into the stone they are called *intaglios*. Onyx has been widely used for cameos because its two colors allow the carver to use one color for the design and the other for the background. Most cameos are made into brooches. The best onyx comes from India and South America.

There is a variety of calcite (crystalline limestone) which is sometimes confused with onyx because it has similar markings. It is called "onyx marble" and is used for much larger articles. The ancient Egyptians, Greeks, and Romans used it for their temples, and the mosques in many Moslem countries have pillars of it. Algeria, Morocco, and Egypt are important sources of supply.

OPERA. An opera is a type of play set to music. It is performed on a stage with scenery, and the singers wear make-up and costumes and act as well as sing. The musical accompaniment is played by an orchestra seated in the orchestra pit which is usually in front of, and lower than, the stage.

The first operas were written in Italy at the beginning of the 17th century. The very first surviving opera was composed in 1600 by Jacopo Peri (1561–1633). Peri was one of a number of Italian composers who wanted to revive what they thought was the art of the classical Greek theater. Thousands of operas

The great Spanish-born tenor Placido Domingo in Giuseppe Verdi's opera *Otello*.

have been written since Peri's time, and the successful ones are performed at the great opera houses, such as Covent Garden in London and the Metropolitan Opera in New York.

There are many different kinds of opera. In Italy in the 18th century there were serious operas (*opere serie*) and comic operas (*opere buffe*); the first kind were based on historical and legendary subjects and the second were gay Italian comedies. In England at the same time there was ballad opera, which was based on well-known songs of the day, and of which the most important example is *The Beggar's Opera*. In France in the 19th century operas were produced with large choruses and sometimes with battle scenes. This was grand opera or romantic opera. In the middle of the century Offenbach, a German who had settled in Paris, amused everyone with a new sort of comic opera called operetta. Operettas usually made fun of well-known people living at the time and were enjoyed by everybody in Paris who read the newspapers. The operas on serious subjects by the German composer Wagner, who also lived in the 19th century, are called music dramas.

The music of the earliest operas consisted of two distinct kinds: there were recitatives (a kind of reciting accompanied by the harpsichord), and arias, duets, trios, and so on,

which are all formal songs accompanied by the full orchestra. When the characters wished the audience to know what was happening in the plot they sang recitatives, but when they expressed their feelings they sang formal songs. Some of Mozart's operas are written in this way. But Mozart also wrote operas in which the recitatives were replaced by spoken dialogue. This kind of opera was called a *Singspiel* (song play). Beethoven's only opera, *Fidelio*, is a *Singspiel*. In later operas, those of Verdi for example, there is less difference between recitatives and arias, and in the music dramas of Wagner they do not appear at all. In his operas special themes, or tunes, "belong" to each of the important characters, and the tunes are heard whenever the characters appear in the story.

Mozart's last opera *The Magic Flute* was written in 1791. It is a classic of the opera repertoire.

The play on which an opera is written is called a *libretto*. This is an Italian word meaning "a little book", and in former times people who went to the opera could read the libretto of the opera in their opera-boxes by candlelight. The plural of the word is *libretti*.

Some libretti are based on the lives of famous people and the events in which they took part. For example, Modest Mussorgsky's opera *Boris Godunov* tells the story of a nobleman of that name who became tsar (emperor) of Russia at the end of the 16th century. Some libretti are based on legends—nearly all Wagner's operas are about legendary subjects.

Clive Barda

The Romanian-born soprano, Ileana Cotrubas (foreground), as Violetta in Verdi's *La Traviata*.

Others are taken from novels and plays. Several of Shakespeare's plays have become operas.

When the composer has the libretto and is ready to write the music he must decide what kind of voices he needs for his singers. Among the many types of operatic voices are the coloratura soprano (the woman's voice that is extremely high, light and agile), the dramatic soprano, a voice of great power, the dramatic tenor and the heroic tenor (also powerful voices), the light baritone, and the deep bass called the basso profundo.

The composer makes the voices suit the parts. The part of a young girl is generally written for a light soprano voice, that of the hero is usually for a tenor voice and that of an older man is usually given to a baritone or bass voice. An older woman is usually sung by a contralto. In addition to the solo voices (that is, those which sing alone) most operas also have a chorus, made up of all kinds of voices and playing the parts of crowds, soldiers, and so on.

Making an Opera

In order to see exactly how an opera is made we will study Verdi's *Aida*. Giuseppe Verdi was the most famous of all Italian opera composers and lived from 1813 to 1901 (see VERDI, GIUSEPPE). He was asked to write an opera to be performed in 1871 at the new opera house in Cairo, the capital of Egypt, and the libretto was based on a story of Egypt in ancient times.

The story tells how Egypt is being invaded by the Ethiopians. A young officer called Radames is chosen to lead the Egyptian army against the invaders. He is loved by two women: Amneris, the daughter of the Egyptian king, and Aida, who is the slave of Amneris. (Aida is actually the daughter of the Ethiopian king, Amonasro, and has become

Clive Barda

Puccini's realistic tragic opera *Tosca* dates from 1900. In this scene, the heroine Tosca (Josephine Barstow, soprano) rejects the attentions of the cruel police chief Scarpia (Neil Howlett, bass).

a slave because she was captured in an earlier war between the Egyptians and Ethiopians.) Radames loves Aida. He is victorious against the Ethiopians and returns from the war, bringing Aida's father, King Amonasro, as one of his prisoners. Aida recognizes her father but nobody else knows that he is the Ethiopian king. Amonasro forces Aida to find out a military secret from Radames. Aida and Radames are overheard by Amneris, who is jealous of Aida. Amneris has Radames arrested, and he is condemned to death as a traitor. He is left to die, locked in a dungeon, where Aida has hidden herself so that she can die with him.

Verdi gives the part of Aida to a soprano, of Amneris to a mezzo-soprano, of Radames to a tenor, of Amonasro to a baritone, and of the king and high priest of Egypt to basses. There is a large chorus which plays the parts of the crowd, priests and priestesses, soldiers, and Ethiopian prisoners.

The opera is divided into four acts. Before the curtain goes up the orchestra plays a prelude, which contains melodies that will be heard in the opera itself. During the course of the opera there are arias, duets (songs for two voices), trios (for three voices), ensembles (for several voices singing together), and choruses. In one scene there is also a ballet (see BALLET).

Benjamin Britten's entertainment for children, *Let's Make an Opera*, first produced in 1949, has as its story the preparation and performance of an opera. In the first part you see the composer choosing a libretto and setting to work to write the music. In the second part the audience joins in the opera he has composed, which is called *The Little Sweep*.

Before an opera is shown to the public a great number of rehearsals are needed. Two men are mainly responsible for managing these rehearsals: the conductor and the producer. The conductor is concerned with the music, and he rehearses the orchestra and the singers; at first separately and later together. The conductor, or his deputy, also teaches the chorus its music. The singers and chorus must also learn to act their parts and to move about

the stage easily and confidently. It is the producer who teaches them how to do this. To put it simply, the conductor is responsible for what is *heard* in opera, the producer for what is *seen* (acting, movements, make-up and lighting). The scenery is designed by a stage designer and usually made by carpenters and painters employed by the opera company. Costumes for the singers are supervized by the wardrobe department in accordance with the stage designer's requirements. Amateur opera companies usually rent scenery and costumes.

The Best-Known Operas

GERMAN

Orpheus and Eurydice by Christoph Willibald von Gluck (1714–87). This is based on the Greek myth about the musician who went to the underworld to rescue his dead wife. (See ORPHEUS AND EURYDICE.)

The Marriage of Figaro by Wolfgang Amadeus Mozart (1756–91). This comic opera is based on a satirical (mocking) story by the French writer Beaumarchais (1732–99). Figaro is Count Almaviva's servant and marries Susanna, the countess's maid. This opera makes fun of the habits of the 18th-century nobility.

Don Giovanni by Mozart. This is another comic opera based on the story of Don Giovanni, or Don Juan, the man who could not be faithful to any woman.

The Magic Flute by Mozart. This is a story about the adventures of a prince, a birdcatcher, and an imprisoned princess. Both the prince and the princess undergo tests before they can be united in marriage.

Fidelio by Ludwig van Beethoven (1770–1827). This is Beethoven's only opera and its subject is a wife's love for her husband, whom she rescues from prison.

The Flying Dutchman by Richard Wagner (1813–83). Like most of Wagner's operas, this opera is based on a legend. It is about a man who is condemned to sail the seas until, coming ashore once in every seven years, he can find a woman who will love him for ever.

Tannhäuser by Wagner. This story of medieval knights and minstrels tells of a magic cave in Germany where lives a beautiful goddess who beguiles any mortals who come her way.

Lohengrin by Wagner. Again based on a legend, this opera tells the story of one of the knights of the Holy Grail.

Tristan and Isolde by Wagner. Considered by many to be Wagner's greatest work, this tells a story of the conflict between love and duty in the hearts of two medieval lovers. Isolde is an Irish princess and Tristan is a Cornish knight.

The Mastersingers of Nuremberg by Wagner. This is the only one of Wagner's operas with completely human characters and with some comedy. It tells the story of a 16th-century singing contest in Nuremberg, Germany.

The Ring of the Nibelungs by Wagner. This is a series of four operas—*The Rhinegold*, *The Valkyrie*, *Siegfried*, and *The Twilight of the Gods*. They tell a continuous story about the ancient gods and dwarfs of German legend. The story tells of a magic ring and how its power destroys the world of the gods.

Parsifal by Wagner. This was Wagner's last opera and tells a story about the Holy Grail.

Die Fledermaus (The Bat) by Johann Strauss (1825–99). This is a cheery, lighthearted Viennese opera. "The Bat" is the name given to a merry young man who loves night life and enjoys flirting with pretty girls.

Der Rosenkavalier (The Knight of the Rose) by Richard Strauss (1864–1949). This opera is set in Vienna in the 18th century, and the story tells of a princess flattered by the devotion of a younger man.

ITALIAN

The Barber of Seville by Gioacchino Rossini (1792–1868). This charming and lighthearted opera was written by Rossini in less than three weeks. Based on one of Beaumarchais's plays, it tells the story of Figaro, the barber who arranges the love affairs and marriage of Rosina and Count Almaviva. (His later story is told in Mozart's *Marriage of Figaro*, described above.)

Rigoletto by Giuseppe Verdi (1813–1901). This is a tragic opera based on a story by Victor Hugo. It tells the story of a duke's jester, whose daughter falls in love with the duke and finally gives her life for him.

Il Trovatore (The Troubadour) by Verdi. This is a romantic tragedy of a high-born child who is kidnapped by gypsies.

La Traviata by Verdi. This tragic opera, whose title means "The Woman led astray", concerns a courtesan who gives up her genuine love for a young man so that his career will not be ruined.

Aida by Verdi. The story of this opera is fully told in the earlier part of this article.

Otello and *Falstaff* by Verdi. These two works are considered to be Verdi's finest operas and are based on Shakespeare's plays *Othello* and *The Merry Wives of Windsor.*

La Bohème (Bohemian Life) by Giacomo Puccini (1858–1924). This tells a story of the happy-go-lucky life of poor artists in Paris. The word bohemian describes a carefree attitude to life and comes from the French word for gypsy, which is *bohémien.*

Tosca by Puccini. This tragic opera is the story of Tosca, an opera singer, Cavaradossi, the painter she loves, and Scarpia, the wicked chief of police who covets her.

Madam Butterfly by Puccini. This is a sad story of a Japanese girl, Madam Butterfly, who is deserted by an American naval officer, Pinkerton.

I Pagliacci (The Clowns) by Ruggiero Leoncavallo (1858–1919). This tells the story of a group of strolling players.

Cavalleria Rusticana by Pietro Mascagni (1863–1945). This short opera is about love and revenge in a Sicilian village. It is often performed on the same program as *I Pagliacci.*

FRENCH

Faust by Charles Gounod (1818–93). This tells the story of Dr. Faustus, who regains his youth by making a bargain with the devil.

Carmen by Georges Bizet (1838–75). This opera is full of color and movement and tells the story of a Spanish gypsy girl named Carmen.

The Tales of Hoffmann by Jacques Offenbach (1819–80). This opera is based on three stories by the German writer

E. T. A. Hoffmann (1776–1821). Offenbach wrote many light operettas but this is his only dramatic opera.

Pelléas and Mélisande by Claude Debussy (1862–1918). This opera tells a strange story of love and fate. The music is dream-like and poetic.

BRITISH

Dido and Aeneas by Henry Purcell (1659–95). This is one of the earliest English operas and one of the most beautiful. It is based on a story by the Latin poet Virgil. (See AENEID).

The Beggar's Opera, of which the music was arranged by John Pepusch (1667–1752) and the libretto was by John Gay (1685–1732). This ballad opera, which consists of popular tunes of the day, tells of thieves and highwaymen and was written to make fun of important people of the time.

Trial by Jury
H.M.S. Pinafore
The Pirates of Penzance
Iolanthe
Patience
The Mikado
The Yeoman of the Guard
The Gondoliers

by W. S. Gilbert (1836–1911) and Arthur Sullivan (1842–1900). (See GILBERT AND SULLIVAN). These are all comic operas. Gilbert wrote the words and Sullivan the music.

All are full of jokes about people and events of the period.

Peter Grimes by Benjamin Britten (1913–76). One of the most famous modern British operas. The story, based on a poem by George Crabbe (1754–1832), is about life in a fishing village in Suffolk.

Billy Budd by Britten. An opera based on the story about a young sailor by the American author Herman Melville (1819–91).

The Turn of the Screw by Britten. This eerie opera was taken from a ghost story by the American writer Henry James (1843–1916).

RUSSIAN

Boris Godunov by Modest Mussorgsky (1839–81). This is a story based on a play by Pushkin (1799–1837) about a Russian nobleman who became tsar of Russia in 1598.

Prince Igor by Alexander Borodin (1833–87). The story takes place in the 12th century and tells how a Russian prince, Igor, goes to fight against the Polovtsy tribe, who are invaders from central Asia. The Polovtsian dances from this opera are famous.

The Golden Cockerel by Nikolai Rimsky-Korsakov (1844–1908). This is based on a fairy tale by Pushkin about a king who acquires a magic cockerel who warns him every time his kingdom is in danger.

OPIUM is a powerful drug made from the opium poppy. When taken too often, opium damages the health, and if taken in large enough quantities it is deadly poison. Nevertheless, it has many uses in medicine.

Opium poppies are grown in India, Iran, Turkey, China, and southeast Asia, legally and illegally, and sometimes in Europe. In India the seeds are sown in November in rich, well-cultivated soil. The large flowers, which are white or purple, open in January,

Camera Press

Close-up of a seed-head of an opium poppy. It has been scored, and the white juice has hardened to a dark-colored gum. This is raw opium from which medical drugs such as morphine are extracted.

and when they fall green seed-cases are left.

When these cases are about the size of eggs, their outer coverings are slit and the milky juice that oozes out is collected, dried, and drained until it is thick. Then it is shipped to factories, dried further and kneaded into reddish-brown cakes. This is the opium of commerce.

When used properly, opium is a helpful drug. It can stop pains and spasms, produce perspiration and quell sickness. It contains a large amount of morphine, which brings about sleep, and from it are made pain-relieving drugs such as heroin and codeine. Paregoric, which is a mixture of opium and other drugs, is useful for soothing coughs; laudanum, a tincture of opium in alcohol, and Dover's powder quiet the nerves and produce sleep.

Unfortunately, opium and the drugs made from it or related to it are all habit-forming. If they are taken too often the patient depends on them and becomes a drug addict. The health of a drug addict becomes poor, he grows pale and thin and suffers from indigestion and itching of the skin. His energy is drained and he grows lazy and listless. Worse still, he will go to any lengths to obtain supplies of the drug he craves. However, because opium makes people feel cheerful and happy for a time, it is often deliberately taken in large quantities, and this habit was particularly widespread in China. There it is generally smoked, the pipe being held over a flame.

The Chinese realized the dangers of opium, but other countries which made money from its sale refused to cut down opium production. For many years the sale of opium for anything except medical purposes has been forbidden in many countries. Even so, some opium is still smuggled into some countries and sold illegally. Because the local peoples of countries such as Turkey depend on the opium crop for their livelihood, efforts to limit or end the growing of opium have not so far been very successful.

OPOSSUM. The only marsupials that do not live in Australia or the islands near by are 66 species of American opossum (see MARSUPIAL). The common Virginia opossum (*Didelphis virginiana*) lives in the United States. It has a large head, hairless ears, and a long pointed snout, so that it looks rather like a rat, but it

Frank Lane Picture Agency

A North American opossum "playing possum" pretends to be dead to protect itself from being attacked.

NHPA/M. Morcombe

The common brushtail possum, a familiar Australian marsupial, weighs up to 4 kilograms (9 pounds).

is as large as a cat. The tail is bare except at the base and can be used for gripping objects. It lives in trees and eats roots, insects, nuts, green corn, mice, and small birds. At night it raids orchards for fruit and henhouses for poultry and eggs. If it is frightened it collapses, closes its eyes and looks as if it were dead. From this comes the expression "to play possum", meaning to pretend death.

The female opossum has between 7 and 13 young at a time. Each is blind and naked and less than 2 centimeters (0.7 inches) long and weighs only a few grams (less than 0.1 ounce). There is not a true pouch, as in the kangaroo, but the young cling to their mother with their tails and feet and are suckled for two months.

The water opossum or yapok (*Chironectes minimus*) is a fierce carnivorous animal of Central and South America that has webbed hind toes.

Australian possums. In Australia the word possum (not "opossum") is used for over 40 species of marsupials of the phalanger family, in which the second and third toes are joined by a web of skin. In some kinds, the webs stretch between the limbs and allow the possum to glide to the ground from the treetops, steering with its long plumed tail. Gliding possums (sometimes called flying squirrels) can glide more than 100 meters (100 yards) in this way. They feed mainly at night on insects, nectar, gum sap, and fruits. Australian possums unable to glide include the ringtail possums, whose long tails are curled into a ring at the tip. The common ringtail (*Pseudocheirus peregrinus*) builds a round nest of tightly woven twigs in the branches of a shrub. The rather smelly and fox-like brushtail possums (*Trichosurus*) were killed in large numbers for their dense, woolly fur but are now protected animals.

OPPENHEIMER, J. Robert (1904–67). The American theoretical physicist Julius Robert Oppenheimer was born in New York City. He was educated at Harvard University. After graduating in 1925, he undertook research at various European scientific centers, including the Cavendish Laboratory in Cambridge, England, and universities in Göttingen (Germany), Leiden (the Netherlands), and Zurich (Switzerland). He became aware of the latest developments in atomic physics and met several pioneers in the field.

From 1929 to 1942 Oppenheimer taught physics at the University of California at Berkeley, and at the California Institute of Technology. He researched in the application of quantum mechanics to the behavior of elementary particles. From 1947 until 1966 Oppenheimer was director of the Institute for Advanced Study at Princeton, New Jersey.

Oppenheimer is famous today for his leadership of the team of scientists who worked on the Manhattan Project, at Los Alamos, New Mexico. This was a top-secret military program for using uranium and plutonium to make an atomic bomb. Oppenheimer and his colleagues were working on this problem in competition with scientists in Hitler's Germany. The American atom bomb was successfully tested at Alamagordo, New Mexico, on 16 July 1945, not long after the surrender of

German forces. A month later the first nuclear bombs to be used in war were dropped on the Japanese cities of Hiroshima and Nagasaki.

The last 20 years of Oppenheimer's life were clouded by political controversy. Ever since the 1930s he had had communist sympathies and, although not a communist himself, he gave financial aid to members of the Communist Party. From 1947 to 1952 Oppenheimer was chairman of the General Advisory Committee of the US Atomic Energy Commission. Deeply concerned about the destructive power of nuclear weapons and convinced of the need to control them, he spoke against the development of the hydrogen bomb, and the Commission duly opposed the project in 1949. Military and political supporters of nuclear weapons accused Oppenheimer of Soviet sympathies. In 1954 his security clearance for work on secret government projects was canceled. Few people doubted Oppenheimer's loyalties to his country, however, and many scientists defended him. In 1963, the US government sought to make amends by presenting to Oppenheimer the Enrico Fermi Award of the Atomic Energy Commission.

ORACLE. Oracles are the places where pagan gods are supposed to speak to their believers, who ask them questions about the future or about the meaning of things that have happened to them. People who consult oracles believe that events are caused by gods, spirits, or witches. When a person is suddenly sick, or when disaster comes, such as flood or famine, then people consult the oracles to discover the reasons, thinking that their own bad or careless behavior may have angered the gods or spirits. The oracle then tells them how to make amends.

Oracles are found in many parts of the world. Among the Azande, a people living in the Sudan in Africa, for example, a man who is ill tries to discover the reason by asking the gods and spirits to answer him through a chicken. The sick man gives poison to the chicken, and while he does so he asks the chicken whether perhaps he will be successful, or whether he is ill because of the anger of a spirit or a witch. If the chicken dies, the answer is that he *will* be successful or that his sickness *is* due to the anger of a certain spirit and not to a disease of his body.

The most famous oracle in Europe was the oracle of the Greek god Apollo at Delphi, in ancient Greece. (See DELPHI, ORACLE OF.) In ancient Rome there were officials (called augurs) who consulted oracles and omens in order to make decisions of state. They examined the entrails (insides) of dead birds and animals and from them claimed to be able to tell the future.

Even in modern Western countries people try to read the future by looking at the lines on their hands or the pattern of tea-leaves left in a cup. This is done mostly as a game or a joke, but in countries where oracles are really believed in, people run their lives by following the answers given by their oracles.

See also MAGIC; WITCHCRAFT.

ORANGE. The orange is described as a citrus fruit, for it belongs to the genus, *Citrus*. The trees on which the fruit grows are sturdy and evergreen, rarely growing taller than 9 meters (30 feet). They thrive in warm climates where there is no frost and many also grow well in the tropics. The leaves are usually deep green and glossy, and the white flowers are richly scented.

Besides the tangerine or mandarin orange there are two main types of orange: sweet and sour. The sweet orange (*Citrus sinensis*) is, after the apple, the most widely grown fruit in the world, and is the kind eaten raw and used for juice. The Jaffa and Valencia are well-known varieties and some of them are seedless. The sour orange (*Citrus aurantium*), also known as the Seville or bigarade orange, has a rough skin and acid juice and is used for making marmalade.

Both sweet and sour oranges are probably natives of China and southeast Asia, where they have been cultivated from very early times. The Arabs are said to have brought the sour orange to southwestern Asia in about the

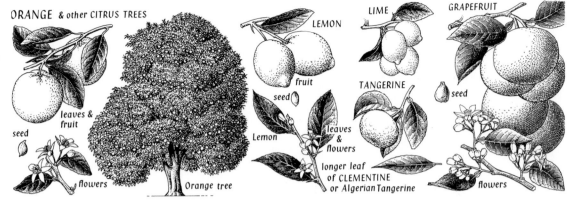

ORANGE & other CITRUS TREES

leaves & fruit

seed

flowers

Orange tree

LEMON

fruit

seed

Lemon

leaves & flowers

longer leaf of CLEMENTINE or Algerian Tangerine

LIME

TANGERINE

GRAPEFRUIT

seed

flowers

9th century AD, and most European languages get their name for the fruit from the Arabic word *naranj*. The sweet orange reached Europe later, but by the 16th century it was commonly grown in Italy.

Today both kinds are found in all countries where citrus fruits are grown. The most important orange-growing areas are California and Florida in the United States, where almost half of all the oranges grown in the world are produced. Brazil, Spain, Italy, South Africa, Japan, Mexico, and Israel also grow much of the fruit, as do India, Australia, and Jamaica. Blood oranges, so called because the pulp is deep red in color, are grown round the Mediterranean.

Usually orange trees are grown by budding (see GRAFTING). The sour orange has been the rootstock most widely used for budding the required plant, because it is strong and the stem and roots can resist a serious fungus disease. It has, however, been found to carry a disease which kills a sweet orange budded on to it, and so more attention is being paid to other rootstocks, such as the rough lemon.

A fully grown tree may bear up to 1,000 oranges each year, and go on bearing good crops for 50 to 80 years, sometimes longer. The fruits are picked when they are fully ripe, and care is taken not to scratch the skin, for if that happens the orange will become moldy. In large packing houses the fruit is thoroughly washed, rinsed and dried, then graded, disinfected, wrapped in paper, and finally packed carefully in boxes to be shipped overseas. (See CITRUS FRUIT; GRAPEFRUIT; LEMON).

ORANGE FREE STATE is a landlocked province of the Republic of South Africa. It is 127,983 square kilometers (49,418 square miles), making it the second smallest of South Africa's four provinces. The whole province is a tableland more than 900 meters (3,000 feet) above sea-level and the higher parts in the east are called the high veld. Peaks over 2,000 meters (7,000 feet) high rise from the Drakensberg Range along the Natal border. (See DRAKENSBERG MOUNTAINS.) The Caledon River forms the boundary with Lesotho in the southeast and across the Orange River in the south is Cape Province. Across the Vaal River in the north is the Transvaal.

Except in the mountainous eastern part, most of the Free State is flat country with an occasional *koppie*, or hill, dotted here and there. There are no trees on the vast rolling plains, most of which are covered with grass. The climate is pleasant but the rainfall is insufficient, especially in the west, and drought is common. Frost is quite usual from May to September.

Peoples, Towns, and Industry

More than three-quarters of the people in the Orange Free State are Bantus who speak Sesotho, the language of Lesotho. Most of them work on the farms of white farmers or in the towns. The white inhabitants are chiefly of South African Dutch descent and speak Afrikaans. The province, and the river, are named after the Dutch kings who were also titled "Prince of Orange".

Bloemfontein is the capital of the province.

Satour

Welkom, founded after World War II, was planned around this shopping area, behind the park.

Kroonstad in the north is an important agricultural and industrial center, and west of it are the big modern gold-mining towns of Welkom, Virginia, and Odendaalsrus.

The most fertile land in the province is in the Caledon valley, where wheat, apples, and plums are grown. Important crops of corn (called "mealies" in South Africa) are grown in the north. Sheep are kept in most parts, as well as many cattle and horses.

Diamonds are found in several parts of the Orange Free State and coal is mined in the extreme north. Gasoline, oil, and chemicals are extracted from this coal. Valuable quantities of gold and uranium are also mined. Many towns in the Orange Free State have flour mills and creameries and at Bloemfontein, Kroonstad, and Harrismith there are factories making engineering products, metal goods, furniture, textiles, and clothing.

White children in the Orange Free State must attend school between the ages of 7 and 16. Bantu children attend community schools, where attendance is not compulsory. The population of the Orange Free State is 2,080,000 (1983).

ORANGEMEN. In 1795, after a bitter fight between Protestants and Roman Catholics in County Armagh (northern Ireland), the northern Protestants founded the Orange Society. It was named after William of Orange, the Protestant Dutch prince who,

together with his English wife Mary, ascended the British throne in 1689, after James II had been driven out because he supported Roman Catholicism. After ascending the throne William had to fight against James II and his Catholic supporters in Ireland, and he defeated them at the Battle of the Boyne and the Battle of Aughrim. So in 1795 the Protestants called their new society after him. It was secret and violently anti-Catholic, and caused great numbers of Catholics to be expelled from the northern counties into Connaught in the west.

BBC Hulton Picture Library

Orangemen march in Northern Ireland every year on 12 July, the anniversary of the Battle of Aughrim.

The Orange Society still exists vigorously in Northern Ireland, and has branches in England, Scotland, and Canada. The Orangemen celebrate 12 July each year with parades and meetings, in memory of the Battle of Aughrim fought on that date in 1691. They are a focus for the strong anti-Catholic feeling that still exists among many Protestants of Northern Ireland.

ORANGUTAN. The orangutan (*Pongo pygmaeus*) is among the apes most closely related to human beings. It lives in the swampy forests of Borneo and Sumatra in the East Indies, and its name means "man of the woods" (see APE). The orangutan is covered with long reddish hair. Its eyes are small and it has a wide, bulging mouth. An old male may be over 1.5 meters (5 feet) in height. He can at once be distinguished from a female by his large cheek pads and the huge fleshy throat sac which hangs down from his face and covers his throat and the upper part of his chest.

Orangutans live high up in the trees, moving about by reaching with their long strong arms from branch to branch rather than by leaping. When they come down to the ground they usually walk on all fours, resting their weight on the outsides of their feet and on their knuckles. They live alone or in small family groups and produce single young.

The food of orangutans is young shoots, leaves and fruit, and they tear open the durian, a fruit with a tough, spiny hide, with their fingers. They build platforms of sticks for

ARDEA

The orangutan uses its long arms and prehensile toes to climb with ease among the forest trees and vines.

themselves on the trees and sometimes sleep on the same platform for several nights running.

Orangutans are rare animals that are classed as endangered by conservation organizations. The main reason for their decline has been the loss of their forest habitat and the taking of young animals for zoos.

ORATORY. The art of making speeches to produce a response from an audience is called oratory. A person who makes speeches in public is called an orator. He or she may be a lawyer in a law court, a senator in the United States Congress, a councillor in a committee, a clergyman preaching a sermon, a statesman speaking on the radio, or a man on a soapbox on a street corner. In all these cases the orator is speaking to an audience, if he can get one. He is speaking because he wants to persuade his audience to think or feel in a certain way about the subject of his speech.

To the ancient Greeks the art of oratory, at that time called *rhetoric*, was an important subject. It was first developed to help men to put a case well in a court of law, and later the great Greek thinker Aristotle wrote one of his books on rhetoric, setting out the rules for making good speeches. Rhetoric was also much studied by the Romans. It was one of the main parts of education in Europe during the Middle Ages. Among the great orators down the ages have been Demosthenes in Greece, Cicero in Rome, Jacques Bossuet in France, Edmund Burke and W. E. Gladstone in Britain, and Abraham Lincoln in the United States. Fine English-speaking orators of the 20th century have included David Lloyd George, Sir Winston Churchill, Franklin D. Roosevelt, and Martin Luther King, Junior.

Aristotle said that a speaker has three main ways of trying to persuade his audience. He may appeal to their reason by giving them proofs of what he says, showing that certain things are true or likely to be true. He may also appeal to their feelings, rousing them to anger or fear or pity. He may also use words so as to make them believe in him and accept whatever he says. The rise to power of Adolf Hitler in Germany in the 1930s rested largely on his ability to persuade huge crowds with his oratory.

ORCHESTRA. An orchestra is a group of musicians which may be large or small and which plays together usually under the direction of a conductor. The word comes from ancient Greek and originally meant the semi-circular space in front of the stage in a theater where the chorus in a Greek play danced or sang. When the first operas were given in Italy at the beginning of the 17th century a small group of musicians accompanied the singers. They were seated in a similar space before the stage, and the word orchestra eventually came to mean the musicians themselves.

The large orchestras of about 100 musicians that are heard today in concert halls, on the radio, or on records are sometimes called symphony orchestras, although they play other music as well as symphonies. The name came to be given to such orchestras because many of the symphonies they play need a large number of instruments. Or they may be called philharmonic orchestras. "Philharmonic" simply means "loving harmony or music". In many large cities there is at least one large orchestra – the London Symphony Orchestra, for instance, or the New York Philharmonic Orchestra – and many of them are famous throughout the world.

Besides this large type of orchestra there are several smaller types. The chamber orchestra, so named because it could be comfortably seated in a large room of a mansion, has about 20 players. It usually plays works of the 18th century, by Bach or Mozart, for example, but works have been written for chamber orchestra by modern composers. The string orchestra, in which only stringed instruments are played, is about the same size, and also plays both classical and modern music. The theater orchestra of up to 60 players accompanies musical comedies, ballet, and some opera. Finally there is the small orchestra, a modern and slightly larger version of the chamber orchestra, heard in certain modern works by such composers as Stravinsky, Britten, and Hindemith. When the wind instruments play alone they are usually called a band (see BAND). However, the word "orchestra" is used to describe any large group of musicians playing together. There are jazz orchestras, which

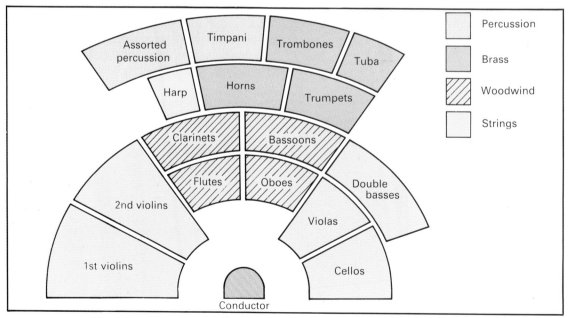

The seating layout of a typical symphony orchestra.

use a wide range of instruments, and concert, or light, orchestras, which play and record light music, a form of music more popular in character than the so-called serious music of the classical repertoire.

Instruments of the Orchestra

The symphony orchestra has three main kinds of instruments: those of the string family, the various wind families, and the percussion family. The stringed instruments are the violin, the viola, the cello, the double bass, and the harp. Although there are only these five members of the string family, string players make up two-thirds or three-quarters of the entire orchestra. There are about 32 violins (divided equally into two sections, called the first and second violins), 12 violas, 10 cellos, and 8 double basses. There may also be one or two harps. (See HARP; VIOLIN FAMILY.)

The wind families consist of the woodwind and the brass instruments, which together number about 25. The woodwind instruments consist of flutes, oboes, clarinets, and bassoons. In the music of some composers – Haydn, Mozart, and Beethoven – there are usually two of each of these, but in the music of later composers such as Tchaikovsky, Richard Strauss, and Stravinsky, there may be three or four of each. One player out of each of the woodwind sections mentioned above usually "doubles" on a lower or higher version of the instrument. Thus one of the flute players will also play the piccolo, while one of the oboists will play the cor anglais. (See CLARINET FAMILY; FLUTE FAMILY; OBOE FAMILY.)

The brass instruments consist of trumpets, horns, trombones, sometimes cornets and usually at least one tuba. Brass instruments are used more in modern music than in the older music. In the symphonies of Haydn and Mozart we find only two trumpets and two horns. In modern works there may be as many as six trumpets, eight horns, four trombones, and two or three tubas. The works of Richard Wagner sometimes require a low instrument called a Wagner tuba. (See HORN FAMILY; TROMBONE FAMILY; TRUMPET FAMILY; TUBA FAMILY.)

The percussion instruments, those which are shaken, rubbed, or struck, are the least numerous but they are the most noticeable, for they generally produce a loud, startling effect. There are four or five players of percussion instruments in a symphony orchestra. The chief among them is the player on the timpani, or kettledrums, called the timpanist. Two, three, or four timpani are set out in a semi-circle before him. Other percussion instruments are the tam-tam, cymbals, triangle, tambourine, several other kinds of drums, rattles, and some of the percussion instruments heard in jazz bands, which composers have introduced into modern works for symphony orchestras. (See DRUM; PERCUSSION INSTRUMENTS.)

The xylophone, glockenspiel, celesta, vibraphone, and piano also come under the category of percussion instruments. They and the timpani, which are set up to play specific notes, are known as tuned percussion. The piano is seldom used in a symphony orchestra but is sometimes found in a small orchestra or theater orchestra.

Arrangement of the Orchestra

In a concert hall the orchestra is seated on the stage in a large semicircle, with the conductor in front on a raised stand, often called a rostrum. To the conductor's left are the violins, and to his right are the violas and cellos, with the double basses behind them. Some conductors vary this seating arrangement, but in all orchestras the whole body of the stringed instruments is in front of the others. In the center of the orchestra are the woodwind instruments: the flutes and clarinets to the left, the oboes, bassoons and double bassoons to the right. Behind these are the brass instruments: the trumpets and trombones are usually to the right, the horns to the left. At the back of the orchestra are the percussion instruments, with the harp just in front of them. All the players have before them the part of the music to be played by their instrument. The conductor has the full score. This is the music as written by the composer, with each of the parts set down one under the other. The conductor can thus see what each instrument is to play.

The Role of the Conductor

What do conductors do as we see them directing the orchestra? They indicate with their arms and with the baton, held in the right hand, at what speed the music should be taken, the kind of rhythm it should have, the kind of expression (meaning), and whether an instrument should sound softer or louder in a particular passage. Of course conductors must also see that the instruments come in at the right place, and correct them during a rehearsal if they play wrong notes. At rehearsals the conductor often talks to the players and discusses with them the best way of playing a certain passage. Each musician may have ideas about how best to play the music, but the members of an orchestra, like those of a football team, must play together, and so they require a conductor who is their captain. It is the conductor who, through the orchestra, gives the music its life and character.

Each section of the orchestra – that is, each group of instruments such as the violins, violas, cellos, double basses, flutes, clarinets, oboes, and so on – is led by a musician chosen for his or her talents on the particular instrument concerned. Each section head is called a principal. The principal first violin is the leader of the orchestra. The leader is responsible for discipline among the musicians during rehearsal. He or she also represents the other players in negotiations with the management of the orchestra. In small orchestras that perform without a conductor, the performance is often directed by the leader.

Besides the big orchestras of professional musicians there are many amateur orchestras that give public concerts. There are also student orchestras and school orchestras. In many European countries, as well as in the United States, there are youth orchestras consisting of amateur musicians aged less than 20, who rehearse together for pleasure and give concerts. Many of these are national youth orchestras, which perform under famous conductors. Players must be of a high standard to enter a national youth orchestra. There they receive a useful musical training, and many of them take up careers in music later on. Youth orchestras sometimes pay visits to other countries, performing on concert tours and attending youth music festivals.

ORCHID. In the second half of the 19th century people spent more money on orchids than they ever had on any other flower, because of their lovely colors and strange, beautiful shapes. They were expensive because the plants had been brought from tropical rain forests in eastern Asia or South America and

NHPA/James Carmichael

The strange tendril-like parts of an orchid flower unfold. This species grows in the tropical forests of northwestern South America.

could not be kept alive in northern climates. Tropical orchids often grow on the tops of the tallest trees or perched on a mossy rock ledge, and these have special roots which hang down like a tangle of thick white ropes. Their family is Orchidaceae and there are as many as 35,000 species.

Orchids vary very much in shape, size, and color. The Lady's Slipper (*Cypripedium*) kinds grow mostly in the northern hemisphere and are so named because of their shape. They have a large pouch in the center in front, like the toe of a slipper, and a small opening where the insects go in and out. The pouch or lip is often spotted or striped and the flowers may be green, brown, white, purple or other colors with darker markings. Another group is called *Cymbidium* and these are tropical orchids that generally grow on trees. They also have a lip,

NHPA/James Carmichael

The startling flower of a ground-growing orchid from the lowlands of the Himalaya Mountains, India.

NHPA/John Shaw

The showy lady's slipper orchid is a North American species which grows in swamps and wet woods.

although it is not shaped like a pouch, and there are often several flowers hanging from one stem. These flowers too are often striped or spotted and may be yellow white, green, deep velvety purple, brown or other colors.

Orchids grow all over the world, from the treeless Artic bogs to the dense rain forests near the equator. The vanilla orchid, which climbs over trees in Mexico, was used by the ancient Aztec people to flavor chocolate, but now vanilla flavoring is made artificially.

One of the first exotic orchids brought to Europe in 1731 was a purple-flowered one from the Bahama Islands in the West Indies. Today many large and splendid orchids from Central America and Brazil are grown in special greenhouses known as orchid houses. They have to be heated and the plants are kept damp in order to make conditions like those of the tropical forests where they grow.

Wild orchids of temperate regions often have flowers that resemble animals, which have given the orchids their name; thus there are frog, fly, spider, butterfly, bee, lizard, monkey, and man orchids.

Orchids are pollinated by many different kinds of insects, each one often special to a particular orchid (see POLLINATION). White orchids, wherever they grow, are generally pollinated by moths. They often have long parts into which the moth pushes its proboscis (a long part of the mouth) for the sweet liquid known as nectar. Orchids give off smells to attract insects, some of the smells being pleasant and some unpleasant.

In Australia there are two kinds of orchid that grow underground. The first was turned up by a plow at Corrigin in Western Australia in 1928, and three years later another kind was found at Bulahdelah in New South Wales.

Both kinds have a scaly stem and a cluster of small flowers in a daisy-like head at the top. They develop and open their flowers well below the surface, but push up above ground to scatter their seeds.

Almost the only plant of the orchid family whose products have any commercial value is vanilla, on which there is a separate article.

OREGON, on the northwest coast of the United States, could not be more different from its southern neighbor, California. Both states have extensive coastlines along the Pacific, but that is where similarities end. In California the greatest concentrations of population are along the coast, while in Oregon they are inland, in the beautiful Willamette Valley. Unlike California, the government of Oregon has been laying claim to all the Pacific beaches to make them public property, open to public use.

Oregon is the chief timber-producing state in the Union, and leans heavily on its vast resources of timber for economic growth, while California has purposefully developed a highly diversified economy. California has long been a magnet drawing population westwards. Oregon, despite its great natural beauty, has never attracted great numbers of people. During the 1970s, in fact, it made a point of telling people not to move there. As unemployment skyrocketed in the 1980s, this policy of unwelcome was reversed. But while California ranks first in population in the United States, neighboring Oregon ranks 30th.

The most distinctive feature of Oregon is its scenic splendor. In addition to the beautiful valley of the Willamette River, where the bulk of the population lives, there are mountain ranges: the Klamath Mountains, the Coastal Ranges, and the Blue-Wallowa Mountains. Tourists can visit more than 200 state parks, as well as thousands of camping and picnic sites. Crater Lake, one of America's finest natural wonders, is in Crater Lake National Park in the Cascade Range. In northeastern Oregon is the Grand Canyon of the Snake River, with Hell's Canyon, going as deep as 2,400 meters (7,900 feet) thus making it the deepest gorge in North America. Multnomah Falls, with a total drop of 259 meters (850 feet) are in northwestern Oregon near Bonneville. To preserve its natural heritage, Oregon has the nation's most advanced laws protecting the environment.

Mount Hood can be seen beyond these fruit trees. It is the highest peak in Oregon, and an extinct volcano.

Of special historical interest is the western end of the Oregon Trail. Along with the Santa Fe Trail, this was one of the two main routes to the Far West during the 19th century. Its eastern starting point was at Independence, Missouri. From there it has stretched 3,200 kilometers (2,000 miles) west and north to the area near present-day Portland at the north end of the Willamette Valley. Over the trail Marcus Whitman, Henry Spalding, and their wives traveled in 1836 to start a mission among the Indians. The wives were the first white women to make the journey. The first emigrant train left Independence in 1842. Thousands followed the trail in the next several decades. It was still in use in 1880, in spite of the transcontinental railroad.

The Land

Oregon is in the Pacific Northwest. It is bounded on the north by the state of Washington, although the great Columbia River follows the boundary line for a long distance. On the east is Idaho, which shares the Snake River as a boundary for more than half the border length. To the south are California and Nevada, and to the west is the Pacific Ocean. The coastline is 476 kilometers (296 miles) long. From east to west Oregon is 636 kilometers (395 miles), and from north to south it is 475 kilometers (295 miles).

Oregon has nine natural regions. Four of them comprise the western third of the state, while the other five cover the eastern two-thirds. The western four are the Klamath Mountains, the Coast Ranges, the Willamette Valley, and the Cascade Range. To the east are the Columbia Basin, the Blue and Wallowa mountains, the Malheur-Owyhee Upland, the Harney High Lava Plains, and the Great Basin.

The Klamath Mountains occupy the southwestern corner of Oregon. The Coast Ranges, immediately to the north, are a series of low, rolling mountains along the Pacific. In the far

ZEFA
Oregon has roughly 500 km. (300 miles) of Pacific coastline, with many fine beaches and views.

ZEFA
The deep Crater Lake is famed for its rich blue color. About 10 km. (6 miles) in diameter, it is the remains of a mountain which exploded about 6,000 years ago.

north the Columbia River cuts through the mountains to reach the ocean. At this point is the state's lowest elevation, at sea-level.

The Willamette Valley is a narrow, fertile trough between the Coast Ranges and the Cascades. It extends for about 290 kilometers (180 miles) south of Portland. Within it are all the major cities of Oregon, including Portland, the largest city; Salem, the capital; Eugene, home of the University of Oregon; Springfield, a timber and wood products center; and Corvallis, home of Oregon State University. Medford, located well to the south in the Cascade Range, is the only major city outside the valley.

The Cascade Range has high slopes covered with evergreen forests. The state's highest peak, Mount Hood, is in the north. Its height is 3,428 meters (11,248 feet). At the southern end of the range are Crater Lake National Park and Upper Klamath Lake.

The Columbia Basin occupies upper north-central Oregon. It is a plateau which slopes northwards to the Columbia River. The Blue-Wallowa Mountain region occupies the northwest corner of the state. At its eastern border is the Grand Canyon of the Snake River. To the south of this region is the Malheur-Owyhee Upland, reaching south to the Nevada border. It is a dry plateau named after its main rivers, the Owyhee and the Malheur.

The Harney High Lava Plains are in the center of the state, south of the Columbia Basin. This is a barren and thinly populated upland, with some desert area. The Great Basin of southern Oregon stretches from the Cascades east to within some 50 kilometers (30 miles) of the Idaho border. It is part of the vast semi-desert that reaches southward into California, Nevada, and Utah. The large Goose Lake is in the region on the California border.

Such varying regions bring equally differing climates. Western Oregon benefits from the prevailing Pacific winds and has cool summers and mild winters. Eastern Oregon has a continental climate, with hot summers and cold winters. Growing season in the west is 200 days, while in the east it varies from 200 to 100 days depending on location. Precipitation along the coast averages 1,520 millimeters (60 inches) a year, while in the east it is much less.

The People

Oregon was originally settled by white Protestants from the East, and it has remained a largely white Protestant state ever since. Its New England background (see NEW ENGLAND) is suggested by the names Portland and Salem for its leading cities. Long before the first settlers arrived, there were about 125 Indian tribes in the region. Among them were the Nez Percé, the Chinook, the Yakima, the Paiute, the Klamath, and the Modoc.

Fur trappers came west early in the 1800s, and John Jacob Astor's Pacific Fur Company founded Astoria in the far northwest in 1811. Astoria claims to be the oldest city west of the Mississippi settled by citizens from the United States. The Spanish cities of the southwest are, of course, much older. Many immigrants came from Canada, Finland, Norway, and Sweden. New waves of immigrants arrived in the 20th century, making the population more diverse than it had been. By 1980 there were about 37,000 blacks, 66,000 Hispanics, and 35,000 Asians from various parts of the Pacific Basin.

The Economy

Oregon has about 12,141,000 hectares (30,000,000 acres) of forest. Added to this are 2,104,440 hectares (5,200,000 acres) of cropland and 4,451,700 hectares (11,000,000 acres) of pastureland. These figures indicate that Oregon's economy is extremely dependent on natural resources. The chief industry is the processing of timber. The state supplies about 20 per cent of the timber produced in the United States. Forest products account for 40 per cent of the state's 5,700 manufacturing establishments and 40 per cent of total industrial employment. Public agencies control about 60 per cent of the state's commercial forests, while the rest belong to private owners. Sawmills, planing mills, and plywood plants make up about one-third of the state's manufacturing capacity. This is followed by food processing, the manufacture of paper and pulp, primary metals, fabricated metal products, and printing and publishing.

In agriculture, livestock products contribute more than one-third of the income, led by cattle and calves. Dairy products, pigs, and poultry are also quite significant. There are about 4,000 farms. Wheat is the main crop. Others are cranberries, filberts (hazelnuts) and English walnuts (a type of walnut), flax, hops, pears, alfalfa seed, clover, oats, barley, potatoes, and sugar beet.

Fishing thrives along the Pacific Coast and in the Columbia River. Salmon are the most valuable catch, followed by shellfish. Other catches include flounder, tuna, ocean perch, and rockfish.

Mining is a less significant part of the economy. The only nickel mine in the United States is located near Riddle. There is quarrying for rock in every county. There is some gold and silver produced in Jefferson County.

Education

French Prairie, now Wheatland, was the site of the state's first school, in 1834. Fifteen years later the territorial legislature established the basis of the modern public school system. For higher education there are three state-supported universities: the University of

Oregon, Oregon State University, and Portland State University.

History

The first Europeans to visit Oregon were Spanish sailors looking for a northwest passage to the Far East. Sir Francis Drake anchored at an inlet in 1579 on his way north from California. He took possession of the land for England. But the Oregon country remained unexplored until the third quarter of the 18th century. Captain James Cook, discoverer of Hawaii, visited Oregon in 1778, and his sailors bought fur pelts from the Indians to sell in China. (There are separate articles on these explorers and the Northwest Passage.)

The first claim by the United States to the Northwest occurred in 1792, when Boston merchants sent two trading ships to its coast. Shortly afterwards, English fur companies approached by land to open routes to the Pacific. The American explorers Lewis and Clark reached the mouth of the Columbia River in 1805 (see LEWIS AND CLARK EXPEDITION). John Jacob Astor's fur company arrived in 1811.

Migration by Americans from the Midwest began in the 1830s. Conflicting claims to the territory – with Great Britain – were settled in 1846, and the Oregon country was added to the United States. Territorial status was granted in 1848. In 1853 the Washington Territory was separated from Oregon, and Oregon entered the Union as the 33rd state in 1859. A long series of Indian wars lasted from 1847 to 1880, and shortly afterwards the transcontinental railroads entered the territory from the north, east, and south. This improvement in transportation led to a rapid expansion of agriculture and of the timber industry.

Industrialization was also promoted by the contruction of dams for hydroelectric power. The Bonneville Dam on the Columbia River was completed in 1937. McNary Dam was finished in 1953 and The Dalles in 1957. Detroit Dam was built on the North Santiam, and Look-out Point on a fork of the Willamette. There are also dams on the Snake River. Since 1940 there has been some movement of the economy away from dependence on timber, and also an increase in the number of people moving to Oregon from other states.

FACTS ABOUT OREGON

AREA: 251,418 square kilometers (97,073 square miles).
POPULATION: 2,842,321 (1990).
CAPITAL: Salem, 107,786.
CITIES: Portland, 437,319; Eugene, 112,669; Salem, 107,786; Gresham, 68,235; Beaverton, 53,310; Medford, 46,951.
HIGHEST POINT: Mount Hood, 3,424 meters (11,235 feet).
PRODUCTS:
  Agriculture: Hay, wheat, potatoes, peppermint, ryegrass seed, pears, onions, green beans, sweetcorn, barley, cattle, dairy products, potatoes.
  Minerals: Gold, industrial minerals, nickel, sand, gravel, stone, silver.
  Manufacturing: Electrical equipment, timber and wood products, machinery, paper products, metals, transportation equipment.
STATE EMBLEMS: Flower: Oregon grape. Tree: Douglas fir. Bird: western meadowlark.
JOINED THE UNION: Oregon became the 33rd state in 1859.

ORFE. The golden orfe (*Idus idus*) is, unlike most fishes, light colored on the back and is an attractive fish to put in ornamental ponds, since it can clearly be seen in the water. It belongs to the same family as the carp and goldfish.

The orfe is a silvery fish that lives mainly in rivers. The golden form is a popular ornamental fish.

The orfe is a variety of the ide, a fish found in many lakes and rivers of Europe and western Siberia. The wild orfe, also called ide, is silvery, with a dark, olive-green back, but by careful breeding the rich, orange-gold aquarium fish has been obtained.

Golden orfe prefer moving, cold, water, but they are excellent pond fishes. They are sensitive to changes in temperature and may die in shallow pools during a hot summer. They also need a lot of oxygen, and fewer orfe than gold-fish can live in a pond.

During the summer, golden orfe may find plenty of natural food in the pond but in the winter, particularly during warm spells, they should be fed with earthworms, chopped meat, or a good fish-food. If they are given plenty of space and food, golden orfe will live for a long time and reach a length of 0.6 meters (2 feet).

ORGAN. The organ is by far the largest of all musical instruments, and the many sounds it produces are as different as those of a whole orchestra. It is a wind instrument, and sound is produced from it in the same way as from other wind instruments; that is to say, by the vibration of air in a pipe. The difference between the organ and other wind instruments is that the organist does not himself set the air vibrating in the pipe by blowing, as the flute player or the clarinet player does. He uses machinery.

Organs are built in three main sections. These are (1) the pipes of various kinds and sizes, (2) the wind chest containing pressurized air supplied from a bellows, or nowadays, from an electrically operated rotary fan, and (3) the console, where the organist sits and which is really the control board of the organ.

The Pipes

The organ pipes are arranged in rows, or ranks, standing on top of the wind chest with their "mouths" pointing downwards ready to receive air from it. The pipes are of graded sizes. The shortest produce the highest notes, while the longest produce the lowest notes. The pipes, which are of wood or metal, may be either open or closed at the end opposite to the "mouth". Because of an effect of acoustics (the way in which sound behaves), a closed pipe produces the same note as an open pipe of twice the length. This helps to make the manufacture and positioning of organ pipes much easier. Pipes are of two basic kinds: *flue pipes* and *reed pipes*.

Flue pipes are basically just whistles. The tube of each flue pipe is fitted with a "mouthpiece" in which air from the wind chest passes over a sharp edge and sets a column of air vibrating inside the pipe. Flue pipes make flute-like or recorder-like sounds. Reed pipes, which are less numerous than flue pipes, are also fitted with a "mouthpiece" in which a tongue of thin metal is made to vibrate against an opening in the side of a little brass tube. This sets up a buzzing noise, which in turn causes the air column inside the pipe to vibrate. The sound reproduced by a reed pipe is similar in tone to that of an oboe or trumpet.

The Console

The organist at his console has several keyboards in front of him, each like that of a piano. Those played with the hands are called manuals and the large one on the floor, which he plays with his feet, is called the pedal board, or pedals. Each key on a manual is connected to several pipes, all playing the same note but each sounding different.

How does the organist obtain the sound of one kind of pipe or another when he presses down the keys? You may notice to his left and right a series of knobs which he pulls out or pushes in again. These are called stops. They are connected to wooden sliders, one under each rank of pipes and each one having a hole for each pipe. When the organist wishes to play on a particular rank of pipes he pulls out its stop, which moves the slider so that the holes are underneath the pipes of that rank. Now when he presses down the keys the air is fed from the wind chest to the pipes of that rank and they sound. When the organist pushes the stop in again, the sliders for that rank move back to their original position so that the holes no longer line up with the pipes. Because a rank of pipes is controlled by a stop, it is itself often called a stop. Another name for a rank is a *register*.

Organs are used mainly for church music and for occasions when many people gather together. An organ is built specially for the particular hall or church where it will be housed, and so no two organs are the same.

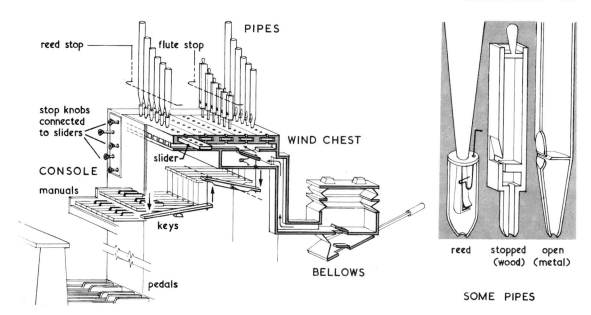

PIPES

reed stop

flute stop

stop knobs
connected
to sliders

slider

WIND CHEST

CONSOLE

manuals

keys

pedals

BELLOWS

reed   stopped   open
(wood)   (metal)

SOME PIPES

Left: How an organ works. Wind is now often supplied from an electrically driven fan rather than from a bellows.
Right: In a reed pipe the air column is vibrated by a tongue of metal. Flue pipes (center and right) work like whistles.

They also vary very much in size. Some of the older organs have only a few stops and one or two manuals. Those that were used in the time of Johann Sebastian Bach, who wrote some of the finest organ music, are of the smaller kind. Although over 200 years old, their tone is still very beautiful and some people think that it is finer than that of the modern organs. Some modern organs are very large indeed. The largest in the world is at Atlantic City in the United States. This organ, in a hall seating over 40,000 people, has more than 33,000 pipes and 7 manuals.

Other Organs

We have described the church organ, but in fact many instruments function in the same way as an organ, or attempt to imitate it.

The most ancient type of organ was the hydraulus, or water organ, invented in Egypt in about 250 BC. It was fitted with pipes and a type of manual. Air was forced into the pipes by the flow of water. The hydraulus was an outdoor instrument used by the Romans at gladiatorial shows. In medieval times, organs were either positive (non-movable) or portative (portable). One type of portative organ, the regals, had only reed pipes.

Reed organs make up a notable class of organs, of which the best-known is the harmonium. This is an instrument that has only a single manual and a foot-operated bellows that blows air over the reeds. An American organ is similar to a harmonium, except that the bellows both blow and suck air past the reeds. Other instruments that are classed as reed organs include the accordion and the harmonica, on which there are separate articles.

An electronic organ is a modern instrument in which a keyboard and pedal board operate switches that allow notes to be produced by electronic means. One of the most advanced instruments of this kind is the synthesizer, in which the notes are produced by oscillating (rapidly changing) electric currents. The range of tone colors that a synthesizer can produce is very great. It is capable of copying any sound, from that of a single instrument to that of a full symphony orchestra.

ORIENTAL ART. The word oriental means "of the East", and oriental art is the art of the Eastern countries of the world, that is, of Asia.

In the continent of Asia there are many nations where there have been artists for many thousands of years, and its art includes

Top left: Chinese tomb figure decorated in colored glazes (AD 618–906). **Top right:** 16th-century painted lacquer bookbinding from Persia. **Above:** Chinese flask in underglaze blue (14th century). **Right:** 16th-century Persian painting: Zal, a king and folk hero, courts Rudabah who stands on the balcony.

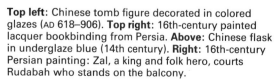

*Courtesy, (top left and bottom right) Victoria and Albert Museum;
(bottom left) G. J. Winner; (top right) Museum of Fine Arts, Boston*

Top left: An 18th-century Mogul jade bottle with rubies and emeralds set in gold. **Top right:** Ladies ironing a silk, detail from an earlier 8th-century Chinese painting. **Left:** The fairy "Queen Mother of the West", Hsi Wang Mu, riding above the clouds, a Chinese coral carving of the Chi'ing dynasty. **Above:** *Attendant leading a black buck* by Indian artist Manohar, *c.*1615.

sculpture, pottery, and carvings of countless different kinds. If you go to a museum or an art gallery and look at things that have come from the East, from China or India, for instance, you will see that they look very different from the kind of pictures and statues and carvings that people are used to in the Western world. Nowadays Asian pictures and carvings are often rather like Western ones, but the style of the older ones was quite different. Occasionally this is because the artists used different materials for their work. For example, Chinese and Japanese painters painted on cloth, silk, or board, but not on canvas as many Western artists have done. The actual method of drawing or painting was different too. Chinese artists used their brushes to make outlines in the same way that they used them to make the delicate characters of their "picture writing". In both China and Japan, where these characters are used for writing instead of alphabetical letters like those of Western writing, and in Arabia and Persia too, much attention is paid to writing as an art. The characters or script are often used as part of a picture or are hung on a wall by themselves to be admired for the elegance and the skill of the writer.

The main reason for the strangeness of oriental art, however, is that we do not know the stories that the artists were telling in their paintings or their sculpture, and the ideas that lay behind them. Most of their work was done to serve either the religion of their country or else their king. Many European paintings tell the stories of the Christian religion, and in just the same way many of the paintings of the East are about the various Eastern religions. In times and countries where most of the people could not read, artists were especially important because they could tell the stories and express the ideas which few people would have known about if they had only been put into books.

Stories and Symbols

Because the Eastern artists often set out to tell stories or to remind people of them through their paintings and carvings, they had to make quite certain that the people who looked at them could recognize each particular story very clearly. To do this they put in special signs and reminders so that there should be no mistake. If a picture was to include a great hero, for instance, the artist would make sure that everyone realized he was a hero by painting him as an ideal and wonderful person, not as an ordinary one like the people to be seen in everyday life. To show the power and greatness of a king, an artist might make him much bigger than the other figures in the picture or carving. The sculptors of Persia, for instance, did this when they carved a scene which included the mighty emperor Darius. Indian artists showed a king as much bigger than his queen, and the queen as much bigger than her maidservant.

When it came to making a picture or carving of a god it was rather more complicated. In India, for instance, priests and artists gradually worked out a set of symbols, or signs, which stood for the character and powers of the various gods. When a god was supposed to possess many different powers, the artists used to paint him (or her) with many arms and hands, each hand holding one of the symbols of power. Used like this, the various symbols showed at once which god was which; and if a picture was about some special event, the place where it happened was shown not by painting in the whole scene, but simply by one object to stand for the whole. In this way the Indian artists could remind people of quite a detailed story in a single painting or carving, by using the symbols that had been handed down from one generation to another and were familiar to everyone. In Christian countries a simple cross stands for a whole event—the crucifixion of Jesus Christ. The oriental artists used their symbols in just the same way.

For example, here is how Buddhist artists showed one of the scenes connected with their religion. The Buddha was a great religious teacher who died in India at the beginning of the 5th century BC. His first sermon, to five men who became his followers, was preached in a deer-park near the city of Benares, and is known as "The Setting in Motion of the Wheel of the Law". This scene can be shown in a straightforward picture or carving: the Buddha, who can be recognized by certain special features and marks on his body, seated and preaching to the five with a few deer included in the picture to show where it is taking place. But this event can also be shown in a single statue. The Buddha can be seated on a pedestal with his hands in front of his chest in such a way that he seems to be spinning a wheel with his right hand—setting in motion the Wheel of the Law. On the pedestal are carved the five men and the deer. More simply still, an artist may show the same scene just by a wheel set between two deer. (See also BUDDHA AND BUDDHISM.)

People, Animals, and Countryside

Another thing that sometimes seems strange to us in oriental pictures is that the people in them do not look like people do in real life. We are used to realistic pictures in which the human beings and animals and the scenery look natural to us, because artists in Europe have been painting in this way for hundreds of years. However, the oriental artists were trying to do something quite different. They did not often paint portraits— likenesses of actual people—but when they did they probably made a picture of what they thought the person *ought* to look like. A king, for instance, ought to look powerful and majestic. A portrait that showed him like this did not necessarily give a clear picture of him as a *person*—he may have been a small fat man, not at all majestic—but what it did do was to show the *idea* of a king, the idea the artist and everyone else had of what a king should be like.

In many other kinds of painting and sculpture besides portraits, Eastern artists wanted to do this same kind of thing—to show the most important ideas about the subject, not necessarily to paint it just as the eye sees it. So, to make a picture of a human figure absolutely clear and definite, a painter might paint each part of the body in the way that showed it most clearly—the face turned sideways, to show the nose and chin, but the eye front view, because that is how eyes show most clearly. The body can be shown from the front, but with the legs and feet sideways. This may seem strange to us, but it is easier to understand once we know the reason for it.

Chinese painters were particularly good at landscapes—pictures of the countryside. They, too, showed the most important ideas about the landscape and not a complete impression of some actual view. They tried to express the strength and ruggedness of mountains and their enduring nature, the peace of the country as a place of escape from the noise and worries of the town. In a Chinese picture of this kind, the presence of deer may be used to show that it is winter. Again, when one particular Chinese painter did a picture of the emperor's famous stallion called *Star of the Night*, he did not really want to make a realistic likeness of the horse's body. Instead he emphasized the animal's fiery, unbroken spirit by showing its flowing mane, its nostrils stretched wide, and its pawing hooves.

When oriental artists painted religious pictures or pictures of historical events, they had a chance to portray the lives of villagers and ordinary townspeople in the settings and backgrounds. They enjoyed doing this, and put in plenty of details. A house would not be drawn just from one point of view, as Western artists would show it. Instead the artist would show each part of the house and its garden and fence in the clearest way he could (just as he did with human figures). A picture of a tree would not be an accurate drawing, but would have its most important features—the grace of its branches, or its berries, perhaps— emphasized. The artists of central Java in the 8th century did this so well that it is possible to make a list of the flowers and trees and animals of the country by studying the carvings on the monuments. In many parts of Asia carvings and paintings tell us a great deal about the ordinary things people used in their lives: pots and pans, weapons, tools and farm implements, boats and houses, musical instruments, clothes, and jewelry.

You can find information about the work of

the artists of Asia and the countries where they lived in other articles, including ARCHITECTURE; FAN; POTTERY AND PORCELAIN; RUG AND CARPET; SCULPTURE; WOODCUT; CHINA; INDIA, REPUBLIC OF; JAPAN; PAKISTAN; PERSIA, ANCIENT. The best thing of all is to go and look at the examples you will find in museums and galleries and try to learn to understand them for yourself.

ORIENTAL LANGUAGES AND LITERA-TURE.

There is a great variety of languages spoken in East and Southeast Asia, the region which is generally referred to as the Orient. Three of the principal languages are Chinese, Japanese, and Korean. The writings in these languages form a huge body of literature.

Chinese

Chinese is the most important member of the Sino-Tibetan family of languages and is spoken by the most people. Other Sino-Tibetan languages include Tibetan, Burmese, and Lao.

ZEFA

A teacher in a Chinese elementary school points out some of the 50,000 characters of the Chinese language.

The history of written Chinese goes back more than 3,500 years. Chinese writing has always been ideographic rather than phonetic. This means that words, or "characters" as they are called, represent their meaning rather than spell out their sounds. You often cannot tell by looking at a word how it should sound. There are about 50,000 characters in Chinese, although only about 3,000 to 4,000 are necessary for everyday use.

The characters have traditionally been read in columns from top to bottom. They start at the upper right-hand corner of the page. The beginning of a Chinese book is on what is the last page of a Western book.

Some of the oldest characters were originally pictures. ⊙ meant "sun". Over the centuries, as the writing evolved, this became 日. ☽ meant "moon" and has now become 月. "Mountain" was ⋀⋀ and is now 山. 久, or "child", is now 子. ψ, or "hand", changed to 手.

Characters are built up from two basic units. These are called radicals, of which there are 214, and phonetics or primitives. Phonetics, which may be radicals themselves, give a broad clue to pronunciation; if no such clue is given, the unit is called a primitive, of which there are about 20 to 30. A character may even be made up of only one radical. Each character is pronounced as a single syllable.

Two characters were often combined to use the sense of both together. The character, 木, means "tree"; two of them, 林, mean "forest". "Sun" and "moon" combined is 明, or "light". Hand in the old form is 彐; two hands modernized, 友, mean "friend".

In spoken Chinese the Mandarin dialect is used by about 70 per cent of the Chinese people. In fact, Mandarin has the largest number of speakers of any language (about 610 million). Several other dialects that sound completely different from one another are also spoken in different parts of the country. A person living in Peking, in northern China, cannot understand a native of Canton, in the south. Neither of them can understand someone from Foochow, in the southeast. All educated people today, however, understand *kuo yü*, "national language" (also called Pu-t'ung-hua, "common language"), which is similar to Mandarin. Unlike spoken Chinese, the written language is the same throughout the whole of China.

None of the dialects of Chinese has more than a few hundred sounds for whole words. The Chinese add a special tone system to give greater variety to those sounds. Just as in English the tone of voice often rises or falls from one syllable to another. Mandarin uses four tones, each within a single syllable: level, rising, falling-rising, and falling. The meaning of a word depends on the tone as much as on the combination of vowels and consonants. The sound *ma* spoken in one tone may mean "mother"; *ma* in another tone may mean "flax"; in still another, a questioning "horse"; and in the fourth, a questioning "what".

Japanese

Japanese is spoken by more than 122 million people living in Japan, and by about 1 million Japanese outside the country. The speakers of one Japanese dialect cannot always understand the speakers of another. But nearly everyone can speak and understand standard Japanese, which is taught in schools throughout the country.

Japanese is an Altaic language, and is most closely related to Korean. But it is still quite unlike other languages of the Altaic language family, which includes various Mongolian languages and Turkish.

Typical Japanese words have several syllables, and in Japanese there are only about 100 syllables altogether. The words are spoken without heavy stress. Hiroshima, for example, is not pronounced HI-ro-SHI-ma, as many Westerners think, but rather HI-RO-SHI-MA, with an equal stress on all the syllables.

Written Japanese is the most complicated writing system in the world. Until about 1,500 years ago, there was no way of writing Japanese. Then, Buddhist monks from China and Korea worked out a system. They began to use thousands of Chinese characters, called *kanji*, to write Japanese. The character 人 was read as *ren* in Chinese, but as *hito* in Japanese, although in both languages it means "man". Words which are Japanese in origin but use Chinese lettering are known as *kun* words. In the course of time, the Japanese

not only adopted Chinese characters but also took over certain Chinese words, although they often gave these words a new meaning. These words of Chinese origin are known as *on* words.

Japanese was so different from Chinese that it was impossible to write Japanese by relying entirely on the existing Chinese characters. Many parts of words, including word endings, could not be written in kanji. Thus, in the 8th century, the Japanese invented a way of writing these uniquely Japanese particles and syllables, based on kanji. These new syllabaries (sets of characters representing syllables) were known as *kana*. In time, kana developed into two parallel syllabic systems, called *hiragana* and *katakana*, which each contained some 50 characters. (It was possible to have only 50 characters because the Japanese language has very few syllables compared to English, for example.)

Originally hiragana was used by women, while katakana was used by priests and officials, who also used to write in pure Chinese, which women never learned. Today hiragana is generally used in all texts, while katakana is reserved for words of Western origin (such as *te-re-bi* for "television"). But many kanji characters continue to be used together with kana, so one word may contain a combination of kanji and kana.

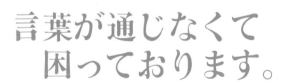

言葉が通じなくて困っております。

I am having trouble since I don't speak Japanese. A Japanese sentence (with English translation) is written in both kanji and kana characters.

After World War II, the Japanese government modified and simplified the system of writing. The number of kanji (Chinese) characters was considerably reduced for official or daily use, to less than 2,000, and their forms were simplified. Some people have urged that kanji be dropped entirely, because anything in Japanese can be written in kana, which children learn in the first years of primary school. But kanji flourishes, and both popular books and textbooks use a combination of kanji and kana. Books written in kana only are for children.

Korean

The Korean language, also a member of the Altaic language family, is spoken by about 57 million people, 39 in South Korea (The Republic of Korea) and 18 in North Korea (Democratic People's Republic). There are some differences between the language of the North and of the South.

Some Korean words come from Chinese. These words are written in Chinese characters, kanji. But unlike Japanese, words of Korean origin are never written in kanji.

During the 15th century, a local phonetic script called *en-mun* (today known as *hangul*) was invented. It was not based on Chinese models like the Japanese script, but on Sanskrit, the phonetic alphabet of ancient India. For a long time, the script was used only by the common people. The royal court and the most important writers continued to use Chinese characters until the late 19th century. Today, however, hangul is used by everyone in North Korea. In the South the use of borrowed Chinese characters as well as hangul is discouraged but nevertheless still accepted.

When the Japanese took over control of Korea in 1910, they abolished the use and teaching of Korean. But after the end of World War II, hangul was revived, although Chinese writing is still taught in schools in South Korea.

Chinese Literature

The earliest Chinese literature dates from the 6th century BC. It consists of several books known as the earliest Confucian Classics. Confucius himself, China's great philosopher and teacher, often referred to one of them, *The Book of Songs* (c.1000–600 BC), as the proper starting point for all study. The other Classics were written later and became part of the Confucian religious literature.

A collection of Confucius' wise sayings called the *Analects* was made by his pupils after his death. From it we get a good impression of Confucius' personality and the way he taught. *The Book of Mencius* was made up perhaps 200 years later and consists of the sayings and doings of Mencius (Meng-tzu), one of the greatest Confucian teachers. (See CONFUCIUS AND CONFUCIANISM.)

Three other writers of this Classical period also produced works of relgious importance but opposed to Confucianism. Lao-tzu wrote *The Way and Its Power*, brief essays on the natural life later used as the basis for Taoism, the religion based on the teachings of Lao-tzu. Chuang-tzu sought for the "perfect" man because he believed that only such a man could be free. Mo-tzu, often considered China's greatest religious writer, spent most of his efforts writing against war.

With the beginning of the medieval period in the 4th century AD, Chinese literature entered its golden age. Most of the greatest writers were poets. They were divided into many different schools and styles, and their subjects varied from nature to wine, from the war ballads of the North to the love songs of the South.

Tao Chien tried to behave and write as one of the common people. He wrote personal poems about nature. Wang Wei was an artist and musician as well as a poet. It is said that there were always pictures in his poems and poems in his pictures. Li Po was a rather wild hermit-poet who wrote some of his most beautiful verse about wine and the carefree life.

Tu Fu wrote of the bitterness of war, of injustice and hunger. He is known as the first poet with a social conscience. Po chu-i was the first important Chinese poet who attempted to write in the plain language of the people. Su Tung-po was a great experimenter who brought new vigor to Chinese poetry when it had become too formal.

The Chinese also wrote fiction. There are popular short tales that go back as far as the 8th century AD, but it was not until the Ming Dynasty (1368–1644) that fiction matured. *The Water Margin* (*All Men are Brothers*), perhaps the first true novel, was a violent adventure yarn. It was probably written by the prolific mid-14th-century novelist Lo Kuanchung, but this is not certain because most early Chinese fiction was published anonymously (without naming the author).

Early in the 16th century, *Journey to the West* (or *Monkey* as it is often called) by Wu Cheng-en appeared. It is about the strange adventures of a stone monkey. Feng Menglung arranged several collections of folk tales early in the 17th century, and they have remained both popular and influential. In 1792 the first complete edition of *Dream of the Red Chamber* by Tsao Chan was published. This is a long romance often considered the greatest of all Chinese novels.

In the 19th century both prose and poetry seriously declined. There were many poor imitations of older forms, but none of the writers could compare with the old masters. After the Communist take-over in 1949, all writing was government controlled. But since 1976 there has been a change and China has become more open to Western influence.

Japanese Literature

The first important works of Japanese literature appeared in the 8th century AD. They are: the *Kojiki* (*Records of Ancient Matters*), which recounts the mythological backgrounds of Japan; the *Nihongi* (*Chronicles of Japan*), history up to AD697; and the *Manyoshu* (*Collection of Ten Thousand Leaves*), an anthology of more than 4,500 poems and one of the world's greatest collections of poetry. The *Manyoshu* contains work by all of Japan's important early poets and established the form of the *tanka*, a brief 5-line, 31-syllable poem. Most of Japan's greatest poetry was written in this form, and it remains extremely popular. Poetry is in fact an important part of the culture; great occasions are marked with poems, and there are annual poetry competitions.

About 300 years later the great age of Japanese fiction began. The oldest novel is *The Tale of the Bamboo-Gatherer*, a charming story about a beautiful maiden only 8 centimeters (3 inches) high. *The Tale of Ise*

appeared about 950 and was the first of a number of disconnected stories about young noblemen.

Two important women writers followed: Sei Shonagon, who wrote *The Pillow-Book*, a witty diary-like collection of comments and gossip; and Murasaki Shikibu, who wrote *The Tale of Genji*, the robust story of Prince Genji, which remains Japan's greatest work of fiction.

About 1250 *The Tale of the Heike* was written by an unknown author. This epic novel concerns the civil war that tore Japan apart during the 12th century. Conditions were so unsettled that little important writing was done during the next several hundred years.

The next development was the rise of Japanese drama: *Noh* (classical theater); *bunraku* (puppet plays), and *Kabuki* (popular theater). Japan's greatest playwright was Chikamatsu Monzaemon. He wrote mainly for the puppet theater but his work was often adapted for *Kabuki* performances.

Early in the 17th century a new poetic form appeared, the *haiku*, a tiny poem of only 17 syllables arranged in 3 lines. The finest *haiku* poet was Matsuo Basho, who wrote thousands of these small poems. He is regarded by many as Japan's greatest poet.

The later part of the Tokugawa period (1603–1868) was another era of fine novels. Among the most important is *Life of an Amorous Woman* by Ihara Saikaku, which is a harsh look at the place of women in a feudal society. Another is *Hizakurige*, meaning "a journey on foot" but translated as *Shank's Mare*, by Jippensha Ikku. It tells of the wild adventures of Yaji and Kita, both of whom have become Japanese folk heroes. Another Tokugawa novel is *Eight Dogs*, the best of about 300 novels by Kyokutei Bakin. It is a dramatization of the eight virtues.

Japan was opened to Western ideas and visitors in 1858. The event brought many changes to both Japanese poetry and prose. World War II brought further changes. Modern authors write in both Western and traditional Japanese forms. Yukio Mishima's novels are often compared with those of

Some Leading Oriental Writers and Works of Literature

China

6th century BC	The Early Confucian Classics; *The Book of Songs.*
551–479 BC	Confucius—*The Analects*; wise sayings.
born *c.*570 BC	Lao-tzu—*The Way and Its Power*; philosophy.
*c.*480–*c.*390 BC	Mo-tzu—*The Book of Motzu*; religious philosophy.
*c.*365–*c.*290 BC	Chuang-tzu—*The Book of Chuang-tzu*; philosophy.
*c.*372–*c.*289 BC	Mencius—*Book of Mencius*; philosophy.
AD 32–92	Pan Ku—*History of the Former Han Dynasty.*
365–427	Tao Chien—poems.
699–759	Wang Wei—poems.
701–762	Li Po—poems.
712–770	Tu Fu—poems.
772–846	Po Chu-i—poems.
1036–1101	Su Tung-po—poems.
1125–1193	Fan Cheng-ta—poems.
1125–1210	Lu Yu—poems.
Mid-14th century	Lo Kuan-chung—*Romance of the Three Kingdoms, All Men are Brothers*; novels.
1500–1582	Wu Cheng-en—*Monkey*; novel.
Mid-17th century	Anonymous—*The Golden Lotus*; novel.
1715–1797	Yuan Mei—poems.
1719–1763	Tsao Chan—*Dream of the Red Chamber*; novel.

Japan

712	Anonymous—*Kojiki* (*Records of Ancient Matters*); history.
720	Anonymous—*Nihongi* (*Chronicles of Japan*); history.
*c.*760	*Manyoshu* (*Collection of Ten Thousand Leaves*); poetry.
Early 10th century	Anonymous—*Tale of the Bamboo-Gatherer*; novel.
Mid-10th century	Anonymous—*The Tale of Ise*; novel.
	Anonymous—*The Tale of Lady Ochikubo*; novel.
*c.*967–*c.*1025	Sei Shonagon—*The Pillow-Book*; diary.
*c.*978–*c.*1031	Murasaki Shikibu—*The Tale of Genji*; novel.

1153–1216	Kamo no Chomei—*Ten Foot Square Hut*; philosophy.
Mid-13th century	Anonymous—*The Tale of the Heike*; novel.
1283–1350	Yoshida Kenko—*Essays in Idleness*; philosophy.
1363–1443	Seami Motokiyo—*Noh*; plays.
1642–1693	Ihara Saikaku—*Life of an Amorous Woman, Five Women Who Loved Love*; novels.
1644–1694	Matsuo Basho—poems.
1653–1725	Chikamatsu Monzaemon—plays.
*c.*1715–*c.*1783	Yosa Buson—poems.
1765–1831	Jippensha Ikku—*Shank's Mare*; novel.
1867–1916	Natsume Soseki—*Botchan*; novel.
1886–1965	Junichiro Tanizaki—*The Makioka Sisters, Some Prefer Nettles, The Key*; novels.
1892–1927	Ryunosuke Akutagawa—short stories.
1898–1973	Jiro Osaragi—*Homecoming*; novel.
1899–1972	Yasunari Kawabata—*Snow Country, Thousand Cranes*; novels.
1925–1970	Yukio Mishima—*Temple of the Golden Pavilion, The Sound of Waves, After the Banquet*; novels.

Korea

*c.*858–*c.*910	Cho Chi Won—*Pen Plowings in a Cassia-Garden*; poetry.
1075–1151	Kim Pu-sik—*Samguk sagi*; history.
1168–1241	I Kyu Bo—poems.
1287–1367	I Cheh Yon—poems.
1337–1392	Chong Mong-ju—poems.
1536–1584	Yul Kok—poems.
1607–1689	Jong Sir-yoi—poems.
1637–1692	Kim Man-jung—*The Cloud Dream of the Nine*; novel.
1640–1723	Im Bang—short stories.
1670–1717	Kim Chun Daek—novels.
20th century	Choe So Hae—novels.
	Pak Hyong Hui—novels.
	Kim Ki Jin—novels.
	Lee Kwang Soo—novels.
	Choo Yohan—poems.
	Han Yong Woon—poems.

Ernest Hemingway. He is the first Japanese writer to achieve international fame. Ryunosuke Akutagawa, Jiro Osaragi, Junichiro Tanizaki, and Yasunari Kawabata, who won the 1968 Nobel Prize for literature, are popular novelists.

Korean Literature

All early Korean literature was wholly dominated by Chinese models. Much of it, especially the poetry, was actually written in Chinese. The first works were histories and collections of short poems. Kim Pu-sik is generally considered the finest early historian, and Cho Chi Won, the foremost poet.

By the 14th century, Korean literature began to emerge. A few poets started to use the new Korean alphabet, although they still used Chinese poetic forms for their models. Novels began to appear. Among the most famous are: *The Cloud Dream of the Nine* by

Kim Man-jung, a story of the rebirth of a hero; and *The Adventures of Hong Kil Dong* by a Buddhist monk, Kasan. Also, about this time, Im Bang wrote in Korean many of his popular short tales. Several important encyclopedias and literary anthologies were also compiled.

Korean literary nationalism emerged in 1910, and most writing was done for the first time in the native alphabet. Poems and stories began to appear showing Western influences. Patriotism was the most important subject, and Choe So Hae, Pak Hyong Hui, Lee Kwang Soo, and Kim Ki Jin were the most important writers.

Since Korea regained its independence at the end of World War II, and especially since the Korean War of the early 1950s, Western influence has been very pronounced in both poetry and prose.

ORIENTEERING. The sport of orienteering began in Sweden in 1918. Since 1950 it has become widespread throughout Europe, and is particularly popular in Scandinavia. It has an even greater following than soccer and athletics in Sweden, where it is taught in schools to all pupils from the age of ten onwards, and where there is an orienteering club in every town.

Orienteering is cross-country running with a map and compass—rather like a car rally on foot. Races are held in hilly forest areas where there is little private property to hinder the runners. Unlike a normal cross-country race the actual course is not told to the competitors when they start, but only the positions of various controls along the course are shown on a map. The runners start at intervals of one minute, and soon disappear into the trees, so that each runner has to work out from his map the direction he must take to reach the next control.

There are usually between six and ten controls in a course, and the distance between them varies from about 180 meters (200 yards) to more than 1.6 kilometers (1 mile). Controls are placed on top of small hills, on stream and path junctions, or at any other small but recog-

nizable feature. At the start of the race each competitor is given an unmarked map. Then the runners are shown a master map on which all the controls are marked, and which also gives a short description of each control. Each runner must then swiftly transfer all these positions and details on to his own personal map, and the quicker he does so the sooner he can set off.

The key to success is accurate navigation at speed. But as the fastest runners are not always the cleverest map readers you do not need to be a top-class athlete or necessarily young to be a successful orienteer.

The International Orienteering Federation was founded in 1961. World and European championships are held.

ORIGAMI is the Japanese art of paper folding. It has been practiced for many centuries and probably developed originally from the earlier art of folding cloth. In origami, there are hundreds of intricate folds, and new ones are being invented all the time. The paper is *never* cut, pasted, or decorated. By folding paper in various ways, it is possible to produce

Courtesy, Japanese National Tourist Office

Origami, the art of paper folding, originated in Japan, and is a popular craft there, and elsewhere.

all kinds of beautiful designs of animals, birds, fish, figures, flowers, and other objects. Some parts of a finished object may be able to move: birds' wings can flap, animals can wag their tails, and frogs can be made to hop by moving their legs. Many of these origami creatures are highly amusing. Other objects may have ceremonial significance. *Noshi*, for example, are folded decorations which the Japanese attach to gifts.

Origami has become a popular hobby in the West. Miguel de Unamuno, a Spanish writer and artist, became fascinated by the art early in the 20th century. He wrote about it and was responsible for inventing several new folded forms. He made it popular in many Spanish-speaking countries. Exponents of the art in the United States include George Rhoads and Guiseppe Baggi.

ORINOCO RIVER. The northernmost of the great South American rivers is the Orinoco. It rises in the Parima Mountains between Venezuela and Brazil and flows for about 2,150 kilometers (1,336 miles) through Venezuela until it reaches the Atlantic Ocean opposite the island of Trinidad. The tributaries from the north and west pass through wide grassy plains called *llanos*, where cattle are grazed. The tributaries from the south rise in the highlands near the Brazilian frontier and join the Orinoco through dense tropical forest, tumbling through many rapids.

The Orinoco reaches the sea through a delta of many branches where the land is so swampy that no port can be built. Therefore the main port of Orinoco is the city of Ciudad Bolivar about 400 kilometers (250 miles) from the mouth of the river. Here goods arriving by steamer are repacked in smaller vessels that take them further upstream, and gold, diamonds, hides, minerals, and timber from the Orinoco basin are loaded in outgoing ships. The chief mineral is iron ore, mined from the Cerro Bolivar mountain. Ciudad Guayana is the other major port.

Fish found in the river include the razor-toothed piranha, and catfish weighing over 90 kilograms (200 pounds). The Orinoco crocodile is one of the longest in the world, reaching 6 meters (20 feet).

ORIOLE is the name of two different groups of perching birds both of which have contrasting black and colored plumage.

There are 24 species of Old World orioles, thrush-like birds closely related to crows

Frank Lane Picture Agency

The European oriole makes its nest slung between the end branches of a tree.

and jays that live in the tops of forest trees and have a strong, slightly curved bill. They build hammock-like nests slung between twigs.

The only European species is the golden oriole (*Oriolus oriolus*), not easily seen but detected by its fluting bubbling song. In the breeding season it feeds mainly on insects, including hairy caterpillars. Later in the year it eats fruit such as figs. The yellow oriole (*Oriolus flavicinctus*) of Northern Australia is mainly a fruit eater.

There are 30 species of New World orioles, slightly smaller birds with a shorter bill. The male Baltimore oriole (*Icterus galbula*) is orange and black, the female a softer brown with yellow and white markings. This species is also a treetop songster, the call consisting of a series of loud whistles. It feeds on insects and some fruit, and builds a bag-like nest, narrow at the top and about 15 centimeters (6 inches) long.

The orchard oriole (*Icterus spurius*) is also a North American breeding bird. The male is black with a deep chestnut colored breast, belly, and rump. It prefers orchards and farmlands with scattered trees where it sings its pleasant warbling song.

The family of New World orioles, the Icteridae includes North American blackbirds, meadowlarks, and grackles. (See BLACKBIRD; LARK.)

ORKNEY ISLANDS.
The Orkneys are a group of islands lying to the north of Scotland, and separated from it by the Pentland Firth. Further north lie the Shetland Isles. There are about 70 islands in the group, 20 of which are inhabited. The islands form a local government area known as an island authority.

They are hilly green islands where the wind blows all year round. Some of their cliffs are steep and splendid. Porpoises can be seen rolling in the waters around the Orkneys, and many seals live along the coasts. There are also many kinds of sea-birds, including gulls, gannets, puffins, and great skuas, which are large, fierce birds.

Scottish Tourist Board

These ancient tall stones, set on end, make up a circle called the Ring of Brogar on Mainland.

Scottish Tourist Board

Stromness is one of only two towns on the island of Mainland—the largest of the Orkney Islands.

The biggest island is called Mainland, where Kirkwall, the chief town of the islands, stands. Kirkwall is a picturesque town with granite houses and a small cathedral which is built of red sandstone. On the west side of Mainland is the smaller town of Stromness.

Across the water from Stromness is Hoy, the second largest island of the group, and off the west coast of Hoy is a tall, narrow rock like a pillar, called the Old Man of Hoy. South of Mainland is South Ronaldsay, which is joined to Mainland by a series of raised roads across the water called the Churchill Barriers. These were built during World War II by Italian prisoners of war. They also left behind a beautiful little chapel, built from scrap materials.

The People

Most Orcadians, as the people of Orkney are called, live by farming. Many beef cattle are kept. On North Ronaldsay, the most northerly of the Orkneys, is a breed of sheep which feeds chiefly on seaweed and sea grasses and has very fine wool. Oil has been discovered southeast of the islands and a pipeline carries it ashore to storage tanks on the island of Flotta.

People have lived in Orkney since the Stone Age. Skara Brae is a village of stone huts that those early people built on Mainland and which can still be seen today. Maeshowe, a mound containing many rooms, was also built by Stone Age people. Other remains of ancient people on Mainland are two stone circles forming the Ring of Brogar and the Ring of Stenness. These consisted of tall stones set on end, similar to Stonehenge (see STONEHENGE). After the Stone Age, people called Picts built underground burial chambers, and round towers called "brochs" to protect themselves against invaders. Vikings arrived later, and in the 9th century the islands became part of Norway. Eventually they were transferred to Scotland, in the 15th century.

The population of Orkney is about 18,000.

ORPHEUS AND EURYDICE.

ORPHEUS AND EURYDICE. A Greek legend tells of Orpheus, son of the god Apollo and the muse Calliope, who played the lyre so beautifully that all the animals in the forest gathered round to listen to him and even the trees and rocks were charmed by his music.

Orpheus was married to a nymph called Eurydice, but a terrible day came when she trod on a snake and died, leaving him distracted with grief. He took his lyre and went down into the underworld to look for her. There he found Hades, king of the Underworld, and his wife Persephone. He sang to them, begging them to release his beloved wife, and even the spirits of the dead who were suffering eternal torture forgot their pain and wept for him. Hades was so moved that he agreed to release Eurydice on condition that Orpheus did not look at her until they had reached the mortal world. Just as they were coming out into the light of day Orpheus turned to see if Eurydice was really following him and she vanished. For seven months Orpheus sang of his sorrow in a cave by the Strymon River and then he was torn to pieces by the women worshippers of the god Dionysus because he despised their love. The muses, who were goddesses of music, poetry, and learning, buried the fragments of his body and it is said that a nightingale sings for ever over his grave. Orpheus' lyre was placed among the stars.

ORTHODOX CHURCHES see EASTERN ORTHODOX CHURCHES.

ORYX is the name of three species of large antelope that live in herds in dry deserts and plains. All have beautiful light-colored coats and darker markings that blend well with the scrub, rock, and sand of their arid homelands. Oryx feed on shrubs and grasses, and bulbs. The males use their horns in combat with other males and also in head-to-head sparring with the females during courtship.

The gemsbok (*Oryx beisa*) of South Africa has a gray fawn coat and a black nose patch and stripe uniting to form a "bridle" around the eye.

The other two species are extremely rare animals. The scimitar-horned oryx (*Oryx dammah*) of North Africa exists in the wild only in the Sahel scrubland south of the Sahara Desert, in the countries of Chad and Niger. It has been hunted to the edge of extinction for its meat and skin by local peoples, and by foreigners as a hunting trophy, mainly for its magnificent backward-sweeping horns.

Fortunately these rare animals breed well in captivity, and in December 1985 ten individuals bred in captivity, were released into the rugged terrain of the Bou-Hedma National Park in Tunisia, an area in which oryx once lived but had become extinct.

The survival story of the Arabian, or white, oryx (*Oryx leucoryx*) is even more dramatic, for in the early 1960s the last wild animals were rounded up and used as the basis for a captive breeding herd. By the end of 1984 the world captive herd numbered 239 individuals of which 44 were reintroduced into Oman and 75 to Saudi Arabia. Most of the captive animals were bred at San Diego zoo, California, in the United States.

NHPA/Anthony Bannister

The gemsbok, one of three species of oryx antelope, has a cream-colored coat and chocolate "stockings".

OSAKA is Japan's third largest city and, together with the neighboring city of Kobe, is its second largest commercial and industrial center. It is located in south Honshu on Osaka Bay, facing Japan's Inland Sea. Osaka with Kobe ranks as Japan's major seaport. The region enjoys a temperate climate, but it often snows in winter, and typhoons have struck the area causing terrible damage.

Courtesy, Japanese National Tourist Office

Osaka is an industrial and financial center. The Yodo River is near the harbor area.

The city was once an important textile center, but machinery manufacturing has become its leading industry. Osaka is also noted for shipbuilding, steel, electrical equipment, food processing, printing, textiles, chemicals, cement, and clothing. The city is the center of an industrial belt that extends for more than 30 kilometers (20 miles) along the north shore of Osaka Bay. At the western end of this cluster of industrial cities is the port city of Kobe.

Osaka also serves as the financial and commercial capital of western Japan and is noted for its many large banks, trading firms, department stores, and wholesale outlets. The modern downtown business district has wide streets lined with tall Western-style office buildings and large department stores. Lying on a river delta, the city is crisscrossed with canals. The canals are used for barge traffic and they are crossed by many bridges. Osaka is a major junction point for the railroads, and the famous high speed "bullet" trains (*Shinkansen*) pass through it. Osaka International airport links it with other major cities in Japan and overseas.

A number of important universities are located in the city, including Kansai and Osaka universities. The city is a center for theatrical productions, particularly for puppet shows (*bunraku*).

In the 16th century the shogun (warlord) Toyotomi Hideyoshi set up his headquarters at Osaka, and the city's importance as a commercial center dates from that time. The city was heavily bombed during World War II, but it has been largely rebuilt. Osaka was rather slow in re-establishing its prewar commercial greatness because of the loss of China as a trading partner after World War II. (China had been a major customer for Osaka's products.) The rise of the Tokyo–Yokohama area as an economic competitor also weakened Osaka's industrial importance. The population of the city if 2,634,000 (1985).

OSIRIS. Among the gods worshipped by the ancient Egyptians were Esit and Usire, or Isis and Osiris, as the Greeks called them in their versions of the Egyptian myths. These stories are very old and were first written down between 4000 and 3000 BC. Like other Egyptian myths, they had a great deal to do with religious beliefs and ceremonies and were connected with the worship of the sun, the honoring of the River Nile which made the land fertile, and the funeral rites which were intended to preserve the bodies of the dead for a future life.

Osiris was the son of the Earth-god and was descended from the Sun-god, Ra. He became king of Egypt and taught the people how to farm their land and how to make bread, wine, and beer. He married his sister Isis, and together they brought civilization to the whole country.

However, Osiris was hated by his brother, Set, whom the Greeks called Typhon. Set plotted to kill him and finally tricked him into lying down in a coffin which he then fastened and threw into the Nile. It drifted to a place called Byblos in Syria, where a sycamore tree grew up around it and hid it. The king of Byblos, not knowing the coffin was there, cut the tree and made a pillar from it. Meanwhile Isis had set out to look for the body of her husband and when she found it she brought it back to Egypt. But Set, his hatred still alive, cut the body into pieces and scattered them throughout all Egypt.

Isis then perseveringly collected the pieces and, by magic performed by her and some of the gods, Osiris was restored to eternal life. He had become a god risen from the dead, and he came back to Earth to teach his son, Horus, who finally defeated Set and was declared the rightful heir.

Some of the events in the story are thought to represent actual happenings in history. The struggle between Osiris and Set, later carried on by Horus, is something like the struggle which actually took place between the rulers of Upper and Lower Egypt. The death and resurrection of Osiris probably stand for the rising and falling of the Nile. In the religious ceremony connected with the myth, figures of Osiris used to be made of Nile mud sown with seeds and thrown into the water. When the seeds began to sprout it was taken as a sign of the god's coming to life again.

Michael Holford

Osiris with his grandsons. Dating from 1050 BC, this painting was found in the ancient city of Thebes.

OSLO is the capital as well as the largest city and seaport of Norway. It was founded in 1050 by King Harald Hardraade. After a great fire in 1624, King Christian IV rebuilt the city and named it Christiania (from 1877, Kristiana), but the old name was restored in 1925.

ZEFA

Oslo harbor is the busiest and largest in Norway, and handles cargo and passenger ships.

Oslo lies at the head of Oslo fjord in the southeast of the country, among pine-clad hills. It is the center of Norwegian banking, industry, and shipping. Over its busy harbor towers the vast modern city hall. Immediately to the east is the 14th-century fortress of Akershus. The chief street, Karl Johans Gade, runs from the main railroad station to the royal castle with its statue of Karl Johan in the west. (Karl Johan was King Charles XIV of Sweden and Norway.) Along this street are the older buildings of Oslo's university, the national theater with huge statues of playwrights Henrik Ibsen and Björnstjerne Björnson, the parliament building and office buildings, stores, restaurants, and cinemas. On the Bygdöy peninsula in the harbor is a large folk museum with old farms and churches and examples of household crafts from the earliest times. It is also the site of the Viking ship hall holding several old Viking ships. Another building holds the famous ship *Fram* built for the explorer Fridtjof Nansen, and near it is the raft *Kon-Tiki* on which Thor Heyerdahl and his companions sailed from Peru to Raroia in the south Pacific in 1947. (See Nansen, Fridtjof; Heyerdahl, Thor.)

Oslo's industries, located mostly in the northern and eastern parts of the city, produce woolen garments, paper, chemicals, glass, machinery, and other goods. The city, which has grown very rapidly, has many large modern apartment buildings and a number of garden suburbs on the outskirts. High above the city to the north and linked with it by a special railroad is Holmenkollen with its world-famous ski-jump and ski museum. International competitions are held there.

The population of Oslo is 477,400 (1984).

OSMOSIS is the movement of water from an area in which it is relatively abundant to one in which it is relatively scarce, across a type of barrier called a semi-permeable membrane. The process is "passive", that is, it does not require energy. Semi-permeable membranes only allow the passage of certain molecules across them (water is one molecule which crosses such membranes very easily), and are found surrounding all living cells.

Science Photo Library

Left: A white carnation is placed in a bottle of blue ink. **Right:** Six hours later ink has traveled up the stem and through the petals by osmosis.

All water movement into and out of living cells occurs by the process of osmosis. For example, the uptake of water by plant roots, the movement of water from one plant cell to another, the entry of water through the gills of a freshwater fish, and the "saving" of water by the kidneys in human beings and other mammals all occur by this process.

If too much water enters an animal cell by osmosis it causes the fragile cell membrane to burst; thus the water content of the body must be accurately controlled to avoid such damage. This does not happen in plant cells because their tough cellulose cell walls resist bursting.

OSPREY. Because it is a fish-eating hawk, the osprey is called a fish hawk in the United States. There is only one kind of osprey (*Pandion haliaetus*) with an extremely wide distribution. It nests near water in most lands of the northern hemisphere and in New Guinea and Australia, and migrates across or winters in all other land masses.

The osprey is white and dark brown in color. Its under parts and breast are white, though there may be a brown band across the breast. The upper parts are brown and the head is mostly white with a dark stripe down each side and brown streaks. The head has rather a ruffled appearance. Female ospreys are larger than males, and may be nearly 60 centimeters (24 inches) long. Their outstretched wings measure almost 2 meters (6.5 feet) across from tip to tip.

For a bird of prey the osprey has quite long legs, greenish in color and half hidden in white feathers. The beak is black and hooked with a pale blue patch, called the cere, just behind it, and the eyes are fierce and yellow. The usual call of the osprey is a short whistle, which seems rather shrill for such a big bird.

The osprey's main food is fish. It may rise to 30 meters (nearly 100 feet) above the water, gliding and flapping alternately as it watches for its prey. When it sees a fish it may hover for a moment, dropping its legs like the undercarriage of an airplane. Then it plunges, usually in a slanting line, into the water. If it is very high it may zigzag several times before the final dive. There is a tremendous splash and beating of wings and, if it has caught

An osprey lands on its bulky nest built on a rock stack by the sea.

a fish, the osprey rises almost straight into the air. It carries its catch head foremost in its claws, which have special rough pads underneath for gripping slippery fish.

Having caught its prey, the osprey takes it to a perch, often a bare branch, where it may sit for hours without moving. It catches several kinds of fish and may also eat small mammals, frogs, and insects. On fine days ospreys sometimes soar high in the clear sky on slightly bent wings.

Ospreys may nest on rocky islands, but usually choose the tops of trees. The nest, known as an eyrie, is used year after year, and so a great pile of sticks and other materials is built up. The female osprey generally lays three eggs, white with heavy brown blotches, in late spring. In North America ospreys nest in colonies, and there is a famous one at Gardiner's Island, New York. People in America also put cartwheels on the top of poles to encourage the birds to nest.

OSTEOPATHY is a form of medical treatment in which the practitioner, who is called an osteopath, "manipulates" the body by pushing, pulling, pressing, and twisting. It is often successful in treating backache, neck pains, and aches in the muscles and joints.

Osteopathy was founded by an Ameri-can doctor, Andrew Still (1828–1917). In 1892 he opened the first School of Osteopathy in Kirksville, Montana. He believed that almost all illnesses are caused by the body's bones being out of alignment. This produces strains in the tissues and affects the blood supply to nearby organs. Since the body works as a co-ordinated whole and will heal itself if helped a little, putting the bones back into their correct positions cures the illness.

For a long time osteopathy was viewed with suspicion, and as an alternative to the drugs and operations of traditional medicine. Today the form of medicine practiced by properly trained and qualified osteopaths is seen as part of the overall treatment of a patient. It is complementary, rather than alternative. Osteopaths are aware that osteopathy cannot really cure diseases such as cancers or serious infections, and that it is limited to structural or mechanical problems in the body such as slipped disk, frozen shoulder, neckache, and tennis elbow.

Most treatment sessions last from 15 to 45 minutes. The person lies on a couch or sits in a special chair, and the osteopath feels for areas of tension and distortion. The parts of the body are then manipulated, sometimes quite strongly, to correct the problem. People with severe backache have reported great relief after only one session. Usually follow-up sessions are required, and the osteopath may give advice on sitting, standing, and moving about.

Some osteopaths are qualified doctors. They prescribe drugs and carry our surgery in combination with their manipulative skills. Others are experts in osteopathy itself, and patients are usually sent to them by a family doctor. In the United States osteopaths must train for up to seven years before they receive qualifications from the American Osteopathic Association. In Britain the training is shorter and in fact anyone, qualified or not, can set up as an "osteopath" and begin to treat people. Obviously if you need to see an osteopath it is sensible to make sure that he or she is properly qualified.

OSTRICH. The largest bird in the world is the ostrich (*Struthio camelus*), which cannot fly and lives in Africa. A fully grown male ostrich may be as much as 2.4 meters (8 feet) tall and weigh about 130 kilograms (286 pounds). The ostrich has three living relatives, the cassowary, emu, and rhea (there is a separate article on each of these). It was also related to the moa of New Zealand, which is now extinct and was even larger than the ostrich (see also MOA).

Nigel Dennis/NHPA

A male ostrich giving a courtship display. Some ostrich chicks can be seen in the scrub at the bottom.

The ostrich has a flat head and a long bare neck. Its body is covered with black feathers and it has beautiful white plumes in its wings and tail. These were once of great value and birds were raised on special farms. Its legs are strong and thick and, unlike all other birds, it has only two toes on each foot. It can deliver vicious kicks if annoyed. The ostrich is a wonderfully fast runner. When going at full speed (nearly 65 kilometers (40 miles) an hour), it is faster than the antelope, which also lives on the sandy plains and open country that are the ostrich's home. Ostriches go about in small troops of five or six — one cock and four or five hens.

The food of ostriches is plants and some insects. Sometimes they swallow hard substances, such as stones, which help their digestion.

Several female ostriches lay their eggs in a shallow hollow in the sand. Sometimes there are as many as 15 eggs in one hollow. They are white and very large. The hens take turns in looking after them in the daytime and the cock takes charge at night. Often the eggs are left by themselves to hatch in the heat of the sun, but the mother birds stand guard over them.

OTTAWA is the capital of Canada. It is in the southeastern part of the province of Ontario, and stands on the high southern bank of the Ottawa River near its junction with the Rideau River. West of the Rideau Canal, some 48 meters (155 feet) up on a rocky cliff overlooking the Ottawa River, are the Parliament Buildings of gray stone with green copper roofs. They have a tower 90 meters (295 feet) tall containing a beautiful war memorial chamber and a carillon of 53 bells. (A carillon is a set of bells on which tunes can be played.)

The city's main business is the government of the country. Unlike Washington, the capital of the United States, and Canberra, the capital of Australia, Ottawa is not situated in a federal district. The city has a municipal government. It elects members to the Ontario Legislature and to the Canadian House of Commons. The Governor-General of Canada

Barnaby's

People fish and relax by the Ottawa River which borders the city on the north side.

lives at Rideau Hall near the eastern end of the city.

Other important buildings in Ottawa are the Chateau Laurier hotel, the Royal Mint, the National Museum, the art gallery, the National Centre for the Performing Arts, and the observatory. There are two universities and two cathedrals. A number of public parks and a scenic driveway add greatly to the beauty of the city. To the north, the picturesque valley of the Gatineau River descends from the blue Laurentian Mountains and to the south is the main airport at Uplands.

Ottawa is a producer of wood pulp and paper, and it also manufactures many other goods. Electricity for the factories is made by water power obtained from the Chaudiere Falls a short distance up the Ottawa River.

Samuel de Champlain in 1613 was probably the first European explorer to visit the site of the present city of Ottawa (an Indian word meaning "to trade"). In 1800, Philemon Wright started the first settlement on the north side of the Ottawa River. For some years the high cliffs above the river discouraged settlers on the south side, although in about 1820 a farm was cleared by Nicholas Sparks in what is now the heart of Ottawa. Then the British government decided to join Lake Ontario with the Ottawa River by a canal, completed in 1832, part of which followed the course of the Rideau River. The village at the north end of the canal was called Bytown and became prosperous as the timber and fur trade developed. In 1854 its name was changed to Ottawa. Political rivalry between Toronto and Quebec, and between Montreal and Kingston led Canadian leaders to ask Queen Victoria to establish a new capital. In 1858 Queen Victoria named Ottawa as the capital of the province of Canada, which consisted of what is now Quebec and Ontario. In 1867, when the confederation of Canada was formed, Ottawa became its capital. Had Ottawa not been made the capital of Canada, it might have remained a small town. The presence of the national government in the city greatly spurred its development. In 1937 Prime Minister William Mackenzie King had the capital district redeveloped.

The population of the metropolitan area is 756,600 (1984), the fourth largest in Canada.

OTTER. Among the relatives of the weasel is the otter, which lives in rivers and streams and sometimes on the seashore. Otters have a wide distribution throughout Europe, the Americas, Asia, and Africa. As they hunt only at night they are seldom seen.

The otter is usually about 1 meter (3.3 feet) long, of which nearly half is taken up by the

R. J. Johns/Bruce Coleman

The otter's flattened head, lithe slender body, and short legs are typical of the weasel family to which it belongs.

thick, muscular tail. The head is small, the neck thick, and the body narrow and eel-like. Its brown fur is long and there is a fine soft underfur. The legs are short and the toes webbed for swimming. Otters can travel submerged for up to 0.4 kilometer (0.25 mile). They travel widely and, although mainly aquatic, can run on land faster than a man.

The otter builds a home of grass and leaves in a hole in the river bank or at the foot of a tree. This home is known as a "holt". Otters live on fish, shellfish, frogs, and small animals, such as rabbits, and also on carrion (dead animals). The female otter has from one to three young, called whelps, which are usually born in the spring. She calls to them and to her mate with a soft whistling sound.

Otters are wonderful swimmers, diving, twisting and turning and performing somersaults in the water. Unlike almost all other animals, otters are playful even as adults. They frolic in grass and slide down river banks and in snow, and throw stones into the water, diving to catch them as they sink. A young otter is easily tamed and trained, showing considerable intelligence.

The sea otter (*Enhydra lutris*), which lives off the west coast of North America, is larger than the river otter and has darker fur. The fur is very valuable, and the sea otter has been so much hunted for it that it is now very rare. However, strong efforts have been made to protect it, and it is now no longer in danger of dying out. The sea otter eats no fish, but lives on clams, mussels, crabs, and similar creatures. It sometimes smashes them on a flat stone resting on its chest as it floats on its back.

The giant otter (*Pteroneura brasiliensis*), also very rare, is a South American species up to 2.2 meters (7 feet) long including the tail.

OTTOMAN EMPIRE is the name of the empire that was started by the Ottoman Turks in western Asia and southeastern Europe in the 14th century and lasted into the 20th century. There were many different branches of

National Maritime Museum

The battle of Lepanto in 1571 provided a slight check to the spread of the Ottoman Empire in Europe.

the Turkish peoples and it was the Ottomans who set up this empire. They ought really to be called Osmanli, from the name of their leader Osman who ruled from 1281 to 1324, but in western countries Osmanli became changed to Ottoman.

The country now called Turkey takes its name from the Turks, and it was in the northwestern part of this country that they first began to establish their empire. Having become strong there, they crossed into Europe about 1346. In 1453, under Sultan Muhammad the Conqueror, they captured the great European city of Constantinople and made it their capital (see CONSTANTINOPLE). In the reign of Suleiman the Magnificent (1520–66) the Ottoman Empire stretched from Hungary in Europe to the Persian Gulf in Asia (see SULEIMAN). In 1683 a great Turkish army invaded Austria and laid siege to Vienna, the capital. However, the Polish king Jan Sobieski saved the day by attacking the rear of the Turkish army and defeating it. From this time the Turks began to be defeated by European countries, and their empire slowly fell apart. The story of how this happened is told in the article TURKEY.

One of the most amazing things about the Ottoman Empire is that, until the 18th century, most of its officials were slaves. They were men who had been born Christians but who had been taken, as children, to be brought up by Turks. Most of them were trained in barrack schools and joined the army, becoming known as janissaries, but those who showed special ability were trained for important government posts. Even the grand vizier (prime minister) was usually a slave.

OWEN, Robert (1771–1858). Born at Newtown, Wales, on 14 May 1771, Robert Owen was attracted as a boy to the rapidly developing cotton industry in Manchester. He became a successful businessman, and, at the age of 29, moved to New Lanark in Scotland, where his cotton mills, which were the biggest in the United Kingdom, became a showplace of the Industrial Revolution (see INDUSTRIAL REVOLUTION).

Unlike many businessmen of his time Owen was concerned with the welfare of his workpeople as well as with the amount of work they did. He shortened working hours, built decent houses for his employees, and opened a school for their children. He believed that if people's working and living conditions improved, their characters would improve too.

In the difficult years of unemployment and distress which followed the Napoleonic Wars, Owen tried to spread his ideas more widely and to influence important people. He urged parliament to limit children's working hours, suggested national programs to relieve unemployment, and demanded wide reforms in education.

When influential people would not follow his advice, Owen created at New Harmony in the United States a small community of people which he hoped would put into practice the idea of co-operation between individual people for the good of the community. After this community had failed, he returned to Britain in 1829 and became involved in a working-class movement, which finally resulted in the foundation of large-scale trade unions. (See TRADE UNION.) Scattered throughout the country there were working men who called themselves "Owenites", studied his writings, and started experiments in co-operation. They continued to carry on Owen's ideas with great energy, even after 1834, when the trade union movement collapsed because of opposition from the employers, and when Owen himself had given up many of his activities. In the long run Owen's most important influence was on the co-operative movement (see CO-OPERATIVE MOVEMENT). By the time that Owen died on 7 November 1858, the movement was well established, although it was based on retail stores, in which Owen had never been very interested.

OWEN, Wilfred (1893–1918). Wilfred Owen was a young poet who became famous after his death for the poems which he wrote during World War I.

He was born in Oswestry in England, and received his education at the Birkenhead

Institute and the University of London. He moved to France in 1913. Some of his poems from this period survive, though they were not published at the time.

Owen enlisted in the army in 1915, and his experience of trench warfare became the subject matter of his poetry. His poems express anger and sadness at the cruelty of war. These lines are from his "Anthem for Doomed Youth":

What passing-bells for these who die as cattle?
Only the monstrous anger of the guns.

Among his other poems are "Arms and the Boy", "Futility", and "Strange Meeting".

When he was wounded in 1917, Owen was sent to a hospital near Edinburgh. There he met Siegfried Sassoon, another young poet who felt as he did about war.

In August 1918, Owen returned to France. He was killed in November 1918, a few days before the war ended. After his death his poems were collected and published by Sassoon.

OWENS, Jesse (1913–80). James Cleveland Owens was a black United States athlete who established several world records and is recognized as one of the greatest runners of all time. He was born at Danville, Alabama. He showed enormous promise at his Cleveland high school. This bore fruit at Ohio State University. At a college track meeting in 1935 he broke on the same day, 25 May, three world records (the long jump, 220-yard sprint, and 220-yard hurdles) and equaled a fourth (100-yard sprint).

Owens's greatest triumph was in the 1936 Olympic Games held in Berlin. The German dictator Adolf Hitler (see HITLER, ADOLF) hosted the games in the hope of showing off to the world the physical superiority of Aryan (Germanic) athletes. But Owens, competing for the United States, won four gold medals, breaking the world records in the 200-meter and long jump events and equaling the Olympic record in the 100-meter sprint. In addition he was a member of the team that broke the world record for the 4 × 100-meter relay. Hitler personally refused to award

BBC Hulton Picture Library

At the Berlin Olympics in 1936, Jesse Owens set track and long jump records which stood for over 30 years.

Owens his medals. His records lasted more than 30 years. After his retirement he took part in youth activities, went on goodwill visits to India and the Far East, and was secretary of the Illinois Athletic Commission.

OWL. There are very many different kinds of owl, from the tiny American elf-owl (*Micrathene whitneyi*), 15 centimeters (6 inches) long, to the eagle owl (*Bubo bubo*) which is nearly 75 centimeters (30 inches) long. Usually they are only seen dimly in the dusk, for they are active at night, but they are quite unmistakable because of their stumpy bodies, hooked beaks, and round heads. Their eyes are very large and the feathers round them grow so as to form rings which make them look very wise. The bird sacred to Athena, the Greek goddess of wisdom, was an owl.

Owls are birds of prey; they catch and eat other animals. But unlike hawks and eagles, owls seek out their prey by sound rather than sight. They hunt quite silently, for their plumage is so soft that the feathers make no sound as they fly.

Owls are found in most parts of the world, and their food varies with their habitat. Most common types of prey are mice, rats, voles, rabbits, insects, and small birds. Prey is usually swallowed whole. However, owls cannot digest bones and fur, so some time after their meal they bring these up in pellets. These are neat little packets of bones wrapped in the fur.

Many owls do not make proper nests, and they are unlike most other birds in their way of hatching their eggs. A bird such as a thrush lays a whole clutch of eggs and then begins to sit on them. An owl, however, lays one egg and sits on it for a day or two before laying the next. As a result, the eldest of a family of young owls may be several days old when the youngest is newly hatched. Owls' eggs are always white in color.

Owls can see and hear extremely well in poor light. The eyes are quite large and have stereoscopic (three-dimensional) vision.

Frank Lane Picture Agency

Owls can surprise their prey because they make no sound as they fly. Here, a North American saw whet owl is about to strike a white-footed mouse.

Although the eyes themselves cannot move around very much, the head is extremely flexible. It can swivel from side to side, making nearly three-quarters of a circle, and can turn almost completely upside down (180 degrees). The disk of feathers that frames the face of many owls is thought to reflect sound to the ear openings that lie just behind and to the side of the eyes. This allows them to judge how far away their prey is.

Hans Reinhard/Bruce Coleman

The European eagle owl is a powerful bird that can kill and carry off animals as large as young deer.

Frank Lane Picture Agency

The burrowing owl of the Americas lives in burrows made by animals such as prairie dogs and viscachas.

Although most owls hunt at night, there are several species that hunt during the day, such as the burrowing owl (*Speotyto cunicularia*) of the grasslands of North and South America, and the short-eared owl (*Asio flammeus*) of the northern hemisphere.

Most owls have repetitive calls that can be heard over long distances. The North American great horned owl has a deep "hoo-hoo-hoo-hoo hoo-hoooooo" call while the calls of some other species are a mixture of screams and screeches.

OX. The word ox (plural "oxen") can refer to any kind of cattle, but it generally means a bull (*Bos taurus*) that has been operated on so that it cannot breed and is more gentle-tempered than an ordinary bull. Oxen are extremely useful animals for plowing, drawing carts, and carrying burdens, but in many countries, they have been replaced by horses or tractors.

Oxen have been used since ancient times, and probably they were used to plow fields soon after men learned how to grow crops. The Bible has many references to them, including directions as to how they should be treated. From Abraham's day onward the amount of oxen a man possessed was a sign of wealth, just as it is today among many African tribes.

Perhaps oxen are most renowned for the part they played in the early settlement of South Africa. Dutch and British pioneers would never have been able to explore and settle in that country without the teams of oxen that drew their wagons. Oxen were used on the Great Trek, when Boers, or farmers of Dutch descent, left Cape Colony to get away from British rule (see GREAT TREK). Ox-drawn wagons were also used by the pioneers in Australia and North America.

In India and other tropical countries the humped cattle called zebus are used in the same way as oxen (see CATTLE).

OXFORD is a famous and historic English city on the River Thames at the mouth of the River Cherwell, about 80 kilometers (50 miles) northwest of London. In the city is Oxford Uni-

ZEFA

Quiet college courtyards are minutes away from Oxford's busy streets. This is Christ Church, with the clock tower.

versity, England's oldest university. The city also includes the industrial area of Cowley, which is known for motor-vehicle manufacturing.

Oxford came into existence during Saxon times and became a major market town and also a religious center. The city developed along with the university, which dates from the 12th century. During the English Civil War (1642–52) Oxford became the headquarters of the Royalist (king's) forces. The king retreated there, after several defeats (see CIVIL WAR, ENGLISH). The city also became an important coach, canal, and rail center. For many centuries the town depended economically upon the university, but now the city has a range of industries, including motor-vehicle manufacturing, publishing, and small-boat building. In addition there is a wide variety of educational facilities, such as language schools, as well as business and conference facilities. The population of Oxford is about 127,700.

Oxford University

Schools may have existed in Oxford from the early 12th century, but the university was not properly established until the end of that century. Many English students were barred from the University of Paris in 1167 and this may have prompted the establishment of a rival university at Oxford, which, indeed, was modeled on that at Paris.

Oxford University has over 36 colleges. University College, the oldest, was founded in 1249. The next to be founded were Balliol (1263) and Merton (1264). The colleges originally took male students only. In the 19th century five colleges were founded for women. Now most colleges take both men and women as students.

Scholarships are offered to students from all over the world. Rhodes scholarships are awarded to students from the United States and the Commonwealth countries (see RHODES, CECIL). Oxford has produced many scholars of great distinction. Robert Boyle the scientist, John Wesley the religious leader, Percy Bysshe Shelley the poet, and Christopher Wren the architect, among others, all studied there.

Among the historic buildings are the Bodleian Library, with over 7 million books and manuscripts; Merton College library, the oldest in England; and Christ Church, the college begun by Cardinal Wolsey in 1525, with its cathedral and clock tower housing the bell, Great Tom. Many of the colleges have beautiful gardens, and in the grounds of New College (founded 1379) are parts of the ancient city wall.

OXFORDSHIRE is a county in England, bordered on the north by Warwickshire and Northamptonshire, on the east by Buckinghamshire, on the south by Berkshire, and on the west by Gloucestershire. The River Thames, known as the Isis when it passes through the county town of Oxford, forms the boundary with Berkshire. The Evenlode, Windrush, Cherwell, and Thame are smaller rivers. The county has an area of 2,608 square kilometers (1,007 square miles) and a population of 555,700 (1984).

Oxfordshire includes three distinct regions. On the northwest are the Cotswold Hills, where many buildings are made of limestone quarried in the area. In the southeast, on the boundary with Buckinghamshire, are the chalk hills of the Chilterns, which rise to a height of more than 250 meters (820 feet) at

ZEFA

The central plain of Oxfordshire has many large arable and livestock farms. This is the Windrush valley.

Shirburn. Beechwoods grow on their slopes. The Chilterns are divided from the Berkshire Hills by the Thames as it flows to the sea. The basins of the Thames and Cherwell form the central plain of the county.

Towns and Industries

The chief city of Oxfordshire is Oxford itself, known for its university, its beautiful buildings, and its car industry centered on the suburb of Cowley. (See also OXFORD.) Banbury, on the Cherwell, was made famous by the nursery rhyme "Ride a cock-horse to Banbury Cross". (See also NURSERY RHYME.) The cross in the town center is not the one of the nursery rhyme, that was destroyed by the Puritans in 1601. Banbury is also famous for its cakes, which have been baked there for about 350 years. Henley-on-Thames in the Chiltern region is known for the regatta, or rowing contest, that is held on the river each July. Thame, which stands on the River Thame, is a market town with a 16th-century school.

Cars are made in Oxford, but the county is mostly agricultural, although there are a few other industries. Two of the oldest are stone-quarrying carried out near the Gloucestershire border, and paper-making near Oxford. Witney, on the banks of the Windrush, has been a blanket-making center since the 14th century.

Iron ore was discovered in north Oxfordshire in the 1850s and mined in the Hook Norton, Adderbury, and Wroxton areas. It was found near the surface, making it possible for the top soil to be replaced and the land to be cultivated after the iron ore had been extracted and sent to the steel mills of Wales to be melted down.

Two cement factories were also set up in Oxfordshire, one at Shipton on Cherwell, north of Oxford, and one at Chinnor, southeast of Thame. Car accessories are made at Witney and aluminum at Banbury. Abingdon, long famous for carpets and clothing, is now also linked to the car industry. Oxfordshire also has several nuclear research sites.

In the Chiltern Hills there is woodworking, while boat-building and marine engineering take place beside the Thames at Henley. Malting and brewing of beer are other notable industries of the county.

Elsewhere in Oxfordshire the land is farmed. Oxford Down sheep are still kept in the Cotswolds, and in the Chiltern region large arable farms spread across the downlands. On the hills, small farms are found. The White Horse Vale is noted for fruit.

History

A reminder of prehistoric times in Oxfordshire is the stone circle near Chipping Norton known as the Rollright Stones. Another ancient landmark is the ancient White Horse, carved on a hill above Uffington some 2,000 years ago. It is 114 meters (374 feet) long, and cut out of the land by removing the turf to reveal the white, chalky soil beneath.

The Romans made only two important settlements in Oxfordshire, one at Alchester, near Bicester, and the other at Dorchester, on the Thame. In Saxon times, Dorchester, now a quiet village, became a cathedral city. The abbey still remains and has a remarkable window (called a Jesse window) with pictures showing the ancestors of Christ from Jesse, the father of King David. After the Norman Conquest in the 11th century, Burford in the Cotswolds became an important center, with its own market and guild, or band of craftsmen. Woodstock was used as a hunting center by many kings of England.

At the time of the Civil War between Charles I and Oliver Cromwell, most of Oxfordshire supported the King, who made his headquarters at Oxford.

The most splendid building in Oxfordshire is Blenheim Palace at Woodstock. It was built by the great architect John Vanbrugh for John Churchill, first Duke of Marlborough, after he had won the Battle of Blenheim. The gardens were designed by "Capability" Brown, who planted the trees in the battle formation of the victorious troops. Sir Winston Churchill, a descendant of the Duke, was born in the palace in 1874.

The peace and beauty of the Oxfordshire

Robert Harding Picture Library

Blenheim Palace at Woodstock was built in 1705. Winston Churchill was born in the palace in 1874.

countryside has attracted many writers. The poet and craftsman William Morris lived for a time in the manor house at Kelmscott and is buried in the church there.

OXYGEN is a gas without color, taste or smell. It is the commonest of all elements, forming one-fifth of the air. When combined with other substances such as calcium and silicon, oxygen makes up nearly half the Earth's crust. When a person breathes, the oxygen from the air drawn into the lungs is carried by the red blood corpuscles in a constant stream to the body cells, where it combines with the food to release the energy needed to keep the body going.

Human beings cannot live without oxygen for more than a few minutes. Mountaineers sometimes carry a supply of pure oxygen for use at great heights where the thin air contains little natural oxygen. Sometimes a sick person is put in an oxygen tent to ease his breathing, but pure oxygen by itself is poisonous if breathed for any length of time. Water contains oxygen, and fishes breathe by taking in water through their gills and extracting the oxygen dissolved in it. Divers carry their own oxygen cylinders when working underwater, and oxygen must also be carried aboard high-altitude aircraft and spacecraft. (See also SPACE FLIGHT.)

Oxygen is necessary for combustion, or burning. Any substance that burns in air will burn even better in oxygen. A burning wax taper flares brightly in a jar of oxygen and causes a glowing splinter of wood to burst into flame.

Oxygen was discovered independently by the Swedish chemist Karl Scheele (1742–86) in 1772 and by the English scientist Joseph Priestley in 1774, although Priestley was the first to announce the discovery. (See PRIESTLEY, JOSEPH.) The French chemist Antoine Lavoisier burned substances such as carbon and sulfur in the new gas, and found that the resulting ash or gas gave an acid when shaken up with water. In 1777 he named the gas oxygen, from Greek words meaning "acid making", because he believed, wrongly, that oxygen was present in all acids. It was Lavoisier who showed that combustion is simply the chemical combination of the burning substance with oxygen. (See LAVOISIER, ANTOINE.)

Oxygen combines with nearly all other elements to form the substances known as *oxides*, and is present in many complex substances. Some substances when heated give off oxygen, examples being potassium chlorate, present in match-heads and fireworks; potassium nitrate (saltpeter), used in gunpowder; and potassium permanganate, used as a disinfectant when dissolved in water.

The combination of another element with oxygen is called *oxidation*. When hydrogen burns it is oxidized to form hydrogen oxide, which is water. Carbon oxidizes to form carbon dioxide, and so on. Burning in a flame is really a very rapid oxidation. Gasoline vapor burns very fast in the cylinders of a motor vehicle engine to give carbon dioxide and water, together with much heat. The reverse of oxidation occurs when oxygen is removed from a substance, and this process is called *reduction*. Important examples of reduction occur when metals such as iron or zinc are obtained from the ores (rocks and earth) containing them.

When an electric current is passed through water, bubbles of oxygen and of hydrogen are given off, as explained in the article ELECTROLYSIS. This method is used for producing oxygen in countries where plentiful water power makes electricity very cheap. However, oxygen is usually obtained from the air by the method described in the article AIR. The oxygen used in industry is supplied either in the liquid state or as gas compressed inside cylindrical steel bottles.

Oxygen in Industry

By far the biggest use of oxygen is made in the steel industry (see IRON AND STEEL). Extremely hot flames are produced by burning fuels in oxygen. The flame of an oxyacetylene burner may be up to 3,000°C (5,400°F). An oxyacetylene flame will heat, cut, or weld such metals as steel, aluminum, and cast iron (see ACETY-

LENE). An oxyhydrogen flame, using oxygen and hydrogen mixed, burns at about 2,400°C (4,300°F) and is used for cutting steel under water when clearing away sunken wrecks or salvaging ships (see SALVAGE, MARINE).

A powerful high explosive can be made by soaking porous charcoal, or some other substance easily oxidized, in liquid oxygen. This has the advantage that the explosive becomes dead if not fired, because the oxygen evaporates. Oxygen is also used in the oxidation of ammonia to nitric acid and the manufacture of many organic chemicals.

Ozone

Ozone is a form of oxygen in which each molecule (see MOLECULE) contains three atoms instead of the normal two. It is formed when electricity passes through air. It has a strong seaweed smell. The word ozone comes from the Greek verb *ozein*, meaning "to stink". Ozone is used for purifying water, as it kills harmful germs and leaves no taste. Air mixed with ozone is sometimes used to provide a refreshing and germ-free atmosphere in theaters, auditoriums, and public buildings. Ozone is a powerful oxidant and in the pure state it attacks substances such as rubber and cork.

The Earth's upper atmosphere contains a layer of ozone, which filters out harmful ultraviolet rays from the Sun before they can reach the Earth's surface. Ozone is destroyed by chemicals used industrially known as Chlorofluorocarbons (CFCs). Quantities have entered the atmosphere and caused a thinning of the ozone layer (see AEROSOL; ATMOSPHERE).

OYSTER. The oyster is a mollusk (see MOLLUSK) which spends its life lying on the bottom of the sea. It has two shells, very different in shape. The lower shell is saucer-shaped and very thick, and the upper shell is thinner and nearly flat. When the oyster gapes, or opens, the lighter shell is lifted. The shells are hinged together by a strong muscle, and it is extremely difficult to open an oyster.

The soft body of an oyster is in parts that are arranged rather like the pages of a book. Lining each shell is a flap of flesh known as the

Oysters live in shallow coastal water.

mantle. Within the mantle are several thin, flattened gills which draw in water and the tiny plants and animals on which the oyster feeds. At the center of the gills is the foot, but once the oyster has found a suitable place in which to live the foot pours out a cement-like substance which anchors the lower shell firmly to the seabed. Oysters are eaten in all parts of the world, and are specially bred for food in oyster beds.

They have many enemies besides human beings. Octopuses prey on them and starfishes tear their shells open and absorb the soft body. There is also a sea snail called the oyster drill that bores a hole through the oyster's shell, and sucks out the living animal. To make up for this, oysters lay many millions of eggs. Oysters are said to be "white-sick" when they have young inside. As the young oysters develop they become a darker color and the parent oyster is then said to be "black-sick". When ready, the parent oyster opens the shell and blows out the spat, as the young are now called. They are then swimming larvae, with the valves of the shell already formed, which swim freely for 2 to 3 weeks before settling.

There are very many species of oyster, several of which are harvested commercially. They include the American oyster (*Crassostrea virginica*), the Australian Sydney rock oyster (*Crassostrea commercialis*), and the European oyster (*Ostrea edulis*).

Oysters are eaten raw, cooked, canned, and frozen. They have been eaten by people for many centuries as shown by the shell deposits found in kitchen rubbish heaps in coastal regions. For example, some shells of Australian oysters show them to have been eaten by aboriginal peoples as many as 6,000 years ago.

Pearls are formed by oysters by the accumulation of nacre, the material that lines the shell. The best natural pearls come from some Oriental species (see PEARLS AND PEARL FISHING).

OYSTERCATCHER. There are several species of oystercatcher (*Haematopus*), wading birds that can often be seen on the seashore running over the stones or flying across the waves. The European oystercatcher (*Haematopus ostralegus*) can be recognized by its smart black and white plumage and its long red beak and legs. The head and back are black and the under parts, including most of the tail, are white. There is a broad white band on each black wing. The bird flies rapidly with a regular beat of the wings.

The oystercatcher has a loud piping call which it utters as it flies. It is an excitable bird, easily disturbed, and lives in flocks in autumn and winter. It is found on both rocky and sandy coasts and on mud flats.

As its name shows, the bird can open oysters, but it usually eats limpets, mussels and cockles (which it opens with its bill), and small

Gunter Zeisler/Bruce Coleman

The oystercatcher has black and white plumage and a red eye and beak. Here a female nests in a hollow.

crabs. It often goes inland in the breeding season, and sometimes follows the plow, picking up worms and insects from the soil. Another name for the oystercatcher is the mussel picker.

The female oystercatcher lays her eggs in a shallow hollow in the ground without any lining or simply with a few small stones or bits of shell. Sometimes this hollow is on the seashore, sometimes it is on the side of a river where there are banks of shingle, or small pebbles, and sometimes it is in a plowed field. There are usually three eggs, buff with brown blotches in color. The downy young can run about at once.

Oystercatchers are found throughout Europe as well as in Asia, Australia, New Zealand, and North and South America. The black oystercatcher (*Haematopus bachmani*) of western North America and the sooty oystercatcher (*Haematopus fuliginosus*) of Australia are dark except for their red bills and pink legs.

P

PACIFIC ISLANDS. The Pacific is the largest of the oceans, with an area greater than that of all the world's lands put together. Its northern and western borders are fringed with chains of islands, the *outer Pacific islands*. In the western chain are the large islands of Japan, Taiwan (Formosa), and the Philippines, and also some of the islands of Indonesia, which are described in separate articles. To the east, the Pacific is bounded by the coasts of North and South America and, to the southwest, by Australia. To the southeast there is no large land area other than the continent of Antarctica and the lower portion of South America.

Between these fringing chains and continents the ocean stretches over one-third of the Earth's surface. There are many thousands of islands and vast expanses of empty sea. Some of these islands are high and volcanic, and may be quite big. Others are low coral rings called atolls (see ATOLL), and still others are mere specks in the ocean. Together they make up the *inner Pacific islands*.

Outer Pacific Islands

The Aleutians. The southwest peninsula of Alaska continues in a chain of volcanic islands stretching westwards for about 1,900 kilometers (1,200 miles). As far as Attu Island these belong to the United States, but the Komandorskije Islands, at the western end, are Russian. This chain divides the Pacific from the Bering Sea.

The Aleutian Islands are rainy, foggy, and cool, with hardly any trees but plenty of grasses and plants. The Aleuts, who are a people related to the Eskimos (see ESKIMO), live chiefly by hunting seals and birds and by fishing, although some breed blue foxes for their fur. The chief island is Unalaska and the main air and sea port is Dutch Harbor.

The Kurils. The islands which stretch in a chain between the Kamchatka Peninsula in Siberia and Japan are called the Kurils (in Russian, Kurilskije). In all there are 56 of them with a total area of 15,600 square kilometers (6,000 square miles). They are volcanic islands mostly covered with dense forests and fern and surrounded by seas which are thickly tangled with seaweed and rich in fish. Among the people in the Kurils are a few Ainus, who were the people living in northern Japan before the present inhabitants came across from China. The islands were Japanese from 1875 until the end of World War II, when they were handed over to the USSR.

Ryukyus. From the south of Japan to Taiwan stretch the Ryukyus, forming a chain of 73 fertile islands and having a warm climate. Although there are few wild animals, the Ryukyus have many poisonous snakes. The people, who are rather like the Japanese, grow vegetables, rice, sweet potatoes, and tobacco. Sugar-cane and pineapples are exported. Fishing is also important. Most of the people live on Okinawa. The capital and largest city is Naha City.

For many years the Ryukyus were claimed by both China and Japan, but towards the end of the 19th century the Japanese took control. One of the fiercest battles of World War II was fought when United States troops invaded Okinawa in 1945. After the war, the Ryukyus were occupied by the United States, but in 1972 the last of the islands were returned to Japan.

The Inner Pacific Islands

The thousands of islands of the inner Pacific are divided into three main groups. Their names come from Greek words meaning black, small, and many. The groups are: Melanesia ("black islands"), Micronesia ("small islands"), and Polynesia ("many islands"). Outside these main groups there are a number of other islands such as Pitcairn; Norfolk Island; the Galapagos Islands, near Ecuador; Easter Island; and the Bonin Islands and Volcano Islands, both belonging to Japan and known as Ogasawara-gunto. These other islands are described in the last section of this article.

Further west are Taiwan, the Philippines, Borneo, and New Guinea. New Guinea is one of the largest islands in the world. It is larger than either Texas or France and the United Kingdom put together, and at least four times as large as all the inner Pacific islands combined. (See PAPUA-NEW GUINEA.)

Melanesia

The Melanesian group of islands lies in the western Pacific, south of the equator. It includes high, mountainous islands which were formed by volcanic action, and also low coral atolls. The largest island is *New Britain*, which is about 36,500 square kilometers (14,100 square miles) in area. It lies in the Bismarck Archipelago (an archipelago is a chain of islands). New Britain is mountainous, with a damp tropical climate and very fertile soil. The people grow coconuts, cocoa, and other crops, and there is a good harbor at

Hutchison Library

Solomon Islanders are mainly Melanesians with a sprinkling of Polynesians (about 4 per cent).

Rabaul. New Britain is part of Papua-New Guinea.

Southeast of the Bismarck Archipelago are the *Solomon Islands*. Further to the southeast are the islands of *Vanuatu*, formerly the New Hebrides and under joint French and British rule. (See VANUATU; SOLOMON ISLANDS.) To the east of the Vanuatu is *Fiji*, where there are more people of Indian descent than native Fijians. Fiji produces sugar, coconuts, fruit, and gold. (See FIJI.)

South of Vanuatu are the islands of *New Caledonia* and the *Loyalty Islands*, both of which are French. New Caledonia is mountainous. The island is not only fertile, growing coconuts, coffee, cotton, and many other crops, but also rich in minerals. The most important metals mined are nickel and chromium. New Caledonia has good roads and a railroad. Its capital and chief port, Noumea, has a fine

harbor. The Loyalty group to the east consists of three large and several small coral islands. Many of its inhabitants spend part of their lives working in New Caledonia.

The Melanesian people are an ancient southeast Asian group, who appear to be related closely to the Australian Aborigines. They have very dark skin and curly hair.

There are perhaps 500,000 Melanesian languages, but little is known about them. Fijian is the most important of these languages, but "pidgin" or "sandalwood" English, a mixture of English and local words, is widely spoken.

Micronesia

The small islands of Micronesia lie north of Melanesia. They include Guam and the groups known as the Mariana Islands, Caroline Islands, and Marshall Islands. Other groups in Micronesia are the Gilbert Islands, the Phoenix Islands, and the Line Islands, which now form the republic of Kiribati. The Micronesians seem to be a separate racial group, but they may be a mixture of Malay and Polynesian peoples.

The *Mariana Islands* lie in the north along the Mariana Ridge, which runs north from Guam to the Tropic of Cancer.

Guam, the southernmost of the Marianas, is a fertile and hilly island, discovered in 1521 by the Portuguese explorer Ferdinand Magellan. It was Spanish from the end of the 17th century until 1898, when it was handed over to the United States. It is thickly populated, most of the people being Chamorros, who are a mixture of Micronesian, Filipino (from the Philippines), and Spaniard. The other islands in the Marianas include some in the north that are still active volcanoes. There are deposits of phosphate rock, from which fertilizer is made, in Saipan, Rota, and Tinian.

South of the Marianas are the *Caroline Islands*, of which those in the west are coral atolls and include the Belau (Palau) group. The island of Yap has a fine harbor and contains deposits of bauxite, the mineral from which aluminum is made. Further east is Chuuk (Truk), the remains of a huge volcano almost surrounded by a coral reef. Pohnpei (Ponape), still further east, is another volcanic island. Bauxite and iron are found there, and there are ruins of ancient stone walls and tombs. Similar ruins exist on Yap and Kosrae and in the Belau group.

The *Marshall Islands* lie east of the Carolines. They are atolls, each consisting of an island or ring-like group of islets on a coral reef. A reef is built up around a submerged mountain peak, and the stretch of water it encloses is called a lagoon. Kwajalein and Majuro are the chief atolls in the Marshall Islands, and the lagoon at Kwajalein is the largest in the world.

In World War I, the Japanese took possession of the Marianas, Caroline, and Marshall Islands, which had formerly been German. They were later ruled by the United States on behalf of the United Nations as the Trust Territory of the Pacific Islands (TTPI). Nuclear weapons were tested on the Marshall Islands, and the inhabitants of Bikini and Eniwetok atolls had to be moved to other islands. The Marshalls later became internally self-governing, as did the Carolines (as the Federated States of Micronesia) and Palau (as Belau). The Marshall Islands and the Federated States of Micronesia became fully independent in 1991. The northern Marianas remain in close association with the United States.

South of the Marshalls are the Gilbert Islands, which are part of *Kiribati* (see KIRIBATI), and the Ellice Islands, which now form *Tuvalu* (see TUVALU). The Gilbert and Ellice Islands were ruled by the United Kingdom until 1978/79. Kiribati also includes Banaba (Ocean Island), which is composed largely of phosphates and where intensive mining has made it necessary to evacuate the population. The *Phoenix Islands*, eight atolls of which the chief are Hull, Gardner, Canton, and Enderbury islands, lie at the center of Kiribati. The tiny independent republic of *Nauru*, to the west (see NAURU) is also a "phosphate" island.

The *Line Islands* are so called because they are near the equator, which sailors sometimes call "the line". Those in the northern group include Kingman Reef, Jarvis Island, a small coral islet; Kiritimati (Christmas Island), which was discovered by Captain James Cook on Christmas Day, 1777, and Fanning, Washington, and Palmyra islands. Palmyra, Jarvis, and Kingman Reef belong to the United States but the others lie within Kiribati. The southern Line Islands, which are also in Kiribati, include Caroline, Flint, Vostok, Starbuck, and Malden. Most of the Line Islands once had rich guano or phosphate deposits, but these have been mostly used up. Some now have large coconut plantations.

Before civilization reached them, the people of Micronesia depended very heavily on the coconut, every part of which they used. The coconut is still very important, not only for food but for the making of copra (the dried flesh of the coconut). The copra is exported to other countries, where the oil is extracted and used in the manufacture of soap, margarine, and other products. The Micronesians were bold and skillful mariners and had graceful and speedy outrigger sailing canoes, whose design is copied in the present-day catamaran.

Polynesia

Most of Polynesia is within a triangle drawn between Hawaii in the north, New Zealand in the south and Easter Island in the east. Some of the Polynesian islands are among the most beautiful in the world. The Hawaiian Islands are part of the United States, and their capital Honolulu is the largest city in the Pacific Islands (see HAWAII; HONOLULU).

In the center of Polynesia lies *French Polynesia*. It includes the Society Islands, so called by Captain James Cook because he was sent there by the Royal Society in 1769 to make astronomical observations. Tahiti is the most important of the Society Islands. It is a fertile land of great beauty, with many lovely streams flowing from the central mountains, of which Orohena 2,236 meters (7,334 feet) is the highest. Besides many Frenchmen, numbers of Americans and Europeans settled there to enjoy the beautiful and friendly atmosphere of the islands. The great French artist Paul Gauguin (1848–1903) painted some of his best pictures in Tahiti (see GAUGUIN, PAUL). Papeete is the capital and port of Tahiti, west of which is the even lovelier island of Moorea, whose jagged peaks give it a skyline of almost unearthly beauty. About 240 kilometers (150 miles) to the northwest are Huahine, Raiatea, Tahaa, and Borabora, which are beautiful volcanic islands surrounded by coral reefs. Makatea, about 210 kilometers (130 miles) northeast of Tahiti, is the only phosphate island in the Society group.

ZEFA

The dramatic mountains and lush vegetation of Bora Bora are typical of many islands of the Pacific.

To the north and east of the Society Islands is the Tuamotu Archipelago, a wide group of low atolls and bare reefs which are dangerous to ships because they are difficult to see. Tuamotu is also in French Polynesia. The people collect coconuts and dive in the lagoons for oysters, which are valuable for their shells ("mother of pearl") and for the pearls sometimes found in them. It was at Raroia in the Tuamotus that the Norwegian scientist Thor Heyerdahl and his companions landed from the raft *Kon-Tiki* in 1947, having sailed from Peru. They were seeking to prove that the early inhabitants of South America, who were known to have had rafts of that kind, could have sailed into the Pacific and settled in the

islands. (It is now known, however, that the original inhabitants came from Southeast Asia). Southeast of the Tuamotus is the Mangareva group of four inhabited islands surrounded by a coral reef. Southwest of the Tuamotus are the Austral Islands, most of which are well-wooded, and the island of Rapa, which is mountainous and dotted with ancient stone forts built in the days when there were frequent tribal wars.

Another group in French Polynesia are the Marquesas, lying to the north of the Tuamotus. The Marquesas, of which Nuku Hiva and Hiva Oa are the largest, are rugged and mountainous. During the 19th century, diseases, strong drink, and opium brought by Europeans did much to reduce the numbers of the original inhabitants.

Samoa, to the west of French Polynesia, includes the islands of Savai'i and Upolu, independent since 1962 as Western Samoa (see WESTERN SAMOA), and an eastern group of small islands belonging to the United States and known as American Samoa. South of Samoa is *Tonga*, which consists of the three groups of Vavau, Ha'apai, and Tongatapu. (See TONGA.)

The *Cook Islands* lie between Tonga and the Society Islands and are a self-governing state in association with New Zealand. The chief of them is Rarotonga, a quite large and mountainous island which was not generally known to the western world until 1823. The Rarotongans are closely related to the Maoris of New Zealand. Their fertile island has a delightful climate and is noted for its oranges and tomatoes.

The northern Cook Islands are mostly lonely atolls. They include Penrhyn; Rakahanga; Manihiki; and Suwarrow, which is a bird sanctuary; Palmerston, where the part-Polynesian descendants of an early British settler speak an old-fashioned English; and the Danger Islands, chief of which is Pukapuka.

Niue, which lies between Tonga and the Cook Islands, is a self-governing state in association with New Zealand. It is a raised coral atoll about 60 meters (195 feet) high with a central tableland that once formed the floor of a lagoon.

Coconuts and bananas are grown, but the soil is poor and the people have to work hard.

Near Samoa are several other Polynesian islands. Due north are the four small atolls of the Tokelau group. One of these, Swain's Island, was settled many years ago by Polynesians, but, when discovered by Europeans, it was deserted. About 100 years ago it was taken over by white men with a number of Polynesian women and laborers. Some of the present inhabitants are descended from one of those early colonists, an American named Eli Jennings. Swain's Island is governed as part of American Samoa, but the other Tokelau Islands, Atafu, Fakaofu, and Nukunono, belong to New Zealand. These three islands are inhabited by Polynesians whose ancestors are believed to have gone there many years ago from Samoa. The Tokelau Islands, like the northern Cooks and Fiji, lie in a region where tropical hurricanes occasionally develop and cause great destruction and loss of life.

To the west of Samoa is the French-governed territory of Wallis and Futuna. There are three principal islands: Uvea (Wallis Island), Futuna, and Alofi. Still further west is the fertile volcanic island of Rotuma. Although inhabited by Polynesians, Rotuma is part of Fiji.

There are also several islands outside the Polynesian area where the inhabitants are people of the Polynesian type. These include Tikopia, Ontong Java, Rennell, and a number of other islands in the Solomon and Santa Cruz groups (in Melanesia). It is interesting, too, that the Lau Islands, between Tonga and the main Fijian group, are populated by a mixed Polynesian and Melanesian people. This kind of information on the scattering and mingling of Pacific races is very important, for it reveals some of the facts about the movements of the people before the islands were discovered by Europeans. In many parts of the world such early history would be recorded in manuscripts or on stones, but very few of the Pacific islanders had a written language. Therefore, one must examine the appearance of the people, together with their spoken languages, their folk-myths and their customs, in order to learn more about their past.

Other Pacific Islands

There is a separate article on *Pitcairn Island*, whose people are partly descended from the mutineers of HMS *Bounty* (see BOUNTY, MUTINY OF THE). *Easter Island*, or Rapanui, in the southeast of the ocean, is scattered with great stone statues of long-eared, stern-faced men. (See EASTER ISLAND.)

On the equator off the South American coast are the *Galapagos Islands*, which have some animals found nowhere else. They gave Charles Darwin valuable evidence to support his theory of evolution (see DARWIN, CHARLES). Their most famous animals are the giant tortoises, some of which are about 400 years old, and the remarkable marine iguanas (giant lizards). *Juan Fernandez* off the Chilean coast is a group of islands where the Scottish sailor, Alexander Selkirk, spent more than four years when put ashore after a quarrel with his captain in 1704. He told his adventures to Daniel Defoe, who used them in his book *Robinson Crusoe*.

Norfolk Island, about 1,450 kilometers (900 miles) northeast of Sydney, Australia, is a fertile volcanic island where much fruit is grown. It is also known for a special kind of pine tree rather like a monkey-puzzle tree. The island belongs to Australia. The Volcano and Bonin Islands (Ogasawara-gunto) near Japan grow sugar-cane and fruit. They were returned to Japan by the United States in 1968.

PACIFIC OCEAN. The Pacific Ocean is the largest and deepest of the world's oceans. It has an area of 165 million square kilometers (64 million square miles), twice that of the Atlantic Ocean and greater than the total of all land surfaces in the world. The Pacific and its adjacent seas cover more than one-third of the surface of the Earth. At its greatest width, from Panama to Mindanao, the Pacific measures 17,220 kilometers (10,700 miles), almost half the distance around the Earth. It extends from the Bering Straits on the Arctic circle, to Cape Adare, Antarctica, a distance of 15,450 kilometers (9,600 miles).

Among the larger seas bordering the Pacific are: Bering Sea, Sea of Okhotsk, Sea of Japan, Yellow Sea, East China Sea, South China Sea, Coral Sea, Tasman Sea, and the Gulf of California. Many other small seas separate the islands of Indonesia and the Philippines.

The chief rivers draining into the Pacific or its adjoining seas are the Changjiang (Yangtze), the Amur, the Huanghe, the Mekong, the Yukon, the Colorado, and the Columbia.

Commercial fishing is important chiefly in the North Pacific where salmon, halibut, mackerel, and sardines are caught. From Oregon south to the waters off Central America tuna is the chief commercial fish. In the tropical waters of the Pacific are shellfish, crabs, shrimps, clams, oysters, and prawns.

Winds and Currents

The surface conditions of the ocean change with latitude. A belt near the Equator has very little wind. It is called the doldrums, or equatorial calms. North and south of the doldrums is the trade wind belt. Although the trade winds are usually warm and gentle, violent storms called typhoons begin in this belt. (In the Atlantic these winds are known as hurricanes.) Beginning about latitude 40 degrees north and south of the equator is the belt of westerly winds. This belt often has storms and high seas followed by fair weather. The surface of the Pacific is not often calm in the higher latitudes. (See also WIND.)

Within the ocean are great circular water movements called currents or drifts. Currents are close to the surface and flow at a speed of 3 to 6 kilometers (2–4 miles) per hour. They affect the temperature of the air above them and thus the climate of nearby land.

The currents move in a clockwise direction in the North Pacific. In the South Pacific they move counterclockwise. Warm currents flowing away from the Equator are cooled as they meet Arctic currents. Thus, the currents returning to the Equator are generally cold.

Islands and Ocean Floor

Thousands of islands are scattered in the Pacific Ocean. It is thought that the islands near the continental shores, such as the Japanese islands, the Philippines, the Marianas, New Guinea, the Solomons, New Hebrides, most of the Fiji Islands, and New Zealand, may once have been part of the Asian and Australian continents. For this reason, most of the islands of the western Pacific are called *Continental Islands*.

The islands of the central Pacific are known as *Oceanic Islands*, for they are of volcanic or coral origin. They are the tops of undersea mountains, which rise from the ocean floor. Among the many oceanic islands are the Hawaiian Islands, the Marshalls, the Carolines, the Cook Islands, the Tuamotus, and the Marquesas Islands. Some of them rise from depths of almost 5,500 meters (18,000 feet). Coral islands are formed from the skeletons of tiny sea animals called coral polyps. The coral builds up on the slopes of undersea mountains. (See ATOLL; GREAT BARRIER REEF; CORAL REEF.) The floor of the eastern Pacific is fairly level at a depth of nearly 5,500 meters (18,000 feet). For this reason there are very few islands in the eastern Pacific. The western Pacific is heavily dissected by a complicated pattern of ridges and trenches. The ridges in this region support most of the Pacific's oceanic islands. The trenches, with depths greater than 7,500 meters (24,500 feet) are the lowest parts of the Earth's surface. In one of them, the Marianas Trench, a depth of 11,034 meters (36,200 feet) has been measured near the island of Guam. One surprising fact about the ocean is that four-fifths of the world's active volcanoes are in the Pacific or in the lands bordering it. These areas of volcanic activity are also the regions where earthquakes are commonest.

The Pacific was the last of the world's oceans to be known to Europeans. In 1513 the Spanish explorer Balboa crossed the Isthmus of Panama and sighted the "Great South Sea", as it was called then (see BALBOA, VASCO NUNEZ DE). This discovery led to Ferdinand Magellan's famous voyage across the Pacific in

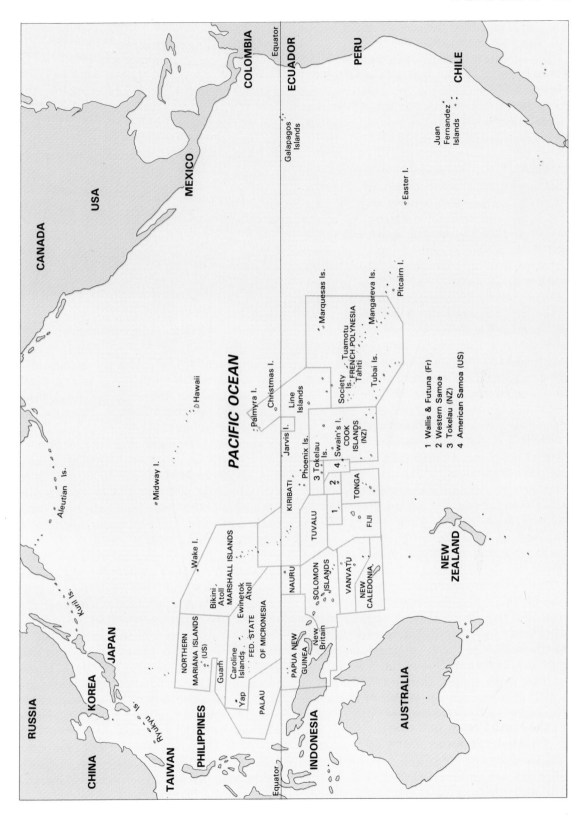

1520–21. He named the ocean Pacific "peaceful". (See MAGELLAN, FERDINAND).

The greatest Pacific explorer was an Englishman, Captain James Cook. Cook led three Pacific expeditions between 1768 and 1779. By the time of his death in 1779, most of the Pacific's islands were correctly mapped. (See COOK, JAMES.)

PAGEANT. In the Middle Ages a pageant was a part or a scene of a play. Plays in those days were often performed in the market square, in front of a church, or in the street, and each scene was acted by a different group of players with their own platform or stage, mounted on wheels. The platform itself was also sometimes called a pageant. It was pulled from one place to another and whenever it stopped the scene was acted. If you had been standing in a street in the city of Chester in England several centuries ago you might have seen a whole series of scenes or pageants acted before you, all of them based on stories from the Bible or about the lives of saints. Plays of this kind are described in the article MYSTERY PLAY.

These pageants were performed only on special occasions. At first they took place on religious festival-days, but they became so popular that eventually they were included in other celebrations, too. At the coronation of Anne Boleyn, wife of King Henry VIII of England, in 1533, for instance, there was a great procession of all kinds of scenes in honor of the occasion.

In this way a pageant came to mean a procession of scenes that were interesting or beautiful to look at. There are many of this kind today, in which the actors do not usually have any lines to speak but are there to form part of the picture. One of the most famous of these processions is the Lord Mayor's show which goes through the streets of London in November each year, when the Lord Mayor of London takes office.

Nowadays, however, the word "pageant" has another meaning as well, and this is probably the one most people think of first. A pageant is now a special kind of dramatic

Picturepoint

A modern pageant: a colorful procession as London's Lord Mayor rides through the City in his coach.

entertainment which shows the history of a town or district in a number of scenes. Most old towns in Great Britain have some exciting happenings in their history. Perhaps the ancient Britons fought the Romans near by, or invaders from Denmark attacked the town, or Queen Elizabeth I was entertained by the citizens. With crowds of people in costumes appropriate to the scene, with horses and coaches, banners and pennants, and with music and words, history comes to life in a vivid and exciting way.

In Siena, Italy, the annual *palio* is a horse race and a festival which in many ways is like a pageant. Similarly, the Spanish bullfights combine pageant, sporting event, and parade. An attractive modern variation of the pageant idea, first introduced in France in 1952, is called *son et lumière* (French for *sound and light*), and is most effective after dark. Multi-colored lights are shone on to a historic building, such as a cathedral or castle, and as music is played, a dramatized narrative of its history is broadcast to the audience.

The article PASSION PLAY describes one of the most famous European religious pageants, which takes place every ten years at Oberammergau in Germany.

PAINE, Thomas (1737–1809). Thomas Paine was an English-American political writer and activist, whose pamphlets *Common Sense* and *The Rights of Man* influenced both the American Revolution and the French Revolution, respectively. He was born at Thetford in Norfolk, the son of a Quaker corset-maker. After a rather unhappy life in England including some years as a customs officer, he went to America at the age of 37. At that time the country we now know as the United States consisted of colonies belonging to Britain, and the colonists wanted to become independent (see AMERICAN REVOLUTION). In 1776 Paine published a pamphlet, or written speech, called *Common Sense*. This urged America to break away from Britain, and George Washington said that it "worked a powerful change in the minds of many men".

For more than ten years Paine remained in America, publishing pamphlets and seeing the success of the colonists' struggle for independence. In 1787 he returned to England after 13 years' absence, and set to work to persuade Britain and France to overthrow their kings and become republics. In 1791 he published a book called *The Rights of Man*, which urged revolution in Britain. He was accused of treason, but he managed to escape to France. There the leaders of the French Revolution, who had driven out their king (see FRENCH REVOLUTION), welcomed him. Paine, however, made himself unpopular by opposing the execution of the king, and he was imprisoned for nearly a year.

Paine also wrote a book called *The Age of Reason*, which was looked on as an attack on religion. He himself once said that his religion was "to do good". Paine died in New York, having spent the last seven years of his life in the United States.

PAINTERS AND PAINTING. There is only one way to know what great painting is and that is to see it and then think about it. This article does not try to *explain* great painting, therefore; but it tells you a little about how painting has grown and changed during its long history and about some famous artists.

This means that the article has had to be arranged in chronological order (the order in which things happened) like a history book. It has been divided into sections, each with its own heading, so that you can find information about any special time you are interested in without reading the whole article. Many painters are mentioned, and some of the most important ones have separate articles to themselves. At the end of each section is a list of the painters mentioned in it on whom there are separate articles.

All through the history of painting artists have tended to group together, and the artists of each group have tended to paint in a similar manner. Such groups are usually described as "schools" of painting. These schools were not necessarily schools where painting was taught but rather gatherings of artists, often in one city or area, to share ideas about painting and often to work under some great painter.

At different periods painting has been done for different purposes and the painters have wanted to express different things; there have also been many different methods of painting. For instance, painting large pictures directly on to the wall, which is not much done today, was the commonest form of painting until quite modern times. Most English churches had pictures painted on their walls, but these were covered up or destroyed after the Reformation (see REFORMATION). There are many different methods of wall-painting, and perhaps as many of painting on canvas or wood or paper. Even from generation to generation and from school to school, there have sometimes been big differences. However, all painting has to be done with paint of some kind, and all paint must have two ingredients. The colour comes from the first, the *pigment*, which was usually a powder made from some kind of earth or stone. It is often called after the place from which it came originally, such as sienna from Siena in Italy. The earth may be used raw or roasted—burnt sienna. The other ingredient in paint is what makes it stick to the brush and flow on to the surface to be painted. It is called the *medium* or *vehicle*, and must be a liquid, such as water, melted wax, egg, or oil. Water is often used for the biggest and the smallest paintings, for wall-paintings (usually called frescoes) and for water-colors on paper. The early Italians mostly used egg for their pictures on wood, and sometimes in their wall-paintings. Oil paint, which is much the commonest today, was not much used before the 15th century.

Ancient Egypt—Art and Religion

We know that some of the very earliest men were painters because some of the paintings they did on the walls of caves can still be seen today (see CAVE ART). In ancient Egypt, centuries later, some painting was connected with religious beliefs. One of the beliefs of the Egyptians was that, as people went on living after death in another world, they would need there the same kinds of things as in their life on Earth. For this reason the Egyptians put a dead person's belongings in his tomb with him, and they painted pictures of similar things on the walls.

Egyptian tomb pictures often form beautiful decoration, but that was not what they were meant for in the first place. They were *diagrams* of real things and people, and therefore everything had to be simply and clearly shown. When nowadays we see a newspaper photograph of several people close together, it is sometimes difficult to tell at first glance which arms and legs belong to which person, especially if the photograph is of some violent action like a moment in a football game. The Egyptian artist made sure there was no doubt about such things. If he wanted to paint one man who was behind another, for instance, he painted him immediately above, where he could be fully seen, and if one of the crowd was a person of great importance—perhaps the pharaoh, or king, himself—he painted him larger to show without any doubt that he was the most important person. The paintings were like diagrams in another way too, for the figures in them look quite flat, like cardboard cut-outs, whereas the people in paintings done in Europe in later ages look rounded and solid, and therefore appear more as they really are.

For thousands of years Egyptian painting remained almost exactly the same because the painters always had to obey the orders of the priests and paint in the traditional way.

Greeks and Romans

The ancient Greeks excelled at art. Wonderful Greek statues and carvings in stone still exist; but hardly anything is known about Greek painting, for none of it has survived except for the special kind which was done as decoration on vases. However, the ancient Greek writers mentioned painters in their books and obviously admired their work. Like the sculptors, the painters seem to have loved to portray beautiful human figures, making them lifelike but always as nearly perfect as they could. Some of the pictures were of gods and goddesses, or illustrations of ancient legends; others were scenes of everyday life. One drawing on marble made about 400 BC shows a group of women playing a game of knucklebones—the modern "jacks". It is signed by Alexander the Athenian, but was probably done in Italy, and is now in the museum at Naples.

The Romans imported Greek artists and copied the art of the Greeks a great deal. Something of Roman wall-paintings is known to us today because of a terrible disaster that happened 1,900 years ago. In AD 79 the volcano Vesuvius erupted and completely buried the nearby town of Pompeii with ash. Underneath this covering of ash the houses of Pompeii were preserved from decay, and when they were at last uncovered, the paintings on the walls of some of the houses were almost as fresh as on the day of the disaster. There were groups of people, events, or stories like that of the voyages of the Greek hero Odysseus (described in the article ODYSSEY), and scenes of land and sea, gardens and vineyards, hunters and fishermen—all painted in clear natural colors. There were also some paintings of the kind known as "still life". These are pictures of a group of objects chosen for their beauty and color, such as fruits and flowers.

Romans liked to have their portraits painted and their books illustrated, as well as their

Courtesy, Trustees of the British Museum

Above: *Fowling in the Marshes,* from the wall of an Egyptian tomb (*c.* 1450 BC). **Top right:** Portrait of a Roman boy painted in wax (2nd century AD). **Below:** 12th-century illuminated manuscript shows Moses preaching to the Hebrews. **Bottom right:** *Christ Discovered in the Temple,* painted on wood by Simone Martini (1342).

Courtesy, The Master and Fellows of Corpus Christi College, Cambridge

Courtesy, the Metropolitan Museum of Art, New York, gift of Edward S. Harkness 1917–78

Courtesy, The Walker Art Gallery, Liverpool

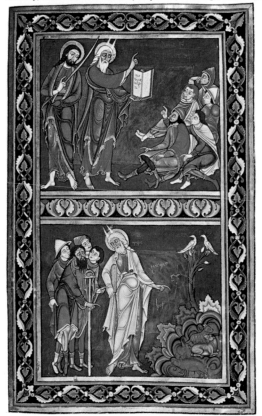

houses decorated, and so painters had many opportunities to practise their art.

Paintings in Byzantium

The ancient city of Byzantium (now Istanbul, in modern Turkey) was in early Christian times the capital of the eastern part of the great empire built up by the Romans. In AD 323 its ruler, the Emperor Constantine, said that all his subjects must accept Christianity as their religion, and artists began to use their skills in the service of the Church. Their task was not an easy one. They wanted to decorate the churches with pictures which would tell the stories of the New Testament to the congregation, many of whom could not read. But the second of the Ten Commandments forbade anyone to make any image or likeness of God. They felt that if they painted Jesus looking like an ordinary man they would be breaking this commandment. The painters therefore painted Jesus and the apostles, saints, and prophets as awe-inspiring and majestic figures, full of dignity and mystery. The walls and ceilings of many churches were covered with great pictures of this kind painted straight on to the plaster. Byzantium was most famous, however, for its mosaics (see MOSAIC). These are not paintings, but are pictures made with thousands of tiny pieces of coloured glass or stone. Gleaming gold and vivid colours make the mosaics more splendid than paintings.

Smaller religious pictures called *icons* were also painted, and in them, too, the figures were solemn and holy rather than human and natural (see ICON). It was considered wrong and even sinful for an artist to paint a picture in any other way and so for hundreds of years icons looked very much the same.

Painting in the Middle Ages

Another type of painting, on a still smaller scale, was the decoration of books. This developed in the monasteries, and from the beginning of the Middle Ages until printing was invented in the 15th century there were monks who devoted themselves to "illuminating" manuscripts in the great monasteries all over Europe. There were famous schools which taught the art of illuminating manuscripts at Winchester and Canterbury in England. In the early Middle Ages this was perhaps the chief form of painting, but as church building developed wall-painting developed with it. A beautiful English example of Norman times has survived in St. Anselm's chapel in Canterbury Cathedral.

By the 13th century the Italian painters had far surpassed all others; and among the Italians Cimabue of Florence stood out above the rest. Great wall-paintings by him with gigantic figures have survived at Assisi in the church built to commemorate St. Francis. There, too, some years later Giotto, who was also a Florentine, painted frescoes which were far more lifelike and natural than Byzantine pictures. Giotto's paintings told the story of St. Francis naturally, with real people showing feelings such as joy and sorrow. They are great, bulky figures, and the paintings give us a feeling of the space and light that they stand or move in. Almost at the same time in Siena, a city south of Florence, a painter named Duccio was painting pictures on panels, which were less powerful but more lovely with graceful lines and rich colours. The one which he painted to go above the altar in Siena Cathedral, with a great Madonna (Virgin Mary) on the front and with small scenes from the life of Christ on the back, seemed so wonderful to the people that the whole town carried the picture in state from Duccio's studio to the cathedral. Another of Siena's artists, Simone Martini, painted a series of frescoes for St. Francis' church at Assisi, in St. Martin's chapel, showing scenes from St. Martin's life. One of his pictures in Siena was important for quite another reason. It showed a famous soldier of the day, Guidoriccio dei Fogliani, riding across a landscape, and it was painted not for a church but for the city's Public Palace.

Duccio, Simone, and others of the Sienese school painted in sympathy with the style of building, and of other arts, called the Gothic style (see ARCHITECTURE), which was becoming fashionable all over Europe. But Giotto's ideas could not be bounded by any style. As Florence became the richest and strongest town in central Italy, it also became the center of new ideas and the finest art.

The 15th and 16th Centuries

These two centuries were the age of a great "awakening" in Europe that is known as the Renaissance (see RENAISSANCE). To make it more convenient to read about the many magnificent artists who lived and worked during these two centuries, this section of the article is divided into smaller parts. Each part deals with the painting styles of a particular country or group of countries, or (in the case of Italy, with which the section begins) of the particular cities of Florence and Venice.

Florence. The new ideas in Florence were introduced by an architect named Brunelleschi, who built the famous dome of the cathedral, and the sculptor Donatello. But soon the new spirit came into painting too in the works of Masaccio. He found out from the mathematicians how to draw buildings in perspective. When things are in perspective it means that solid objects are drawn so that they *look* solid and not flat, and so that their shapes and sizes and the distance between them seem to be exactly as the eye sees them in reality (see DRAWING). Even more important, Masaccio studied light and learned how to show light in painting falling on all his figures as if it came from the nearest window; so that the light bound the whole picture together as well as making it look natural and spacious. Masaccio studied anatomy too (that is, the construction of the body with its skeleton of bones), and therefore he could draw human figures looking as they really are.

One of his immediate followers was Uccello, who was particularly fascinated by the idea of drawing in perspective. His figures, unlike Masaccio's, are portrayed in movement, and he delighted in painting animals. Two pictures by Uccello that are in the National Gallery in London reflect an important change in the idea of a picture. One, a great battle scene, is painted on wood and was part of the fixed decoration of a room. The other, a little picture called *St. George and the Dragon*, is on canvas and is perhaps the first picture to survive which was intended to be framed and hung up as pictures are today.

Fra Angelico was a very different kind of painter. "Fra" means brother, for he was a monk, and he was called Angelico probably from the nature of his paintings, which were in the freshest, most delicate colors, full of natural details and bright light, always expressing the greatest love and reverence for God. He belonged to a monastery in Florence, where he painted a fresco on the walls of each of the simple cells in which the monks lived.

The painters of Florence were joined by artists from all over Italy. One of the greatest, who came from Umbria, further south, was Piero della Francesca. As well as being a painter Piero was a mathematician, and his interest in mathematics made a great difference to the way he painted. Like Uccello, he was especially concerned with perspective. Piero's pictures have a sense of space and dignity and quietness partly because of the care and study he gave to their perspective. The people in them are almost like statues, and the buildings that form the backgrounds are correct, beautiful, and cool.

Many painters were still employed by the Church, but in fact it was often the members of the powerful families that ruled Italian cities who paid for the pictures and hung them in their own chapels. Benozzo Gozzoli, who had learned painting perhaps under Fra Angelico, was asked to decorate a chapel in one of the palaces in Florence with a painting of the three wise kings visiting the infant Jesus. But he produced a picture of a Florentine procession in fancy dress, with Lorenzo de Medici, the greatest man of the city, as one of the three kings. In earlier times no artist would have been able to paint a religious subject in this way, but soon many paintings were not of religious subjects at all. Two of the most famous and delightful of all the pictures of the time are *Primavera* (Spring) and *The Birth of Venus*, painted

Above: *Madonna with Chancellor Rolin*, oil painted on wood by Jan van Eyck (*c.*1435). Chancellor Rolin commissioned this picture from Van Eyck in order to display his wealth and piety. **Right**: *The Last Judgment* by Michelangelo, part of the Sistine Chapel frescoes which he painted between 1508 and 1541. **Below**: *La Primavera* or *Spring*, tempera on wood by Sandro Botticelli (1477–78). The meaning of this allegorical painting is still a mystery.

by Sandro Botticelli, who expressed in his paintings the ideas of the poets and scholars at the Medici court.

Most famous of all, however, were three men born in the second half of the 15th century and living and working into the 16th century, whose names, unlike those of many earlier artists, were never to be forgotten. They were Leonardo da Vinci, Michelangelo, and Raphael. Leonardo was a sculptor and a scientist, as well as a painter. In his pictures there are not only beautiful human figures and ideal landscapes, but also a greater beauty that comes from the mystery and the meaning which Leonardo saw in life and was able to put into his painting. Michelangelo, too, was not only a painter but an architect and sculptor as well: indeed he was at first unwilling to undertake the task of painting the ceiling of a great chapel in the Pope's palace in Rome. Yet he did paint the ceiling of the Sistine Chapel, as it is called, and later returned to paint a whole wall with his *Last Judgment*, the mightiest of all pictures. Raphael painted noble frescoes in the rooms of the Vatican, the Pope's palace in Rome, as well as many beautiful and tender Madonnas. He and Michelangelo, who worked in Rome, were greatly influenced by the ancient sculptures and buildings which they saw there. Perhaps because they were sculptors too, these three men gave the human figure even more importance in painting.

See also BOTTICELLI, SANDRO; LEONARDO DA VINCI; MICHELANGELO BUONARROTI; RAPHAEL.

Venice. In the early 15th and 16th centuries there lived in Venice a family of craftsmen whose name became famous in the history of painting: the Bellini family. The father was Jacopo, a fine painter of religious pictures, and his two sons were Gentile and Giovanni. Giovanni Bellini was among the first Italian painters to use oil paints, although artists in northern Europe (see the next section of this article) had already learned to use them. These new colors were particularly good for making the objects in a picture look solid and real and also for creating effects of light and shade and atmosphere.

Among Giovanni Bellini's followers in Venice were two painters who were to become even more famous than their master: Giorgione and Titian. The painters of Venice differed from their rivals in Florence because of a new feeling that they put into their pictures. They still painted religious pictures, but they made them less mysterious and more human than ever before. As Michelangelo and Raphael were turning away from nature, the Venetians brought nature in again. They loved to paint rich fabrics for the sake of their colors and textures, and they delighted in landscape, perhaps because they lived surrounded by water. Many Venetian pictures were of beautiful nude (naked) women, often against a background of natural scenery which added its own beauty to the picture.

Paolo Veronese was another painter of Venice. He was a great designer in the classical style of the late Renaissance and he loved to people the white marble palaces he painted with groups of beautiful young women and noble senators dressed in the richest silks and brocades.

After Titian the best-known painter is probably Tintoretto. He had a wonderful imagination and became famous for the way he could make his figures seem to come out at all angles from the darkness into the light, and for the tremendous speed at which he worked. He painted many large pictures, and one of them—*Paradise*, in the palace of the Doge (the head of the Venetian state) at Venice—is said to be the biggest canvas in the world. It is 22.5 meters (74 feet) long and 9.1 meters (30 feet) wide.

See also BELLINI, GIOVANNI; TITIAN, TIZIANO.

Northern Europe. During the time of these artists in Italy, painting had been growing in a rather different way in the northern countries of Europe. North of the Alps the Renaissance in architecture, which had begun in Italy with its adaptation of Roman design and decoration, came only by degrees, and very much later. The new styles did not really have much effect in England, for instance, until the time of Charles I, though they came earlier to France. Instead, northern churches and cathedrals were built in the Gothic style, with huge windows of stained glass. During the 14th and 15th centuries windows more or less took the place of wall-painting, for there was not much space left on the walls that would have been suitable. Gothic paintings were therefore usually either altarpieces (pictures to be placed above an altar), usually with very elaborate gilt frames, or book illustrations. The style of these Gothic paintings spread all over Europe and is often called the International Style, for the different schools were sometimes very much alike.

The most famous miniature-painters of the time (see MINIATURE PAINTING) were employed by the Duke of Berry, brother of King Charles V of France, who had a wonderful library. One of his books, made about 1415 by three brothers, contained, besides scenes from the life of Christ, a calendar picture for every month of the year, in colors glowing and rich like jewels. Each calendar picture showed a scene suitable to the time of year. The January one, for example, was of a feast in the Duke's hall, with the sparks of a great fire flying up the chimney, while for July there was sheep-shearing and harvesting in the fields.

The miniature painting of the three brothers, who were known by the name of Limbourg, had a great influence. Such scenes as these, with their delight in landscape and even with a feeling of weather, led to a new freedom of painting in larger pictures, especially in the Netherlands, where the brothers originally came from. There, early in the 15th century, a new school of painting developed at much the same time as Masaccio was changing everything in Italy. In the Netherlands, Robert Campin and Jan van Eyck were the leaders. Although these men painted Gothic architecture in their pictures, for that is what they saw around them, they broke away from the Gothic style of painting and arranged their figures in groups bathed in light and with the effect of surrounding space. They did not get this effect, as the Italians did, by mathematical perspective, but by looking at everything even more keenly—above all at how the light fell upon the shapes of things, how it was reflected by a certain surface or absorbed by another. Oil paint is more transparent than the egg-medium paint called tempera, which was still used in most Italian pictures of the 15th century, and therefore it is better for painting light. So the artists of the Netherlands probably painted in pure oil paint, a thing the Florentines did not often do until the time of Leonardo.

Van Eyck was probably younger than Campin, but it is he who has been credited with the invention of oil painting. He and Rogier van der Weyden, the pupil of Campin, are the most famous of the early Netherlandish painters. Van Eyck's largest and most famous picture is the great altarpiece called *The Adoration of the Lamb* at Ghent in Belgium. There is also a wonderful picture in the National Gallery, London, of *The Marriage of Giovanni Arnolfini*. It shows Arnolfini swearing a promise of faithfulness to his bride, and its beauty is not only in the serious calm faces of the man and wife or in all the lovingly painted details of the scene reflected in the mirror on the wall behind them, but also in the atmosphere which makes the scene so real.

Later on, in the 16th century, came Pieter Bruegel, who was not a portrait artist, but a painter of scenes from real life. Some of them are happy and humorous pictures of country feasts and jollifications, full of all the uproarious fun and energy that they must have had in real life. Others show the grim facts of war with which everyone of the time was well acquainted. Bruegel was much influenced by an older Netherlands artist, Hieronymus Bosch, who filled his pictures with odd and frightening figures which he drew from his imagination.

There were great French painters in these days, but not very much of their work has survived, and none of them became as famous as the Netherlands painters or as the greatest of the Germans. In Germany, Gothic painting flourished, especially in Cologne, and towards the end of the 15th century there were two great painters. Matthias Grünewald painted the wonderful *Isenheim Altarpiece* at Colmar.

One side of this shows the terrible suffering of Christ on the cross, but it is balanced on the other side by scenes of incredible richness and gorgeous color, where Christ is shown as a child with his mother and at the Resurrection. The second of the two painters, Albrecht Dürer, was a much more famous painter in his lifetime. He traveled and wrote and painted many pictures, but he was perhaps at his best as an engraver.

Another German, Hans Holbein, settled first in Switzerland and finally in England. He painted pictures of every kind, book illustrations, and designs for stained glass and jewelry, but he is best known for his portraits. Some of these were very small pictures, called miniatures like the old book illustrations, and he shows his great skill in characterization as much in these little portraits as in his larger oil paintings. Holbein used glowing colors and painted the most delicate details with great skill, but above all he painted the character of his sitters with great dignity, as if each were master of the world he knew. Holbein eventually became court painter to King Henry VIII.

See also BRUEGEL, PIETER; DÜRER, ALBRECHT; HOLBEIN, HANS.

Spain. Churches of the north of Spain that were built in the old Romanesque style which came before the Gothic (see ARCHITECTURE), have wonderful wall-paintings stark and strong, but the names of the painters are unknown to us. The Gothic paintings in Spain were not so interesting, though there are a great many altarpieces in enormous gold frames which make them splendid church furniture. But in the second half of the 15th century, at least one great painter emerged. He was Bartolomé Esteban Bermejo. Very few of his pictures were seen anywhere but in Spain, and it was not until the 17th century that a Spanish school of painting developed, which is known to all the world. The new ideas of the Renaissance did not become widespread in Spain, and the first of the great 17th-century painters, El Greco, painted very few pictures which were not of religious subjects. El Greco was not his real name. It is Spanish for "The

Greek", and his proper Greek name was Domenikos Theotocopuli. He learned to paint in Venice, while Titian and Tintoretto were still alive, then went to Rome, and then, when he was still quite young, settled in Toledo, the religious capital of Spain. His paintings were glowing and rich like the Venetians', but the saints in them are holy and unworldly and have their eyes only on heaven.

Velazquez, the most famous of all Spanish painters, was born in Seville, a rich commercial town. At 25 he was appointed painter to King Philip IV in Madrid. The royal palaces there were crammed with pictures by Titian, and Velazquez, much impressed by them, decided to visit Italy. His picture called *The Toilet of Venus*, in the National Gallery, London, is one of the most famous of all paintings of nudes. Velazquez excelled in portrait painting, however. He painted the princes and princesses of the royal family and the nobles of the court, and the dwarfs too. But all his portraits are equally serious, completely natural and simple.

See also EL GRECO; VELAZQUEZ, DIEGO RODRIGUEZ.

The 17th Century: Flanders and Holland

Spain now ruled the Netherlands, where, in Antwerp, Peter Paul Rubens lived. He was court painter to the Spanish regents (rulers) at Brussels and painted for all the courts of Europe, including the court of King Charles I of England. Rubens painted some of the richest, most colorful, and energetic of all pictures. The beauty of the human figure and all the joy and gusto of life filled his paintings, and he painted all kinds of subjects, including religious scenes, portraits, and landscapes. He was the first great painter of pure landscape. As well as being a painter, Rubens was involved in state affairs and traveled to Italy, Spain, and England. His pupil Anthony Van Dyck came to England and became court painter to King Charles I.

Holland and other northern provinces had broken away from the Spanish Netherlands, and in Holland in the 17th century a new kind of painting developed. Prosperous Dutch

Archivo Mas, Barcelona

Infanta Margarita, oil painting by Diego Velazquez (1660).

Courtesy, The Art Institute of Chicago

Assumption of the Virgin, oil painting by El Greco (1577).

Courtesy, The National Gallery of Art, Washington, DC, Andrew Mellon Collection

Mrs. Sheridan, oil painting by Thomas Gainsborough (c. 1785).

Courtesy, the Staatliche Museum zu Berlin

The Lamentation over St. Sebastian, oil painting by Georges de la Tour (1645).

merchants wanted paintings for their houses, and the artists gave them just what they wanted: pictures of their solid comfortable homes, their loyal wives and sturdy children, their fertile lands, and the sea that brought them their wealth. Dutch painters also gave details of other aspects of life in Holland, and not only the life of rich people. Some artists were interested in painting both poorer people living in simple houses and the statelier rooms of their wealthy neighbors. The most famous painters of indoor scenes were Jan Vermeer and Pieter de Hooch. There were landscapes, sea pictures, and flower paintings, and even the less dignified side of Dutch life was not left out. For instance, Dutch painters such as Jan Steen loved to show scenes of drunken and vulgar jollity, and painted them so vividly that you can almost hear the noise of the shouting and music. A Dutch portrait painter of this time was Frans Hals, who has a museum named after him in his native city, Haarlem.

The greatest of all the Dutch portrait painters was Rembrandt, for he was much more than a portrait painter. He was the greatest story-teller in paint of all time. His religious pictures, full of light and shade, were deeply moving, and he learned to put into these portraits of men and women the whole story of their lives.

See also REMBRANDT; RUBENS, PETER PAUL; VERMEER, JAN.

French Painting Before 1789

Many Dutch painters—although perhaps none of those who are best known now—went to Italy as well as Rubens, Van Dyck, and Velazquez. However, the most famous of all painters who lived in Italy in the 17th century were two Frenchmen, Nicolas Poussin and Claude Lorrain. Both lived in Rome. Poussin believed that Greek and Roman times were perfect and painted even Bible scenes as if they were part of Roman history. Like the later Renaissance painters, he painted many scenes from Greek and Roman legends. Lorrain painted such scenes too, but his figures are usually small and his real interest was in landscape, always bathed in light. He loved the part of Italy called the Roman Campagna, with its castles, palaces, and ruins, and all the country between Rome and Naples.

Another Frenchman, Simon Vouet, started his career in Rome, but he returned to Paris and founded a French school. In time, Paris became the chief center of European painting. Under Louis XIV, with his glittering court, France became the great center of style and culture, and the French Royal Academy was founded in 1634, more than 100 years before the English Royal Academy. The court and the Academy were the center of everything; but in the 18th century, long before the Revolution of 1789, there was a great freedom of ideas. For instance, Antoine Watteau would not paint the classical subjects the Academy preferred him to paint, but invented a make-believe world of his own. In his pictures actors and actresses from the theater were mixed with elegant young men and women in silk and satin, wandering in parks with grassy glades, tall trees, and marble fountains and statues.

Jean Baptiste Chardin went further, painting mostly still-life pictures or scenes in kitchens and parlors like those the Dutch had painted. François Boucher painted classical subjects with naked gods and goddesses, but they behave very frivolously and do not pretend to be more than pretty young men and women. Jean-Honoré Fragonard, who lived on after the Revolution in retirement, painted in a light-hearted manner. The gaiety of these painters makes their work look easy, but to make work look easily done is really very difficult.

See also WATTEAU, ANTOINE.

English Painting

Much of the English church painting that had been done in the Middle Ages was destroyed during the Reformation in the 16th century, and there was no English Renaissance, except in poetry and drama. Before the 18th century, nearly all the good painting done in England was by foreigners at the court, such as Holbein and Van Dyck. At last, in a time of great peace and prosperity, when there was time and money for many to live well and cultivate the arts throughout the country, an English school of painting appeared.

It began with Sir James Thornhill, who painted the ceiling of the Great Hall in Greenwich Palace, and several other buildings, mostly now destroyed. He painted classical and religious subjects, as the Italian and French painters did. But he was not as good at it as they were, for such subjects and such a way of painting were alien to the English, who were fonder of things than they were of ideas. Thornhill's son-in-law William Hogarth was the first world-famous English painter. The subject of his most famous paintings was the life of London, both of its fashionable and of its poor people. He could make every kind of character come alive in paint and he used this power to show up and condemn the things that he thought silly in the life he observed, including the classical ideas of his father-in-law.

The 18th century was a time of fine craftsmen in England. Town houses and country mansions, furniture and decorations, were perhaps more beautifully designed and made then than at any other time. The same elegance, ease, and craftsmanship came into painting, especially the painting of portraits. Most famous among the many portrait painters was Sir Joshua Reynolds. He was important not only because of his fine portraits but also because he was a learned and intelligent man who did everything in his power to make English painting good enough to be compared with the great works of other nations. He was the first president of the Royal Academy, founded in 1768. A rival of his was Thomas Gainsborough, who, unlike Reynolds, never studied in Italy and who painted more easily and naturally. A popular kind of portrait in the 18th century was a picture of a whole family, or of a group of friends, enjoying a conversation in a fine room or a picnic in a park.

Although Gainsborough became a portrait painter by profession, he loved the country and was in fact one of the great English landscape artists. The first important British landscape painter was Richard Wilson, who started off as a portrait painter but soon turned to landscapes instead.

The poet William Blake was also a painter, but he had little to do with any of the fashions in painting of his time. His solemn and mysterious pictures expressed his deep and private religious feelings so well that we can call them great even though they are mostly in watercolor and on a small scale.

See also BLAKE, WILLIAM; GAINSBOROUGH, THOMAS; HOGARTH, WILLIAM; REYNOLDS, SIR JOSHUA.

The 19th Century: Arguments

The chief French painter at the time of the Revolution was Jacques Louis David. He felt that painters must turn their backs on the frivolity of the old order and once more study the statues and monuments of the ancient Greeks and Romans. The beauty of a statue is its shape and the way it fits into a group, and so David determined that the arrangement and design of the figures should matter most in pictures and that color, and the richness of light and shade, ought to be less important. In this way he and his followers started the first of the great disagreements over painting that were to come in the 19th century, for it was not long before other French artists began to insist once again that light and color were among the most wonderful things a painter could create. One of these, Eugène Delacroix, chose the most exciting subjects possible for his paintings, such as a lion hunt in Africa, or the scene before the battle of Waterloo. His rival was Jean Auguste Dominique Ingres, who had been a follower of David. Ingres said: "Drawing is everything, color is nothing"; but Delacroix asked where line (drawing) was to be seen—he saw only color in nature.

Delacroix was partly influenced by the passionate Spanish painter Goya. Goya was court painter to King Charles IV of Spain. He remained at court during the reigns of four monarchs, but he ended his life in France.

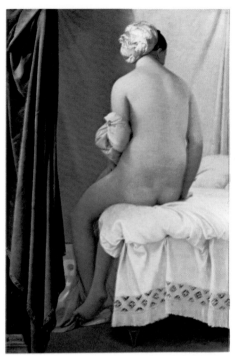

Left: *Valpicon Bather,* oil painting by Jean-Auguste Dominique Ingres (1808). Ingres is noted for his skill in painting light and skin tones.

Below: *Snow Storm—Steam-boat off a Harbour's Mouth . . .,* oil painting by J. M. W. Turner (1842). Turner's ability to portray the changing moods of sea and clouds has never been surpassed.

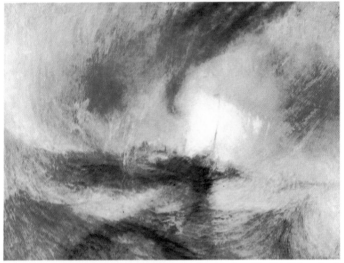

Below: *Impression: Sunrise,* oil painting by Claude Monet.

Unlike most court artists he did not admire or flatter people. In fact he despised the vanity and money-grabbing of the court, and showed his contempt for it by not hiding or altering the selfish, greedy expressions on the faces of his sitters. Goya also painted scenes of Spanish life, including bullfights.

In early 19th-century England there were two great landscape painters who were to become world-famous: John Constable and J. M. W. Turner. Constable loved the domestic aspect of the countryside and said he had never seen anything ugly in nature. His landscapes are full of all the various greens of trees and meadows. Turner traveled much abroad and painted enormous views, and his pictures glowed with brilliant colors and lights.

Later, in Queen Victoria's reign, artists often used their skill to paint "pictures that told a story". They were popular in their day, but the "stories" were rather sloppy and sentimental and so their popularity has not lasted. Even then, however, not everyone thought such pictures were good, and so there were great disagreements in England, too. George Frederick Watts, for instance, painted pictures that had a much more serious meaning, and felt that art should not just be trivial and lighthearted. A group of other young artists were thinking in the same way, but they went further and said that to be really worthwhile painting ought to go back to the ideas and methods of the Italian painters before the days of Raphael. In 1848 they banded together and called themselves the Pre-Raphaelite Brotherhood, and each of them signed some of his pictures with the initials P.R.B. after his own name. They wanted their pictures to be simple with no tricks or cleverness to spoil the simplicity; they were to be in clear colors with precise shape and details. Other painters who did not join the short-lived Brotherhood were also called Pre-Raphaelites, and this name is now used to describe Ford Madox-Brown as well as Holman Hunt, John Millais, and Dante Gabriel Rossetti.

See also CONSTABLE, JOHN; DAVID, JACQUES-LOUIS; DELACROIX, EUGENE; GOYA; ROSSETTI FAMILY; TURNER, J. M. W.

Modern Painting

The Pre-Raphaelites wanted to paint naturally and study every detail carefully, as the early Netherlands painters had done; but they mostly turned away from the life around them. If they painted landscape, for instance, they were apt to go to distant places where no railroads or factories were to be seen. Holman Hunt, for example, went to the Holy Land in order to paint scenes from the Bible with perfect accuracy. In France the more revolutionary painters did the opposite. Instead of painting in great detail, they painted broadly, with great sweeps of the brush, and increasingly, they painted the life of France in their day. Gustave Courbet, for instance, painted landscape, still-life, and every kind of scene from the life both of well-to-do farmers and of peasants. Jean François Millet painted mostly peasants, often working in the fields. A school of landscape painters settled at Barbizon, not far from Paris, and painted scenes in the forest around them. They were known as the Barbizon painters.

In Paris, Edouard Manet painted the life of the streets and cafés, scenes in houses and studios, and picnics out-of-doors. His most famous picture, *Le Déjeuner sur l'Herbe* ("Lunch on the Grass"), shocked people because the ladies at the picnic had been bathing and were not wearing any clothes. Like Delacroix, Manet thought color was all-important. He tried to model form, as Velazquez had done, by matching his colors and tones to those he saw in nature. So his painting had an influence on a new school of landscape painters who were called Impressionists (see IMPRESSIONISTS), from their dislike of detail, and who wished to paint as if light were everything and shadows were even more richly colored than the light. Until then, painters had got brilliance by laying one transparent layer of color over another brighter one—this is called "glazing". The Impressionists preferred to put thick touches of bright, contrasting color side by side. This makes the color "vibrate". The leading Impressionists were Claude Monet (not to be confused with Manet), Alfred Sisley, who was born in

Right: *Violin and Palette*, oil painting by Georges Braque (1910). Together with Picasso, Braque was one of the major artists of the Cubist movement.

Above: *I and the Village*, oil painting by the Russian, Marc Chagall (1911). **Below:** *Autumn Rhythm*, oil painting by Jackson Pollock (1950). Pollock's abstract paintings have been a powerful influence on other 20th-century American artists.

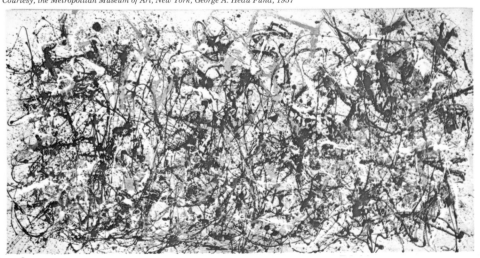

England, and Camille Pissarro. Edgar Degas, though he scarcely ever painted landscape, was often called an Impressionist because he too wanted to show things just as they are seen. He studied effects of light and even used photographs to catch the movement of dancers or race-horses in action and make his pictures look like slices of real life.

The Impressionists were not at all popular when they first began their new way of painting. People could not see nature as they saw it and thought the brightness of their colors was shocking compared with the brownness (due to the old varnish on them) of the pictures in the museums.

The Impressionists would not use varnish. They deliberately broke away from the old ideas of what painting ought to be, so that they could be free to paint their pictures as they wished. It was not only the Impressionists who did this: all great artists, today and in history, have always been explorers, leaving behind what is old and finding new subjects to paint and new ways of painting them. Three painters who did this in the years towards the end of the 19th century were Paul Cézanne, Paul Gauguin, and Vincent Van Gogh. Gauguin left his family and his friends in France to devote his life to painting, and eventually went to live in the island of Tahiti in the South Seas, away from everything that could prevent him from painting in his own way. His most famous pictures are of the scenes and people he lived among there, painted in broad masses of brilliant and startling color.

Van Gogh expressed his passionate feelings in brilliant color too; but while Gauguin's paintings often look still, Van Gogh's almost seem to move as you look at them. He applied the paint thickly, and in broken touches, often in twists and swirls of color, to create such things as scurrying clouds and rippling grain-fields.

Cézanne, on the other hand, although he used pure colors like the Impressionists and Van Gogh and Gauguin, thought that they were only painting the surface of things. He studied the paintings of the old masters and, above all, of the Venetians. He mostly painted the subjects that he could see before him, the landscape of the south of France, where he lived, the fruit and the dishes on his table, or the people of his household; but he rearranged the scene when he painted it. He wanted to paint with color, like the Impressionists, but also to make the forms, or shapes, of things look as solid as the old masters had. When a painter makes you feel that the figures and objects in his pictures are as strong and as interesting on the other side, which you cannot see, as they look on the side that you *can* see, and when you feel that there is air and space all around them, then these figures and objects are said to have form. Though Cézanne's pictures are full of the bright light of southern France, he had such strong ideas about the importance of form—of making rounded things, for instance, look really round and square things look like cubes—that a younger generation of artists, the Cubists, thought for a time of nothing else. The Cubists were not interested in making landscapes or still life look natural, but only in constructing in their pictures forms which made you feel that they had three dimensions, almost like sculpture.

The Cubist movement began a few years before World War I. The most famous of the Cubist painters was Pablo Picasso, a Spaniard who worked mostly in France. He changed his way of painting an extraordinary number of times, and his pictures are so powerful that each style invented by him has come to serve as a model for younger and less original painters, some of whom have gone on painting in the same way for most of their lives. Another Cubist was Georges Braque, whose Cubist pictures were hard to tell from Picasso's. He, too, changed his style a good deal. Both painters went further than Cubism in painting pictures in which it is hard to recognize the actual objects which they looked at before beginning to paint. Yet these objects gave them an idea, by their shape and color, of how to make a beautiful design. Such pictures, which do not pretend to represent anything and are all design, like a carpet, are usually called "abstract". This is a useful label for them, though all good painting is abstract in the proper sense of the word: that is, it is not made up of the ordinary material things of life. The people and things shown in the pictures may be actual and real enough, but a great painter does not want his canvas just to be like a mirror which reflects things—he wants to make something new out of them that has never existed before. It is this "new creation" that makes a great picture, and so the greater the picture the more "abstract" in the true sense of the word it is likely to be.

Getting the materials right: British artist Bridget Riley mixes paint, surrounded by some of her work.

Henri Matisse, who was another of these revolutionaries, died in 1954. He once said that he wanted to create an art that could not have any "troubling subject matter" but would be pure and calm and "like a good armchair in which to rest from weariness".

Today there are more painters than ever in almost every country, and in each country very many influences are at work.

The painters of the Bauhaus (an art school founded in 1919 by the architect Walter Gropius) included the Russian-born Kandinsky, the German Feininger and the Swiss Paul Klee. These painters have had a great influence on abstract painting in many countries. Paul Klee described his special kind of abstract fantasy as "taking a line for a walk". If you look at his paintings you will see exactly what he meant.

In the 1920s the movement called Surrealism (see SURREALISM) broke away from all other previous developments. The Surrealist painters created pictures from the subconscious mind. Sometimes these took the form of pure fantasy. Sometimes they were the reconstruction of a dream world. A few of Picasso's paintings in the late 1920s belonged to this type, but the painters most often associated with Surrealism were Chirico, Tanguy, Picabia, and Salvador Dali.

Piet Mondrian was a Dutch painter who lived in Paris until 1938 and then in New York. He was trained in Germany and his geometrically inspired paintings, always in primary colors with black, gray, and white, had a strong impact on many painters. Among these are Ben Nicholson, Nicolas de Stael, and William Scott.

After 1940, the center of painting moved from Paris to New York where Robert Motherwell, Jackson Pollock, Willem De Kooning, and Mark Rothko were all important figures.

The movement known as Pop Art appeared in the late 1950s and early 1960s, both in England and the United States. Painters of this movement used advertising material, photography, and strip cartoons blown up to an enormous size as their source of inspiration. They used a hard-edged style with strong, garish colors. Roy Lichtenstein and Andy Warhol in New York are the best-known artists using this style. In England, the movement is associated with Peter Blake, R. B. Kitaj, and David Hockney.

See also CÉZANNE, PAUL; DALI, SALVADOR;

Degas, Edgar; Gauguin, Paul; Manet, Edouard; Matisse, Henri; Monet, Claude; Picasso, Pablo; Pisarro, Camille; Van Gogh, Vincent.

PAINT, LACQUER, AND VARNISH.

Houses, bridges, ships, and automobiles are painted not only to decorate them and improve their appearance but also to protect them. The skin of paint acts as a protective layer against the effects of weather and the corrosive (damaging) atmosphere in industrial towns. Paint is also used for identification, or marking objects such as mailboxes so that they stand out.

Paints consist mainly of substances of two groups called *pigments* and *vehicles*. The pigments are solids, usually in the form of fine powders, and provide the coloring matter. The vehicles are so called because they carry the pigment. They are liquids, usually vegetable oils. In making the paint, a pigment powder in very fine form is thoroughly mixed with the liquid vehicle by special machinery.

Pigments are usually classed either as prime pigments or as extenders. Prime pigments give paints "hiding power", which is the property of hiding the surface of the object beneath. Most prime white pigments are made from the ores of metals (that is, the earth or rock from which the particular metal is obtained) by roasting or chemical treatment. White lead, zinc oxide, and titanium oxide are three of the most important. Extenders are cheap substances, such as chalk, limestone, and various clays, which are added to increase the bulk of the paint.

The chief part in paint vehicles is played by the drying oils, obtained by crushing oil-bearing seeds, nuts, plants, and fishes. These oils have the property of absorbing oxygen from the air and thus they form a thin but elastic skin. Chief among the drying oils is linseed oil, obtained from the seeds of the flax plant (see Flax). Others are tung oil, obtained from the Chinese tung nut, soybean oil, and a number of other vegetable and fish oils. Oils obtained from petroleum are also used.

Paint vehicles may also contain resins, thinners, and dryers. Resins help to bind the paint together and make it easier to apply with a brush. They may be natural gums obtained from the sap of trees or synthetic (artificial) resins made from chemicals. Thinners are solvents such as turpentine and kerosine which make the paint more fluid and easier to apply. Dryers are chemical substances obtained from metals such as cobalt, manganese, or lead. They help the paint to dry quickly when spread thinly over a surface.

Paints can be classified according to their use. Paints for outdoor use need to be more lasting and hard-wearing than those for use indoors. Outdoor house paints contain plenty of drying oils but little turpentine. This makes them slow to dry but gives a glossy finish and a long life. Indoor paints do not need to have as much luster (shine) and resistance to weather as outdoor ones, and therefore contain less oil and more turpentine. Some indoor paints may not have oil vehicles, as, for example, the water-mixed paints such as the latex paints that are used on walls and ceilings. Radiator paints may be made by mixing powdered metal in quick-drying varnishes or lacquers. There are also special enamels for baths and furniture, floor paints, stovepipe enamels, and floor stains.

An interesting development was the production of latex emulsion paints which contain synthetic rubber. Their advantages are that they are easy to use, have practically no smell, flow well, and dry quickly.

For painting stonework out of doors, a paint consisting of tung oil with fine sand or ground rock as a pigment may be used. The special "anti-fouling" paints used on ships' bottoms contain chemicals poisonous to weed and barnacles. Other special paints are used to resist heat and to discourage fire, to prevent the growth of fungus in places such as greenhouses and dairies, and for use on the hands and figures of instruments so that they glow in the dark ("luminous" paints).

Varnishes and Lacquers

Varnishes and clear lacquers are really paints without pigments. Varnish is made by dissolving resins in drying oils. Lacquer is named after the lac insect (*Kerria lacca*), a scale insect which lives on trees in the tropics (see SCALE INSECT). It makes a natural resin called shellac, which is often used as the resinous substance in varnishes. There are also vegetable and synthetic resins that can be used instead. The resin or shellac makes the varnish hard and shiny and the oil makes it tough and lasting. The varnish used on boats, for example, contains plenty of an oil, known as tung oil, because it needs to be flexible and to resist water and weather.

Lacquer is an opaque colored varnish. Although lacquer is named after the lac insect, the true oriental lacquers used for hundreds of years in China and Japan have nothing to do with shellac but are obtained from the sap of a tree. With this kind of lacquer, which is used for decorating wooden and metal articles, anything up to 30 coats are applied, each being dried, smoothed, or polished. It may be made red, black, gold, or silver in color. It gives a hard surface with a brilliant polish like fine porcelain.

A different kind of lacquer is often used for applying the topcoat of an automobile. It usually consists of nitrocellulose (see CELLULOSE) with a natural or synthetic resin added to give gloss and to help the lacquer stick to the metal.

The paints used by artists are described in the article PAINTERS AND PAINTING.

PAKISTAN is a republic in Asia. It lies on the northwest of the Indian sub-continent, and is bordered on the west by Iran, to the north by Afghanistan, and to the south by the Arabian Sea. Much of Pakistan is mountainous. To the northeast the western Himalayas run into the Hindu Kush mountain range. The average height is 6,100 meters (20,000 feet), and includes some of the world's highest peaks such as K2 and Nanga Parbat. The Baluchistan Plateau, to the west, contains deserts, salt lakes, and a narrow coastal plain. From north to south runs the great Indus River, which with its

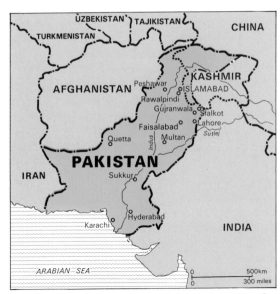

tributaries has created a great plain. In the northeast the Karakoram Mountains run through the territory of Jammu and Kashmir, which is disputed by Pakistan and India.

The capital of Pakistan is the new city of Islamabad. The two largest cities are Lahore and Karachi, the main port. (See ISLAMABAD; LAHORE; KARACHI.) Other important cities are Hyderabad, Faisalabad, Rawalpindi, Multan, and Peshawar.

People

The people of Pakistan vary considerably from area to area. In the mountains of the northwest live a hardy warlike people called Pashtuns, formerly known as Pathans. They also

Barnaby's

Oasis town of Nushki in Pakistan's desert region.

make up the majority of the population of Afghanistan and, unlike other Pakistanis, they belong to tribes and sub-tribes. Occasionally the tribes still fight among themselves. Some of the villages in this part of Pakistan have watch-towers which date from the days when tribal warfare was common. The city of Peshawar lies at the foot of the Khyber Pass and there traders from the whole of Asia exchange their wares. Islamabad, the new capital of Pakistan, lies to the east.

Nearly half of the population are Punjabis. They take their name from the Punjab, or Land of the Five Rivers (the Jhelum, Chenab, Ravi, Sutlej, and the Beas), part of which is now in India.

Pakistan is a country of many languages. The official language is Urdu, the language of the educated upper classes, but more people speak Punjabi. English is often spoken.

The Muslim religion makes life in Pakistan different in many ways from life in a Christian country. Friday is the day of worship and in the afternoon hundreds of people go to worship at the mosques. In a traditional Pakistani household the women of the family live in a separate part of the house, known as the *zenana* and wear a veil when they go out of doors. Although there are now women doctors, lawyers, and a woman prime minister, Pakistani women still have low status, as they do in

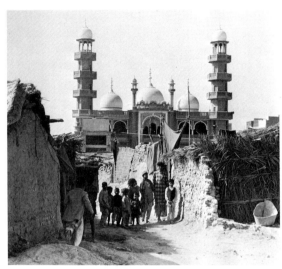

Barnaby's

Sukkur's old town, on the west bank of the Indus, has many mosques. It is near a famous irrigation project.

many strict Muslim countries (see ISLAM).

Only about a quarter of Pakistan's population can read and write. The government has opened more schools and now most boys receive at least primary education. However, so far the girls have not benefited. Only one girl in three receives any education at all. Pakistan is developing its universities. In 1947 there were only three, but since then others have been founded. These include universities at Karachi, Hyderabad (Sind), Lahore, and Peshawar.

Agriculture and Industry

Agriculture has been much improved by the increasing use of fertilizers, better quality seeds, and irrigation in the dry areas. The main crops are wheat, rice, cotton, sugarcane, and tobacco. Cattle, water buffaloes, goats and poultry are kept and hides and leather are exported. More than 70 per cent of Pakistan's working population works on the land, many as peasant farmers.

Pakistan is not rich in natural resources, but it does have supplies of petroleum, natural gas, chromite, and limestone. There is also some poor quality coal. The amount of electricity produced from hydroelectric and gas-fired power plants is increasing. Pakistan also has nuclear power.

Barnaby's

A busy fruit-stall in Lahore with several different types of mango for sale.

Industry employs only a small proportion of the population. Textiles are the chief manufacture and are a leading export. Small-scale "cottage industries" such as wool and cotton weaving are developing rapidly. Newer industries include the manufacture of sodium silicate, chocolate, paint and varnish, and also the tanning of hides. Embroidery and pottery are made for export.

FACTS ABOUT PAKISTAN

AREA: 796,095 square kilometers (307,390 square miles).
POPULATION: 118,820,000 (1989).
GOVERNMENT: Independent republic.
CAPITAL: Islamabad, 204,364 (1981 census).
GEOGRAPHY: The Indus River flows through Pakistan, which is mountainous in the north and west.
CITIES: Karachi, 5,208,132; Lahore, 2,952,689; Faisalabad, 1,104,209; Rawalpindi, 794,843.
ECONOMY. Products and exports.
  Agriculture: Sugar-cane, wheat, rice, cotton, corn, tobacco; goats, sheep, cattle, buffalo, camels, poultry; timber; fish.
  Minerals: Coal, petroleum, natural gas, limestone, rock salt, gypsum, marble, silica, china clay, bauxite, chromite.
  Manufacturing: Petroleum products, cement, chemical fertilizers, steel products, refined sugar, textiles, paper, beverages, cigarettes, bicycles.
  Exports: Cotton, rice, leather, carpets, fish, sporting goods.
EDUCATION: Primary education is free, but not available to most girls. Only about one-quarter of Pakistan's population can read and write.

Separation from India

Pakistan came into existence on 15 August 1947, when the single country that had previously been known as India was divided into two. Before that date India had been ruled by the British, but in 1947 they agreed to hand over the government of the country to the people who lived in it. One country would come into being where most people were Muslim and the other where most people were Hindu. The Muslim country would be called Pakistan.

Before independence British India had consisted of provinces ruled by the British and the princely states. In most cases Muslim states joined Pakistan while Hindu states joined India. But in some of them the ruler belonged to a different religion from his people and a difficult decision had to be made about which country to join. The problem was most acute in Kashmir, which had Muslim people and a Hindu Maharaja (see KASHMIR).

In British India, there were two separate areas where most people were Muslims, and therefore the new state of Pakistan came into existence as two provinces, East Pakistan and West Pakistan, separated from each other by more than 1,500 kilometers (950 miles) of the Republic of India.

Even so, there were still many Muslims living in India and many Hindus living in Pakistan. This led to trouble, particularly in the Punjab where the boundary cut through an area where many Sikhs lived (see SIKH). The Sikhs sympathized with the Hindus and began fighting the Muslims on both sides of the border. Dreadful massacres took place and refugees were soon on the move: Sikhs and Hindus trying to get from Pakistan into India and Muslims trying to reach Pakistan from India.

From Monarchy to Islamic Republic

From 1947 to 1956 Pakistan was a dominion within the Commonwealth, with the British sovereign as head of state (see COMMONWEALTH). In 1956 it became an independent republic, but remained within the Commonwealth. From 1958 to 1969 the country was ruled by President Ayub Khan. There was growing discontent in East Pakistan, which felt that its needs were neglected by the more prosperous West Pakistan. Riots broke out and Ayub Khan resigned in 1969. He was succeeded by Yahya Khan.

Discontent grew and in 1971 the East Pakistanis (who were mainly Bengalis) broke away from West Pakistan altogether and declared their country independent as the Republic of Bangladesh. Civil war broke out and was followed by full scale war between Pakistan and India, which supported Bangladesh. Pakistan was defeated and Bangladesh became a separate state. (See BANGLADESH.) Yahya Khan resigned and was replaced by Zulfikhar Ali Bhutto.

After the war Pakistan, now consisting of

what had formerly been West Pakistan, left the Commonwealth in protest at Britain's recognition of Bangladesh. In 1977 the army, led by General Zia ul-Haq, took over the government and imposed a strict Islamic code of law on the country. Bhutto was executed. In August 1988 Zia was killed in a plane crash and the following November Bhutto's daughter Benazir was elected prime minister in Pakistan's first elections since 1977. She made many enemies and was removed from power, officially for corruption, in 1990. Pakistan rejoined the Commonwealth in 1989.

PALESTINIANS are Arab people, believed to be some 4.5 million in number, who live in and around what was the ancient region of Palestine in the Middle East. This region ceased to exist politically in 1948, when it became the state of Israel. Palestine was a narrow strip of land bordering the eastern Mediterranean and backing on to the vast Arabian desert. The modern state of Israel stands today on much of Palestine's ancient lands (see ISRAEL).

When Israel declared independence in 1948, some quarter of a million Palestinians fled to neighboring Arab states, and became refugees (see REFUGEES).

Palestine was considered the Holy Land by Christians, Jews, and Muslims alike: by Christians, because it was the home of Jesus Christ; by Jews because Moses led his people there after fleeing from Egypt; and by Muslims because certain places are associated with the prophet Muhammad. Jewish tribes first settled there 4,000 years ago. In the 7th century it was invaded by Muslim Arabs and remained largely under Muslim control until World War I (1914–18).

By the beginning of the 20th century many Jews were seeking to re-establish a homeland in Palestine. The Zionist movement was the chief force behind this (see ZIONISM). In 1917 Britain gained control of Palestine when General Allenby defeated the Turkish forces there. At the same time the British government came to recognize the aims of the Zionist movement. The Balfour Declaration made in 1917 by the prime minister, Lord Balfour,

Barnaby's

In the Middle East there are many Palestinian refugee camps such as this one in Egypt.

recognized the right of the Jewish people to a national home in Palestine.

In 1920, the League of Nations (forerunner of the United Nations) put Palestine under British control and protection.

Jewish settlement of Palestine had increased dramatically since the end of World War I, and had led to clashes between the Jews and the Arabs, who wanted Palestine to be an independent Arab state. In the mid-1930s another large wave of Jewish refugees followed from Europe, to escape persecution in Hitler's Germany. Britain tried to restrict this immigration but succeeded only in angering both Jews and Arabs. In 1947 Britain handed over the problem to the United Nations, which recommended that Palestine be divided into two small countries, one Jewish and one Arab, with Jerusalem as an international zone. While most Jews favored this, the Palestinian Arabs did not. Nevertheless, the British withdrew in 1948, and immediately the Jews proclaimed the new state of Israel. This not only caused a massive exodus of Palestinians to other Arab countries and to refugee camps, but also provoked surrounding Arab states into a series of Middle East wars.

Palestine Liberation Organization (PLO)

The Palestine Liberation Organization (PLO) was established in 1964 to represent the displaced Palestinians and to press for a Palestinian homeland. Its charter called for the elimination of Israel. Yasir Arafat became chairman in 1969. The PLO launched military operations against Israel from Jordan until it came into conflict with the government of King Hussein and in 1971 was forcibly expelled. From there it shifted its headquarters to the Lebanon.

In the early 1970s several other nationalist groups emerged alongside the PLO, including al-Fatah (the Palestine Liberation Movement) and the Popular Front for the Liberation of Palestine (PFLP). Each had an extremist wing which throughout the 1970s and 1980s used terrorist tactics to draw attention to the Palestinian cause and to harass Israel (see TERRORISM). The PLO itself became increasingly moderate. In 1973 Arafat withdrew his support for terrorism outside Israel. In 1974, the Arab League recognized the PLO as the sole representative of the Palestinian peoples. Arafat addressed the United Nations on the Palestinian problem later that year.

The Palestinian cause suffered its worse setback in 1982, when Israel invaded the Lebanon and surrounded Beirut, then headquarters of the PLO. Under international supervision the PLO forces were deported to other sympathetic Arab countries while the remaining Palestinians stayed in the refugee camps. Later in the year many hundreds were killed in an attack on the camps by Lebanese Christians. The PLO now has its headquarters in Tunis, North Africa.

Israel has continued to occupy some of the territory it captured from the Arabs in the Arab–Israeli War of 1967. The occupied territories include the West Bank (of the River Jordan), the Gaza Strip, and east Jerusalem. The population is mainly Palestinian. In December 1987 an uprising (*intifada* in Arabic) broke out among Palestinians living in these areas. The Israeli government used troops in an attempt to suppress it.

Peace initiatives by the United States and moderate Arab governments aimed at settling the problem of a Palestinian homeland continued. In 1988 Arafat announced that the original charter of the PLO, calling for the destruction of Israel, was null and void. He recognized the right of Israel to exist and called for a "two-state" solution whereby there would be separate homelands for Jews and Arabs, as had been envisaged by the UN in 1948. However, the Israeli government refused to negotiate directly with the PLO.

The extremist Palestinian groups rejected Arafat's peace initiatives and allied themselves with other Muslim terrorists seeking the destruction of Israel.

PALLAS ATHENE, or Athena, was the goddess of war, worshipped by the ancient Greeks. Later, she also became the goddess of wisdom. The Romans had a similar goddess called Minerva. The ancient Greeks believed that Athena was the daughter of Zeus, king of the gods, and that she sprang fully grown from her father's head. They thought of her as tall and handsome, wearing helmet and armor. She was the guardian of cities, especially Athens, which was named after her, and was wise in both the arts of war and peace. She was the goddess of weaving, spinning, and other handicrafts, and was supposed to have invented the plow.

One story tells how Zeus decided that whoever gave mortals the most useful gift should possess the city of Athens. Poseidon gave them a horse but Athena drove her spear into the ground and an olive tree sprang up. Athena's gift was judged the better and so she was given the city.

The Athenians held a festival called the Panathenaea on her birthday and built the most beautiful of Greek temples, the Parthenon, in her honor.

PALM. A typical palm tree has a straight, slender trunk with no branches and a cluster of leaves at the top. There are over 2,500 different species of palm, and some have branching stems, while at least one is a trailing vine. Palms also vary in height, from a few centimeters to over 30 meters (98 feet).

The trunks of palms do not have the rings by which one can tell the age of many trees when they are cut down. The shiny, leathery leaves are either fan-shaped or feather-

PALM, OIL

PALM, ROYAL

flower head

flower spathe

oil nut (enlarged)

FAN PALM

flowers

male flowers

edible flowers & shoots

female inflorescence

violet fruit

shaped, and the largest are nearly 12 meters (39 feet) long. The small flowers, which are usually greenish-white or yellowish (though they can be orange or red) grow in clusters near the tops of the plants. Often male and female flowers grow on separate trees.

There are palms in Asia, Africa, Australia, Europe, and North and South America, and many grow on the tropical islands of the Pacific. Some grow in dry deserts and some in rich, damp earth. Palms bear various fruits, the best-known being probably the coconut and the date. Betel nuts, which when chewed turn the lips red, come from the areca, or betel palm (*Areca catechu*), of southeast Asia. Ivory palm nuts are carved into buttons, and from the red fruits of the oil palm (*Elaeis guineensis*) come palm oil and palm kernel oil, both used in soap and as edible oils. The *coco de mer* is a palm (*Lodoicea maldivica*) that grows only in the Seychelles Islands in the Indian Ocean. It reaches a height of 30 meters (98 feet) and its nuts may be 30 centimeters (12 inches) long.

As well as their fruits, many other parts of palms are also useful. Their stems and leaves, when tender, can be eaten. Strong wood and cane come from the trunks and branches; the large leaves are used for thatching and from them and the bark are made twine, rugs, baskets, hats, and brushes.

The sago palm provides sago, which is extracted from the trunk. The sap of some palms is made into sugar, wine or honey. The stately royal palm (*Roystonea regia*), which is crowned with graceful, feathery leaves more

than 3 meters (10 feet) long, is often planted along streets in hot countries.

There are separate articles COCONUT; DATE; and SAGO.

PALMER, Geoffrey (born 1942).

Geoffrey Winston Russell Palmer was prime minister of New Zealand from 1989 to 1990.

Geoffrey Palmer was born at Nelson, a seaside resort in the north of the South Island. His father was a journalist and edited the city's newspaper. He graduated with arts and law degrees from Victoria University of Wellington and worked as a solicitor (lawyer) for two years. After a period studying and teaching in the United States, during which he gained a doctor of law degree from the University of Chicago, he returned to his old university in New Zealand as professor of English and New Zealand law in 1974.

Palmer joined the Labour Party and became MP for Christchurch Central after winning a by-election in 1979. When Labour came to power five years later he held several posts including those of minister of justice, and leader of the house. He was a strong advocate of open government and introduced important reforms concerning the way parliament worked. He became prime minister on the resignation of David Lange in August 1989.

PALMERSTON, Henry John Temple, 3rd Viscount (1784–1865).

Lord Palmerston was one of the most popular of Britain's 19th-century prime ministers and one of its greatest foreign ministers. He went to Harrow School and, later, Cambridge University, having inherited the title of Viscount when he was 17. In 1807 he became a member of parliament, but he did not hold any important posts until 1830, when he was made foreign minister. The Whig party then formed the government.

Palmerston's first achievement was to help establish Belgium, which had just broken away from its Dutch rulers, as an independent country. He also did much to suppress the trade in African slaves. In 1842 he succeeded in adding the Chinese territory of Hong Kong to the growing British Empire.

Palmerston was out of the government from 1841 to 1846, when the Tories (Conservatives) were in power. He came back as foreign minister, and established his high-handed, blustering manner, which included blockading Greece over a minor incident involving a British subject in Athens. This sort of action made him popular with the people, but not with Queen Victoria and important politicians. He was eventually dismissed, but re-emerged as a reforming home minister.

Palmerston became prime minister in 1855, as it was felt he was the best person to lead Britain during the difficult time of the Crimean War (see CRIMEAN WAR). He successfully brought the war to an end and remained prime minister until his death, except for one year.

"Pam", as Palmerston was often called, was rather bullying and sometimes rude. But his respect for liberty and love of his country gave people a very high opinion of him, both at home and abroad.

PAMPAS is a vast fertile plain that forms one of the major regions of Argentina. It lies east of the Andean foothills and south of Argentina's dry, scrub Chaco region. The word *pampas* comes from a Quechua Indian word meaning "plains".

The northern end of this great plain lies in the interior of the South American continent. In the south it ends in a cliffed coast. The pampas slopes gradually upward from southeast to northwest where it reaches heights of more than 450 meters (1,500 feet). The Argentine pampas has an area of almost 760,000 square kilometers (293,000 square miles). The deep, fertile soils of the region have been deposited by wind or by streams draining the eastern slopes of the Andes.

The pampas is divided into two distinct climatic zones. The western portion of the pampas is known as the dry pampas. The moister eastern portion is called the humid pampas and is the most productive farming area of the entire country.

The original vegetation of much of the dry

and humid pampas is thought to have been *monte*, a covering of low scrubby trees and coarse grasses. When the Spaniards first arrived in what is now Argentina in the early 16th century, they saw the Indians burning the *monte* for purposes of hunting game and for warfare. The result of prolonged burnings, plus a possible reduction in rainfall over the past 1,000 to 2,000 years, was a decrease in the woody vegetation and an expansion of grasses.

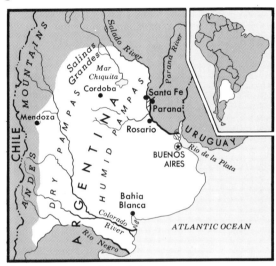

The pampas area of South America.

The original Indian inhabitants were wandering hunters and gatherers, unlike the farmers of the Inca Empire in the central Andean highlands. They did little farming and had few domestic animals. The Spaniards in the 16th century introduced many totally new and different domesticated plants (wheat, oats, vegetables, fruits) and animals (horses, cattle, sheep, goats, pigs, chickens). Escaped cattle and horses multiplied rapidly on the open grasslands. At this time the Indians learned how to ride on horseback.

For about 300 years, Spanish settlement was concentrated in a small area surrounding Buenos Aires. The principal activity was extensive cattle raising, and income came chiefly from the sale of hides, meat, and tallow. It was the mestizo gauchos ("cowboys" of mixed native and Spanish parentage) who herded the cattle and fought with the Indians his reed pipe. When shepherds heard the wind sighing through the rushes, they used to say that it was Pan playing.

The Athenians worshipped Pan because they believed he had helped them in the Battle of Marathon (see MARATHON, BATTLE OF). In later times Pan came to be thought of as a very powerful god. All nature was his and he seemed to the early Christians to stand for all that the pagans worshipped. There was a legend that when Jesus Christ was born, the hills of Greece resounded with the cry: "Pan is dead!"

One sign of Pan's power was that he could fill mortals with terrible fear: it is from his name that the word *panic* comes.

Sergio Larrain/Magnum

The pampas region is important for crop growing as well as for raising livestock.

in the no-man's-land beyond the area settled by the Spaniards.

In the mid-19th century the pampas was transformed: the Indian tribes were pushed back and subdued in the campaigns of 1879–84; the government-sponsored immigration, beginning in the 1860s, attracted new settlers who introduced new ideas for developing the land; the growth of railroads spurred on development, as did the use of refrigerated ships (to transport meat) from around 1875, and the development of a deepwater port at Buenos Aires.

The wealthy landowners of the vast ranches (called *estancias*) began to employ immigrants, chiefly Italians, to cultivate their lands, sowing alfalfa, flax, and corn. The *estancias* were fenced in, and the gauchos gradually became more like hired laborers. Tractors took over from horses. Farmers near the urban centers, such as Buenos Aires, now grow fruit and vegetables and produce milk.

See also ARGENTINA.

PAN was the Greek god of the countryside and of flocks and herds of animals. He was the son of the god Hermes and had the body and face of a man but the legs, horns, and tail of a goat. Attended by goat-like beings called satyrs and fauns, he roamed over hills and dales, playing

PANAMA is a republic which occupies the isthmus, or neck of land, joining South America to Central America. This isthmus runs roughly east-west. To the west of Panama is Costa Rica and to the east of it is Colombia. Panama is about 772 kilometers (480 miles) in length, and varies from 60 to 177 kilometers (37–110 miles) in width. Across the middle of the country runs the Panama Canal, which links the Atlantic and Pacific Oceans (see PANAMA CANAL).

Mountain ranges form the backbone of the country, dipping to about 26 meters (85 feet) above sea-level where the canal is. The highlands in the west include several extinct volcanoes, the highest being Baru, at 3,475 meters (11,401 feet) the country's highest

peak. From the Canal Zone a series of narrow ranges rising to 1,200 meters (4,000 feet) extends in a southeasterly direction. Lowlands make up about 85 per cent of the country's territory. The climate alters little with the seasons, being generally hot and damp with a heavy rainfall, especially in the north. More than half of Panama is covered by tropical rainforest. Animal life includes anteaters, tapirs, ocelots, and jaguars. Crocodiles abound in the coastal creeks.

Most of the people are of mixed blood, being descended from Spaniards, American Indians, and black Africans. There are a few Indians and descendants of immigrants from Asia. Spanish is the language generally used, although many business people speak English, and most of the people are Roman Catholic. Nearly all children attend school between the ages of 7 and 15, and almost 90 per cent of the people can read and write. Panama has two universities, one of which is in the capital, Panama City.

ZEFA

The old-town area of Panama City.

Hilary Bradt/South American Pictures

A young woman with baby, of the Cuna Indian tribe of Panama.

Panama City is near the Pacific entrance to the canal. It is a mixture of old Spanish architecture and modern office buildings and hotels. The port of Panama City is Balboa. Other towns in the republic are Colon at the Caribbean (Atlantic) end of the canal, and David in the center of the farming province of Chiriqui. San Miguelito is the second largest city.

Industry and Agriculture

Much of Panama's wealth comes from the Panama Canal. Ships using the canal pay a toll, and the canal attracts many tourists to the country. Panama is one of the world's most important financial centers, with many large banks having offices there.

Farming is important both in providing employment and produce for export. The main crops are rice, corn, beans, bananas, sugarcane, coffee, and cacao. Fishing is a growing industry with shrimps, lobsters, and prawns becoming major exports. Panama has huge deposits of copper, thought to be the largest undeveloped reserves in the world. Small factories make foodstuffs, cement and building materials, clothing, and furniture. Panama hats, despite their name, are made in Ecuador, not Panama. They are called Panama hats because they were first seen there by European visitors.

The section of the Pan-American Highway in Panama is not quite complete (see PAN-AMERICAN HIGHWAY), and although a road and a railroad cross the isthmus beside the canal, there are few good roads elsewhere. Many merchant ships fly the Panamanian flag because it is cheaper to register ships in Panama than in the countries where they are owned. Tocumen, near Panama City, is an important airport.

History

The original Indians of Panama were mostly of the Cuna, Guaymi, and Choco tribes, but their numbers dwindled when European explorers arrived at the beginning of the 16th century. Vasco Nunez de Balboa, about whom there is a separate article, founded the first Spanish settlement in 1513 and Panama became a major thoroughfare for trade between Spain and its South American colonies.

FACTS ABOUT PANAMA

AREA: 77,082 square kilometers (29,762 square miles).
POPULATION: 2,370,000 (1989).
GOVERNMENT: Independent republic.
CAPITAL: Panama City, 439,996 (1987).
GEOGRAPHY: Coastal lowlands with very heavy rainfall rise to thickly forested upland valleys and plateaus or tablelands. In the west, near the Costa Rican frontier, are some volcanic mountains, rising to about 3,400 meters (11,000 feet).
CITIES: San Miguelito, 231,920; Colon, 68,688; David, 50,621.
EXPORTS: Bananas, shell fish, coffee, raw sugar.
EDUCATION: Education is free and compulsory between the ages of 7 and 15.

In 1821 the people of Panama declared themselves independent of Spain and joined the new state of Colombia. The canal began to be discussed in about 1840. France, Great Britain, and the United States were all interested in it. Panama remained a part of Colombia until 1903 when, with the help of the United States, it gained its independence. The Panamanians signed a treaty allowing the United States to cut the Panama Canal and to occupy for ever the land either side of it, known as the "Canal Zone". However, in 1979 the United States officially handed back the Canal Zone to Panama, though the two countries agreed that the United States would continue to operate the canal until the end of the century.

After 1979 Panama suffered economic decline and became increasingly unstable. An army general called Manuel Noriega took advantage of the political upheavals and established a dictatorship. His threats against the United States, where he was wanted on drug charges, finally provoked an American invasion of Panama. In 1989 United States forces overthrew Noriega and he was taken to the United States for trial. The opposition leader Guillermo Endara was installed as president.

PANAMA CANAL is a great international waterway connecting the Atlantic and Pacific Oceans through the Isthmus (a neck of land) of Panama in Central America. It lies entirely within the Republic of Panama.

The canal is located near the geographical center of the western hemisphere and is a vital link in the world's ocean trade routes. Just over 12,000 ships pass through its locks each year. It saves a vast amount of money in shipping costs by reducing the distances that goods must travel by sea.

The canal is more than 80 kilometers (50 miles) long and at least 150 meters (500 feet) wide in the channels, with a minimum depth of 12 meters (39 feet). It is 26 meters (85 feet) above sea level. Because of the geography and layout of the isthmus, the canal was built in a northwest-southeast direction. This put the Atlantic entrance about 30 kilometers (19 miles) *west* of the Pacific entrance.

Canal installations include three sets of twin locks; each lock is about 33 meters (110 feet) wide and 300 meters (1,000) feet long. Ships entering from the Atlantic are raised 26 meters (85 feet) in three steps at the Gatun Locks. They then cross Lake Gatun for 37 kilometers (23 miles) and pass the Continental Divide in the 13-kilometer (8-mile) Gaillard Cut. Further on they are lowered 25 meters (85 feet) in three steps to the level of the Pacific Ocean. Dams on the Chagres River create Madden Lake reservoir and the much larger Lake Gatun.

Cargo from all over the world passes through the canal, but more than half of the tonnage moves to or from the United States. Other areas sending large volumes of trade through the canal are eastern Asia, western South America, and western Europe. In 1988, 159 million tonnes (175 million US tons) was carried through the canal.

There are modern port facilities at Cristobal on the Atlantic side and at Balboa on the Pacific. The Panama Railroad runs along-

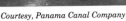

Left: The Miraflores basin on the Panama Canal. Beyond the locks is Miraflores Lake, on the other side of which lie the Pedro Miguel locks. **Right:** A ship passes through the Miraflores locks.

side the canal for 76 kilometers (47 miles), and there are a number of paved roads. The Pan-American Highway crosses the canal near Panama City over a 1.6-kilometer (1-mile) long bridge (see PAN-AMERICAN HIGHWAY).

History

The first serious attempt to build a canal was considered at an international congress held in Paris, France, in 1879. Various plans for canal construction were put forward, and the one chosen was that of the French engineer, Ferdinand de Lesseps, successful builder of the Suez Canal. A company was formed, and rights were obtained from the Republic of Colombia to build a canal across its province of Panama. Digging began in 1881. The effort failed, however, because of unhealthy conditions and bad use of funds. More than 22,000 canal workers died, mostly from yellow fever and malaria, and the attempt was given up in 1889.

During the Spanish-American war of 1898 the United States found it very awkward to have its navy divided between the Atlantic and Pacific. In 1902 the United States bought the property of the French company and tried to persuade Colombia, in whose land the isthmus then was, to allow the canal to be made. Colombia was unwilling, but Theodore Roosevelt, President of the United States, persuaded the

people of Panama to break away from Colombia and form their own republic. The new republic agreed to the building of the canal. Construction took seven years and was directed by John Stevens and George Goethals. As many as 65,000 men were employed at one time, and more than 153 million cubic meters (200 million cubic yards) of soil and rock were removed. The canal opened to ships in August 1914, and effectively cut the sailing distance from New York to San Francisco by 13,000 kilometers (8,000 miles). To safeguard the canal, the United States acquired control over the Canal Zone, extending for about 8 kilometers (5 miles) on either side, and paid an annual rent to Panama. In 1979 the land around the canal was handed back to Panama, though the United States continued to operate the canal. There are plans to build a second canal, for the existing one cannot take more than 15,000 ships a year and many modern vessels are too big for it.

PAN-AMERICAN HIGHWAY is a road system that connects the capitals and major cities of South and Central America and is linked to the road systems of the United States and Canada. The Central American part of the highway, running 5,390 kilometers (3,350 miles) from Mexico to Panama City, is also called the Inter-American Highway. The Pan-American Highway has helped the economies of the countries through which it passes and has been valuable to travelers and tourists.

The idea of building a Pan-American Highway goes back more than a hundred years. In one of the earliest moves toward inter-American travel, the First International Conference of American States in 1889 began a project for building a Pan-American Railroad. The railroad was never built, but at the Fifth International Congress in 1923 a proposal was made to study the possibilities of a Pan-American Highway. In 1925 the Pan-American Highway Congress was established as a permanent institution. The congress is now a part of the Organization of American States. Great progress on the highway was made in the 1930s and by the early 1940s more than 60 per cent was completed.

World War II spurred the road-building activity, and by the end of the war only some of the toughest sections remained to be completed. These sections were finished one by one through the 1950s and early 1960s and by the 1980s only one gap needed to be closed to connect a single highway system through Central and South America. This gap is called the Darien Gap, and runs some 400 kilometers (240 miles) through jungle on the Panama–Colombia border.

The Pan-American Highway, today, is really a number of inter-connecting roads. The country using the highway decides upon the additional roads within its boundaries that will make up part of the total highway system. The United States had given considerable financial aid to those countries that could not otherwise afford road building. United States finances and engineers are involved in the planning of the road through the Darien region.

Not all of the Pan-American Highway is paved, and in some places it is not passable in bad weather. A trip on the Pan-American Highway covering the entire road network would take a traveler over some 26,000 kilometers (16,000 miles) of road,

and through passes 5,000 meters (16,000 feet) high.

PANDA is the name of two Asiatic animals, the giant panda (*Ailuropoda melanoleuca*) and the common, or lesser panda (*Ailurus fulgens*). They are thought to be related but are not much alike in appearance.

Thumb-like structures on a giant panda's front paws give it a good grip on bamboo, which, although it is not very nutritious, is the animal's main food.

The giant panda is the better known of the two and lives in the forests of bamboo that cover the mountainside in parts of Szechwan province in central China. It is rather like a good-natured black and white bear, about 1.5 meters (5 feet) in length from nose to tail. Its eyes are surrounded by black patches like spectacles, its head is large, and its tail is very short.

Giant pandas eat great quantities of bamboo shoots, leaves, and stems. They usually live alone but sometimes they are found in pairs. Most of the time they are very quiet, but they can whine and make a growling noise. Giant pandas have dens under overhanging rocks in dense bamboo thickets, where they make nests of broken bamboo stalks.

A mother panda has one cub at a time in the early spring. It grows up in four or five years and probably stays with its mother for more than a year. As they are good-tempered animals and attractive to look at, giant pandas are very popular in zoos. They are difficult to breed in captivity. However, since the early 1980s a number of zoos have been successful. Examples are Mexico City, Madrid, Tokyo, and zoos in China. Breeding has been mainly achieved by using artificial insemination. This means that sperm is taken from the male panda and introduced by a syringe into the female.

The common panda, which is also known as the catbear, lives in the foothills at the bases of the Himalaya Mountains, from India to western China. It is about the size of a large cat and has a ringed tail. In color it is rusty red with black legs and underside. There is some black fur round the eyes. The sides of the muzzle (nose), insides of the ears, and spots under and over the eyes are whitish.

Common pandas live on bamboo shoots and leaves, fruit, and nuts. Occasionally they catch and eat a small bird or mammal. As they have sharp curved claws they are good climbers and often spend the day high up in a tree, waking up at night. When angered they spit and hiss like cats and occasionally growl, standing up on their hind legs and boxing with their paws.

Usually the female has two young ones. They are blind when first born but their eyes open after three weeks or a month. Common pandas are easier to keep in zoos than giant pandas.

PANDORA. In Greek mythology, Pandora was the first woman in the world. Soon after the world had been created, when (according to the story) it was only inhabited by men and there were no women, the gods Zeus and Prometheus had a quarrel. Zeus did not want men to have fire on Earth so he hid it away, but Prometheus found it and brought it back

again. Zeus was so angry that he decided to send something down to men which would cause trouble, and he made the first woman. She was called Pandora, which means the "all-gifted", because the gods and goddesses gave her gifts to bring with her, including beauty, charm, and the art of flattery. Zeus's present was a special box which she was forbidden to open.

Pandora became the wife of Prometheus' brother Epimetheus and at first all went well, until she grew so curious about what was inside her box that at last she opened it. At once a swarm of little winged monsters flew out. They were disease, envy, anger, revenge, and all the other curses that brought the happiest times of the world to an end and left man miserable. Pandora tried to close the box, but it was too late. They had all escaped and flown over the world and only hope was left.

PANGOLIN see ANTEATER.

PANSY. Garden pansies, which may be grown in many beautiful colors—yellow, red, purple, almost black, maroon, bronze, and white—were all developed from the little wild

The petals of the garden pansy have beautiful markings and a velvet-like sheen.

yellow and purple pansies called heartsease (*Viola tricolor*). They were first cultivated early in the 19th century.

The petals of the pansy flower are unequal in size and generally of two colors. They have a long part, known as the spur, which contains the sweet liquid called nectar. A bee visiting a pansy alights on the large lower petal to get at the nectar. In collecting nectar, it also picks up pollen from the stamens. In order to prevent the flower's own pollen from falling on to its stigma, a little flap on a hinge closes over it. However, when the bee visits the next flower, it pushes open the flap as it reaches for the nectar, and leaves some pollen from the first flower on the stigma. When ripe, the fruit splits into three boat-shaped parts, throwing out the seeds.

There are several different species of wild pansy that grow mostly in exposed places in mild regions and in the mountains of the northern hemisphere. They belong to the family Violaceae, and so are related to violets (see VIOLET). As well as reproducing by seeds, they send out shoots from the same place on the stem as the solitary flowers. Pansies should be picked often, for then the later ones will be larger. They grow best in a rich soil, in a damp, cool climate.

PANTOMIME. At Christmas time in Great Britain, and in many other countries too, people go to the theater to see a special kind of play called a pantomime. The theme is usually a well-known fairy story—*Cinderella, Aladdin, Dick Whittington, Robinson Crusoe*, or perhaps *Babes in the Wood, Mother Goose, Puss in Boots, Jack and the Beanstalk*, or *The Forty Thieves*—with music, singing, dancing, and jokes as well. The hero is usually an actress dressed as a boy in tunic and tights and known as the principal boy. His mother or the heroine's ugly sisters are usually men dressed as comic old women. The heroine sings sentimental songs, and there is often a fairy queen and either a demon (in the shape of a rat, spider, wicked godmother, or other unpleasant character) or a regular villain. Other pantomime characters are a rough and

funny pair dressed as workmen, and an animal which, if a horse or cow, consists of two men inside the skin.

The pantomime usually starts in a seaport or market-place where chorus girls wander about singing until the main characters arrive to introduce themselves, some suffering undeserved poverty and others enjoying equally undeserved riches. As the pantomime goes on, the heroes or heroines win their way to riches, weddings, and living happily ever after. There are plenty of changes of scenery. Acrobats or jugglers perform while the scenery is being changed, and the comedian persuades the audience to sing a song. He usually plays the comical old woman part, or pantomime dame.

Barnaby's

The fairy tale, *Sleeping Beauty*, dramatized as a pantomime with singing, dancing, clowning, and jokes.

Harlequinade and Fairy Tale

Pantomimes developed from an older kind of entertainment called a *harlequinade*. The word pantomime used to mean (and often still does) "dumb show"—acting without using any words—and the harlequinade began as a kind of play acted in that way. There were certain "stock" characters, that is, characters who were in every harlequinade. They were Harlequin, Pierrot, Columbine, and Pantaloon. Harlequin ran away with

Columbine and was pursued by her father Pantaloon, whose servant, called Clown, got up to mischief. Pierrot, rather simple-minded and awkward, was funny and sad at the same time.

To lengthen this story there were opening scenes to show how a pair of lovers escaped from their enemies by changing into Harlequin and Columbine and then, in the end, changed back. This explains how the "transformation scene", such as when the fairy godmother changes Cinderella from a poor kitchen girl to a princess ready for the ball, came into pantomimes. Thousands of stories were used for the opening scenes of the harlequinade and some became favorites. Over time, nursery tales and fairy stories came to be used, and during the 19th century the entertainment that had first been designed for grown-ups changed to a treat mainly for children.

In the 18th-century pantomimes, the most important person was the actor playing the part of Harlequin. Then one day a young dancer named Joseph Grimaldi who played Clown made Londoners laugh so much that this character – called "Joey" after him – took first place instead of Harlequin. Since then it has nearly always been the leading comedian in a pantomime who matters most, although of course the principal boy is very important too. (See CLOWN.)

From 1880 onwards pantomimes were acted by performers from the music-hall. One famous one was Dan Leno, a wiry little figure with bright little eyes, a smile which seemed to spread right across his face, and remarkably agile legs. He acted the pantomime comedian at the Drury Lane theater, London, from 1888 to 1903. The best of the many pantomime comedians since his day was George Jackley, in the period between World Wars I and II. He was so great a favorite with children that he could win liking even for such unpleasant characters as Idle Jack, who stealthily put stolen money into Dick Whittington's wallet. Today comedians and actresses well known for their performances in films and television and on the radio often appear in pantomimes during the Christmas season.

See also MIME.

PAPER AND PAPER-MAKING.

Paper is used not only for writing and printing on, but also for wrapping and packing. It is the base material for some kinds of plastics, including those made in sheet and panel form. It is a valuable insulator for preventing the leakage of electricity (see CABLE, ELECTRIC) and is used to filter impurities from liquids.

Paper is believed to have been discovered in China in about AD105. The Arabs learned about it from some Chinese prisoners they took in the year 751 at Samarkand (now in Uzbekistan). The knowledge was carried to Sicily and Spain by the Moors and reached Italy in about 1276. The first paper mill in England is believed to have been set up near Stevenage (Hertfordshire) in about 1490. Nearly all the early paper mills were started in unused flour mills, which were generally beside rivers. Water is necessary to make paper and the water-wheel of the mill provided power to drive the simple machinery then used.

If you tear a sheet of paper and look closely at the torn edges you will see tiny hair-like fibers sticking out. These are the fibers of cellulose, the substance from which the cell-walls of plants and trees are made (see CELLULOSE). To make paper, the trees or plants that are used are broken down until every fiber is separated and the fibrous pulp is then mixed with water.

Until early in the 19th century all paper was made by hand. The paper maker took a large flat mold consisting of a sheet of cloth woven from wire and dipped it into a vat containing a mixture of fibers and water. When lifted out covered with a layer of pulp, the mold was shaken from side to side and backwards and forwards to make the fibers form an even mat and to drain the water. The wet sheet thus made was "couched", or laid on a sheet of woolen felt, followed by another sheet of felt and another of paper, and so on to form a pile of sheets. The pile was then squeezed in a

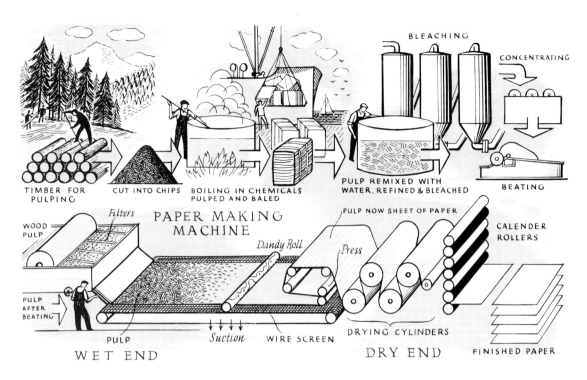

BLEACHING

CONCENTRATING

TIMBER FOR PULPING   CUT INTO CHIPS   BOILING IN CHEMICALS PULPED AND BALED   PULP REMIXED WITH WATER, REFINED & BLEACHED   BEATING

PAPER MAKING MACHINE

WOOD PULP

Filters

Dandy Roll

Press

PULP NOW SHEET OF PAPER

CALENDER ROLLERS

PULP AFTER BEATING

PULP   *Suction*   WIRE SCREEN   DRYING CYLINDERS   FINISHED PAPER

WET END   DRY END

press to remove the water and the sheets of paper were hung in a loft to dry. The sheets were then *sized* by dipping them in a bath of gelatin to prevent them from being too absorbent (like blotting paper). Hand-made paper, unlike that made by machinery, is as strong in one direction as in the other.

The paper-making machine was invented in 1799 by the Frenchman Louis Robert, and in 1804 the brothers Henry and Sealy Fourdrinier, together with the English engineer Bryan Donkin, made a machine of this type in England. This machine made it necessary to build other machines for preparing the fiber. Most modern paper is made from tree fibers whose cellulose is called *wood pulp*. There are two main kinds: wood pulp which has been cleaned by a chemical process, and mechanical pulp made by grinding the logs with rough grindstones turned under water. First the logs are tumbled together in "barking drums" to strip off the bark. For chemical pulp the logs are then cut into chips before being boiled in chemicals in tall, sealed vessels about 12 meters (40 feet) high. The pulp is bleached with other chemicals if it is

required for making white paper. If the pulp mill is close to the paper mill, the liquid pulp is pumped direct to the paper mill. Otherwise, after straining, the pulp is dried and cut into sheets which are packed into bales of about 200 kilograms (440 pounds). Wood pulp is prepared in Canada, the United States, Scandinavia, Russia, and other abundantly wooded countries. Much of the wood pulp used in Great Britain is obtained from overseas, although it is being produced increasingly from home-grown timber. The articles in this encyclopedia are printed on paper made from chemical pulp.

In the Paper Mill

In the paper mill the wood pulp goes to a beating engine or *beater*, which is a large vat of water in which the pulp goes round and round a central division, passing between a revolving roller fitted with knives and a set of fixed knives. These "develop" or cut the pulp into separate fibers of the length required for the type of paper being made. In most mills, the beater is being replaced by a *refiner*, which consists of a revolving cone fitted with cutting blades.

During beating or refining, size and coloring are added. Size consists of starch or rosin whose particles settle on the fibers, producing a flat surface that does not blur when inked. Dyes are "loaded", or added, to color the paper. Even if the paper is to be white some coloring is added, as without it the paper has a muddy, yellowish look.

The pulp is now ready for the paper-making machine, which may be 120 meters (400 feet) long and 10 meters (33 feet) wide and produces the paper in a continuous ribbon. The machine has a "wet end" and a "dry end". At the wet end is a tank in which the pulp from the beaters is mixed. At this stage the mixture is about 99 parts of water to 1 part of fiber. The milky pulp flows on to a moving belt of finely woven wire mesh called the *wire* which moves forwards at up to 650 meters (over 2,000 feet) per minute. This is supported on rollers or foils and is shaken slightly from side to side as it advances. The shaking movement prevents the fibers from lying all in the same direction and helps the water to drain away. The wire then passes over vacuum boxes which suck away more water. By the time the end of the wire is reached enough water has been removed to leave a continuous sheet of paper.

Often a *watermark* is added. This mark, which can be seen when the paper is held up to the light, is made by a large wire-mesh roll on which the letters or design of the watermark are raised from the surface. It is called the *dandy roll* and revolves as the paper passes beneath it, impressing its design in the soft sheet.

The "web" of the paper, as it is called, is lifted from the wire on to a moving belt of woolen or nylon felt which carries it forward to the drying cylinders. These are large heated rollers of which there may be as many as 50. The web passes over each cylinder in turn and the heat causes moisture to be drawn from the paper. At the dry end of the machine, the web consists of about 93 parts of fiber and 7 parts of water.

Paper making really ends at this point. But there are other processes to make papers suit-able for particular uses. Among these is *tub sizing*, in which resins, starch and clays are at times added to the pulp preparation in order to improve the surface. This process is sometimes carried out on the paper-making machine itself and is then called "surface sizing". Another separate process is the coating of the paper with china clay (see CHINA CLAY) and then polishing it by passing the web through a set of polished, swiftly revolving rollers called a *calender*. This makes "art" paper, the glossy kind used for pictures. Modern coating processes are of three main kinds: blade coating, air knife coating, and roll coating. Blade coating is normally done "off" the paper machine, as is air knife coating. But roll coating is done "on" the paper machine and can either be a complete coating, or a first coat followed by "off-machine" coating by the blade or air knife process.

After the "on" machine treatments, the paper is wound on to spindles, each of which may contain up to 28 kilometers (17.5 miles) of paper, 6.6 meters (22 feet) wide. When a spindle is full, it must be replaced by an empty one without interrupting the flow of paper.

Besides wood pulp, paper can be made of other materials such as cotton, linen, esparto grass, sugar-cane, and flax. Also, paper-like substances are made from man-made materials. Waste paper, too, is used to make pulp. It is first broken up mechanically into pulp, and then treated with chemicals to remove ink and any unwanted materials. Finally it may be bleached if white paper is required. Recycled paper is also widely used for packaging such as egg boxes.

PAPUA NEW GUINEA. In the eastern half of the large island of New Guinea, between northeast Australia and the equator, is Papua New Guinea. (The western half is Indonesian and is called Irian Jaya.)

Papua New Guinea is an independent parliamentary Commonwealth state, consisting of two territories formerly governed by Australia, the Territory of New Guinea in the north and Papua in the south.

A high range of mountains runs like a

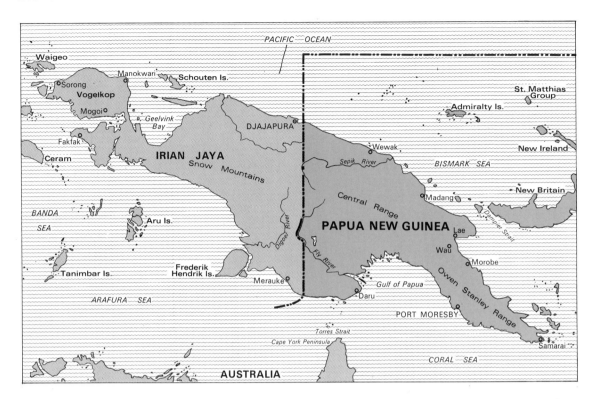

backbone along the middle of the island. The climate is hot and there is a high rainfall. Much of the country is covered with forest, and some of its animals, such as the wallaby, are like those of Australia. The big fruit-eating bats called flying foxes are very common and birds of paradise are also found. There are also approximately 70 species of non-poisonous snake.

More than 700 different ethnic groups live in Papua-New Guinea. These can be divided into two main groups, Papuan and Melanesian. About 80 per cent of the people are Papuan, while less than 17 per cent are Melanesian. The remainder are Polynesian, Chinese, or European. About half of the population speaks a Melanesian pidgin language (a mixture of English and local language) which is one of the country's two *lingua francas* (a language which people who normally speak different languages use to communicate with one another). The other is Hira which is spoken by 150,000 people. Even though English is the official language, only 2 per cent of the population can speak it.

Although town populations are growing, most people live in villages and live on vegetables, coconuts, pigs, and fish.

Coconuts, rubber, and some coffee and cocoa are important to the economy. Papua New Guinea is rich in minerals. Petroleum (oil) and gold are found, and one of the world's largest copper deposits is mined on Bougainville. Tim-

Courtesy, Papua New Guinea High Commission

A primary school class displays craft work in a Papua New Guinea village.

Courtesy, Papua New Guinea High Commission
Traditional stilt houses on M'Buke Island in the
Admiralty Islands, now part of Papua New Guinea.

FACTS ABOUT PAPUA NEW GUINEA.

AREA: 462,840 square kilometers (178,703 square miles).
POPULATION: 3,499,000 (1987).
GEOGRAPHICAL FEATURES: A range of mountains over
 4,870 meters (16,000 feet) high in places, runs through
 the whole length of the island. In the north and south
 are broad plains, swampy and thickly forested.
CAPITAL: Port Moresby.
CHIEF PRODUCTS: Copra and coconut products, rubber,
 sugar-cane, sago, cocoa, forest products; gold,
 petroleum, tuna.

---

ber, and fishing (particularly for tuna) are also
growing industries. River and air transportation are important as roads and railroads
are few. The capital of Papua New Guinea is
Port Moresby in southeast Papua where the
university is established.

History

Peoples from Southeast Asia may have
migrated to the island as long as 50,000 years
ago. The first Europeans to see the island were
the Portuguese and Spanish in the early 16th
century. The British were the first to attempt
to colonize the land, in 1793, but the Dutch
claimed the western half in 1828 as part of the
Dutch East Indies. John Moresby, after whom
the capital is named, surveyed the southeast
in the 1870s. This was eventually claimed for
Britain.

The Territory of New Guinea included the
group of islands called the Bismarck Archipel-

ago, of which the most important are New Britain
and New Ireland, and Bougainville and Buka,
two of the Solomon Islands. The territory came
under German control in 1884, but after World
War I, it was given to Australia to govern on
behalf of the League of Nations. Papua, on the
other hand, was taken under British protection
in 1884 and later claimed as a British possession, control of which was gradually handed
over to Australia.

In 1942 Papua and New Guinea were captured by Japan, and after World War II the
United Nations agreed that New Guinea
should continue as a trust territory, administered by Australia. From 1949 Papua and New
Guinea were governed jointly from the capital,
Port Moresby in southeast Papua.

Papua New Guinea became independent in
1975.

PAPYRUS. The ancient Egyptians used the
stems of the papyrus (*Cyperus papyrus*), a
reed-like plant belonging to the sedge family,
to make a form of paper. They cut the stem
into long strips, the center one being the
broadest and most valuable. These strips were
laid side by side, their edges overlapping
slightly, and other strips were placed across
them. They were then stuck together, either
by soaking them in water from the Nile or with
wheat-flour paste. The sheets were hammered
or rolled flat and dried in the sun.

The papyrus plant itself grows to a height of
up to 3 meters (9.8 feet). The stems are soft
and sometimes as large as a man's wrist at
the base. At the top of the stems are drooping,
slender branches which look like shaggy,
coarse hair. The leaves are small and the roots
strong.

The Egyptians also wove baskets from the
slender stalks of the papyrus and made mats
and sails from the thicker ones. The pith
inside the stems was dried and used for fuel,
or boiled and eaten by the poorer people.

The papyrus is still found in Ethiopia and
the region of the upper Nile, but it does not
grow as abundantly as it once did in lower
Egypt (the area round the Nile delta).

The papyrus plant is often used as an orna-

Papyrus reeds were cultivated in ancient times for the writing material, papyrus, made from the stems.

mental water plant in warm areas. The dwarf papyrus (*Cyperus isocladus*) is sometimes grown as a pot plant.

PARACHUTE. When an object is dropped through the air, the force of gravity will tend to make it fall faster and faster. However, as its speed increases, the air resistance or "drag" will build up until it just equals the mass of the falling object. Once these two forces are in balance, speed will remain constant; this speed is known as the object's "terminal velocity". The human body, being fairly dense, has a terminal velocity of about 190 kilometers (118 miles) per hour. (See GRAVITY; VELOCITY.) However, by attaching himself to a device which greatly increases his air resistance, without adding much to his mass, a man can reduce his terminal velocity so that a gentle descent can be safely made. The name given to this device is "parachute", from the French words *parer* and *chute*, meaning "to avoid" and "a fall".

Leonardo da Vinci (1452–1519), the great Italian artist, designed the first model parachute, and his sketch shows a man attached to four ropes beneath a pyramid-shaped linen tent. No practical progress was made for 250 years, however, and then it was the parasol that inspired parachute inventors. In about 1777, the French balloonist Joseph Montgolfier dropped a live sheep attached to a parachute from a high tower, and in 1785 his fellow countryman J. P. Blanchard dropped a dog

from a balloon. L. S. Lenormand jumped from a tower in 1783, but the first person to make parachute drops regularly and successfully was André-Jacques Garnerin, also a Frenchman. He descended from a balloon over Paris on 22 October 1797. In the 19th century, parachuting from balloons became a popular form of entertainment.

All the successful early parachutes were umbrella-shaped, with rigid ribs and silk or canvas covering. The first limp-canopied parachutes appeared in the 1880s. They were flat disks of material with a number of shroud lines attached around their circumference. Like the earlier types they were dropped,

A parachute takes advantage of air resistance to slow the descent of someone falling to earth.

As it comes in to land, a high-speed jet aircraft can be slowed down by means of a brake parachute.

already open, from balloons, or were pulled from a container attached to the balloon when the parachutist made his jump. In 1908 the American A. L. Stevens developed a parachute carried in a pack and opened by the parachutist pulling a rip-cord after falling freely for as far as he dared.

The first successful parachute jump from an airplane was made in 1912 by Captain Albert Berry of the US Army. In World War I parachutes were seldom provided for pilots, other than balloon crews. Only in the last few months of the war, and only in Germany, were parachutes issued to aircrew. The parachutes used were of the attached kind, and not until 1918 was the pack type, rip-cord-operated parachute considered as a means of escaping from a damaged or burning aircraft. The man who patented this kind of parachute in 1918 was an American, Floyd Smith, but another American, Leslie Irvin, is associated with the later worldwide development of parachutes.

Modern parachutes are usually made of nylon with canopies about 5 to 6 meters (16 to 19 feet) across when opened. The canopy is attached by cords called shroud lines to a webbing harness round the airman's body. The parachute and shroud lines are packed in a canvas-covered bundle which may form a seat or back cushion for the wearer in the aircraft. Parachutes usually weigh between 9 and 15 kilograms (20 and 34 pounds).

When an airman uses a parachute, he steps or falls out of the aircraft and after a few seconds' pause the parachute is opened, either by a manually operated rip-cord, or by an automatic timing device, or by a line fastened to the aircraft. Elastic cords pull back the flaps of the parachute pack and release a small "pilot parachute" about 75 centimeters (30 inches) across. This fills with air and drags the main canopy and shroud lines from the pack. As the canopy unfolds, the air rushing past opens it fully. The parachutist drops at about 6 meters (19 feet) per second and can exercise some control over his gliding angle and point of landing by pulling the shroud lines on one side or the other, so spilling some of the air out of the parachute. To make landing easier he can turn himself to face the direction of drift. The harness is fitted with a quick release mechanism.

During World War II thousands of airmen saved their lives by parachuting to safety. By 1945, however, aircraft were flying so fast that it was difficult for pilots to climb out of the cockpit into the airstream. Also, when the aircraft was flying close to the ground, there was not enough time for a parachute to open. The Germans used a spring-assisted catapult in some of their fighters, but the best answer was found to be an ejector seat fired out of the aircraft by one or more explosive charges. These seats were developed in Great Britain, notably by James Martin. The modern system is fully automatic. When the pilot pulls the ejection lever, the cockpit canopy is jettisoned, his seat is fired clear of the aircraft, his emergency oxygen supply is turned on, and at the right height the seat drops away and the parachute opens.

Parachuting is a popular sport and experts use special parachutes with open panels to try to land precisely on a given target. These give the parachutist a useful forward speed, so that he can make corrections and counteract the effect of the wind. New shapes of parachute, called ram-air parachutes, are in use which look more like curved nylon wings.

Modern aircraft land at such a high speed that they run a long distance after touching down. To reduce this run, some aircraft are fitted with a parachute which opens at touchdown and acts as a brake. Parachutes are used to land spacecraft safely after they have re-entered the atmosphere.

PARAGUAY is a landlocked republic in South America. No part of its territory is closer than 950 kilometers (600 miles) to the ocean. It is divided into two by the Paraguay River, the eastern part containing far more people than the Chaco region, to the west. Part of Paraguay's eastern boundary with Brazil is formed

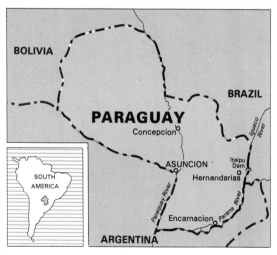

by the great Parana River which reaches the Atlantic as the Plata River (see PARANA, PARAGUAY, AND PLATA RIVERS). Part of the southern boundary with Argentina is formed by the River Pilcomayo and to the northwest of Paraguay is Bolivia.

The hilly district east of Paraguay River is thickly wooded and has wide valleys with fertile red soil. The Chaco, west of the river, is mostly an area of flat grasslands with trees growing in groups, and much of it becomes flooded during the rainy season. Being south of the equator, Paraguay has its summer from

Tony Morrison/South American Pictures

Chaco grassland with motacū and totai palms in the background.

October to March, during which it is wet and very hot. The winters are warm and fairly dry.

In eastern Paraguay the trees are mostly evergreens and include one of the holly family whose leaves are used to make *yerba mate*, a kind of tea which is very popular in Paraguay and in neighboring countries. The wood of the quebracho tree, which grows in the higher parts of the Chaco, is so hard that it will break an axe (*que-bracho* is Spanish for "break-axe") and is used for making railroad ties, while the tannin obtained from its bark is used in making leather. Another valuable tree is the bitter orange, whose leaves give oil of petitgrain, used in the manufacture of perfumes.

Animals found in Paraguay include jaguars, pumas, tapirs, anteaters, armadillos, and deer, as well as snakes and brilliantly colored parrots in the forests. There are red stumplike ant hills everywhere.

The Guarani Indians, who were the early people of Paraguay, form the basis of the population, but there are also many *mestizos* of mixed Indian and Spanish descent and a few people of pure Spanish descent in Asuncion, the capital. Many Paraguayans speak both

Tony Morrison/South American Pictures

Yerba trees being checked for their quality. These trees produce yerba maté, or Paraguayan tea.

Spanish and Guarani and most of them are Roman Catholic.

Asuncion, on the east bank of the Paraguay River, is the republic's capital and chief river port. Concepcion, about 210 kilometers (130 miles) higher up the river, is the center of the cattle industry. Villarrica is an agricultural and manufacturing center on the railroad between Asuncion and Encarnacion in the southeast corner of the country.

Tony Morrison/South American Pictures

Asuncion, the capital of Paraquay, with the River Paraguay in the distance.

Agriculture and Industry

The people of Paraguay grow manioc (a plant whose root is used for food), corn, rice, and peanuts. Cotton, sugar-cane, fruit, tobacco, and coffee are other crops, and there is a large cattle industry supplying hides and meat, much of which is canned in Paraguay.

The country has few minerals, but cement is made from limestone and other factories make tannin from quebracho bark, cotton cloth, vegetable oils and a spirit drink called *cana* which the cattle herders enjoy. Paraguay is famous for its delicate cobweb lace called *nanduti*.

One of the world's largest hydroelectric projects is being built by Paraguay and Brazil at Itaipu on the Parana River. Two other projects, in collaboration with Argentina, the Corpus and Yacyreta-Apipe schemes, are also being planned. Paraguay could become a leading exporter of electricity by the end of the 1980s.

FACTS ABOUT PARAGUAY

AREA: 406,752 square kilometers (157,048 square miles).
POPULATION: 3,897,000 (1987).
GOVERNMENT: Independent republic.
CAPITAL: Asuncion.
GEOGRAPHICAL FEATURES: In the east, between the Parana and Paraguay rivers, are thickly forested ridges rising to about 600 meters (2,000 feet); in the west is a district called the Chaco, mainly marshes and poor quality grasslands.
CHIEF EXPORTS: Cotton, timber, quebracho extract (tannin from the quebracho tree), meat products, hides, tobacco, oils, coffee.
IMPORTANT TOWNS: Asuncion, Villarrica, San Lorenzo, Lambare, Fernando de la Mora, Concepcion, Encarnacion.
EDUCATION: Where schools are available, children must attend between the ages of 7 and 14.

Most goods are carried by water. Fairly large steamers come up the Parana only as far as Corrientes in Argentina and smaller ships are used to reach the Paraguayan river ports. The Paraguayan main railroad from Asuncion to Encarnacion is linked by a ferry to the Argentine railroad at Posadas. Visitors to Paraguay also travel by air, and it is now possible to reach Paraguay by road from Argentina and Brazil on the Pan-American Highway (see PAN-AMERICAN HIGHWAY).

History

Asuncion was founded by the Spaniards in 1537 and became a center of Spanish rule in South America. It is the oldest permanently inhabited settlement in the interior of South

America. In 1608 Jesuit missionaries came to convert the people, gathered them into settlements known as "missions" and taught them agriculture and handicrafts. The missions were prosperous and successful. But the local landlords desired the land and its willing workforce. In 1767 the Jesuits were driven out of Paraguay and, indeed, out of all South America, by Spain who feared that they were becoming too powerful. The Indians were unwilling to return to their former, less effective, methods of agriculture and set to work on the large Spanish-owned estates in return for food and shelter.

In 1810 the people of Argentina began their struggle for independence and soon afterwards the Paraguayans too broke away from Spain. After that Paraguay was ruled by one dictator after another. The dictator Francisco Solano Lopez (1827–70) plunged his country into war with Argentina, Brazil, and Uruguay. This ferocious war began in 1865 and did not end until Lopez was killed in command of the Paraguayan army in 1870. Paraguay was defeated and lost not only a great deal of land but also most of its men, who were killed in battle.

In 1932 a frontier dispute with Bolivia led to another costly war. Both sides claimed the Chaco and the fighting there lasted for three years. Paraguay was victorious and gained about three-quarters of the disputed land, although the war cost more than 100,000 lives.

Paraguay is a republic ruled by a President, who has usually had wide powers of government. President Alfredo Stroessner held office continuously from 1954 until 1989.

PARAGUAY RIVER see PARANA, PARAGUAY, AND PLATA RIVERS.

PARANA, PARAGUAY, AND PLATA RIVERS.

This river system is the second largest in South America, that of the Amazon being larger. The Parana and the Paraguay rise in the tropical regions of Brazil. After flowing about 2,400 kilometers (1,500 miles) southwards the Paraguay joins the Parana

Tony Morrison/South American Pictures

The huge Itaipu project on the Parana River provides much-needed water power.

at the southeastern corner of the republic of Paraguay. The Parana's waters are being harnessed by the great Itaipu Dam, to provide hydroelectric power. Beyond this, the Parana continues southwards across the fertile plains of Argentina for about another 1,100 kilometers (680 miles) before being joined by the Uruguay River. Here it becomes a wide shallow estuary between Argentina and Uruguay, and is called the Plata. The estuary is over 300 kilometers (185 miles) long, and where it reaches the sea it is 221 kilometers (137 miles) wide.

This great river system is used by traffic carrying agricultural products, manufactured goods, and petroleum. However, its winding course, floods, droughts, shifting sandbanks and, sometimes, rapids, tend to make navi-

Tony Morrison/South American Pictures

Fishermen on the River Paraguay near Ascuncion, below Remanso bridge.

gation difficult. The waters are also used for irrigation.

PARAPSYCHOLOGY. Psychology is the study of the mind. Parapsychology is the study of abnormal (or paranormal) phenomena, happenings apparently not explained by the laws of science. (*Para* here means "beyond".)

Normally, we gain knowledge and find out about things through our five senses (see SENSES). For example, we see objects placed in our view. However, some people claim they can "see" things hidden from their view. This is called clairvoyance or "second sight". Others claim to be *telepathic*, to "know" what people are thinking without being told. These are both examples of *extrasensory perception*, or ESP. "Levitation" (making objects rise in the air) is said to be an example of *psychokinesis*, or PK. Another example is the unexplained behavior of objects which is sometimes blamed on a "poltergeist".

Ghosts, magic, and coincidence have all been suggested as explanations for such phenomena. Some people believe that they show the power of the human mind to communicate without using the normal senses. In a typical parapsychology test, a person is asked to guess the symbol on a unseen card. He or she does this many, many times. The results are examined to see if the number of correct guesses is greater than it would be if pure chance was at work. The experimenters are looking for scientific evidence that these curious happenings really do take place.

See also GHOST; MAGIC.

PARASITE AND SAPROPHYTE. A parasite is a plant or animal that lives with, in, or on another living organism. The other organism is called the *host*. A saprophyte is an organism that lives on dead or decaying matter.

All living things depend on one another. However, certain plants and animals could not live at all if they did not live together with a certain other kind of living thing. Very often, one of these partners is a parasite. The parasite takes from the host and gives it nothing in return. The name for this relationship is parasitism.

A parasite may be either a plant or an animal; and it may live off either a plant or an animal. Sometimes a parasite can live with many types of hosts, but more often it can live only with one or a few different types of host.

Sometimes the parasite kills its host by taking too much of the nourishment the host needs. Or it may give off substances which poison the host, making the host weak and sick. This may be unfortunate for the parasite because it depends upon the host in order to live. Unless it finds another host, it will die too.

A parasite may live on after its animal host dies if the flesh of the host is eaten by another animal. The parasite then may enter the other animal and use it as the host. A certain species of threadworm found in dogs can pass from the female dog upon which it lives to the unborn young inside the mother. In this way it goes from one generation of dogs to the next. Certain parasitic germs are carried by insects from one animal to another.

Because theirs is not a safe and certain way of life, parasites produce large numbers of eggs.

Plant Parasites

Many diseases of animals are caused by parasitic plants that cannot be seen except under a powerful microscope. These parasites are bacterial germs. Other parasitic bacteria cause diseases of plants, such as the black rot of cabbage, bean blight, fire blight of pear, and crown gall of apple. Bacteria are very dangerous as parasites because they are easily carried from place to place; they can stand heat, cold, and dryness; and they quickly increase in numbers. (See BACTERIA; PLANT.)

Seed plants that are parasites are not common. This is perhaps because most seed plants are able to make their own food in sunlight, and so do not have to live on other things. Some plants, including the common mistletoe, make some of their food and take the rest from a host plant. These are called semiparasites. True parasites, such as the leafless climbing dodder, feed entirely off host plants. Because they have lost all of their green coloring matter (chlorophyll), they are unable to manufacture any of their own food.

There are many fungus parasites. These reproduce by tiny spores. The skin disease called ringworm is not caused by a worm but by one of these fungal parasites. Rusts, mildews, some blights, and smuts are parasitic fungi that attack plants. (See FUNGUS). Mushrooms are also fungi. A few are parasitic, but most are saprophytic, living on dead plant material.

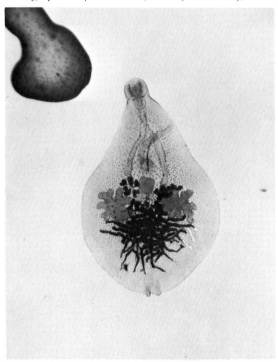

Courtesy, Department of Parasitic Worms, Museum of Natural History, London

The fluke is a flatworm parasite that lives attached to the intestine of sea fishes.

Animal Parasites

Among animals, as among plants, the most important parasites are the smallest ones. These are microscopic, single-celled animals called protozoa (see PROTOZOA). Often they cannot stand extremes of temperature and dryness as bacteria can. Therefore they have come to depend upon some animal, such as an insect, to carry them to a host. The protozoan that causes African sleeping sickness is carried by the tse-tse fly. The malaria parasite is carried by the female Anopheles mosquito (see MALARIA; SLEEPING SICKNESS). In such diseases the parasite is not simply carried from one host to another in the way the typhoid bacteria are carried on the hairy feet of the housefly. These parasites actually live part of their life in the insect, which is their second host. Yaws, recurrent fever, and amoebic dysentery are other human diseases caused by protozoa.

Another important group of animal parasites is the worms. Trichinosis, a disease of pigs, rats, and human beings, is caused by a roundworm, trichina. This worm enters the body when a person eats poorly cooked pork. Hookworm disease is caused by a worm that gets into the body through tiny cuts in the feet (see HOOKWORM). The tapeworm is sometimes more than 3 meters (10 feet) in length. It lives in the intestines, after entering the body through the eating of infected meat or fish (see TAPEWORM). The stomach worms of sheep, dog worms, and the liver fluke of sheep, cows, and pigs are worm parasites.

Higher in the animal kingdom than the protozoa and worms are the insects and mite parasites. One of these is the botfly, the larvae of which live in the stomachs, skins, or noses of horses and sheep and other hoofed animals. Fleas, ticks, and lice are all parasites too.

Parasitic plants must not be confused with *saprophytes*, plants that get their food from dead plants and animals or lifeless products of living things. Examples of saprophytes are bacteria of decay, mushrooms, bread mold, and the bacteria that sour milk and wine and create flavor and aroma in cheese.

Saprophytes, which cause decay, are for the most part very useful organisms. They change

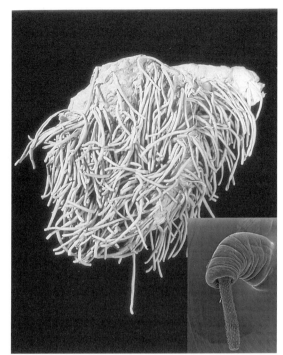

Courtesy, Department of Parasitic Worms, Museum of Natural History, London
A heavy infestation of thorny-headed worms attached to the intestine of a killer whale. **Inset:** Close-up of the head of a spiny-headed worm shows its long proboscis covered with sharp barbs that it uses to attach itself to its host.

dead material into substances that living things can use as food. Without saprophytes higher plants and animals would soon disappear from the Earth. The saprophytes set free the elements and simple compounds that would otherwise be tied up in dead bodies of plants and animals.

Symbiosis and Commensalism

Sometimes a plant or animal lives co-operatively with another plant or animal. Each supplies something which the other needs, and each gets something in return. In such cases, the two are called *symbionts*, or those-who-live-together. Such a partnership is called *symbiosis*.

An example of symbiosis is the case of certain bacteria that live on the roots of such plants as beans, clover, and alfalfa. These bacteria take free nitrogen gas out of the air and make it into nitrates that can be absorbed and used by plants in manufactur-

ing food. The bean plant supplies water, minerals, manufactured sugar and starch, and also protection for the bacteria. (See LEGUMINOUS PLANTS.)

It is not always easy to tell the difference between symbiosis and commensalism. *Commensalism*, however, is a relationship in which one of the partners is helped and the other is neither helped nor harmed. The parasite benefits, but the host is unaffected. Some very small crabs, for example, live under an oyster's shell. They eat the oyster's food and use its shell for protection, but do not harm the oyster.

PARENT AND PARENTHOOD. The love and care of parents, or a parent, plays an important part in human development. But parents are also indispensable in a biological sense. Every living thing comes from some other living thing, for life cannot arise spontaneously (see LIFE). A human baby is conceived when a sperm from its father unites with an ovum from its mother, as explained in REPRODUCTION. Our parents pass on to us

Richard and Sally Greenhill

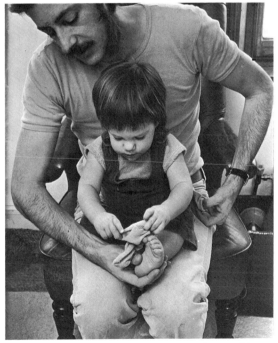

A child's earliest ties are to its parents, who provide love, care, and instruction in basic skills.

certain inherited characteristics. They give us our "genetic potential". (See HEREDITY AND GENETICS.)

As well as passing on physical characteristics (eye color, for example), parents also shape the environment in which we grow up. They play a "caring role". Birds feed their young in the nest and care for them until they can fend for themselves. There are exceptions in nature, however. For example, frogs leave their tadpoles to the mercy of hungry predators. Young frogs therefore have only instinct (see ANIMAL BEHAVIOR) to help them in their struggle to survive.

Frank Lane Picture Agency

Animals, too, depend on their parents for food, protection, affection, and companionship.

In mammals, and particularly in human beings, parents must be providers and teachers for much longer. Compared to most young animals, the human baby comes into the world at an early stage in its development, and is totally dependent on others for survival. A young wildebeest, by contrast, can walk within minutes of being born. It must do so to keep up with the herd, or it will be eaten by predators. But a human baby cannot walk until it is about a year old. (See BABY.)

A long period of dependency, when the young need their parents, means that more information can be passed on from generation to generation. In the case of human beings, an enormous fund of *acquired*, or learned, knowledge, from the art of making fire to advanced electronics, is added to the fund of *instinctive* knowledge. If acquired knowledge had to be rediscovered by each generation, we would still be using flint tools.

The parents carrying out the caring role are not necessarily the biological, or natural, parents. A young cuckoo's parents are a male and female cuckoo, but its caring parents are the unfortunate birds in whose nest the cuckoo has laid her egg. A human baby may be adopted and thus be raised by adults who have no biological relationship.

PARIS. In Greek stories Paris was the son of Priam, king of Troy. When he was born, he was left on a mountainside to die, for his mother Hecuba had dreamed that he would cause Troy's destruction. However, some shepherds found and brought up the boy, and later he was recognized by his parents who reclaimed him.

Paris was chosen by the gods to judge a quarrel between the goddesses Hera, Athena, and Aphrodite about which of them was the most beautiful. Each goddess offered Paris a wonderful gift if he would choose her. Hera promised to make Paris ruler over all Europe and Asia. Athena promised that she would make him a great soldier who would lead the Trojans to victory over the Greeks. Aphrodite promised him that he would win the most beautiful woman in the world. Paris decided to choose Aphrodite's offer. This choice is called the Judgment of Paris.

Aphrodite took Paris to Sparta, in Greece, to the home of King Menelaus. Menelaus' wife, Helen, was the most beautiful woman in the world. When Menelaus was away from home, Paris took Helen with him to his father's palace in Troy. The Greeks demanded that Helen be returned to Greece, but the Trojans refused, thus causing the Trojan War. (See TROJAN WAR.)

During the fighting, Paris was about to be overcome by Menelaus when Aphrodite helped him escape. Later he shot an arrow that killed the Greek hero Achilles. Paris himself was wounded by an arrow and died.

After ten years of terrible fighting, the war ended, and Troy was destroyed. Hecuba's dream had come true.

PARIS is the capital of France, and has existed as a settlement for 2,000 years. It is by far the largest and most important French city and is, in nearly every sense, the center of the nation. It is also one of the most beautiful capitals in the world. It lies on both banks of the River Seine in the midst of the wide fertile plains forming the northern half of France. Paris proper (Ville de Paris) is made up of 20 *arrondissements* (municipal districts) and has a population of just over 2 million. Outside are the suburbs in which three out of four Parisians live. The total urban area has a population of 9 million.

Historic Paris

In ancient times, the easiest way to cross the Seine was at an island in the river. This island, now the Île de la Cité in the heart of Paris, was made into a fortified town by the Parisii, a Gallic tribe, who joined the island to the banks by wooden bridges (see GAUL). The town was called Lutetia by the Romans.

The Île de la Cité became the heart of medieval Paris and the capital of the French kings. On it was built Notre-Dame, a cathedral which was begun in the 12th century and is one of the most beautiful Gothic churches in existence.

By the 12th century, Paris had spread to the river banks and was surrounded by ramparts. Northwestwards the marshes were drained and became a suburb called Marais, where the noblemen lived. The Marais stretches eastwards to the Place de la Bastille, where the famous fortress and prison once stood that was stormed by the Parisians on 14 July 1789, and spurred on the French Revolution (see BASTILLE).

The south side of the river, known as the Left Bank, was the center of medieval Paris. A university was founded there in the 13th century called the Sorbonne. Today, it is part of the University of Paris, which is split into 13 separate universities spread throughout the city, with a total of 300,000 students. For centuries the Left Bank was the home of artists, writers, and students and it is still the main center of French art and culture. Near the Sorbonne is the building called the Panthéon, where many great men are buried.

Also on the Left Bank are the two houses of the French parliament, most of the government offices, and the famous gardens of the Palais du Luxembourg. Further west is the

The cathedral of Notre-Dame, founded in 1163, is one of the oldest and most beautiful Gothic cathedrals in existence. It sits on an island, the Île de la Cité, in the middle of the Seine in the heart of Paris.

Hôtel des Invalides. The French word *hôtel* here means "hostel". It was built by Louis XIV for his wounded soldiers. It contains the tomb of the Emperor Napoleon I, who in his will had asked to be buried "on the banks of the Seine among the French people I have loved so well". To the west again is the Eiffel Tower, Paris's most recognizable landmark, which with its television mast is more than 300 meters (985 feet) tall.

On the north side of the river, known as the Right Bank, stands the Palais du Louvre, which was at one time a royal palace on the north bank, and now contains priceless art treasures. West of the Louvre are the Tuileries Gardens, where a splendid palace once stood, and the Place de la Concorde, one of the largest and finest squares in the world. It was in the Place de la Concorde that people were beheaded during the French Revolution. From here the broad tree-lined Avenue des Champs-Élysées leads to the Place Charles de Gaulle (formerly Place de l'Étoile), from which streets reach out like the rays of a star. In the middle stands the Arc de Triomphe, or triumphal arch, built by Napoleon I to commemorate his victories. Under the Arc de Triomphe lies the memorial to France's Unknown Soldier of World War I. Westwards, broad avenues lead to the Bois de Boulogne, a wooded public park which used to be a royal hunting ground. It contains lakes and the two famous racetracks of Longchamp and Auteuil. To the northwest is a huge modern business center, known as La Défense, with many skycrapers.

Between 1853 and 1870 Georges Haussmann transformed Paris, encouraged by Napoleon III. Crowded slums gave way to broad avenues, and more open spaces. (Broad avenues also made the erection of barricades by rioters more difficult.) New sewers, water supply, bridges, and a new Opera House, one of the largest in the world, were also built. Haussmann planned the system of the boulevards, magnificent wide avenues some of which run along the lines of the old ramparts of Paris. Those in the north, such as the boulevards de la Madeleine, des Capucines, and des Italiens, form a splendid setting for

Hutchison Library

The view looking northwest from the Eiffel Tower towards La Défense business district. The Trocadero Gardens are in the foreground.

the big stores, restaurants, theaters, and hotels. North of them the striking white church of the Sacré Coeur stands on the hill of Montmartre, a district which is known for its music-halls and cabarets.

Paris in the 1990s

Most Parisians live in apartment buildings. Many of the older blocks are of five or six stories and have two or more apartments on each floor that are reached by a staircase from a court behind a single front gate, which is looked after by a *concierge*, or caretaker. Many people like to sit outside a café with a drink while they read, chat or watch the passers-by. They go to work by car, on green single-decker buses or by the *métro*, which is the name for the underground railroad. Traffic on the roads is very heavy.

Since the 17th century the main roads of France have been planned to fan out from

Paris, as do the French railroads. In addition, the city is a port, and the Seine is linked through canals and other rivers with the English Channel, the Mediterranean, Germany, and Belgium and with other parts of France. The city has two busy airports, Orly and Charles de Gaulle. These excellent communications have made Paris a very important industrial center. Most of the factories are in a ring among the outer suburbs. Among their products are automobiles, electrical and engineering goods, chemicals and medicines. Paris is the center of the French film industry. In the southern suburbs there are tanneries, cement works, breweries, and tobacco factories. Within the city itself are manufactured many luxury goods, the chief being women's clothes, jewelry, perfumes, china, and furniture. Modern skyscrapers, such as the group known as La Défense and the 200-meter (650-foot) tower of Maine-Montparnasse, altered Paris in the 1970s. As well as the Pompidou Centre for the Arts (Beaubourg) with its multicolored service ducts outside the building, several other massive building projects were commissioned in the 1980s, including a new museum inside the old Gare D'Orsay (train station) and a new popular opera house beside the Bastille.

The population of Paris is about 2,152,000.

PARK. A park is an open space mainly used for leisure and recreation. Parks are usually found in towns and cities, as they provide a small piece of the countryside when the real countryside is far away. National parks are areas set aside for the preservation of natural beauty and wildlife and are dealt with in a separate article, NATIONAL PARKS AND MONUMENTS.

The earliest parks were hunting grounds owned by royal families. Although other people were often allowed to walk in them and sometimes gather wood, they were not usually allowed to hunt animals. These hunting parks existed in Persia as well as medieval Europe. Gradually, well-worn paths developed and shelters were built where formal gardens became established. Windsor and Richmond parks in London began like this. The word "park" is still used today to describe the land surrounding a large house, which may be partly deer park, partly grazing land for herds of sheep and cattle, and partly formal gardens. After the time of the Renaissance more formal gardens began to be laid out. You can read more about the development of gardens in the article GARDENS AND GARDENING.

Open spaces in towns originated in meeting places such as the agora in Athens and the

Courtesy, Promotion Australia

Hyde Park in Sydney, Australia, provides city dwellers and office workers with a place to relax in the fresh air.

forum in Rome. These were market places where public meetings were also held. There were statues of political leaders and gods, temples for religious worship, and nearby places set aside for athletes to train.

During the Middle Ages in Europe the only open spaces in cities were market squares, often in front of a church. But most cities were so small that it was easy to get to the countryside outside the city walls. Only in the mid-19th century, when cities began to expand rapidly as a result of the Industrial Revolution, did it become necessary to set aside space in cities specially for recreation. People who worked in industry spent most of their time in noisy dark factories. They lived in overcrowded conditions and in badly ventilated houses without proper sanitation, and they needed to spend what little leisure time they had in the open air.

Sometimes landowners gave part of their own parks to the public, or philanthropists (wealthy people wishing to benefit others) provided money to buy land for parks. For example, the Bois de Boulogne in Paris was a royal park given to the city by Napoleon III. Other parks were provided by city governments themselves. Examples are Victoria Park in east London and Central Park in New York city, which was opened in 1876.

Some well-known parks, such as Kew Gardens, London, and the Botanic Gardens in Melbourne, Australia, originated as botanical gardens, which are dealt with in a separate article.

PARK, Mungo (1771–1806). The Scottish explorer Mungo Park was born near Selkirk and became a doctor. When a young man he was chosen to mount an expedition to discover the course of the River Niger. It was known that a great river flowed through West Africa south of the Sahara Desert but no one knew where it went to. Some thought that it flowed into the River Nile.

Park started in 1795 from the mouth of the Gambia River on the west coast of Africa with two black servants. When he reached the lands ruled by Moorish chiefs he was robbed and imprisoned but managed to escape. He reached the Niger at Ségou and followed it far enough to prove that it flowed eastwards. Then he had to turn back. He himself now believed that the Niger flowed into the River Congo.

In 1805 the British government asked Park to lead another expedition to the Niger. This time he had as an escort an officer and 30 white soldiers, as well as 2 sailors, 4 carpenters and 2 other white men including his brother-in-law. However, most of them died of disease and hardships before reaching the river. Park and four companions got as far as Busa, Nigeria, in their boat, but there they were drowned after a fight with the local inhabitants. The Niger was not traced to its mouth until 1830. (See NIGER RIVER.)

PARKES, Sir Henry (1815–96). The statesman Sir Henry Parkes, often called the father of the Australian Commonwealth, was born at Stoneleigh in Warwickshire, England. He was the son of a poor farmer and had little schooling, for at the age of eight he was already working for a wage. When learning a trade in Birmingham he joined workers' political movements and began his lifelong activities in politics. In 1839 he and his wife went out to Sydney, New South Wales, where he began writing political articles. In 1850 he started his own newspaper, the *Empire*.

He was elected to the New South Wales legislative council (parliament) in 1854, and two years later, after the granting of self-government to the colony, to the first legislative assembly. Except for short intervals, he remained a member until 1895 and was five times premier (prime minister) of New South Wales, his terms of office totaling more than ten years. In this time he encouraged education, the development of railroads and telegraphs, and land settlement by people from Britain, but he opposed unlimited immigration by Chinese. He reduced customs duties (taxes paid to the government on goods brought into the colony) so as to give New South Wales almost completely free trade.

Parkes is best remembered for his powerful support for Australian federation, or the idea that all the Australian states should group together to act as one nation in matters affecting them all. A meeting held at his suggestion at Melbourne in 1890 took the first real steps towards federating Australia, and he presided over the Sydney Convention of 1891 which drew up a federal constitution (plan of government) for Australia. Unfortunately, Parkes did not live to see the formation of the Australian Commonwealth in 1901.

Barnaby's

The British House of Commons and House of Lords together occupy the Palace of Westminster in London.

PARLIAMENT. The word "parliament" (from the old French word *parlement*, meaning "speaking") originally meant "talk". Gradually it came to describe a group of people assembled together. It is now most commonly used as the name of the law-making bodies of Great Britain and several major Commonwealth countries.

Parliaments Around the World

As the various parts of the British Empire achieved self-government, their legislatures acquired the designation of parliaments. Canada, Australia, and New Zealand are examples of the British, or Westminster, model – so called from the seat of the British parliament – working along much the same lines as the British parliament itself. Among other members of the Commonwealth, India provides an example of the existence and working of a parliament in a very different social and cultural environment. Outside the Commonwealth, the Dail of Ireland is a parliament in the full sense. So, too, is the Knesset in Israel, where Britain governed at the time of the Palestine mandate.

Most of the countries of Europe have elected legislatures, which can be classified as parliaments, although their own names in the different languages may have other roots. Japan also took its parliamentary system from European examples. It is customary for parliaments to have more than one house, or chamber, often elected in different ways, although Britain is now alone in preserving a hereditary element in one house (that is, in the House of Lords, where most seats are passed on through family succession). New Zealand is an exception to the two-house rule, having only one house.

The sizes of parliaments differ very greatly. Small countries such as Israel and Denmark tend to have small parliaments. The largest in the Western world is the British House of Commons with 650 members. Wherever they exist, parliaments are recognized as the supreme law-making bodies. Governments put forward their proposals – "bills" as they are called in the English-speaking countries – and when they have been discussed and perhaps altered, they are voted upon and, if agreed to, become "acts of parliament" or "statutes", that is to say part of the law.

Parliaments must obviously have very close connections with government and they have various ways of controlling the actions of the ministers or officials who work under them. Indeed, it is usual to keep the term "parliament" for those legislative bodies whose support is required by ministers in order to form and maintain a government (see PRIME MINISTER). Where there is a separation of powers between the executive branch (the President), the judicial branch (the Supreme Court), and the legislative branch (Congress), as in the United States, and where the office of the president does not depend upon a parliamentary majority, it is not usual to call the legislature a parliament.

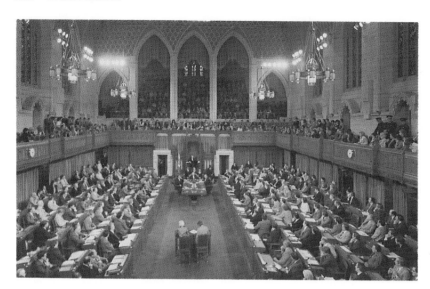

The Canadian House of Commons in session.

Canadian High Commission

So the Congress of the United States would not normally be called a parliament, although it does much of what parliaments do elsewhere. On the other hand, it is usual to speak of the French parliament, even though executive power is divided between the president of the republic and the prime minister, and neither he nor the other ministers sit in the parliament.

Inside Parliament

In parliaments that have followed and adapted the British model, the seating and forms of business reflect the importance of the role of parliament in relation to government. The members sit opposite each other, with the government ministers and their supporters on one side, and the opposition on the other. The Speaker has a very important position as it is his business to see fair play between the two sides and orderly debate. This was not always the case. Originally the English Speaker was the member chosen to convey the wishes of parliament to the king, hence the title. Later on he tended to be identified with the governing majority. He only assumed his modern impartial role in the 19th century. Now on being chosen Speaker he is expected to cut off all party ties he may have had before.

This kind of parliament usually goes with an electoral system that favors the emerg-

ence of only two main political parties, one providing the government and the other an opposition that is ready to step into the government's shoes if it wins the next election. The existence of three or more substantial parties, as has been the case from time to time in Britain, Canada, and Australia, does put a strain on the system.

In parliaments based on the continental model there is a different arrangement. Members are seated in a semi-circle, their positions being dictated by their party membership. Ministers sit separately, and ordinary members as well as ministers make their speeches not from their seats as at Westminster, but from a rostrum. Such parliaments are usually elected by some method of proportional representation, which tends to produce a number of parties, some of which have to get together in a coalition if a government is to be formed and sustained. The strength of a coalition government is that the major party will not propose extreme laws for fear that the smaller parties might withdraw their support.

The working of parliament is further complicated if the confidence of the upper house is also required by the government. Upper houses, as second chambers are also called, have different roles in different countries. They tend to be most important in federal countries where they help to give voice to the provinces or states of which the federation is composed.

Parliamentary Business

It is not only in appearance that the Westminster and continental models diverge. There is also a basic difference in how they go about their business. In the British case, bills which come before parliament, usually from the government, are first looked at from the point of view of the general principle involved. The first vote is taken on the "second reading". After that, detailed examination begins in committee. Membership of committees usually reflects the party composition in the House of Commons itself, so that the government can rely on its majority to see that changes (which it is determined to resist) are not made. In cases of very important bills the committee stage may be taken in a committee of the whole house. (In the House of Lords this is true of all bills.) Since the late 19th century, governments have increasingly been given powers to determine the timetable for parliament so that measures cannot just be talked out without the decisive votes being taken.

The use of committees is one of the ways in which parliaments differ. In continental-style parliaments, bills are usually referred to a committee at once and come before the chamber after the committee has done its work. The governments do not usually have the same degree of control over the timetable, which has to be worked out by bargains between the political parties represented. Since Britain is a country where law-making is very much in the hands of parliament, and where bills are very detailed, the British parliament now sits longer and more often than its continental counterparts.

Committees are not used just to see through bills. In Britain it was thought that ministers could be controlled by being questioned in the house during a regular session known as Question Time, when members could question ministers about their departments and so give voice to criticism. But with the growth of business, this system was increasingly felt to be an outdated one, and there was strong pressure to make more use of committees for acting as parliament's watchdogs over the whole range of government, instead of just on financial matters. During the 1970s and 1980s a series of such committees were set up which can question ministers and, within limits, their officials as well. A problem arises in the fact that, while the House of Commons itself acts on strict party lines, the committees represent the opposition parties as well, and governments are unwilling to give ammunition to their political opponents by telling them more than they want to.

In addition to committees dealing with matters of government, there is a range of domestic committees covering such matters as procedure, the privileges claimed by members, the management of the parliamentary buildings and arrangements for supplying meals to members while the house is in session. This is particularly important in the British House of Commons, which always sits into the evenings.

People in Parliament

The ability to get work done in committee demands from members a good deal of time, and the result has been that membership in most parliaments is now thought of as a full-time occupation. It was not so in the past, when to be elected by one's fellow-citizens was thought of as an honor and when the demands upon members were much fewer. Members did not expect to be paid for their work and could not therefore undertake to serve in parliament unless they had an assured income from property or a profession. In the 20th century, payment of members was introduced into the British parliament largely to allow the Labour Party to be represented, since most of its representatives from the working classes could not otherwise have taken up their seats. Today members of all parliaments are paid, although the sums vary considerably from country to country. And even now, the British House of Commons does not sit in the mornings (although committees do) so that members may have time to pursue their own professional or business interests.

In addition to the members, parliaments have always employed people for the day-to-day running of affairs. The senior officials, called clerks in the British and Commonwealth parliaments, are important elements in the system. In addition there are officials who record what is said, and many other people such as doorkeepers, messengers, and telephonists needed to make things run smoothly and help members to maintain contact with their local supporters and the general public. With the growth of the committee system, the number of clerks and specialist staff has much increased.

As the workload has increased, so members of parliament have demanded what is usual among people with jobs involving a lot of paperwork and correspondence: offices of their own with secretaries and other assistants paid for out of public funds. Again, parliaments differ as to the degree to which these wishes are satisfied; some are more generous to themselves than others.

Besides law-making and keeping an eye on the doings of government, parliaments function as the source of ministers. In most parliamentary countries ministers are chosen from among members of the majority party or parties. By speaking well in debates, ordinary members of parliament (referred to in British-style parliaments as "backbenchers" because they sit behind their leaders on the government side or the opposition side) can attract the attention of ministers or other party leaders, and thus advance their claims to becoming a minister when an opportunity arises. Indeed such ambitions explain the attraction which membership holds for many people, despite the long hours of work and the relatively low levels of pay.

Informing the Public

Parliaments also have an educational function, which is to keep the public informed about the great issues of the day and what the rival parties propose to do about them. This has not always been the case. Until the late 18th century, parliamentary proceedings in Britain were thought of as confidential and reporting what went on or what was said was not allowed. But since that time regular reporting has become the universal rule. In the 19th century in fact, when the newspaper industry had its great period of growth, newspapers used much of their space to report speeches made in parliament. This is no longer true, but some account is normally given in any newspapers that claim to be serious. A new dimension has been introduced with the coming of radio and television, and many countries have allowed one or both of these media to transmit parliamentary proceedings. The British House of Commons was more reluctant than other countries to allow broadcasting from parliament. Radio broadcasts started only in 1978 and television in 1989.

Neither medium is ideal, since both thrive on drama. Although most parliaments have moments of drama – a confrontation between two rival statesmen or a closely fought vote – most of the work is long-drawn-out and of a routine nature. Much of it also is carried on outside the chamber in committees so that the cameras are likely to disappoint viewers who expect to see their member always in his place. On the other hand, the availability of members of parliament for interviews on radio or television, and in discussion programs, means that the faces and voices of the country's politicians are much more familiar to the general public than they were in the past, when only a minority could see them at meetings. The new media have in turn had their effect upon parliaments themselves. The set speech of parliamentary debate, sometimes running to several hours, and the kind of delivery suited to a great outdoor rally do not go down well in the conversational atmosphere of radio or television, and this atmosphere now predominates in parliament itself.

Limited Parliaments

So far we have been describing things as they are in countries where parliaments flourish in freedom, where more than one party is allowed, and where individuals can speak their minds freely inside parliament and outside. But there are countries which have parliaments where these conditions do not apply, and where they are really only assemblies that "rubber-stamp" decisions already taken by the leader or leaders of a single all-powerful party. In many countries in Africa and the Middle East, for example, members of parliament are simply appointed by the ruling tribal or religious group, usually as a reward for having served it faithfully at the local level.

Novosti Press Agency

A bust of Lenin dominates this 1982 session of the USSR Supreme Soviet. The Supreme Soviet was the USSR's equivalent of a parliament. It, however, met rarely and no true debate took place.

In China, North Korea, Vietnam, and Cuba, it is the Communists who control the parliament. All members have to be members of the Communist Party or approved by it and there are no contested elections. The parliaments are used as a platform for the Communist Party leadership to make known its views to the country.

Until the democratic revolutions of 1989 this was also true of the parliaments of the USSR, Czechoslovakia, Hungary, Poland, and other countries of Eastern Europe. After 1989, these countries abolished the article in their constitution that guaranteed the Communist Party's leading role. Poland, Czechoslovakia, and Hungary were able to revive parliamentary traditions of their own dating from before World War II.

In between the democratic parliaments and those that are the puppets of a ruling party, there are parliaments which have at least a limited power to voice grievances, if not actually to influence policy. This is true in many of the Commonwealth countries.

The European Parliament

Parliament is now also the name given to the elected assembly which is one of the institutions of the European Community. It does not, however, have powers similar to those of any of the national parliaments, since the executive of the Community, the council of ministers, is not responsible to the parliament. But it does play an increasing part in the legislative and financial affairs of the Community and is constantly pressing for more notice to be taken of its wishes. It is different from other international assemblies, first because its members are directly elected to it and do not form part of official government delegations, as at the United Nations, and second because its members group themselves in party blocs – socialists, liberals, conservatives, and so on – and not according to the countries they come from. The parliament's procedures and the conduct of business are on the continental rather than the Westminster model.

The European parliament is unique in not having a single permanent site. Its full sessions are held at Strasbourg in France, but its committees normally meet at Brussels, in Belgium, where the other institutions of the Community are situated. Its staff and records, as well as its members, have to be constantly on the move. The huge cost to European taxpayers of such an arrangement has led to calls for the parliament to be moved to Brussels. (See EUROPEAN COMMUNITIES.)

History of Parliament

The beginnings of the English parliament have been traced to the Witan of the Anglo-Saxon kings of England. This body, also known as the Witenagemot, was a council made up of wise men, mainly nobles and the clergy. The members were not elected. The king was the chief power, but the Witan could elect and depose the king, and he did not perform an act of state without its advice and approval. Originally, each of the several king-doms that then existed in England held such a council. After the land was united into a single nation in the 9th century, the Witan became a national council.

Following the Norman Conquest of England in 1066, the Witan was replaced by a feudal council. It was composed of officers of state, clergy, and feudal landlords (see also FEUDALISM) whom the king chose to summon. With his council the king discussed affairs of state.

As a result of the political differences between king and barons in the 13th century, there were moves to strengthen the council by calling on a wider group of people to attend on particular occasions. Such meetings were in effect the early "parliaments". These could either control royal power or reinforce it.

In 1265 Simon de Montfort, the leader of a revolt against King Henry III, called a national assembly that included representatives from the towns of England. This parliament, however, was not truly representative because most of those attending had been selected from De Montfort's supporters. (See also MONTFORT, SIMON DE.)

Henry's successor, Edward I, summoned several parliaments. The most important was the Model Parliament of 1295, which was more representative of the people, and became the model for future parliaments. The bishops and abbots and barons were summoned individually, and every sheriff was directed to have elected two knights from each shire, two citizens from each city, and two burgesses from each borough (town). Thus the nobles, the clergy, and the land-owners and merchants, the rich and powerful of medieval society, were represented in the Model Parliament.

What gave power to parliaments was the need of the kings for money, mainly to pursue their wars for which the rents of their own estates were insufficient. It was only possible to levy taxes if there was consent on the part of those who would pay them and see to their collection. Thus parliaments became

occasions when grievances were put to the king and his putting them right was made a condition of parliament's voting for taxes. But it was a long time before the kings were obliged to concede that there were not taxes that could be imposed without parliamentary authority. The opposing claims to the throne in the 15th century, the Wars of the Roses, also gave parliament a new status, since successive claimants to the throne sought parliament's approval. Parliaments in the 15th century met more frequently than before and began to take on their modern form with Lords and Commons (the elected members) meeting separately.

Parliament gained its permanent place in the English state in the 16th century. The decision of King Henry VIII to break the ties

Queen Elizabeth I presiding over the House of Commons in the late 16th century.

between the English Church and Rome, and the gradual working out of a new Protestant settlement, as well as economic and social changes, made a good deal of legislation necessary. For this the approval of parliament was recognized as essential. Parliament met for quite long periods under Henry VIII and Elizabeth I, and was the scene of debate on vital national questions.

Parliament no longer merely offered advice and presented petitions to the king. By the 17th century it had come forward as a critic of the king and challenged his authority. The English Civil War (1642–51) was fought to decide whether government was to be by the king himself, or by the king and parliament. Charles I and his royalist supporters were defeated in the war by Oliver Cromwell, the leader of the parliamentary forces. Cromwell, however, failed to settle the relationship between the authority of the crown, or of himself as Lord Protector, and the authority of the representative national assembly.

The period of the Restoration of the monarchy after 1660 saw a further gain in the status of parliament as the financial needs of Charles II could not be met without its support. When James II was forced to quit the throne and give way to William III and Mary, parliament played a vital part in the change and its role in the constitution was set out in the 1689 Bill of Rights.

The wars of William and his successor Queen Anne again meant dependence upon parliament to vote the necessary funds. By the Act of Union of 1707, the parliaments of England and Scotland were merged. When George I of the German house of Hanover succeeded Queen Anne, he needed the support of ministers who could assure him of parliament's backing. Legend has it that the position of ministers was strengthened by the King's lack of English and indifference to British politics. In fact the development of a cabinet meeting without the king being present was a gradual one. The monarch still had the right to decide who should form an administration and who should be included,

and his wishes were made known by seeing ministers individually. Nevertheless, it was under the first three Georges that parliament became a regular part of British government with ministers requiring regular majorities to get their measures through and remain in office. (See GEORGE, KINGS OF BRITAIN.)

As parliament became more important, questions arose as to whether it was sufficiently representative. Reform was held up by the impact of the French Revolution late in the 18th century, which made people wary of change. But after the Napoleonic wars, ending in 1815, the reform movement gathered strength.

The Reform Bill of 1832 marked the beginning of more equal voting rights for the people of England. By this legislation the new middle class that was emerging as a result of the Industrial Revolution was able to share in the government. Similar reform legislation was passed in the following years until all adults, regardless of religion, property, or sex, were given the right to vote.

As the British parliamentary democracy developed, traditional practices and institutions had to change to keep pace with the developments. The House of Lords, whose members are not elected, had to be adjusted into a governmental system based on elected representatives. Originally the House of Lords was the more powerful of the two chambers of parliament. It was able to control the majority of seats in the House of Commons. But as more people were given the right to vote, this control was lost.

The House of Commons thus acquired equal power and eventually more power. The House of Lords, however, could refuse to pass legislation submitted to it by the House of Commons. The result was sometimes deadlock. In 1909 the House of Lords rejected the Finance Bill. This brought about legislation in 1911, revised in 1949, that greatly reduced the powers of the upper house. The House of Lords may now delay legislation for about a year, but proposals may then become law without its approval.

Parliament Today

In Britain the 1,200 or so members of the House of Lords are people who have inherited their titles or been appointed peers by the monarch; the law lords, who also form the country's final court of appeal; and the archbishops and bishops. The minimum age requirement is 21. In fact, many members do not attend at all, and others only rarely. The burden of legislation is undertaken by a hard core of "working peers" (mainly life, or appointed, peers) numbering about 400. The average daily attendance is about 300 members.

The House of Commons consists of 650 members, men and women, each elected from a single constituency by the "first past the post" system. Vacancies caused by the death or resignation of a member are filled by by-elections, which attract attention as giving a clue to the strength of support in the country for the different parties. The House of Commons must submit itself to new elections after a maximum period of five years. But the prime minister can ask the monarch to dissolve parliament at any time, and few parliaments run their full course. In both World Wars (1914–18 and 1939–45), parliament prolonged its own life so that there were no general elections between 1910 and 1918 or between 1935 and 1945. (See also ELECTION.)

Canada's parliament, closely modeled on the British parliament, has two chambers, the elected House of Commons and the Senate whose members are appointed on the recommendation of the prime minister. There are 295 members of the House of Commons, elected for a maximum of five years, and 104 members of the Senate, who may hold office until the age of 75. The parliaments of the provinces have a single chamber each, the legislative assembly, operating in the same way as the House of Commons.

The Australian parliament also has two chambers, the Senate, consisting of 76 members elected for six years, and the House of Representatives, consisting of 148 members elected for three years. All the states have parliaments on similar lines, except that Queens-

ZEFA

The Canadian Parliament building in Ottawa replaced an earlier one which burned down in 1916.

land has only one house, the legislative assembly.

Parliament in New Zealand consists of a single chamber, the House of Representatives. There are 95 members elected for three years.

PARNELL, Charles (1846–91). Parnell was leader of the Irish Home Rule party which demanded an Irish parliament in Dublin, in place of government from London. He was born at Avondale in County Wicklow. His mother was American and, unlike most of his Irish followers, he was a Protestant.

Parnell was elected to the British House of Commons in 1875 and soon became leader of the Home Rule party. He tried to force the British to grant home rule by prolonging debates in parliament and opposing all other business there. In Ireland he worked to win for the Irish peasants lower rents and more justice. For a time he was imprisoned for arousing disorder.

In 1886 the Liberal prime minister W. E. Gladstone (see GLADSTONE, WILLIAM EWART) tried to introduce home rule for Ireland, but was prevented by the House of Lords. A year later *The Times* newspaper published letters which seemed to show that Parnell had approved of the murder of Lord Frederick Cavendish in 1882. (With another English politician, Cavendish had been killed in

Phoenix Park, Dublin.) Parnell swore that these letters were false, and won a court case against the newspaper.

Because Parnell's Home Rule party was quite large, consisting of about 80 members, the two great British parties (Liberal and Conservative) had to bargain for his support. He thus seemed likely to win home rule before long. But suddenly, in 1889, one of his colleagues, Captain William O'Shea, brought an action for divorce against his wife Kitty, claiming that Parnell had been involved with her.

In those times divorce was regarded as a most shameful thing. The scandal was so great that Gladstone announced that the English Liberals could no longer work with the Irish party if Parnell continued to lead it. In Ireland too, the divorce turned most of the people against him. Parnell fought fiercely to keep

Mary Evans Picture Library

Charles Parnell had nearly won Irish home rule when he was forced to resign from the British parliament.

the leadership, but was forced to give it up. Soon afterwards he died and was buried in Dublin.

PAROLE see PRISON.

PARROT. Parrots are birds with the ability to mimic (imitate) the human voice. The two species most frequently kept as pets are the blue-fronted Amazon parrot (*Amazona aestiva*) of South America and the African gray parrot (*Psittacus erithacus*). The Amazon parrot is a large green bird with a pale blue forehead and yellow cheeks; it is between 35 and 38 centimeters (13.5 to 15 inches) long. The African gray parrot is ashy gray with beautiful red feathers in its tail; it is slightly larger than the Amazon parrot, up to 40 centimeters (16 inches) long.

There are, however, very many other kinds of parrots and also closely related birds, such as macaws, cockatoos, parakeets (including budgerigars), keas, and lories. These birds are found almost all over the world except in North America and Europe.

Parrots have very strong beaks, the upper part being curved and pointed and hooking over the lower one. In the dense forests that are their home they use these beaks chiefly for pulling themselves from branch to branch as they scramble about in the trees. They climb more than they fly, and generally live in large groups. Their food is mainly fruit, buds, and nuts, and they hold it in one claw while eating. With their strong beaks they are able to crack quite hard nuts. Parrots make their nests in holes in trees and their eggs are white.

The Relatives of Parrots

Cockatoo. The sulfur-crested cockatoo (*Cacatua galerita*) is a handsome, pure white bird with a crest of yellow feathers that it sometimes keeps folded and sometimes expands. One of the most beautiful cockatoos is Leadbeater's (*Cacatua leadbeateri*), which has white feathers tinged with rose and salmon pink and a crest striped with scarlet and yellow. The largest cockatoo is the palm, or

Zoological Society of London

Zoological Society of London

NHPA/Nigel Dennis

Zoological Society of London

great black cockatoo (*Prosciger aterrimus*), up to 75 centimeters (30 inches) long. It has a threadbare crest and bare red cheeks that turn blue when it is is excited.

Cockatoos live in Australia, New Guinea, and some of the smaller islands near by, such as New Ireland, but not in New Zealand. They are very noisy birds. Like all larger members of the parrot family, cockatoos live long, some for more than 100 years.

Parakeet. This name, also spelled paroquet, is generally given to the smaller parrots, particularly those with long tails. One often seen in zoos is the ring-necked parakeet (*Psittacula cyanocephala*), which lives in Africa and Asia. It is pale green in color with a black band running partly round its neck, like an incomplete collar. A band of fiery red runs around the back of the neck.

About 14 species of brightly colored small parrots live in southern Australia. Among the most numerous is the parakeet (see BUDGERIGAR). The turquoise or rock parakeet (*Neophema pulchella*) is mainly green with blue on the wings. It nests in rock crevices. Many of Australia's parrots are now rare, including the night parrot (*Geopsittacus occidentalis*) that feeds at night on grass seeds.

Kea. The kea (*Nestor notabilis*) of New Zealand is as big as a raven and dull green in color. Unlike other parrots, it does not feed only on plant food. It enjoys fat and has been accused of pecking at the flesh of sheep. But it seems likely that the damage done by keas has been much exaggerated. The kea lives high among the New Zealand mountains.

Macaw. Central and South America are the home of the macaws, which are large, vividly colored birds with huge beaks and long tails. Most species nest in holes high up in trees.

Lory. Lories and lorikeets are birds of the Australasian region. They have a slender, wavy-edged beak and a brush-type tongue used to extract nectar from flowers and juices from fruits. Lories have short tails and lorikeets have long pointed ones.

PARSLEY is a herb of the family Umbelliferae to which celery, carrots, and parsnips also belong. It comes from the Mediterranean area, but is now grown in many other parts of the world for use in cooking. It has green, frilly leaves. These are picked and used either as a decoration on food or as flavoring in sauces, soups, and salads.

Parsley was grown by the ancient Greeks and Romans. It takes two years to grow to its full size, but the leaves are best picked in the first year, when the plant is only about 15 centimeters (6 inches) high. If left to grow, it will develop coarse leaves and small yellowish flowers, and may reach a height of 2 meters (6 feet).

Petroselinum crispum is the common parsley with very crisp, crinkly leaves. *Petroselinum sativum* has flatter leaves and is known as plain-leaved parsley. It is often used in Greek cooking to flavor and decorate food. Hamburg or turnip-rooted parsley (*Petroselinum crispum tuberosum*) is grown for its white roots. It is known as celeriac and is eaten raw, grated, as a salad.

PARSONS, Sir Charles (1854–1931). The British engineer and inventor Charles Algernon Parsons is remembered chiefly for his development of the steam turbine. He was a son of William Parsons, Earl of Rosse. In 1884 he became a partner in a firm at Gateshead, England, where he was in charge of the electrical department. At once he tackled the problem of building a high-speed steam engine to drive a dynamo for making electricity, and

Facing page: Members of the parrot family. **Top left:** Orange-fronted parakeets from South Island, New Zealand. **Top right:** Sulfur-crested cockatoo from Northern Australia and New Guinea. **Bottom left:** Palm cockatoo from New Guinea. **Bottom right:** Yellow-streaked lory, also from New Guinea.

Parsons' turbine-driven steam launch, the *Turbinia*, caused a sensation at the naval review of 1897.

in the same year he produced the first successful steam turbine. In 1889 he established his own factory at Newcastle-upon-Tyne.

Turbines are explained in a separate article (see TURBINE). Parsons never claimed to have invented turbines, but he overcame all the obstacles and difficulties in the way of making the steam turbine efficient and economical. The chief difficulty was this: if a jet of high-speed steam strikes blades mounted on the rim of a wheel like the sails of a windmill, the wheel is made to turn but much of the jet is wasted. Parsons arranged to catch the steam from the jet after it had left the blades and then to direct it on to a second row of blades mounted on the same shaft as the first, and so on until the whole force of the steam was used up.

A turbine is most economical when the speed at which its blades move is about half the speed of the jet of steam supplied to it. Steam from a boiler at a pressure of 14 atmospheres leaves the jet at about 3,000 kilometers (1,900 miles) an hour, so the speed of the blades in this case should be about 1,500 kilometers (930 miles) an hour. A small turbine would have to spin very rapidly for its blades to reach that speed, so that Parsons' turbine was at its best when made in large sizes or when used for driving high-speed machinery. The first great use of it was in driving dynamos in power plants. Then in 1897 Parsons' turbine-driven steam launch, the *Turbinia*, made a sensational appearance at the naval review, darting in and out of the lines of anchored warships at a speed of 34 knots (63 kilometers, or 40 miles, an hour), which was much faster than ships of that date could steam.

In 1910 Parsons developed reduction gears (see GEAR) which allowed the turbine to drive low-speed machinery while itself turning rapidly. His other inventions included special mirrors for searchlights and ways of making optical glass for telescopes, binoculars, and instruments.

PARTHENON see ACROPOLIS.

PARTICLE ACCELERATOR. A particle accelerator (often called an "atom smasher") is a device used in nuclear physics to find out how atoms, and the particles they contain, behave. The particle accelerator first pulls the centers (nuclei) out of the atoms and then speeds them up until these nuclear particles are traveling faster than 250,000 kilometers (155,000 miles) a second. The fast-moving particles can be used to turn atoms of ordinary substances into radioactive atoms (see RADIOACTIVITY). Electrical forces are used to accelerate the charged particles (that is, the electrons and protons) of the atom. (See ATOM.)

In a *linear accelerator*, the nuclear particles are pushed along a series of hollow tubes and finally emerge to strike a target. A large linear accelerator can be over 3 kilometers (2 miles) long.

The *cyclotron*, another type of accelerator, was invented by the US physicists E. O. Lawrence and M. S. Livingstone in 1931. In this

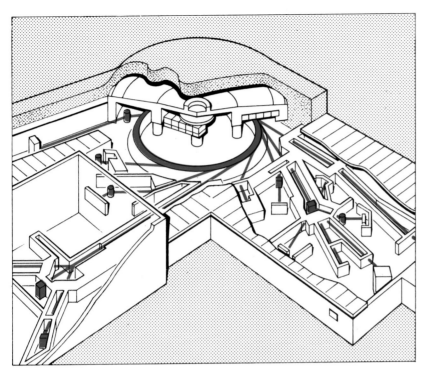

This is a simplified drawing of a cyclotron, an accelerator that speeds up the heavy particles called protons. The particles are fired from the injector (at the top left of the diagram), a kind of electrical gun. The proton stream is controlled by the electromagnet (center), and accelerated by powerful "kicks" of electrical voltage. After they have made a million circuits of the ring, the protons will have reached their greatest energy. They are then released into the experimental chambers and guided towards target atoms with which they collide.

machine, protons are forced to go round and round in a huge magnet and twice each turn they are "kicked" faster by a high voltage of about 100,000 volts. The machine is designed so that however fast or slow the protons are moving they all take exactly the same time to go round one turn.

To stop the protons from being slowed down by atoms in the air, the space inside the huge magnet has the air removed. Atoms of different gases can be fed through a small tube into the center of the machine where, in an electric arc, the particles are obtained.

The *betatron*, designed in 1940 by the American physicist D. W. Kirst, accelerates electrons by a changing magnetic field.

These methods are also used in much larger and more powerful machines called *synchrotrons*. Here, nuclear particles are first speeded up outside by a linear accelerator and then shot into the outer edge of the magnet. After the particles are shot in they are speeded up just as in the cyclotron and make thousands of turns round the magnet. The accelerating particles come close to the speed of light and

gain in mass (see RELATIVITY). As they do so the synchrotron's magnetic field has to be increased. When the magnet's strength can no longer be increased to hold them, the particles fly out.

The largest synchrotrons accelerate particles to more than 500,000 MeV (MeV=one megavolt, or 1 million volts). A large cyclotron can give particles energies of up to 200 MeV, while a betatron can develop energies of up to 350 MeV.

PARTRIDGE. The partridge is a small, rather plump game bird (that is, a bird that is hunted for sport). There are many kinds, all originally from Europe and Asia.

The common, or gray, partridge (*Perdix perdix*), which is often shot and sold as food, is a stout bird with brown upper parts, an orange-brown head, grayish front and under parts, and reddish-brown flanks and tail. There is a noticeable horseshoe-shaped patch of dark chestnut on the breast. In North America it is called Hungarian or hun partridge, and was first introduced there in 1889.

Partridges have loud, grating voices and

their wings make a whirring noise when they fly up. In autumn they gather into family parties known as "coveys" and are frequently seen feeding among corn stubble. Their food includes grass, clover, spiders, and insects.

The birds scrape out hollows in the ground for their nests and line them with dead leaves and grasses. The eggs, which are olive-brown in color, vary in number from 9 to 20.

Left: Red-legged partridge. **Right**: Common partridge.

The red-legged partridge (*Alectoris rufa*) is rather larger than the common partridge, with bright red bill and legs. Its cheeks and throat are white, edged with black, and it has striking black, white, and chestnut stripes on the flanks. It has a sharp double call when alarmed.

Francolins are partridges with leg spurs and come from Africa.

PARTS OF SPEECH. If you look carefully at any sentence or passage of English, you can see that the words used in it are of several different kinds; that is, they do different kinds of work in the sentence. There are eight different kinds of words altogether and they are called *parts of speech*. A good way to understand them is to go through a few sentences and try to pick out words that seem to be doing the same sort of work, making separate lists of them. Then you can compare the lists and see the differences between them. Look, for instance, at this passage from *Alice's Adventures in Wonderland*:

The cook took the caldron of soup off the fire, and at once set to work throwing everything within her reach at the Duchess and the baby—the fire-irons came first; then followed a shower of saucepans, plates and dishes. The Duchess took no notice of them even when they hit her; and the baby was howling so much already, that it was quite impossible to say whether the blows hurt it or not.

"Oh, please mind what you're doing!" cried Alice, jumping up and down in an agony of terror. "Oh, there goes his *precious* nose!" as an unusually large saucepan flew close by it, and very nearly carried it off.

The first thing to notice about this passage is that some of the words have much more meaning than others. Words such as *caldron, throwing, fire-irons, hit, impossible, terror, precious, unusually, close* seem to mean something even when they are used by themselves, but words such as *the, and, to, at* are much weaker in meaning. Used by themselves they do not give us a picture or tell us much at all, for their meaning in a sentence comes from the way they join the other words together.

Now look at the words belonging to the first group, the "meaning" group. Some of them are obviously names of things: *cook, caldron, fire, baby, saucepans*, and so on. These words are called nouns, and all names of persons, places, and things are nouns. Some other words in the passage seem to go very closely with the nouns and tell us more about them—Alice exclaimed about the baby's *precious* nose as a *large* saucepan flew by it. Such words are called adjectives, and they describe nouns or pronouns; they add to, or make more definite, the meaning of nouns or pronouns. (The two very common words *the* and *a* or *an*, are really adjectives, since they usually go very closely with a noun, but they are called by the special name *article*. *The* is called the *definite article*, and *a* or *an* is the *indefinite article*.)

Pronouns are words which stand for or take the place of nouns, to save us repeating the names of people or things over and over again. For instance, the Duchess took no notice of *them* (the things the cook threw) even when *they* (the things the cook threw, again) hit *her* (the Duchess); the saucepan flew by *it* (the baby's nose) and nearly carried *it* (the baby's nose again) off. If the Duchess had been telling the story she would have said "*I* took no notice when they hit *me*", and if the cook had been speaking to the Duchess about the occasion she would have said "*You* took no notice even when they hit *you*". In fact pronouns are movable labels and change according to whether they stand for a person speaking, a person spoken to, or a person or thing spoken about.

Now look at the words *took, came, followed, hit, hurt, flew*. They are words with plenty of meaning and are very important to the sentences—as you can see if you try to leave them out. They tell us what the people or things do; they are doing-words, or action-words, and are called verbs. Every sentence has to have at least one verb in it to be complete and to make sense. Not every verb, however, expresses a definite "action"; a few of them express what things or people are, rather than what they do. Words such as *is, seem, appear* are verbs of this kind.

"The fire-irons came *first*; *then* followed a shower of saucepans." The word *first* obviously goes closely with the verb *came*, rather in the same way as the adjective *precious* goes with the noun *nose*. Words like this, which describe or make more definite the meaning of verbs, are called adverbs. In the passage quoted, *much, already, up, down, there, nearly* are also adverbs; *soon, suddenly, loudly, slowly* are other examples. Some adverbs can go with an adjective or an adverb instead of with a verb. In "an *unusually* large saucepan", the adverb *unusually* adds to the meaning of the adjective "large"; and in "*very* nearly carried it off", *very* goes with the adverb *nearly*.

The five kinds of words mentioned so far—nouns, adjectives, pronouns, verbs, and adverbs—make up the group of "meaning" words. The commonest word of all in the second group, the words that do not seem to have much meaning when they are used alone, is *and*. Its work is to join together other words and groups of words. *And, but, or, nor* are called conjunctions, or joining words.

This leaves a number of other small words in the passage, part of whose work is also to join other words together: *of, at, to, within, in, by*. Look at the words "the caldron of soup". *Of* links together "caldron" and "soup" in a special way; the two words "of soup" form what is called a phrase, which describes "caldron" in much the same way as a single adjective might—for instance, "soup-filled caldron". Alice jumped "up and down *in* an agony of terror": there the phrase "in an agony" tells something about the jumping (how Alice was jumping), and therefore it is doing the same work as an adverb. "*Of* terror" is describing "agony" and so is doing the same work as an adjective. The words which begin these phrases are called prepositions. Prepositional phrases, that do work like that of single adjectives or adverbs but in more detail, are a very useful part of the English language.

The eighth part of speech is not connected with other words in a sentence in the same way as the seven already described. It stands somewhat apart from the other words and is called an interjection. Words such as *Oh! Ah! Alas!* are interjections. An interjection expresses strong feeling of some kind, such as Alice's alarm and anxiety as the saucepans fly by.

Changing Parts

The eight parts of speech, then, are: noun, pronoun, adjective, verb, adverb, preposition, conjunction, and interjection. However, an actual word is not necessarily always the same part of speech. A great many words in English can do the work of several parts of speech. For example, *cook, fire*, and *reach* are nouns in the passage you have been looking at earlier; but they can also be verbs: she *cooked* a meal, *fired* a gun, *reached* the finishing-post. *Hit, hurt*, and *mind* are all verbs, but used in other ways they can be nouns. In "*off* the fire", *off* is a preposition; but in "carried it *off*", *off* is an adverb. Many words which are usually nouns can turn into adjectives when they are put in front of another noun: a *government* order, a *radio* message, a *river* scene. Many adjectives can be used as nouns: into the *blue*, all of a *sudden*, the *poor* shall be comforted, remember the *brave*.

Some words also do the work of two parts of speech at once. For example, in the sentence "He asked the boys who had come away from home where they were going", *who* is a kind of pronoun called a relative pronoun; as a pronoun it stands for the noun "boys", but it also does the work of a conjunction in linking the group of words "had come away from home" to the main sentence. *Where* is an adverb, but in this sentence it too is doing the work of a conjunction as well. All this shows that it is not always easy to decide what part of speech a word is, and rules about them may not always seem to fit. The only answer is to think carefully every time until you can see what work each word is doing in its sentence, and to remember that even if you are used to a word being one part of speech it *can* change and be a different one !

Each of the parts of speech is described and explained much more fully in a separate article.

PASCAL, Blaise (1623–62).

The French mathematician, scientist, and philosopher Blaise Pascal was a mathematical prodigy as a child. At the age of 16 he wrote the "Essay on Conics", a short work on geometry that impressed even the great mathematician René Descartes. Pascal noticed that his father had to spend hours over his accounts and between 1642 and 1644 he invented and made a calculating machine for adding sums of money. This was the first digital calculator ever invented (see CALCULATOR). Among his other accomplishments in mathematics, he aided the development of differential calculus and the theory of probability. (See CALCULUS; PROBABILITY.)

Pascal also made important contributions to physics. In 1643, the Italian Evangelista Torricelli invented the barometer to show that the air exerts a pressure on its surround-

Mansell Collection

The great French mathematician and philosopher Blaise Pascal, who forsook science for religion.

ings. Pascal saw that the pressure should become less as one climbed higher and confirmed this in 1648 by an experiment in which his brother carried a barometer up the Puy de Dome, a mountain in Auvergne (see BAROMETER).

Pascal also formulated an important principle which was called *Pascal's Law* in his honor. This states that if pressure is increased anywhere on the surface of a fluid (liquid or gas) in a closed chamber, the pressure will be transmitted without loss in all directions. The hydraulic brake works on this principle (see HYDRAULICS). The international unit of pressure is also called the pascal.

From 1646 onwards, Pascal became increasingly concerned with religious matters. He was a Roman Catholic, but in 1655 he went to live a religious life with the Jansenists, a religious sect named after Bishop Cornelius Jansen (1585–1638). Parts of Pascal's unfinished written work explaining the truth of Christianity were published under the title *Pensées* ("Thoughts") after his death.

PASSION-FLOWER. There are more than 400 species of passion-flower (*Passiflora*). They grow naturally in the warmest southern and western areas of the United States and in tropical areas of South America, Asia, and Australia, and are cultivated as ornamental plants in other parts of the world.

The passion-flower is a climbing or trailing vine. It was given its name by early explorers who saw in it a symbol of the crucifixion of Jesus Christ. The three pistils, at the center of the blossom, represent the nails used on the cross. The five stamens represent Christ's five wounds. The ten sepals and petals represent the faithful disciples, with Judas and Peter missing. The beautiful fringed corona represents the crown of thorns.

In spite of the sacred tradition built around the passion-flower, it is better known in its native regions by its common name of maypop. The flowers are generally purplish-white. A large scarlet-flowered variety is grown as an ornamental vine. There is also a yellow variety.

The fruit of some passion-flowers, such as the purple granadilla (*Passiflora edulis*), is the size of a small apple and is edible. It is native to Brazil but is grown throughout the tropics for its perfumed, slightly acid-tasting fruit. One kind of passion-flower is grown commercially in southern California. A refreshing drink is made from the pulp and juice of its fruit.

NHPA/James Carmichael

The purple passion-flower from South America is a climbing plant grown in gardens throughout the world.

PASSION PLAY is a drama depicting the Passion, or suffering, of Jesus Christ. Passion plays are mystery plays (dramas based on events in the Bible, see MYSTERY PLAY). They usually dramatize Christ's life from the time of the Last Supper to his death. (See JESUS CHRIST.)

Barnaby's

A scene from the Oberammergau Passion Play, first performed in 1634 and now a world-famous event.

Passion plays were first presented some time in the Middle Ages. They were introduced in the Roman Catholic Church by priests who acted in the plays and presented them in Latin for Christmas and Easter. During the 15th and 16th centuries they were acted by laymen in the languages of the people. In England the plays were presented on wagon stages that were moved from one place to another. In France the actors performed on stationary stages built in village squares or marketplaces. Passion plays were also performed in Spain, and Spanish conquerors introduced the plays into the New World.

In 1633 the village of Oberammergau, Germany, was stricken by a dreadful plague. When the plague ended the grateful inhabitants vowed to present a passion play every tenth year. The first performance was given in 1634. The Oberammergau Passion Play has become a world-famous event. It is seen by visitors from all parts of the world. The actors and chorus singers in the production, numbering about 700, are chosen from the villagers of Oberammergau. The production runs from May until September.

In the United States various groups

present passion plays. Two of the most out-standing are the Zion Passion Play and the Black Hills Passion Play. In Zion, Illinois, the play opens with the Sermon on the Mount and follows the life of Christ as he wandered with his disciples. It closes with Christ's res-urrection and ascension. The Black Hills Pas-sion Play, performed in Spearfish, South Dakota, was first known in the United States as the Luenen Passion Play. It became a permanent company when Josef Meier, sev-enth member of his family to play Christ, settled in Spearfish in 1939. This passion play tells the events of the last seven days of the life of Christ.

Closely related to the passion and other mystery plays were the miracle plays, which presented incidents in the lives of the saints. Morality plays were also popular during the Middle Ages. In these plays actors portrayed roles such as Charity, Vice, and Love and acted out a story. The best-known morality play is *Everyman*, which appeared in England sometime in the 16th century, and was a translation from a Dutch morality play called *Elckerlyc*. From these plays modern drama developed. Early in the 13th century, laymen as well as priests began to write plays, and gradually non-religious as well as religious themes were used.

PASSOVER is the Jewish festival of freedom that celebrates the Exodus of the ancient Israelites from Egypt. The festival is called Pesach by the Jews. The story of Passover is told in the Book of Exodus in the Bible. When Pharaoh refused to allow the Israelites to leave the country, Moses warned that God would bring plagues upon Egypt. (See MOSES.) The festival is called Passover because the angel of death "passed over" the houses of the Israelites to spare their firstborn children from harm. The Egyptian firstborn, however, were killed. After this terrible plague, the Israelites were released.

According to the Book of Exodus, the Israel-ites killed a lamb on the 14th day of the Jewish month of Nisan. The blood was sprinkled on the doorposts of the Israelite homes as a sign for the angel of death to pass by. The lamb later became known as the Paschal lamb.

Passover is now celebrated for seven or eight days beginning with the eve of the 15th day of Nisan (which coincides with March or April). During the entire festival, matzah (unleavened bread, made without yeast) is eaten. This is a reminder that the Israelites baked unleavened bread be-cause they were in a hurry to escape from Egypt.

Stephanie

These children are reading the Haggadah in preparation for the commemorative ritual of Seder night.

Passover is chiefly a home festival. On the first two nights a Seder, or order of service, is arranged at mealtime. This is one of the most colorful and important family occasions in the Jewish calendar. The family reads from a special prayer book called Haggadah, which tells the story of the slavery and freedom of the Israelites. The foods on the Seder table are symbolic ones. In addition to the unleavened bread, there is also a roasted leg bone of lamb, which is a reminder of the Paschal lamb, and bitter herbs (usually horseradish) which recall the bitterness of the Egyptian slavery.

PASSPORT is a travel document issued by a government to its citizens to enable them to enter other countries and re-enter their own.

The word passport comes from two French words, *passer*, meaning "to pass", and *port*, meaning "harbor". The earliest passports or documents of identification were issued to individuals and also to ships that desired safe passage in and out of foreign ports. They are no longer issued to ships.

Although identification documents have been used for centuries, passports as we know them today were not required by many countries until after World War I (1914–18). With the increase in tourism since the end of World War II in 1945, it has become comparatively easy to obtain travel documents.

A passport contains the traveler's photograph and personal details such as name, date of birth, and country of residence. A passport is usually stamped by an official when a traveler enters and leaves a country in order to record how long the traveler has stayed there. Some countries require a visa before permitting a foreigner to enter. This is a stamp on the traveler's passport stating that he or she will be admitted, and it must be obtained by the traveler before reaching the country.

Each country has its own procedure for issuing a passport. The applicant usually has to provide two photographs, one of which is put on the passport and the other kept in the records of the issuing authority. The applicant must also provide proof of birth and nationality. This may be a birth certificate and certificate of naturalization, if appropriate, or may simply be the previous passport. It is also usually necessary to have the photograph and application documents witnessed by a reliable person who has known the applicant for a certain number of years and can verify that he is who he says he is.

The passport is issued for a certain number of years, up to about ten, and may normally be renewed once. After that a new one must be obtained.

A passport holder may have the names of his or her spouse and children added to the passport so that when those people are traveling together they do not need separate passports.

PASTA is a food eaten by people in many countries, but particularly in Italy and China. It is made from durum wheat flour which is rich in gluten, a kind of protein. The flour is mixed with water to make a dough, which is pushed through holes to make a variety of shapes. The dough is then dried, and will keep for a long time. Pasta is usually cooked by boiling it in water, which softens it.

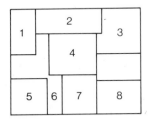

1 Penne; 2 Vermicelli; 3 Ruote di carro (cartwheels); 4 Wholewheat conchiglie; 5 Green tortiglioni; 6 Spaghetti; 7 Conchigliette; 8 Green conchiglie.

ZEFA

Marco Polo is said to have brought the recipe for pasta to Italy from China but a form of macaroni had been eaten in Europe since the time of the ancient Greeks. Among the many forms of pasta eaten today are noodles, macaroni, spaghetti, lasagne, and tortiglioni. Some forms, such as ravioli (square shaped) and tortellini (crescent shaped) are stuffed with a meat or cheese filling. Lasagne is flat and cooked in layers with sauce between and usually cheese on the top. Cannelloni is tube shaped and is cooked in a similar way. The very small varieties such as stelline (tiny stars) are used in soup. Spaghetti and the thinner version known as vermicelli, and the different kinds of noodle (known in different parts of Italy as fettucine, tagliatelle, and pappardelle) are often served with meat and tomato sauce described as *bolognese* (from Bologna in Italy). There are other forms shaped like shells, spirals, bows, cartwheels, and tubes of various shapes and sizes. They may all be eaten with sauces made from any kinds of meat, fish, shellfish, or vegetables, or just tossed in olive oil or butter and topped with a sprinkling of Parmesan cheese.

"Fresh pasta" is made with eggs added to the dough. It has a yellower color, and is usually sold without being dried first. Green pasta is made with cooked spinach in the dough and orange pasta with tomatoes. Brown, or wholewheat, pasta is made from wholewheat flour.

PASTEL. Pastel is made from powder color mixed with just enough gum arabic to bind it and allow it to set in molds. When set, pencil-thick sticks are removed from the molds. These are used for drawing on rough, sometimes tinted, paper. The colored powder of the sticks adheres to the paper, giving an effect almost like painting. Pastel sticks are fragile and their color tends to smudge and brush off the paper easily.

Courtesy, the Louvre, Paris

Courtesy, Art Institute of Chicago

Courtesy, Staatliche Kunstamlungen, Dresden

Top left: A self-portrait by the French artist J. B. S. Chardin (1699–1779). **Left**: *Mother and Child* by Mary Cassatt (1844–1926). **Above**: *The Chocolate Girl* by the Swiss artist Jean-Etienne Liotard (1702–89).

Ornament of Fruit, an abstract in pastel by Henry van de Velde (1863–1957).

Among 18th-century French masters, Jean-Baptiste Chardin and Quentin de la Tour used the softest kinds of pastels for portraits. The harder, grittier pastels give an effect closer to chalk drawing. The 19th-century French painter Edgar Degas used this for his well-known studies of ballet dancers. Pastels feature in the work of such other French artists as Auguste Renoir, Henri de Toulouse-Lautrec, and Pierre Bonnard, and also in the work of the American Mary Cassatt and the Swiss artist Paul Klee.

PASTEUR, Louis (1822–95). The scientist Louis Pasteur was in born in France in a little town in the Jura Mountains near the Swiss frontier. While teaching, he became interested in chemistry and after studying at Paris qualified as a doctor of science. In 1848 he showed that there were two kinds of tartaric acid, thus discovering a whole new class of substances. This discovery brought him fame and in 1854 he was appointed head of the science department at Lille University in northern France.

There were many breweries and distilleries at Lille, which caused Pasteur to consider why beers and wines should go sour. This led to his interest in fermentation. (See FERMENTATION.) At that time processes such as fermentation, "going sour", decay, and the like were thought to be mere chemical changes. Pasteur showed that they were actually caused by germs, or tiny creatures living in the air. Hitherto, scientists had believed that these tiny creatures were the *result* of decay instead of being its *cause*, and that they were examples of *spontaneous generation*; that is, of new life springing from nothing. But Pasteur insisted that all life must come from living parents.

In the course of his work Pasteur showed that the germs could be killed by moderate heat. This led to the process of *pasteurization*, which is a method of preventing milk from turning bad by heating it. The English surgeon Joseph Lister saw the importance of Pasteur's work, and in 1865 he began to use carbolic acid to prevent the infection of wounds by germs (see LISTER, JOSEPH). In the same year Pasteur applied his theory of germs to the silkworm disease which was ruining the French silk industry. He discovered what kind of germs were causing the disease and how to treat it and thus saved the industry from disaster.

Later, Pasteur showed it was possible to protect an animal against a particular disease by inoculation; that is, by introducing into its bloodstream some of the germs causing that disease. The germs used for this vaccination (as Pasteur called it) were artificially grown so as to be rather weak, and they gave the animal a mild attack of the disease, from which it developed a resistance against further attacks. Pasteur developed vaccines of this kind against anthrax (a deadly cattle disease which can attack man), swine plague, and chicken cholera. In 1881 he began work on the terrible disease hydrophobia, or rabies, which is produced in human beings by the bite of a rabid (mad) dog. He obtained a weakened form of the germ and in 1885 successfully inoculated a child who had been badly bitten by an infected dog.

Grateful people from all over the world subscribed money to build the Pasteur Institute in Paris, which was opened in 1888 as a center for making vaccines and as a research

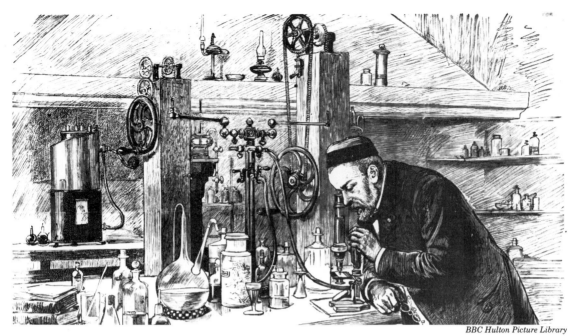

BBC Hulton Picture Library

This drawing shows Louis Pasteur working in his Paris laboratory to find a cure for hydrophobia, or rabies.

institute. There are now Pasteur Institutes in many parts of the world.

Pasteur was a simple, modest, and kindly man, and a devout Roman Catholic. He received honors from many countries for his great work in the fight against disease.

PATAGONIA is a vast region of desert, semi-desert, and treeless scrubland taking up most of the southern land area of South America. With an area of 673,000 square kilometers (260,000 square miles) it is the largest desert in the Americas. The Rio Colorado forms most of its northern border, and the Atlantic Ocean is to the east. It stretches into Tierra del Fuego in the south, and is bordered by the southern extension of the Andes along the west.

The original Indians of Patagonia may have moved up from Tierra del Fuego over 5,000 years ago. The Patagon tribes were nomadic hunters when Spanish explorers arrived near the end of the 16th century. Magellan (see MAGELLAN, FERDINAND) was the first European to explore the coast, and is said to have named the region after "Patagon", a monster from a 16th-century story which, he thought, resembled the natives with their thick furs, bushy hair, and painted faces. After Argentinian independence from Spain in 1816, immigrants were encouraged to settle there. Some came to work on the land, others to find a place with religious

Tony Morrison/South American Pictures

The Moreno Glacier and Lake are in the Patagonian region of South America.

and political freedom, such as the Welsh who established a community there. But the population remains sparse and mostly rural. Oil and iron ore are the major products extracted; but there are also deposits of gold, manganese, lead, and uranium.

PATENT. A patent is a bargain between a person who has invented something and the government of his country. The inventor makes something new and then tells the government all about it. In return he is granted a patent by the government. Unless he tells the government about his invention he cannot be granted a patent. This patent is a document that gives him the right to prevent other people from making and selling his invention. No one can make or sell it unless the inventor allows him to do so, and this gives the inventor the chance to make money out of his invention.

A patent usually lasts for a specified period of up to 20 years; each country has its own rules. However, in some countries, such as France, inventions that are thought to be particularly useful can only be patented for a period of six years. This type of patent is known as a "utility certificate".

In some countries (not the United States or Canada) fees must be paid regularly in order to keep the patent. If they are not paid the patent lapses. The patent can then be used by anyone.

The granting of patents in some form or other has been going on since the 15th century when grants were first made to inventors in Italy. The earliest recorded patent for an invention in Great Britain was in 1449, when "John of Utynam" was granted a patent for his method of making colored glass. There are two main procedures used in applying for a patent. In many European countries a patent is granted to anyone whose application complies with the legal requirements. Court actions can then be brought by anyone who wishes to oppose the patent. During the court action the invention is looked at in detail to see if the person who was granted the patent really has invented something that is new.

The other system is used in the United States, Canada, Australia, New Zealand, Japan, the United Kingdom, Germany, Sweden, and Austria. The applicant must submit documents giving a full description of the invention and explaining how it works. The application and the other documents are examined by experts to make sure that the invention is something new. This means that it has not previously been published or used by others.

When the experts are satisfied that the application is in order, it is accepted and all the information describing the invention is printed and published. Then an interval of time is allowed for any person to oppose the grant of the patent. One of the reasons for opposing the grant of a patent is that the applicant for the patent is not the true inventor. This means that he may have obtained the idea of the invention from someone else. Sometimes a court of law has to decide whether a patent should be granted to the applicant.

There is a slightly different procedure in, for example, the Netherlands. Patents are granted for seven years to start with and then the inventor can ask for a further period if he still wants to keep the patent. This means that the examination by the experts does not take place until the second period is applied for and it eases the burden of time-consuming work on the experts.

PATRICK, Saint (*c*.389–461). Patrick, the patron saint of Ireland, was the son of a British official of the Christian Church, and it is thought that he was born in south Wales.

When he was about 16 a band of Irish raiders carried him off to Ireland, where he was put to work as a shepherd. His Christian training helped him to bear the hardships of the life and after six years he escaped to France. He appears to have spent some years at the monastery on the island of Lerinum (this is a tiny island, now called St. Honorat, off the southern coast of France), and then at the monastery of St. Martin at Auxerre in central France. While there, "the voice of the Irish" came to him, beseeching him to spread the gospel in Ireland. It was not until he was made bishop to Ireland in 432 that he was able to obey this call. His ardor and faith made St. Patrick a persuasive preacher. His courage impressed even the Irish king, Loigaire, who took him under his protection. Many miracles were said to have been performed by the saint during his years in Ireland and often he was forced into contests with the priests of the druids (see DRUID), who did not want to lose their power.

St. Patrick is said to have used the three-leaved shamrock, the national flower of Ireland, as a symbol with which to explain the Trinity. Although Christianity had been introduced into Ireland before St. Patrick's time, he was the first to spread it widely. He found a race of sun and tree worshippers and left a well-organized Christian Church. His introduction of Latin into Ireland as the church language helped to arouse an interest in classical learning. St. Patrick's "Confession", written in Latin, gives an account of his life.

A legend about St. Patrick tells that he called all the snakes in Ireland together, put them into a box and threw the box into the sea. That is why there are no snakes in Ireland today, and the Irish Sea is rough because the snakes are tossing about in their box trying to get out! The anniversary of St. Patrick's death is celebrated on 17 March.

Barnaby's

St. Patrick's day parade in New York. His feast day is celebrated by the Irish throughout the world.

PATTON, George S. (1885–1945).

The American general George Patton became famous in World War II for his daring strategy in tank warfare. He was a tough, colorful soldier who earned the nickname of "Old Blood and Guts".

BBC Hulton Picture Library

General Patton landed in Sicily in 1943 to begin the Allied invasion of southern Europe in World War II.

General Patton was born in California, and graduated from the US Military Academy at West Point, New York, in 1909. In 1916–17 he served with General John Pershing in the army expedition into Mexico to capture the Mexican guerrilla chief Pancho Villa. He also served in France during World War I, commanding an American tank brigade.

During World War II (1939–45) Patton fought in North Africa, where he commanded the US Fifth Army, and in Sicily, where the army was enlarged and renamed the US Seventh Army. General Patton's troops, fighting alongside the British Eighth Army led by General Bernard Montgomery, successfully landed in Sicily in July 1943 and began the Allied invasion of southern Europe.

In July 1944 Patton was moved to northwest Europe to command the US Third Army, which was taking part in the great battles to liberate France and the Low Countries and end the war in Europe by defeating Germany. By the time of the German surrender on 8 May 1945, Patton's Third Army had fought in

France, Belgium, Luxembourg, Austria, and Czechoslovakia. He had proved to be one of the most successful Allied generals, particularly in his use of armored divisions (tanks, guns, and mechanized infantry moving at speed across country).

Shortly after the end of the war, Patton died in Germany as a result of a road accident. He was buried in a US Third Army cemetery at Hamm in Luxembourg.

See also WORLD WAR II.

PAUL, Saint. The story of the life of St. Paul is told by his friend St. Luke in the Acts of the Apostles in the New Testament of the Bible. Paul's own Epistles (letters), which he wrote to the churches he founded and to his friends, give additional facts about his life and show what kind of man he was. He suffered from an illness which he called his "thorn in the flesh", which may have been epilepsy. Until he became a Christian his name was Saul. He was probably born at much the same time as Jesus Christ, and like Jesus he was a Jew, although he was born outside Palestine at the city of Tarsus in what is now known as southeastern Turkey. This was a part of the Roman Empire, and Saul's father had won the right to become a Roman citizen. (This was an honor which the Romans conferred on some people in the countries of their empire, and it gave them special rights.) As the son of a Roman citizen Saul was a Roman citizen also. His family were strict Jews and Saul was sent to Jerusalem to study Jewish law.

Soon after the crucifixion of Jesus (see JESUS CHRIST), Saul began to come across his followers, the Christians, and was horrified at their new religion. To Jews crucifixion was the most shameful death, and they could not believe that the Messiah, or savior, whom they had awaited so long, could possibly have been so humiliated. People began to persecute the Christians and Saul became one of the most violent persecutors and was present at the stoning of St. Stephen, the first Christian martyr. (See MARTYR.)

The missionary journeys of St. Paul. He traveled and established Christianity in many countries.

Then came the turning point of Saul's life. The ninth chapter of the Acts of the Apostles tells how this happened. One day, as he was traveling to Damascus to seek out and destroy a group of Christians, he saw a blinding light and heard a voice saying to him, "Saul, Saul, why persecutest thou me?" Saul asked, "Who art thou, Lord?" and was answered, "I am Jesus whom thou persecutest". When he got to Damascus, still blinded from the brightness of the light, he was looked after by a Christian, and from that moment onwards Saul the persecutor became Paul the Christian missionary.

Some time later Paul returned to Jerusalem and there met the Christian leaders Peter, James, and John. From them he no doubt learned more about Jesus, and Paul soon realized that there was special work for him to do: he was to preach Christianity to the Gentiles (non-Jews) as well as to the Jews.

At first he made Antioch (now Antakya in Turkey) his headquarters and set out with Barnabas and Mark on his first journey to Cyprus and southern Asia Minor, now southern Turkey. He returned to Antioch in time to take part in a crisis in the development of Christianity. Peter thought that if Gentiles wished to become Christians they ought first to agree to keep the religious laws of the Jews. Paul, believing that Christianity was a religion for everyone, insisted that this was unnecessary. He won the day and made possible the great spread of Christianity, but his victory made him many enemies.

From Antioch he set out on another journey. First he visited the churches he had founded earlier in Asia Minor, and at Lystra was joined by Timothy, who was his most faithful disciple. Then he was led to take the gospel further west by seeing a vision of a man from Macedonia (an area north of Greece) who said, "Come over into Macedonia, and help us". He went there and was imprisoned for performing a miracle of healing on a young girl. In prison he made friends with his jailer and converted him to Christianity. When the magistrates heard he was a Roman citizen they were frightened in case they should be punished by the Romans for imprisoning him, and they let him go. Then he went south to Greece and at Athens argued with the philosophers but he did not succeed in converting many people to Christianity. However, at Corinth he succeeded in starting a Christian fellowship, and it was there that he wrote his two Epistles to the Thessalonians in the New Testament. After 18 months in Corinth he returned to Antioch by way of Syria and soon afterwards set out on his third great journey.

His first stop on this journey was Ephesus (in present-day Turkey), where he stayed two years and where he wrote the First Epistle to the Corinthians. Finally he was driven out by the silversmiths, who lived by making images of the Roman goddess Diana. He spent some time in the rest of Greece and in Macedonia, then returned to Jerusalem.

While in the Temple in Jerusalem, he was attacked by hostile Jews but was rescued by Roman soldiers, who arrested him. However, he had to wait two years for a trial and then claimed the right to be tried by the Roman emperor himself—this was the right of a Roman citizen. From this point onwards our knowledge of what happened to Paul is not at all clear. It seems that he remained in Rome for two years, living under guard, but in a house he rented and not in prison. It is even possible that after this he visited Spain. He seems to have been arrested again (perhaps in Asia Minor), to have been taken once more to Rome, and to have been killed in the persecutions of the Emperor Nero (see NERO).

It is sometimes difficult to understand St. Paul's epistles. For one thing he was a man of action rather than a scholar, and never sat down to write a full account of what he believed. For another thing his letters were sent to particular people who were facing particular problems, which we can only guess at. His letters to the Corinthians and Thessalonians are full of advice about how Christians should behave, and his letter to the Galatians deals mainly with the struggle between Christianity and the Jewish devotion to Jewish law. The letter to the Romans is the fullest and most closely reasoned statement St. Paul made about Christianity.

PAUL VI, Pope (1897-1978).

Giovanni Battista Montini, who became Pope Paul VI, was born in Concesio, near Brescia, in Italy. Early in life, he decided to become a priest and was ordained when he was 26 years old. Soon afterwards he went to Rome to study at the university. In 1954 Father Montini was appointed archbishop of Milan, a large industrial city in northern Italy. His particular interest in Milan was the Church's welfare work among the poor. While he was archbishop, about 200 churches and chapels were built or repaired in his diocese. He was appointed cardinal in 1958.

Camera Press

Pope Paul VI brought guidance to the Roman Catholic Church during a period of problems and uncertainties.

Upon the death of Pope John XXIII in 1963, Cardinal Montini was elected pope. He chose Paul VI as his papal name, in memory of the early Christian missionary St. Paul (see PAUL, SAINT). Pope Paul traveled a great deal and became known as the "flying pope". One of his goals was to work for the unity of all Christians, and his first journey was a pilgrimage to the Holy Land where he met the head of the Eastern Orthodox Church. Altogether he traveled to 16 countries on 6 continents urging peace, understanding, and justice.

During his pontificate, or reign, Pope Paul relaxed the regulations on fasting and on Roman Catholics marrying people from other religions. But he reinforced the Church rule against priests marrying, and spoke out against women becoming priests.

Pope Paul also made important changes within the Church organization. He greatly increased the number of cardinals, appointing many new cardinals from Communist countries and Africa, and introduced a retirement age of 75 for bishops and 80 for cardinals. He died on 6 August 1978 after 15 years in office. (See POPE.)

PAULING, Linus (born 1901).

The American chemist Linus Carl Pauling made outstanding contributions to understanding the structure of chemicals and biological molecules.

Pauling was born in Portland, Oregon, in the United States. He graduated in chemistry at the Oregon State Agricultural College (now the Oregon State University) in 1922 and in 1925 received his doctorate from the California Institute of Technology, where he taught until 1963. He was among the first to apply the principles of quantum mechanics to chemistry, notably to the structure of molecules and the nature of the chemical bond. His book *The Nature of the Chemical Bond and the Structure of Molecules and Crystals*, published in 1939, was one of the most influential scientific books of the century.

In the mid-1930s, Pauling began to study the structure of proteins, although during World War II (1939–45) he worked on explosives. In 1949 he showed that red blood cells from patients with sickle-cell anemia contain an abnormal form of the oxygen-carrying protein, hemoglobin. In the early 1950s he proposed a helical model for the secondary structure of proteins, that is, the way in which the amino acid building-blocks of the protein interact (see PROTEIN). In 1954,

Pauling was awarded the Nobel Prize for Chemistry.

Following the development of nuclear weapons, Pauling became active in the campaign for nuclear disarmament and was an outspoken opponent of nuclear testing. He was awarded the Nobel Peace Prize in 1962 and is the only person to have won two Nobel Prizes by himself, without sharing one or both with another person.

During the late 1970s Pauling received publicity for his so-called "megavitamin" idea. He claimed that massive doses of vitamin C would cure the common cold, schizophrenia, and even some forms of cancer.

PAVLOV, Ivan (1849–1936), was a Russian physiologist noted for his experiments on blood circulation, digestion, and conditioned reflexes.

Society for Cultural Relations with the USSR

The Russian physiologist, Ivan Pavlov, conducts one of his classic experiments in conditioned reflexes.

Ivan Petrovich Pavlov was born in Ryazan, Russia. He entered a religious seminary, but his scientific interests led him away from the priesthood. In 1870 he enrolled at the University of St. Petersburg. During the next decade, he became involved with work on the nerve physiology of animals. In 1883 he earned the degree of Doctor of Medicine from the Military Medical Academy in St. Petersburg. After conducting animal research in St. Petersburg and in Germany, he returned to the Academy and became professor of physiology in 1895.

Pavlov's most famous experiments were with the salivation (that is, the flow of saliva in the mouth) of dogs. He demonstrated that some reflexes develop as a result of training. He called these reflexes conditioned reflexes, as opposed to inborn, or inherited, reflexes.

To investigate conditioned reflexes, Pavlov rang a bell every time he fed his dogs. The dogs salivated when presented with the food. Eventually, after several feedings accompanied by the sound of a bell, the dogs salivated when they heard the bell even when they received no food. Thus he had conditioned his dogs to respond to the sound of the bell. Pavlov wrote of his experiments and theories in *The Work of the Digestive Glands* and *Conditioned Reflexes and Psychiatry*.

Continuing his work, Pavlov attempted to link complicated workings of the mind with conditioning. He believed that his conditioning principles could be used to solve the problems of psychiatry. During his life Pavlov received many honors. Among them was the 1904 Nobel Prize for physiology or medicine, which was awarded to him for his important studies of digestion.

PAVLOVA, Anna (1881–1931), was the most famous ballet dancer in the world during her lifetime. Her dance *The Dying Swan* is one of the best-known dances in the history of ballet. It was composed especially for her by Michel Fokine, a choreographer, or dance arranger.

Pavlova was born in St. Petersburg, Russia, of Polish parents. When she was eight years old, her mother took her to see her first ballet, Peter Tchaikovsky's *The Sleeping Beauty*. Instantly she decided to become a dancer. She began her training at the Imperial Ballet School in St. Petersburg at the age of ten. The training was long and hard, but in 1906 she became prima ballerina, or leading dancer, of the Imperial Ballet.

In 1907 and again in 1908 Pavlova joined a group of dancers who toured several European cities. The next year she left Russia to join a new ballet company, Ballets Russes, in Paris, under the leadership of Sergei Diaghilev. Her

A postcard picture of Anna Pavlova, the most famous ballerina of her time. She was best known for her performance in *The Dying Swan*.

partner there was the finest male dancer of modern times, Vaslav Nijinsky (see NIJINSKY, VASLAV). Their most famous performances were in the ballet *Les Sylphides*, choreographed by Fokine. Pavlova studied under Enrico Cecchetti, who continued as her teacher to the end of her life.

In 1910 Pavlova went to London where she was an immediate success. She and her husband, Victor Dandré, a Russian lawyer, bought Ivy House, a pleasant home in London, where she gave ballet lessons. She formed her own ballet company, which was managed by her husband. Pavlova toured in many different countries, taking the art of ballet to places where it was unknown. Among her many well-known dances were *Les Papillons, Autumn Bacchanal, The Magic Flute,* and *Invitation to the Dance*.

She died of pneumonia at The Hague, Netherlands, at the age of 50.

PEA. The pea is a leguminous plant (see LEGUMINOUS PLANTS) and is therefore useful for enriching the soil (see NITROGEN) as well as providing food. It is related to vetch, clover, beans, and sweet peas. Peas can be grown as either a farm crop or a household vegetable. The plant climbs, for the stalk is too weak to stand upright by itself and the compound leaves end in tendrils which cling to supports. It varies in height from about 30 centimeters to 2 meters (12 inches to 6 feet). The peas themselves are enclosed in pods.

The original home of the pea was southern Europe and southwestern Asia, but nowadays it is grown all over the world, although it does best in a cool climate and dislikes hot, dry weather. Peas were eaten in prehistoric times and in ancient Greece and Rome. For a time in Europe they were cooked in their pods. Sugar peas, also known as *mangetout* or snowpeas, are picked when still small and cooked and eaten in the pods.

The field pea is grown on farms and has brown or mottled seeds and purple flowers. It

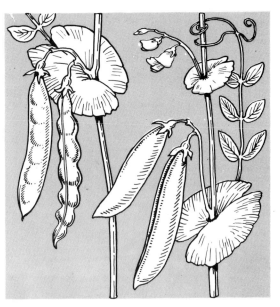

A pea plant with ripened pods (left). Flowers, a young plant, and tendrils are on the right.

is coarser than the garden variety and makes very good food for cattle, horses, sheep, and pigs.

Garden peas (*Pisum sativum*) may roughly be divided into two main types, those with smooth seeds and those with wrinkled seeds. The smooth type, which is the dwarf (smaller) pea, is chiefly sown early because it is hardy enough to withstand the colder weather, and ripens quickly. The wrinkled or tall pea is sown as the main crop because it has more pods and the peas themselves are sweeter and larger. The flowers are white. Other varieties include black-eyed peas and chick-peas, which are an important food in India and the Middle East. The Greek salad hummus is made of chick-peas, oil, garlic, and lemon.

Peas grow best in fairly rich, well-drained soil. The most common diseases that affect them are root rot and mildew.

Besides being sold in pods, peas are also processed (preserved), canned, dried, and frozen. The split peas used for making pea soup are the seeds of dwarf plants harvested when they have dried after ripening.

PEACE CORPS is an agency of the United States government made up of volunteers who live and work in developing countries. Peace Corps volunteers teach in schools, serve as nurses and doctors in hospitals, build roads and houses, work on agricultural projects, and do many other jobs that are useful to these countries. President John F. Kennedy founded the Peace Corps in 1961, and its first director was R. Sargent Shriver, Jr. Many foreign governments responded to its establishment by inviting volunteers to their countries. Thousands of Americans applied for service in the Peace Corps, and more than 700 of the best qualified were chosen, trained, and sent abroad in 1961 to 16 countries around the world. These first experimental projects were so successful that the US Congress passed a bill in September 1961 that officially authorized the US Peace Corps as an agency of the federal government.

The Peace Corps grew rapidly in the early 1960s, and in 1966, at the height of its success, 15,556 volunteers served in 52 countries. Since then, however, the numbers have decreased to 6,000 a year and the budget has been cut. In its first 25 years, 110,000 people have worked as Peace Corps volunteers.

Barnaby's

A United States Peace Corps volunteer supervises a tree-planting project in Turkey.

Applicants for the Peace Corps must be at least 19 years old and in good health. There is no upper age limit, and many people in their 60s and 70s have qualified. In 1986, the average age for volunteers was 29, and roughly two-thirds were college graduates. Since the 1970s, skilled craftsmen have also been recruited, as well as volunteers with families. Volunteers usually serve for two years. They receive a small allowance that enables them to live on the same level as the local people in the host country.

Volunteers must be trained and prepared for life in a Third World country. Training programs are conducted in the country or region where the volunteers will serve, and usually take 10 to 12 weeks. They learn the language of the country and study its history, geography, and culture. In the mid-1980s, 38 per cent of volunteers worked in education; 22 per cent in food production; and 12 per cent in health and nutrition.

There are similar volunteer organizations in a number of European countries. The British equivalent of the Peace Corps is called Voluntary Service Overseas (VSO).

PEACE MOVEMENTS. Peace movements are groups dedicated to the promotion of peace. The first organized peace movement not affiliated to any government was set up in the United States in 1814. An international peace congress met in London, England, in 1843, and by 1914, on the eve of World War I, there were 160 peace groups in the world.

The 20th century has witnessed more bitter and global struggles than any preceding period in history. In the devastation of the two World Wars (1914–18; 1939–45), millions of people, civilians as well as soldiers, lost their lives, and homes and cities were destroyed. The horror of such immense destruction encouraged the growth of peace movements and fired the determination of many to work for a permanent peace. A new threat looming on the horizon following World War II was the development of nuclear weapons with their untold destructive force.

Barnaby's

Members of CND (Campaign for Nuclear Disarmament) join other protest groups on a march in London, 1984.

Pacifists are people who, on the grounds of religious and moral beliefs, oppose *all* wars and violent confrontation between nations. Religious sects such as the Quakers (see FRIENDS, SOCIETY OF) and Mennonites are pacifist. Most members of these sects have been conscientious objectors during wartime; that is, they refuse to fight on religious grounds and serve their country instead in a non-military capacity. While most peace movements oppose specific wars, or specific methods of warfare, they are not necessarily opposed to the waging of all war. They cannot therefore be regarded as truly pacifist.

During the 1960s and early 1970s, peace movements focused their attention on the American war in Vietnam. In the United States itself, there were peace marches, demonstrations, and vigils, which drew thousands of people, and the movement was supported by many prominent Americans. Towards the end of the war, even enlisted soldiers became active in the peace movement.

More recently, peace activists have concentrated on the issue of nuclear war. The Campaign for Nuclear Disarmament (CND), which started in the 1950s in Great Britain and expanded rapidly all over the world in the 1980s, wants all nations to dispense with all nuclear weapons.

PEACH. The juicy, pink and yellow peach grows on a low, spreading, deep-rooted tree. It is related to almonds and cherries and, like them, its leaves are folded in the bud. Some varieties have small red glands at the base of the leaf. The blossom is usually pink and it appears on otherwise bare branches. Cultivated fruits are usually over 7.5 centimeters (3 inches) across, with a fuzzy skin. This is the chief way in which they differ from nectarines, which are very like peaches but have smooth skins. Like peaches, nectarines grow best on well-drained sandy or gravelly soil with plenty of humus material (dead leaves and other decaying vegetable matter).

Peach trees are grown in most regions where the summers are warm and dry. In cooler countries they are often trained to grow in a fan shape against a wall. In many countries the peach is second only to the apple in importance. Most peach orchards in Europe are in France and Italy. Peaches are divided into free-stone varieties, in which the stone separates easily from the flesh, and the clingstone varieties. Freestone peaches are better for drying and clingstone for canning. Yellowfleshed varieties are preferred in America and whiter-fleshed kinds in Europe.

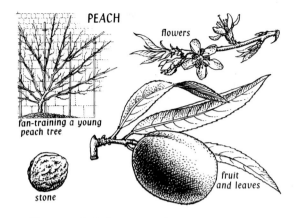

PEACH

flowers

fan-training a young peach tree

stone

fruit and leaves

The peach belongs to the genus, or group, *Prunus*, and its species, or kind, is called *persica*, because for a long time it was thought to have first grown in Persia. Actually it probably came from China, where it grows wild, as it does in Japan and many other Asian countries. The peach is one of the oldest cultivated fruits. The Greek historian Xenophon wrote in the 4th century BC that it was being grown in Persia. It probably spread into France in Roman times and from France into many countries of Europe. Later, Spanish settlers took it to America and now it is also grown in South Africa, Australia, and New Zealand. The United States produces about one-fifth of the world's supply, with Italy the second most important peach producer.

PEACOCK. "As proud as a peacock" is a well-known phrase, and indeed the peacock (*Pavo cristatus*) has reason to be proud of its beauty. Although they are commonly called its "tail", it is actually the feathers called the tailcoverts of the male which are so wonderful. Most of each feather resembles a bronze fern, but at the tip is a disk known as an eye. In the center of the eye is a patch of velvety black, bordered with bright blue. This is surrounded by bronze with an edging of greenish gold. When the peacock wishes to show off to the peahen (female bird) it raises up its train, as these special feathers are called, and spreads it out in an enormous fan, quivering every feather.

Besides its magnificent train, the peacock

has a crest of feathers on its head with fan-shaped tips of black and bluish-green. The head and neck are bright blue, the back is green, marked with black, the wings are reddish cream and the under parts are dark glossy green and black. The skin of the face is bare and white. The peahen is a much more dull-colored bird.

The blue, or Indian, peacock comes from India and Sri Lanka, but has been taken to many other parts of the world, both for zoos and for parks. Peacocks are hardy birds and breed well in captivity. The main drawback in keeping them is their ugly screaming call.

The peacock's nest is a hollow in the ground and the peahen usually lays five buff-colored eggs. In spite of their long trains, peacocks can fly quite well.

NHPA/Michael Leach

A male Indian peacock displays before a female by fanning his magnificent tail feathers, each tipped with an iridescent eye ringed with blue and bronze.

There are two other kinds of peacock besides the well-known Indian one. One is the Javan or green peacock (*Pavo muticus*), which is found in Indonesia, Burma, Thailand, Kampuchea, and Malaysia. This bird has a crest of ordinary feathers, a green neck and breast, blue and yellow skin on the face, and longer legs than the Indian peacock.

The Congo peacock (*Afropavo congensis*) was discovered in 1936 after a search that began in 1913 with the finding of a single feather. The cock bird is mainly blue and green; the hen is reddish and green.

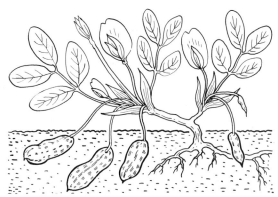

Peanuts are forced into the soil by the growth of their stalks.

PEANUT. Other names for peanuts are groundnuts, earthnuts, monkey-nuts, and goobers. They are grown in warm countries and belong to the large family of plants, the Leguminosae (see LEGUMINOUS PLANTS).

Peanut plants look rather like very large clover plants and have small yellow flowers. After they have been fertilized, the flower stalks bend downwards and force the developing fruit into the soil. This forms a pod containing two or three seeds that ripen underground. Peanuts do best on a light, sandy soil, in frost-free conditions.

Although native to South America, the peanut is now grown on a large scale in over 40 countries. India, China, and the United States are among the top peanut producers.

The peanut is grown mainly for its edible oil, except in the United States where half the crop is harvested to make peanut butter. The peanut plant is also grown as an animal feed. Like related peas and beans, peanut plants are valuable as a fertilizer as they add nitrogen to the soil.

PEAR. The pear is a relation of the apple, but quite a different shape. All pears narrow towards the stem, and swell towards the base around the seed cavities. Pear blossom is white, and the trees do not spread like apple-trees—the branches grow straight upwards and outwards.

Most cultivated varieties of pear were developed from the wild pear (*Pyrus communis*) of southern Europe and western Asia.

Pears were grown in Greek and Roman times, and the Emperor Charlemagne ordered them to be planted for him in about AD 800. The delicious pears eaten today were first produced by Belgian growers early in the 19th century. The best-known varieties are Williams' Bon Chrétien (usually shortened to "William"), the Conference, and the Kieffer, the latter type being widely grown in North America. William has been successful in the western United States. It was taken there by a Mr. Bartlett, who gave it his name, and it became known all over the world as the best pear for canning. Special varieties are grown for making a fermented drink called perry.

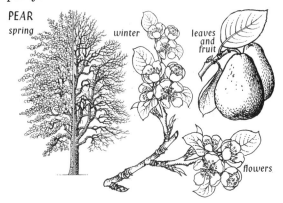

PEAR spring winter leaves and fruit flowers

Italy is the world's leading pear producer, followed by China and the United States. The main areas of production in North America are the states of California, Oregon, Washington, New York, and Michigan, and the province of Ontario in Canada.

PEARL HARBOR is a large, well-protected inlet of the Pacific Ocean on the southern coast of Oahu Island in Hawaii. This excellent deep-water harbor is about 11 kilometers (7 miles) from Honolulu, the state capital. It is an important naval base and the headquarters of United States military forces in the Pacific area.

Two peninsulas extend into the harbor and divide it into three bays. Among the naval facilities around the harbor and on tiny Fords Island (in the east bay) are dry docks, refueling and supply piers, training and communications buildings, administrative offices, and a submarine base. Hawaii's location makes the harbor especially important as a refueling and supply point for ships crossing the Pacific and as an outpost of United States defense.

By a treaty with Hawaii in 1887, the United States was permitted to use the harbor as a repair and fueling station. Maps of the harbor were first drawn in 1897. Congress approved construction of the naval base in 1908.

Peter Newark's Western Americana

The USS *West Virginia* and USS *Tennessee* burning after the Japanese raid on Pearl Harbor on 7 December 1941.

Pearl Harbor was the site of a Japanese surprise attack, on Sunday morning, of 7 December 1941. The attack brought the United States into World War II. Beginning at about 7:55, the first of a series of air attacks was launched from enemy aircraft carriers 320 kilometers (200 miles) northwest of Oahu. By about 9:45 the fighting was over. It had been a great Japanese victory. Nearly 100 United States ships were in Pearl Harbor at the time, but the chief targets were the eight battleships and the aircraft on the island. During the short raid more than 2,000 men were killed, 16 ships were sunk or damaged, and about 150 planes were destroyed. The Japanese losses amounted to about 95 men, 29 aircraft, and several midget submarines. A large number of the United States casualties were sailors aboard the battleship *Arizona*, which blew up and sank. After the attack the harbor facilities

were rebuilt, and many of the ships were repaired and used during the war.

PEARLS AND PEARL FISHING. Not every pearl oyster contains a pearl. In some pearl beds pearls are found in every oyster but in others not one pearl is found. In some pearl fisheries the mother-of-pearl lining of the oyster is more valuable than the pearls.

Pearls are not found in normal healthy oysters. The pearl forms around an irritation in the oyster, perhaps a grain of sand. It becomes enclosed in a pearl sac, and nacre, or mother-of-pearl, is deposited on to the irritation.

The oysters are usually found on the seabed, on either mud, sand, or coral. The pearl oyster lives for up to 16 years but it is generally found that the younger the oyster the better the pearl. The most important species that produce pearls belong to the genus *Pinctada* (or *Meleangrina*). Freshwater mollusks that produce pearls belong to the genus *Unio*. Edible oysters do not produce pearls of any value. (See MOLLUSK; OYSTER.)

Pearls may be round, drop-shaped, egg-shaped, or button-shaped. Those of irregular shape and surface are called *baroque* pearls and those attached to the inside shell of the oyster are called *blister* pearls. Pearls are measured by their weight in grains (4 pearl-grains make 1 carat and 5 carats make 1 gram (0.03 of an ounce)). Pearls weighing less than

Barnaby's

The pearl being removed from an oyster.

Barnaby's

Cultured pearls produced in Japan are sorted according to their color and size.

Often he has a spear to defend himself against sharks. He gathers all the shells he can see into baskets which are drawn up by ropes. The pearls, if round, are drilled through the center and sent to the world markets.

The most important centers today are the Australian fisheries where the "white" pearls are found. The main Australian areas are Broome (Western Australia), Darwin (Northern Territory), and Thursday Island, off the northern tip of Queensland. Here the oysters, which are up to 30 centimeters (12 inches) across, produce pearls larger but less attractive than oriental pearls, and much of the value is in the mother of pearl.

Greenish and rose-tinted white pearls come from the fisheries in the South China Sea the Sulu Sea northeast of Borneo, the Philippine Islands, Tahiti, and other Pacific islands.

a quarter of a grain are called *seed* pearls. The value of a pearl depends on its quality and the *square* of its weight.

The pearl has always been numbered among jewels and has been called "the queen of gems". Sometimes it has been prized more than diamonds and precious stones, although it does not last as long. One of the finest pearls was a drop-shaped pearl called "Star of the West", fished near Broome (Western Australia) in 1917. It was about the size of a sparrow's egg. Some famous pearls have been much larger, such as the Hope pearl of 1,888 grains and Shah Sofi's pearl of 513 grains.

One of the most important pearl fisheries is off the Trucial coast and around the island of Bahrain in the Persian Gulf. The port of Lingeh is a pearl market. Another rich bed is the Gulf of Mannar, between India and Sri Lanka. In these fisheries, a diver jumps from a boat feet first into the sea, with a rope and a heavy stone attached to it to take him down.

Women divers in Japan go as deep as 12m (40ft) to cut the pearl oysters off the rocks on the seabed.

Other pearl fisheries are in the Pearl Islands (Gulf of Panama) and the Gulf of California.

Freshwater pearls are whiter but lack the brilliance of the sea-water pearls. They are found in small quantities in particular sorts of mussels on the beds of rivers in Scotland, Germany, and Russia. They are found in quantities large enough to make them worth selling in the Mississippi and its tributaries in the United States.

Cultured pearls are those which are produced by the artificial introduction of a "nucleus", or core. This is done by introducing a nucleus of pig-toe shell and a graft of live tissue from another oyster. The live tissue grows around the nucleus until it forms a sac which completely covers the nucleus. The oyster then deposits nacre on the nucleus and a cultured pearl is formed. This practice began in South China in the 13th century and was developed into an important industry in Japan and Australia in the 20th century.

Cultured pearls can be distinguished from natural pearls by their different luster (brilliance) and color. Natural pearls last much longer and have a much greater value. The presence of an artificial nucleus can be detected by X-rays or by special instruments.

Mother-of-Pearl

The pearly lining of the shells of pearl oysters and of some other shellfish is called mother-of-pearl. It is used for buttons and for ornamental objects such as knife-handles.

Mother-of-pearl from freshwater mussels is used for buttons in the United States, and in Europe trochus shell is also often used for this purpose. The trochus is a large, top-shaped shellfish found in shallow tropical waters, off the coast of Queensland and around the Malay peninsula, Indonesia, New Guinea, the Philippines, and the Pacific Islands.

PEARSON, Lester (1897–1972).

Lester Bowles Pearson, 19th prime minister of Canada and leader of the Canadian Liberal party, was born in Toronto, Ontario. He entered Victoria College of the University of Toronto in 1913 and received his degree in 1919, after serving in World War I. Following graduate studies in England, he taught history at the University of Toronto.

In 1928 Pearson became first secretary in the Canadian Department of External Affairs. From 1935 to 1941 he served in London as first secretary in the office of the high commissioner for Canada. During World War II he served in the embassy in Washington, DC, becoming Canadian ambassador to the United States in 1945.

In 1948 he was elected a member of parliament for Algoma East in northern Ontario

BBC Hulton Picture Library

Lester Pearson, 19th prime minister of Canada and Liberal leader, began his career as a diplomat.

province. From 1948 to 1957 he was secretary of state for external affairs. In 1951 he became chairman of the North Atlantic Treaty Organization (NATO).

In 1957 Pearson was awarded the Nobel Prize for peace for his part in settling the Suez crisis. (This was a conflict involving Britain, France, and Israel against Egypt in 1956.) The resolution that he presented to the United Nations – which stated that Britain, France, and Israel were to withdraw from Egyptian territory and be replaced by a United Nations emergency force – was accepted, and peace was restored to the area.

Pearson became leader of the Liberal Party in 1958. He was elected prime minister in 1963, and held office until 1968. His period of government was badly affected by political rivalry between the parties of the Canadian parliament and by scandal. But Pearson succeeded in passing many useful laws to improve Canada's social welfare and transportation systems and help the country's poorer regions. During his time in office Canada also acquired a new flag and its armed forces were unified.

PEARY, Robert Edwin (1856–1920), is credited with the discovery of the North Pole on 6 April 1909. He was born at Cresson, Pennsylvania, in the United States, on 6 May 1856. After he graduated from Bowdoin College, Brunswick, Maine, he joined the Civil Engineer Corps of the US Navy. He decided to be a polar explorer after a trip to Greenland in 1886. Between 1891 and 1908 he led five expeditions to Greenland.

Peary's trip to the North Pole from Greenland made use of all his Arctic experience. His ship, the *Roosevelt*, was specially built for Arctic work. On the actual trip a large group set out from Cape Columbia in Grant Land with as much equipment as they could carry. A small advance party selected the route and marked the trail. At intervals small parts of the main party turned back with only enough supplies to reach the base, leaving the others fully provisioned. Finally only Peary, Matthew Henson, and four Eskimos were left to make the last dash of 225 kilometers (140 miles) to the pole. After they believed they had reached it, they remained there for about 30 hours, taking observations and recording scientific data. Peary's records of the event, however, are incomplete, which has caused some experts to question whether he did really reach the Pole.

Peary proved Greenland was an island and learned a great deal about the Eskimos. Information was collected on the polar seas, tides, and winds. Peary made soundings within 8 kilometers (5 miles) of the pole that failed to touch bottom at 2,700 meters (9,000 feet) and proved the North Pole to be in the center of a vast sea covered with ice.

PECAN. The pecan (*Carya illinoensis*) is one of the most popular nuts in the United States. It is the only native nut tree extensively grown in orchards, located chiefly in the southern states, Arizona, California, and Oregon. Georgia is the leading pecan state.

J. Horace McFarland Company

Above: A cluster of pecan nuts. **Left:** The husks removed and the nut cut open showing the kernel.

The pecan tree is one of about 15 species of hickory native to the United States. It grows to as much as 45 meters (150 feet) tall, and has large leaves made up of 9 to 17 tapering leaflets. The tree bears two types of flowers: those from which nuts develop; and pollen-bearing flowers. The nuts grow inside a thin husk of four parts. They ripen from October to December. Nuts from different trees differ in size, thickness of shell, and flavor.

Until about 1900 most of the pecan crop came from wild trees. Many nuts from wild trees are still harvested. The finest quality nuts are from the southern orchards. Budded or grafted varieties of trees are grown in most orchards. They produce the so-called paper-shelled pecans, large nuts with sweet kernels and thin shells.

After harvest, ripe nuts are dried and cured, sorted and graded. They are sold in the shell or as shelled nuts. The nuts have high food value as they are rich in fat and a good source of certain vitamins, calcium, phosphorus, and iron. Pecans were used as food by American Indians. The early white settlers also used them as food for themselves and for their hogs.

Pecan wood is too brittle to be of much value. Some tannin, used in leather preparation, is taken out of shells collected at pecan-cracking factories.

The trees are sometimes planted around homes or along streets and roads, and have been introduced to other countries such as South Africa and Australia.

PECCARY

PECCARY is an American animal of the swine family. It is sometimes called wild pig, musk hog, or javelina. It is not a true pig but is related to it.

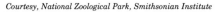

Peccaries differ from pigs in having small erect ears, no tails, and a scent gland under the skin.

Peccaries squeal and grunt. Their snout and body build is pig-like; but their tusks turn downward. They have only three toes on the hind foot instead of four, and no visible tail. On their backs, they have a musk gland which gives off a strong and unpleasant odor. Some-times they live in hollow tree trunks or in a thicket, where they give birth to their young.

Although peccaries will eat almost any-thing, they prefer nuts, grain, and vegetables. Herds of peccaries sometimes uproot whole fields. They kill all kinds of small animals, including snakes.

There are two kinds of peccaries. Both are grayish black with a mane of stiff black hairs down their back. The collared peccary (*Tay-assu tajacu*) has a grayish white band from its shoulder to its chest. It is about 1 meter (3 feet) long and it weighs about 22 kilograms (50 pounds). It is found from southern Texas, New Mexico, and Arizona down through South America.

The white-lipped peccary (*Tayassu pecari*) has a band of white from its chin almost to its eye. It is larger than the collared peccary and lives in Central and South America.

Peccaries are killed for their skins which are used in making gloves and jackets.

PEEL, Sir Robert

PEEL, Sir Robert (1788–1850). Sir Robert Peel was a British prime minister and the founder of the Conservative party. But he is best known for his part in founding the London police force in 1829. British policemen are often known as "bobbies" after him, although they were first known as "Peelers".

Peel was born at Bury in Lancashire, the son of a wealthy cotton manufacturer. He was sent to Harrow School and Oxford University, where he was brilliant at both classics (Latin and Greek) and mathematics. In 1809 he became a member of parliament, and it was soon seen that he was both able and hard working. At 24 he became secretary for Ire-land, which at that time was in a very bad state. Peel would not support Catholic emanci-pation (which aimed at giving Irish Catholics the same rights as Protestants) and this made him unpopular in Ireland.

Peel had great success as home secretary in the Tory governments of Lord Liverpool and the Duke of Wellington (the victor of the Battle of Waterloo). He reformed the criminal law by reducing the number of crimes for which people could be hanged and by improving the prisons. During this time he changed his mind about Ireland and made a speech in favor of Catholic emancipation. This made him unpopular in Britain and also broke up the Tory party.

Peel built up a new party from the Tories, which became the Conservative party that still flourishes today. He was prime minister for a short time in 1834 and would have been so again in 1839 if he had not asked Queen Victoria to give up some of her ladies-in-waiting who belonged to the Whig (opposition) party. This the queen refused to do.

When Peel became prime minister for a second time in 1841, he improved Britain's financial position and repealed (canceled) the Corn Laws. These laws kept the price of grain artificially high to help farmers, but prevented thousands of poor people from buying bread Peel believed this was wrong, but many fellow Conservatives disagreed. They combined with the opposition to bring about his resignation. Peel remained a supporter of free trade ideas. He died on 2 July 1850, three days after falling from his horse on Constitution Hill in London.

PEGASUS. When, in Greek legends, the hero Perseus cut off the head of the monster Medusa, there sprang from her body a winged horse called Pegasus. A young warrior named Bellerophon, after taming the horse with a bridle given to him by the goddess Athena, mounted Pegasus and flew off in search of adventure. He slew the fire-breathing monster Chimera, which was part lion, part goat, and part dragon. He overcame the fierce female warriors called the Amazons. But when he tried to fly to heaven Pegasus threw him. According to some tales Zeus, the king of gods, was angry at Bellerophon's boldness and sent an insect to tickle Pegasus and make him throw his rider. Pegasus went on flying up to heaven and was changed into a group of stars.

The Greeks also said that a blow from Pegasus' hoof caused the fountain of Hippocrene, sacred to the Muses, to spring up on Mount

Helicon in Greece. (See MUSES, THE.) The story probably reached Greece through the ancient city of Corinth, many of whose coins bore a winged horse.

PEKING see BEIJING.

PELICAN. There are many different kinds of pelican, large water birds found all over the world. Some may be nearly 3 meters (10 feet) across the wings.

Pelicans can at once be recognized by the big pouch of skin on the lower half of their very large beaks. The pouch stretches so that the pelican can collect and store an enormous amount of fish in it.

White pelicans. Black wing feathers show in flight.

Pelicans are clumsy-looking birds, being stoutly built with broad rounded wings and rather short tails. Their legs are short, too, with large webbed feet. Nevertheless, they are graceful in flight. The long neck is curved so that the head rests far back on the shoulders and the beak lies on the front of the neck.

They usually live in large colonies on lakes and other stretches of water, but they also visit coasts and the mouths of rivers. Sometimes they dive after fish.

The nest is made of sticks and grass stalks roughly put together and is built on the ground or in a low bush. Sometimes a hollow in the ground is used. The eggs have chalky, bluish white shells. When the young, which are covered with gray-brown feathers, hatch out the parents feed them on partly digested fish. The young birds get this by putting their beaks, and often their heads as well, into the pouch of the parent and helping themselves.

The North American white pelican (*Pelecanus erythrorhynchos*) breeds chiefly on western lakes. It winters on the California coast and along the Gulf of Mexico. The smaller brown pelican, also an American species, breeds along the tropical and subtropical shores. Two kinds of pelican live in Europe. One, the eastern white pelican (*Pelecanus onocrotalus*), is mainly white, tinged with pink, with a tuft of yellowish feathers on the breast, a small crest at the back of the head and black feathers in the wings. The Dalmatian pelican (*Pelecanus crispus*) is like it but has gray-tinged plumage. It nests in southeast Europe and, according to the Latin writer Pliny, once nested on the North Sea coast of Europe. The Australian pelican (*Pelecanus conspicillatus*) is the largest species with a length of 180 centimeters (70 inches). It has black and white plumage.

PELOPONNESIAN WAR.

If you look at a map of Greece you will see that the most southerly part of the mainland is nearly cut off from the rest by a deep inlet of the sea called the Gulf of Corinth. This part of Greece is called the Peloponnese, and the Peloponnesian War was fought in the 5th century BC between Sparta in the Peloponnese and Athens to the northeast. Athens had been the greatest of the city states into which ancient Greece was divided, but its glory came to an end with the war.

Athens and Sparta quarreled for years. Both of them wished to be the leaders of Greece, and Sparta had built up a mighty army and Athens a mighty navy to show their power. Sparta took advantage of rebellions in cities belonging to Athens to make trouble. In 433 BC a settlement on Corcyra (now called Corfu) in the northwest asked Athens to protect it against Corinth, which was a friend of Sparta. Then the long rivalry between the two states broke out into war.

War was declared between Athens and Sparta in 431 BC, when Thebes, an ally of Sparta, attacked Plataea, an ally of Athens. Pericles (see PERICLES) ordered the people to gather together inside the strong walls of Athens while the navy attacked the coasts of the Peloponnese. Meanwhile the Spartans invaded Attica, the region round Athens, and destroyed the crops.

In June 430 plague broke out in Athens and instantly spread in the hot summer weather. Thousands of Athenians in the crowded city died of it and it also spread to the navy. The people turned against Pericles, and a year later he too died of the disease.

After Pericles' death a tanner called Cleon, who had always opposed Pericles, became one of the leaders of Athens. In 425 Cleon went to overcome 420 Spartans trapped on the little island of Sphacteria, west of the Peloponnese. These Spartans resisted the Athenians for a long time, but Cleon, much to everyone's surprise, succeeded in conquering them. Sparta looked on this as a great disgrace and tried to make peace, which Cleon refused.

The Spartans' greatest general Brasidas marched through Greece, causing great destruction. Cleon went out to defeat him and both men were slain. After their deaths at the Battle of Amphipolis in 422 Nicias, another Athenian leader, agreed to end the fighting, and a period of peace called "the Peace of Nicias" lasted for six years.

Athens and Sparta, however, went on plotting against each other. Alcibiades, a brilliant but untrustworthy politician, did much to stir up fresh trouble. It was he who suggested that the Athenians should conquer Sicily in order to gain more glory. However, Alcibiades had to return to Athens, where he was accused of a crime and he escaped to the Spartans. At Syracuse in Sicily the people turned against the Athenians, defeated their army and navy, and killed almost all the invading force, including Nicias.

After some success at sea, chiefly owing to Alcibiades, who had returned to Athens, the Athenian fleet was caught off its guard at Aegospotami near the Hellespont (now called the Dardanelles). The Spartan navy under its great admiral Lysander destroyed the Athenian fleet. He then sailed to Athens and cut off its food supply, until, after six months of starvation, it surrendered in April 404 BC, after 27 years of war.

PEN AND PENCIL. An instrument for writing or drawing with ink is called a pen. Pencils are sticks of mineral substances usually encased in wood.

Development of Pens

Early man scratched pictures on animal bones with sharp flints. The ancient Egyptians, Greeks, and Romans wrote either on wax tablets with a stylus, which was a pointed rod, or on parchment (made from animal skins), or papyrus (a form of paper made from reeds) with split pens made from the hollow stalks of marsh grasses or bamboo. The Chinese and Japanese until recently painted their letters with a fine brush.

In the early Middle Ages paper was invented and it was found that the quills (stems) of the tail or wing-feathers of geese, swans, or crows made good pens. The tip was pointed and split so that the ink could flow down a straight narrow channel to the paper. The small knife with which this shaping was done was called a penknife. The word pen itself is obtained from the Latin *penna*, meaning feather.

These quill pens were not lasting, but metal pens did not come into general use until about 1840, although known to the ancient Romans. The first to make steel pens by machinery was probably an Englishman, John Mitchell, in 1822. The slip pen, or nib that would slip into a nibholder, was invented about the same time by the English inventor James Perry. Nibs are made from sheet steel. They

are punched out as flat shapes, softened, formed into an arched shape, hardened and treated to make them tough and springy, smoothed and polished, and then sharpened and split.

Fountain pens carrying their own ink were hard to make before the discovery in about 1850 of vulcanite and ebonite. These substances were suitable for making the barrel and were obtained by heating rubber mixed with sulfur. The early fountain pens had nibs of gold, which was the only metal that was not eaten away by ink. However, they had to be tipped with a very hard metal, usually iridium, to withstand the wear against the paper. The first fountain pens had to be filled with ink from a squirting device like an eye dropper. The person credited with the invention of the fountain pen is an American, Lewis E. Waterman, whose design appeared in 1884. The basic workings of the fountain pen have not greatly altered since his day.

Self-filling pens appeared around 1910. They work on the principle that as air is sucked or squeezed out of the reservoir, ink flows in. The mechanism may be a pump lever, a plunger or a screw. A modern alternative to filling the pen from an ink bottle is the cartridge which comes ready-filled and merely has to be inserted into the pen.

A design for a ball-point pen appeared in 1888, but was intended only for use on rough surfaces and not as a proper pen. The ball-point as we know it was invented by a Hungarian called Lazlo Biro in 1944, and owed much to the improvements made in ball-bearing manufacture.

The tiny ball in the socket at the brass tip of a ball-point pen applies the ink to the paper. The ball stops ink from escaping from the reservoir, but as it turns, it picks up ink and so continues to write. Ball-point ink is thick and jelly-like, and reaches the ball thanks to capillary action (see CAPILLARY ACTION).

Felt- or fiber-tip pens were first made in Japan in the 1960s. Instead of a nib or a ball, these pens have a tip made of a tough fiber.

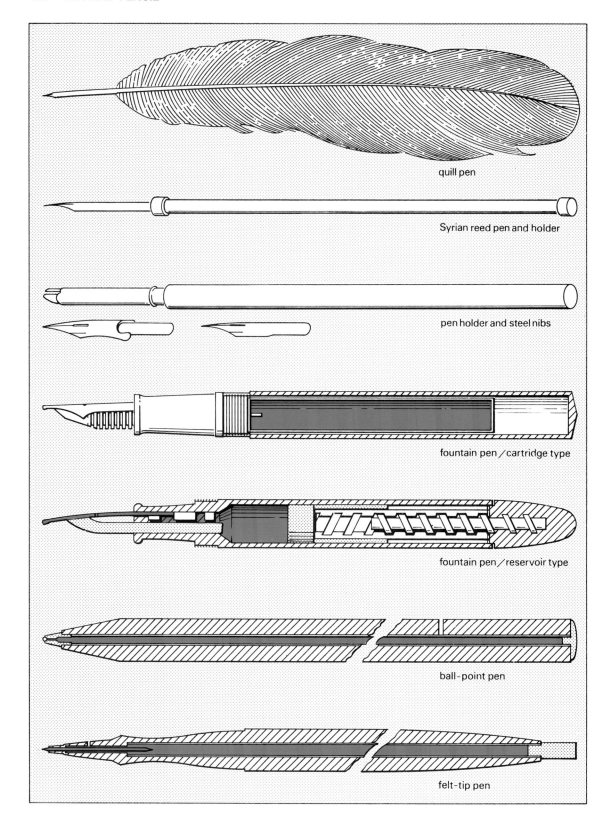

quill pen

Syrian reed pen and holder

pen holder and steel nibs

fountain pen / cartridge type

fountain pen / reservoir type

ball-point pen

felt-tip pen

Courtesy, Parker Pen Company

Above: When a quill was used for writing, sand was sprinkled on to the ink to dry it quickly. **Below:** Pieces of cedar wood are grooved, glued together with leads in between, and shaped into pencils.

Courtesy, Royal Sovereign Pencil Co.

They are useful for marking and coloring as well as for writing. (See also INK.)

Pencils

A "lead" pencil contains not lead but a mineral substance called graphite. Graphite, like lead, leaves a mark when drawn across paper (see GRAPHITE). Because of this it is called "black lead"; hence the name lead pencil.

In pencil manufacture dried ground graphite is mixed with clay and water. The more clay, the harder the pencil will be; the more graphite, the softer the pencil. Pencils are usually marked with letters or numbers to show the degree of hardness or softness of the lead. After the mixture reaches a doughy consistency, it passes through a forming press. It emerges as a thin sleek rope. This is straightened out, cut into lengths, dried, and put into huge ovens to bake.

Meanwhile the pencil case has been prepared. The wood, either red cedar or pine, is shaped in halves and grooved to hold the lead. After the finished leads are inserted in the grooves, the halves of the pencil are glued together. A saw cuts the lead-filled slats into individual pencils, and a shaping machine gives the surface a smooth finish.

Colored pencils are made of kaolin (fine white clay) mixed with waxes, gums, and coloring matter. Sometimes when they are soft the pencils are encased in paper wrapped spirally around the lead. The pencil is "sharpened" by unwinding the paper. Copying and ink pencils are made of a mixture of aniline dye, graphite, and China clay. In carpenters' and markers' pencils, graphite is combined with wax or tallow. In "automatic" or "propelling" pencils the lead is held in a small metal tube inside the shell of the pencil. The lead is pushed out or pulled in by means of a plunger operated by a screw mechanism

PENDULUM. If a weight is hung so that it can move freely and is then given a push, it will swing back and forth. This arrangement is called a pendulum, from the Latin word *pendere*, meaning "to hang". In 1583 the Italian scientist Galileo noticed that a lamp hanging in Pisa cathedral always took the same time to make one complete swing. This is the important principle of the pendulum, and is used to regulate clocks. Although any hanging object set swinging will in time make shorter and shorter swings because the air resists its movement, in nearly all cases the actual time taken for each swing is the same. Galileo used a pendulum for timing the human pulsebeat, just as a doctor or a nurse uses a watch for the same purpose. He is also said to have designed a clock controlled by a pendulum, although the first pendulum clock known was made by the Dutch scientist Christiaan Huygens in 1656.

The simple pendulum consists of a heavy weight called a bob either hung on a fine thread or attached to a light rod pivoted at the top. The length of the pendulum, measured between the point from which it is hung and the center of the bob, is the only thing that affects the time of the swing of a pendulum in a particular place. The weight and material of the bob make no difference, but the longer the pendulum the more slowly it swings. The time that it takes to swing backwards and forwards once is called the period and is proportional to the square root of its length (see SQUARE ROOT). Therefore a pendulum 200 centimeters (80 inches) long takes twice as much time to swing backwards and forwards as a pendulum 50 centimeters (20 inches) long.

Courtesy, W. Barclay Stephens, H.D., Hon. Curator of Horology, California Academy of Sciences

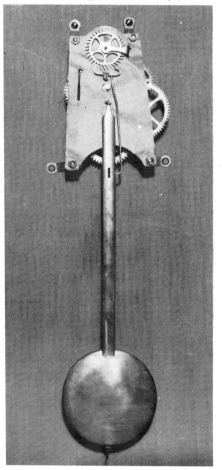

Clock pendulum. The rod and bob are made of a metal that does not contract or expand greatly when the temperature changes.

The time taken for a pendulum to swing also depends on its position on the Earth's surface. The Earth's gravity is greatest at low altitudes and near the poles (see GRAVITY). Therefore a pendulum swings faster away from the equator and at low altitude.

A cuckoo clock usually has a simple pendulum. If it gains, or goes too fast, it can be corrected simply by sliding the bob a little further down the rod, thus making the pendulum longer. A clock with a simple pendulum having a plain steel rod loses time in hot weather because the rod expands, or grows longer, with heat. (Actually, it loses $2\frac{3}{8}$ seconds a day for a rise of 5°C (10°F) in temperature.) For this reason, most pendulum clocks have what are called compensated pendulums. One type has alternate zinc and steel rods so arranged that as the steel rods expand upwards the zinc rods expand an equal amount downwards. Some pendulums are compensated with mercury, which was the first metal used for this purpose. It is placed in a container attached to the steel rod.

A weight hung on a length of elastic or from a coiled spring will bob up and down with a steady beat if pulled and let go. Similarly, if a spiral spring is arranged to oppose the turning of a wheel which is then turned to wind up the spring and let go, the wheel will twist back and forth with a regular beat. This is called a torsion pendulum and is found in the balance wheel and hair spring of a watch.

All types of pendulum have been used to control escapements in clocks. In an escapement a tiny push is given to the pendulum, enough to overcome the friction so that the pendulum does not run down in its swing until the spring or weight that supplies energy to the escapement runs down. Thus, clocks that run 24 hours, a week, a month, or even a year (anniversary clocks) are possible. (See also CLOCK AND WATCH.)

The word pendulum is almost always used in connection with a clock or timekeeper. However, there is another type of pendulum known as the Foucault pendulum. This pendulum has no time-telling function, nor has its rate of swing any significance. It is only the direction or plane of its swing that is important.

The Foucault pendulum gets its name from Jean Bernard Léon Foucault, a French physicist and astronomer. He demonstrated visually the rotation of the Earth, making use of a pendulum for the purpose.

Foucault made a public demonstration which attracted worldwide attention in the spring of 1851 in Paris, France. From the dome of a building called the Panthéon he hung a wire pendulum 67 meters (220 feet) long with a ball at the lower end weighing about 28 kilograms (62 pounds).

On the floor of the Panthéon a large compass dial, showing the north-south and east-west directions, was placed directly below the suspended pendulum. The pendulum ball was then given a north-south motion. After an hour or two it was noted that the pendulum apparently had changed its swing in a clockwise direction. In fact the pendulum was still swinging in its original direction and it was the Earth, which rotates on its axis once every 24 hours, that had turned beneath it.

The rate at which the Foucault pendulum appears to rotate depends on the latitude. At the poles the pendulum rotates once every 24 hours; at the equator it does not rotate at all. In the northern hemisphere it rotates in a clockwise direction; in the southern hemisphere its rotation is counterclockwise. These facts can be seen by rotating a globe (or ball) beneath a weight swinging on a piece of string.

PENGUIN. Among the birds that cannot fly are penguins. They are sea-birds and their narrow wings, which are covered with scaly feathers, are rather like flippers. From a distance penguins resemble solemn little men as they stand bolt upright or waddle along on their large webbed feet, which are set far back under the body.

There are many kinds of penguin. They all live in the southern half of the world. Many live on the mainland and islands of Antarctica. The furthest north they are found is the Galapagos Islands on the equator.

Penguins live in large flocks and breed in groups known as rookeries. Although they look quaint on land, they are wonderfully swift swimmers, both on the surface of the water and under it. They pursue fish, which they catch with their sharp, pointed beaks. On land they sometimes slide down a slope on their stomachs, propelling themselves along with their feet. Penguins have few enemies, though the fierce leopard seal sometimes catches them in the water.

The largest penguin is the magnificent emperor penguin (*Aptenodytes forsteri*), which stands up to 120 centimeters (4 feet) tall. It has the general color scheme of all penguins – black back, head, and flippers and white front – but it is beautifully marked with black on the throat and has a broad, semicircular patch of orange-yellow on each side of the upper neck. Emperor penguins live in the depths of the Antarctic.

King penguins (*Aptenodytes patagonica*) live further north. They are the second largest members of the penguin family, and can be distinguished from the emperors by the different pattern of the orange and black on the neck.

Emperor and king penguins have very interesting breeding habits. Both lay only one egg at a time, and this is balanced on the feet of the parent. A flap of skin hangs down and keeps the cold away from the egg. When one parent gets tired of holding the egg, it rolls it off on to the feet of the other. The young bird stays on its parents' feet and keeps warm there for a time after it hatches.

Other penguins breed on rocky islands and lay two eggs in a hollow in the ground or among rocks. A rough nest is made of bits of grass, or the hollow is lined with small stones.

The rockhopper penguin (*Eudyptes crestatus*) is found from Patagonia in South America to the edge of the Antarctic. The macaroni penguin (*Eudyptes chrysolophus*), which lives in the southern Atlantic and Indian oceans, is a slightly larger bird. It has golden-orange feathers across its forehead and along the side of the crown. The bearded penguin (*Pygoscelis antarctica*) lives in Antarctic seas and in the southern Atlantic. It has a thin black line passing from ear to ear under its chin.

The jackass penguin (*Spheniscus demersus*), found on the coasts of South Africa, has a curious braying call when on land. It makes long tunnels to lay its eggs in. Similar penguins live on the west coast of South America and in the Galapagos Islands. The smallest kind of penguin is the little, or fairy, penguin (*Eudyptula minor*), which lives in the seas around Australia and New Zealand. It stands about 40 centimeters (16 inches) high.

The Adélie penguin (*Pygoscelis adeliae*) is the common small penguin of the Antarctic. It is dark blue-black on its upper parts and head, with a white breast.

PENICILLIN. When Alexander Fleming (see FLEMING, FLOREY, AND CHAIN) discovered penicillin at St. Mary's Hospital, London, in 1928, it brought new hope for many sick people. Doctors and chemists had long been searching for something that would kill germs without harming the patients. Such substances as chloride of lime, iodine, arsenic, and quinine had been found to kill germs, but if given in the wrong way or in too big doses, they could also poison people. Penicillin is not poisonous in normal doses and is effective against many kinds of bacteria (see BACTERIA), although some are resistant to it. However, some people are allergic to penicillin, and in such cases another antibiotic is given.

Penicillin was discovered when a tiny speck of mold fell out of the air into a special plate containing jelly on which Fleming was growing staphylococci bacteria. These are germs which cause blood poisoning and boils. Fleming noticed that around the mold, which was growing on the jelly, the colonies (groups) of germs were being killed.

The mold was an uncommon member of the Penicillium family. Molds related to it are often seen on cheese, stale bread, or damp cellar walls, and are so named because they look like tiny paint brushes, which are called *penicilla* in Latin. By growing the mold in a sugary soup, or broth, and then filtering the broth, Fleming made the liquid that he named penicillin. This stopped the growth of many kinds of bacteria, including those of diphtheria, pneumonia, and sore throats. Penicillin was the first of several drugs which kill germs without harming the body tissues, and those drugs are called antibiotics. (See ANTIBIOTICS.)

Two other scientists, Howard Florey and Ernst Chain, discovered how to mass-produce penicillin as a pure dry powder that could be stored. In 1941, the first patients were treated with the drug. Fleming, Florey, and Chain were awarded a Nobel Prize in 1945 for their work on penicillin.

PENN, William (1644–1718). The state of Pennsylvania in the United States was founded by William Penn. He was the son of a British admiral who had married a Dutch widow. He attended school at Chigwell in Essex and later went to Oxford, where he came under the influence of a Quaker preacher (see FRIENDS, SOCIETY OF). The Quakers wanted religious freedom, which was not a popular view at that time in England, and Penn had to leave the university because of his views. He spent some time studying and traveling in France and Italy, returning in 1664.

In 1667 Penn again got into trouble through attending a Quakers' meeting and was sent to prison. He spent the next few years preaching and writing about religious freedom and tolerance, often from prison, as Quaker meetings were forbidden by law.

His father's death in 1670 left Penn rich. In 1681, in settlement of a debt owed to his father by the king, he was granted a fertile tract of land, about the size of England, in North America. This land was named Pennsylvania ("Penn's woods") in honor of his father. There Penn planned a colony where all could share in the government, and worship as Christians of any kind. The constitution, or set of rules, that he drew up for Pennsylvania had later an influence on the constitution of the United States. The capital of Pennsylvania was chosen at a place which Penn called Philadelphia (meaning "brotherly love") on the Delaware River. Penn went there himself in 1682 and in the following year made a treaty of peace and friendship with the local Indians.

The colony of Pennsylvania prospered, but in 1684 Penn had to return to England to settle a dispute which he had had with the colonists of Maryland. Then King Charles II died, and Penn remained in England hoping to persuade the new king, James II, to grant freedom of worship to the Quakers. This James was willing to do, but the policy of religious freedom was unpopular in England and caused a revolution. King James fled to France and Penn had to go into hiding because of his association with the king. In 1692 the governorship of Pennsylvania was taken away from Penn. It was restored two years later, but when Penn went back to the colony in 1699 he found that nearly everything had gone wrong. Pennsylvania was divided by disputes which saddened the later years of Penn's life. In 1712 he proposed to give up his governorship to the crown but became too ill even to arrange this. He died in 1718 and was buried at Jordans Meeting House, near Chalfont St. Giles, in Buckinghamshire, England.

PEN NAME. An author who for one reason or another does not want to use his (or her) own name when having a book published invents a pen name instead. Mark Twain, for instance, was the pen name of the author who wrote *The Adventures of Huckleberry Finn* and *The Adventures of Tom Sawyer*. His real name was Samuel Langhorne Clemens, but he had called himself Mark Twain when he was a newspaper writer and kept the same name when he began to write books. Another writer well known by his pen name was Lewis Carroll, author of *Alice in Wonderland*, whose real name was Charles Lutwidge Dodgson. The French for pen name is *nom de plume*; another word for the same thing is *pseudonym*, which comes from Greek.

In the 19th century, book publishers and readers did not very much approve of women writers, and so authoresses used to disguise their real names under masculine pen names. The famous novelist known as George Eliot was really Mary Ann Evans. The three sisters Charlotte, Emily, and Anne Brontë first published their books under pen names that kept their own initials: Currer Bell, Ellis Bell, and Acton Bell. Nowadays women when they marry sometimes continue to write books under their maiden names. Occasionally people who write two kinds of book use a pen name for one of them. For instance, the English poet C. Day Lewis wrote detective stories as Nicholas Blake.

PENNSYLVANIA is one of the top five industrial states in the Union. During the 19th century its growth became a focus for the rapid and massive industrialization of the United States, especially in the decades after the American Civil War. The world's first oil well was drilled near Titusville in August 1859, marking the beginning of one of the world's leading industries. Pennsylvania, after decades of mining, still has enough coal under its soil to provide fuel for the United States for several centuries. It was in Pennsylvania that Andrew Carnegie established his steel company, a forerunner of United States Steel. Strategically situated between the northern and southern states of the East Coast, as well as between the East and Midwest, Pennsylvania developed a massive railroad system led by the, now closed, Pennsylvania Railroad. Its ideal location has given Pennsylvania the nickname Keystone State.

By the start of the 20th century the state had become an industrial giant, heavily dependent on coal, steel, and railroads. Its largest city, Philadelphia, was a financial and industrial center, sitting astride a rapidly growing megalopolis that stretched from Boston in the north to Virginia in the south. Pittsburgh, in the western part of the state, was at the eastern end of an industrial belt that extended through Ohio and Indiana to Chicago and Milwaukee. The iron ore to feed the steel mills came from nothern Michigan, and later, from northern Minnesota. The coal to fire the mills was abundant throughout the state.

By the 1980s, Pennsylvania was in serious economic decline. Like its neighbor, Ohio, it had become quite heavily dependent on traditional "smokestack industries". Steel production had begun to slide in the 1920s, when the era of railroad building was over. By the 1980s the future of the steel industry was in doubt. Its facilities, among the oldest in the nation, were outdated and in little position to compete with cheaper imports. Oil had long since ceased to be a major industry, as production shifted to Texas, Oklahoma, Louisiana, California, and other western states. The Pennsylvania Railroad collapsed in 1970, the largest commercial bankruptcy in American history. Coal production dropped dramatically. In 1910 there were nearly 400,000 men working the mines. By the early 1980s there were fewer than 40,000.

The Land

Pennsylvania is a Middle Atlantic state, located near the eastern seaboard. Its eastern boundary is formed by the Delaware River, and across the river are New Jersey and New York. The state is bounded on the north by New York and 82 kilometers (51 miles) of Lake Erie shoreline. On the west is Ohio, and to the south are West Virginia, Maryland, and Delaware. From west to east the state's greatest length is 489 kilometers (304 miles). Its greatest width, north to south, is 280 kilometers (174 miles).

Pennsylvania lies mostly within the Appalachian Highlands. As a result it has an average elevation of 152 meters (500 feet) above sealevel. The highest point is Mount Davis, at 979 meters (3,213 feet). The lowest point is at sealevel, in the southeast along the Delaware River near Philadelphia.

Pennsylvania has seven natural regions. By far the largest is the Allegheny Plateau, which occupies all of the northern and western part of the state, except for the small Lake Plains region along Lake Erie. The plateau is a rough and hilly tableland cut by streams. In the west, at Pittsburgh, two of the largest rivers, the Allegheny and the Monongahela, meet to form the great Ohio River. The Ohio has long been a major transportation artery to the west, where it meets the Mississippi.

The second largest region is the Valley and Ridge. It lies along the southern and eastern edge of the plateau and consists of high, narrow ridges that run roughly parallel in a northeast-southwest direction. Between the ridges are long, narrow valleys. East of the Blue Mountain Ridge is the Great Appalachian Valley, which is cut in two sections by the Susquehanna River.

The Blue Ridge region juts north from Maryland into Pennsylvania. It is the northernmost projection of a range which extends south into Georgia. Just east of the Blue Ridge lies the Piedmont Plateau. It is a series of low hills and ridges about 97 kilometers (60 miles) in width. It is one of the state's more fertile farming areas. To the east of this plateau is a small region, the Coastal Plain. It is a low, fertile region extending northeast and southwest from Philadelphia.

To the north of the Piedmont Plateau is the New England Upland. It lies between the Delaware and Schuylkill rivers. The area is a small projection of the plateau-like highlands of New Jersey, lower New York, and New England.

Climate varies from region to region. The northern part of the Allegheny Plateau is the coolest because of its elevation. The warmest region is the southeast, where summers are hot and humid and the winters mild. The Lake Plains have a mild climate because of the moderating influence of Lake Erie's waters. Rainfall is distributed rather evenly around the state. In winter, deep snows can fall near Lake Erie, and Atlantic storms occasionally bring heavier rainfall in the east. The southeastern section has a growing season of from 170 to 200 days. In the mountainous areas it is only 130 days.

The People

Four major Indian groups lived in Pennsylvania at the time of European discovery. These were the Delaware (or Lenni Lenape), the Susquehanna, the Shawnee, and some segments of the Five Nations of the Iroquois Federation. The Indians fought white settlers fiercely and thus played a powerful role during the colonial era.

Swedes and Dutch settlers were the first whites to arrive in Pennsylvania. They were soon outnumbered by English Quakers, however. The policy of religious toleration initiated by founder William Penn encouraged Europeans who had known religious persecution to immigrate. (See PENN, WILLIAM.) Germans from the Rhineland settled in large numbers in inland counties. By the time of the American Revolution they were known as Pennsylvania Dutch. The "Dutch" is a corruption of "Deutsch," meaning German, and does not refer to people from the Netherlands. Subgroups of Germans form a significant part of the state's population. They are largely religious communities, and include the Amish, Mennonites, Moravians, Schwenkfelders, and Dunkers.

Another major colonial group were the Scotch-Irish, who passed beyond the English and Germans into western Pennsylvania. There were also small numbers of French Protestants (Huguenots), Welsh, Cornish, and Irish.

Because of early opposition to slavery there grew up a sizable black population within the colony, and more blacks continue to settle there from the South. Today they comprise about 8.8 per cent of the population. When industrialization began to transform the state, large numbers of eastern European immigrants began arriving to work in the factories and mines, and on the railroads.

The Economy

Although mainly an industrial state, Pennsylvania has about 59,000 farms. The primary farming counties are Lancaster, Chester, Berks, York, and Franklin. Livestock, poultry, and their products account for about three-quarters of farm income. Hay is the leading crop, followed by corn, wheat, oats, apples, potatoes, cigar-leaf tobacco, buckwheat, mushrooms, grapes, and peaches.

Barnaby's

An attractive old flour mill on Conestoga Creek, near Lancaster.

Coal is the chief mineral. Pennsylvania ranks fourth among the states in coal production. Most of the nation's hard coal (anthracite) is mined in Pennsylvania, and there are large deposits of soft, or bituminous, coal as well. Cement is the second most profitable mineral. Most of it comes from Northampton and Lehigh counties. Cement is followed in value by stone, especially limestone and basalt. There are still sizable reserves of petroleum, and the oil fields also yield natural gas. Oil is also piped in from western states and brought in by tanker from Venezuela to be processed in refineries along

A coal-mining town in the Appalachian Mountains of Pennsylvania. This state is the fourth largest producer of coal in the United States.

Courtesy, Standard Oil Company (New Jersey)

the Delaware River. Sand and gravel are found in many parts of the state.

Pennsylvania's first ironworks was built in Berks County in 1716 and the eastern part of the state was long the leader in iron production. Once ore was discovered in the Great Lakes states, however, the industrial shift to Pittsburgh occurred. In total steel production, Pittsburgh is second only to the steel complex along the southern shores of Lake Michigan from Chicago to Gary.

In addition to steel, Pennsylvania produces high-temperature furnaces for firing clay, truck trailers, paints, glass, metal products, textiles, electrical and non-electrical machinery, food products, and chemicals. There is a Volkswagen automobile plant at New Stanton. Pennsylvania leads the nation in the production of ice cream and frozen dairy products.

Pennsylvania has been a leader in the development of the retail trade. The nation's first department store was opened by John Wanamaker in Philadelphia in the 1870s. Frank Woolworth began the successful chain of what used to be "five-and-ten-cents" stores at Lancaster about the same time. Other state retailers were S. S. Kresge, founder of what is now the K-mart chain, the second largest retailer in the United States.

Another source of income is tourism. Pennsylvania accounts for about 5 per cent of the American tourist industry. There are six national park areas. Gettysburg National Military Park sets aside the battleground of

the major conflict of the Civil War. Other military sites have been preserved from the French and Indian War, the American Revolution, and the War of 1812. Philadelphia has Independence Hall with its Liberty Bell; Elfreth's Alley, the oldest continuously inhabited street in the United States; and Carpenters' Hall, site of the meeting of the First Continental Congress. Harrisburg, a good deal smaller than Pittsburgh or Philadelphia, is the state capital. There are more than 100 state parks and forest sites. The Pocono Mountains are a popular resort area.

Barnaby's

Fort Pitt Bridge and the Golden Triangle of downtown Pittsburgh at night.

Education

William Penn's Frame of Government in 1682 provided for the education of all children. The Friends' (Quakers) Public Grammar School was opened in Philadelphia in 1689. Other religious groups founded their own schools as well. The Free School Law 1834 established a system of free public education by creating school districts and permitting collection of taxes to support them. The first compulsory school attendance law was passed in 1895, and high schools were authorized in every school district.

There are more than 120 colleges and universities in Pennsylvania. The private University of Pennsylvania, in Philadelphia, was founded as a charity school in 1740, but was transformed by Benjamin Franklin into an academy. In 1765, it opened the first medical school in North America.

Pennsylvania State University, in University Park, is a state-supported land-grant institution, as are Temple University, in Philadelphia, and the University of Pittsburgh.

History

Henry Hudson claimed Pennsylvania and nearby regions for Holland in 1609 (see HUDSON, HENRY). Swedes, however, were the first settlers founding a colony on the Delaware in 1638. In 1655 Swedish rule ended when the Dutch of New Netherland (New York) took over the territory. Nine years later the English annexed the territory to New York.

The Quaker leader William Penn decided to establish a colony that would be a haven for people of all religious beliefs. King Charles II of England granted Penn an area of land between New York and Maryland in 1681, west of the Delaware River. The first band of Quakers arrived in July 1681. Penn himself followed the next year and published his Frame of Government, one of the most liberal constitutions of the colonial era. The religious freedom of the colony attracted people from Europe and other colonies. Philadelphia soon became the largest city in America.

Western Pennsylvania played a major role in the struggles between France and England for control of the Ohio Valley. In 1754 the Ohio Company built a fort at the site of present Pittsburgh. The French took it and renamed it Fort Duquesne. In a counter-attack led by George Washington the fort was retaken and named Fort Pitt.

During the revolutionary period Philadelphia was the new nation's capital. The Continental Congresses met there; the Declaration of Independence was signed there; and the Articles of Confederation were formulated there and at York. Pennsylvania witnessed much action during the war. Philadelphia was captured by the British. Washington spent the winter of 1777–78 at Valley Forge, by the Schuylkill River, with his army. (See also AMERICAN REVOLUTION.)

In 1787 the Constitution was drafted at Philadelphia. The city served as national capital from 1790 until 1800, when the federal government moved to Washington, DC.

FACTS ABOUT PENNSYLVANIA

AREA: 119,251 square kilometers (46,043 square miles).
POPULATION: 11,924,000 (1990).
CAPITAL: Harrisburg, 52,376.
CITIES: Philadelphia, 1,585,577; Pittsburgh, 369,879; Erie, 108,718; Allentown, 105,090; Scranton, 81,805; Reading, 78,380; Bethlehem, 71,428.
HIGHEST POINT: Mount Davis, 979 meters, 3213 feet.
PRODUCTS:
  Agriculture: Dairy products, hay, cattle, poultry, eggs, pigs, corn, mushrooms, apples, potatoes, oats, wheat.
  Minerals: Coal, petroleum, stone, sand, gravel, zinc, clay.
  Manufacturing: Food and drink products, chemicals, machinery, electrical and electronic equipment, primary and metal products, printing and publishing, transportation equipment, paper products, etc.
STATE EMBLEMS: Flower: mountain laurel. Tree: hemlock. Bird: ruffled grouse.
JOINED THE UNION: Pennsylvania was one of the thirteen original states in the Union and was the 2nd state to ratify the Constitution, in 1787.

During the American Civil War the pivotal Battle of Gettysburg took place early in July 1863. After Confederate forces were turned back a cemetery was established, and President Lincoln delivered his Gettysburg Address in November at its dedication (see GETTYSBURG, BATTLE OF).

Pittsburgh got its start as a steel center in 1853, when Andrew Carnegie opened his first factory. (See CARNEGIE, ANDREW.) Twenty years later he sold his firm to United States Steel. The industrialization of the state proceeded rapidly. In both World Wars

Pennsylvania's industries were suppliers of iron, steel, arms, and machinery. In March 1979 the first serious nuclear accident in the United States occurred at Three Mile Island, near Middletown on the Susquehanna River.

PENSION. The usual kind of pension is one paid to provide a person with a regular income after he or she has stopped working. For example, in Britain old age pensions are paid to people who no longer work because they have retired. Similarly, social security payments are made in the United States. The age of retirement varies from country to country. In 1986 it was 65 for both men and women in the United States and Canada; 67 in Denmark, 60 in New Zealand and France, and 55 in Japan. In other countries the age of retirement for women is lower than that for men. In Britain, Australia, Belgium, and Greece the retirement age for women in 1986 was 60 and for men 65, whereas in Italy it was 55 for women and 60 for men.

There are other kinds of pension, too. People who are injured or who catch some disease may, if they are disabled, be paid a disability pension either by the state or through a program organized by their employers. If they die as a result of their injuries or illness, then pensions my be paid to their widows, widowers, or dependent children. These are known as survivor pensions.

Before the general introduction of pensions, few of the elderly, disabled, widows, or orphans had much of a life to look forward to. Most people did not earn enough money to save for their old age. Either they had to carry on working until they were too old or ill to continue, or else they became dependent on their relatives who were also poor and struggling to feed their own families. People who were not supported by their own families were forced to rely on charity.

The earliest known pension plans date back to those organized by the European medieval guilds, which were collections of tradesmen who relied on their skills to earn their living (see also GUILD). Old age or injury put an end to these skills, and so they all contributed to a fund that could be used to pay a pension to any member who could no longer continue working. Military pensions have also existed for many centuries. The pensions first paid by the United States government were to disabled veterans of the American Revolution.

In England during the 17th century pensions were seen as a way of rewarding good employees for the work that they had done. They were also a way of getting an old person to leave the job and make way for someone younger. The pension was paid by the younger person who took over the job. Martin Horsham is the first recorded pensioner of this type. He retired on 10 March 1684. Mr. G. Scroope, his successor, had to pay him half his salary every year by way of a pension. Even a person on a low annual income was supposed to pay the former employee a pension; but most found the amount too much, as they only had enough money for their own needs.

In the early 18th century a temporary solution was found. The whole workforce above a certain grade had to contribute to the pensions paid to former employees. This forms the basis of many of today's pension plans where those who are working pay part of their income into a fund which is used to pay the pensions of people who have retired or become disabled. Employers also usually make contributions to such plans.

Organized Pension Plans

During the 19th century several large employers throughout Europe and North America organized pension plans for their workers. Many companies were reluctant to take on the risk of working out pension plans themselves. In the United States, companies, called life insurance companies, offered to provide this service for them. They calculated how much the employer had to pay, operated the plan, and paid the pensions. These were introduced into Great Britain in the 1920s. During the 1930s the Legal and

General Assurance Society became one of the first British companies to specialize in pensions.

Much earlier, during the 19th century, the British government had provided their own employees with a pension plan. Early plans organized by the government were "non-contributory": the workers were not required to make any contribution to the plan from their wages. Because of this many people preferred to work for the government rather than for private companies. A general plan for civil servants began in 1834 and was extended to servicemen in the armed forces in 1874, and to teachers in 1898.

One in four old people in Britain were paupers in 1906 because pensions were only paid to a small number of workers. To overcome this problem the government, and the governments of other countries, introduced plans that guaranteed pensions to all old people. Germany, the first to act, passed its Old Age Pensions Act in 1889. Britain followed in 1908, France in 1910, Sweden in 1913, and Canada in 1918. The Social Security Act in the United States dates from 1935 and the Pensions Act in Japan from 1941. Most countries in the world now have some form of state pension plan.

Many governments today are concerned that they may not be able to raise enough money to continue paying people their pensions. This is because people are retiring earlier and living longer, which means that pension funds need much more money than ever before or than was ever anticipated.

PEONY. Peonies (*Paeonia*) belong to the buttercup family and are among the oldest of garden flowers. They have been cultivated in China for more than 2,000 years. In early times their roots were used for food and in medicines, but they were prized, then as now, for their beautiful flowers. Wild ancestors of garden peonies grew in China, parts of Europe, and Asia Minor. From them have come thousands of varieties.

J. Horace McFarland Co.

Peony plants produce large, beautiful flowers. They grow best in good rich soil in a sunny position.

Most peony flowers are white or shades of pink or red. A few are yellow. The blossoms may measure 20 centimeters (8 inches) across. Several types are known, ranging from single flowers with few petals to ball-shaped double blossoms. In northern United States they bloom in May and June. They make excellent cut flowers, and the bushy plants are attractive all summer.

Peonies are very hardy, and live without winter protection in areas with moderate frosts. The tree peonies, which have woody stems, are less hardy. The plants die down in autumn. Gardeners usually cut the stems close to the ground.

New plants are started by dividing large clumps or are grown from seed. Plants usually are set out or moved in the autumn. They grow best in rich, well-drained soil with plenty of sunlight. Once well started, plants will keep growing for many years. For this reason peonies have been called the "lifetime flowers".

PEPPER is a spice obtained from several kinds of plants. Ordinary black pepper comes from a trailing vine (*Piper nigrum*) which originally grew in India, Thailand (Siam), Indonesia, and the Philippine Islands and has been taken to the West Indies. The center of the pepper trade is Singapore. The berries are picked when they turn red, before they are ripe and black. After drying, they turn black and are

ARDEA

Leaf and fruit of the black pepper plant. The berry-like fruits are dried and become "peppercorns".

ground into pepper grains. White pepper, which is less strong, comes from the same plant. It is made from ripe berries with their outer coats removed. The plant may reach 10 meters (33 feet) in height and has shiny, broad, green leaves arranged alternately. The berries hang on slender spikes in clusters of about 50 at a time.

Cayenne pepper, paprika, and tabasco pepper resemble black pepper only in their taste. They are prepared from a kind of capsicum, the pod-like scarlet peppers, or chilies, of the West Indies and South America (see CHILIES AND PEPPERS).

In the days before food was frozen or canned to preserve it, much meat and fish had to be dried or salted, and this spoiled its taste. Pepper helps to give flavor, and so it was much more valued than it is today. Trading caravans (companies of merchants) brought it overland with other spices from India to Europe, but the price was so high because of the long journey that few people could afford it. In 1488 the Cape of Good Hope, round which ships could sail to India, was discovered. After that the price of pepper fell.

PEPYS, Samuel (1633–1703). The most delightful diary in the English language was written by Samuel Pepys. Until 1819 it lay unread in the library of Magdalene College, Cambridge, England, written in cipher in six faded notebooks. It was turned into ordinary writing by John Smith, an undergraduate, and published in 1825.

The diary gives a very detailed and interesting description of everyday life in England between 1660 and 1669. There are eye-witness accounts of the Plague, of the Dutch fleet sailing up the Thames and frightening everybody, and of the Great Fire. How vividly Pepys described the Fire:

Everybody endeavouring to remove their goods, and flinging into the river or bringing them into lighters that lay off; poor people staying in their houses as long as till the very fire touched them, and then running into boats, or clambering from one pair of stairs by the water-side to another. And among other things the poor pigeons . . . were loathe to leave their houses, but hovered about the windows and balconies till they . . . burned their wings and fell down.

Pepys also wrote about himself, even about his weaknesses and faults. He often slept during sermons. Church services bored him and instead of listening to them he looked for pretty girls in the congregation. He described his home life—a quarrel with his wife and how they made it up, his concern at her illness ("my poor wife in bed in mighty pain, her left cheek so swelled that we feared it might break"), and how he read to her when she got better. As well as books, he liked music, plays, and card games, and parties with good food and plenty of merry-making.

Mary Evans Picture Library   *National Portrait Gallery*

Samuel Pepys saved the Navy Office during the Great Fire of London and wrote up the events in his diary.

Besides all this, Pepys was a very busy man and held various important positions. He was a member of parliament, and at one time president of the Royal Society. Most important of all, however, was the work Pepys did to reorganize the British navy, building it up and making it thoroughly efficient once more. He was Clerk of the Acts in the Navy Office and later Secretary to the Admiralty.

PERCENTAGE. Percentages are another way of writing fractions. The words *per cent* mean "out of a hundred", and the per cent sign % is made from the digits of 100.

20 per cent (written 20%) means "20 out of 100," or $^{20}/_{100}$, which is equivalent to $^1/_5$. So when a store advertises "20% off everything", it means that a fifth is being taken off each price. This is a particularly easy system to use with money, because 20% is equivalent to 20¢ in every dollar, or 20p in every pound. So if an article originally cost $24, a 20% *discount* would mean 20¢ off each of the 24 dollars, 24 × 20¢—that is, 480¢ or $4.80.

Percentages are often used to express changes in values, such as falls in prices. They are also used to describe the rise in the cost of living. If this rises at the rate of 10% a year, it means (usually for any given month) that if that rise in prices continued every month for a whole year, at the end of the year you would be paying 10% more for the same goods. In practice, the way this is worked out is quite complicated because some prices rise more than others and not everyone buys the same

items each month. Increases in wages are also described by percentages.

Percentages are widely used in business, particularly when people are borrowing money. If someone borrows money from a bank, interest is charged on the loan (see INTEREST). If the loan is of $8,000 and the interest charged is $12^1/_2\%$ *per annum* (that is, per year), the interest the borrower has to pay will amount to $^1/_8$ of the loan, or $1,000.

At school, percentages are often used for examination scores. If all subjects are marked out of 100, the idea is that the scores are easier to compare. In fact, of course, you could get 60% in mathematics and have the highest score, and get 60% in history and have the lowest! If the examination is marked out of 50, the teacher can double the mark to make it out of 100. So if you got 45 out of 50, this would be equivalent to 90 out of 100 or 90%.

On the other hand, if you read that 40% of men are color-blind, although this sounds like "40 out of 100", it does not mean "40 out of *every* 100". It is perfectly easy to find 100 men, none of whom is color-blind. What it means is that *on average*, 40 out of every 100 men are color-blind, or (better still) that $^{40}/_{100}$ or $^2/_5$ of men are color-blind.

Another popular wrong idea is that you cannot have more than 100% of anything. True, you cannot get more than 100% of the answers correct in a test, and you could not have more than 100% of men color-blind, and if a storekeeper gave more than 100% discount, *he* would be paying *you*! However, inflation (see INFLATION) could run at over 100%, and a wage increase of 200% would mean that you would receive three times as much as you are earning at the moment.

Another thing to watch for is how the percentage is worked out. For instance, a storekeeper may sell you something for $1 and say that 20% of that is profit. That means it cost him 80¢ and he makes 20¢ on the sale. But the 20¢ is in fact 25%, or ¼ of what it cost him (80 × ¼ = 20).

Most calculators have a % key which can be used to calculate percentage increases or decreases. The most frequent use for this is probably for adding sales tax or value-added tax (VAT) onto prices of goods or services. Let's suppose that this additional tax is 15%. If a book costs $8.80 without tax and the bookseller wants to know the price with tax, he must add $8.80 and 15% of $8.80. By pressing the following calculator keys

$$8.80 + 15\%$$

he can easily arrive at the full price, $10.12.

To calculate the VAT only we need 15% of $8.80, and on a calculator we press

$$8.80 \times 15\%$$

which gives $1.32.

Sometimes customers who know the full price, $10.12, want to know how much of it was tax. You cannot use the % key for this. If you try to subtract 15% then you get $8.60, which is not correct. This is because the VAT is 15% of the original $8.80, not of $10.12. In fact then, the $10.12 is 115% of the $8.80. If we divide 10.12 by 115 we find 1%, and we can then multiply by 100 to find 100%. On the calculator

$$10.12 \div 115 \times 100$$

gives $8.80.

PERCH is any of several freshwater fishes that make up the family Percidae. The family is divided into three subfamilies: those species commonly referred to as perch; the walleyes (also called walleyed pike or pike perch); and the darters. All the members are carnivorous, spiny-rayed fish with two dorsal fins.

The yellow perch (*Perca flavescèns*) is found in the lakes, ponds, and streams of North America. It is a popular game fish and forms

North American perches. **Above:** The yellow perch likes lakes and streams with plenty of water plants. **Below:** The walleye lives in clear, deep lakes and large rivers.

the basis of an important fishing industry in the Great Lakes region of the United States. It is a small fish, usually 10 to 30 centimeters (4 to 12 inches) long and weighing less than 0.5 kilogram (1 pound). It is a brassy, yellow color with several blackish bars on the side of the body.

The European perch (*Perca fluviatilis*) is found in northern Eurasia. It is similar to the yellow perch but slightly larger. It is greenish in color with dark bars. Both these perch species have sharp spines on each anal fin and the first dorsal fin.

Perch begin to spawn when three years old. They lay their eggs in the spring. A female may produce from 10,000 to 40,000 eggs. She strings them together in long bands of gelatine-like material and deposits them on water plants. A single female has been known to produce a string of eggs more than 200 centimeters (80 inches) long.

Walleyes are the largest members of the family. They reach a maximum length of 0.9 meters (3 feet) and may weigh as much as 11 kilograms (25 pounds). Their identifying features are their coloring, which is olive to blue, mottled with brown or black, and their many small canine teeth. Walleyes are excellent food fish and are a popular catch among sportsmen.

Darters are small, quick fish. They are usually less than 10 centimeters (4 inches) in length. Their coloring varies greatly. Some darters are among the most brilliantly colored freshwater fish.

PERCUSSION INSTRUMENTS. Musical instruments in which the sound is produced by striking, shaking, or rubbing belong to the percussion family. There are two separate groups; those instruments which themselves vibrate to produce sound (see SOUND), such as bells, gongs, and rattles; and those instruments which produce sound through the vibration of a stretched skin or membrane, such as drums. Percussion instruments are found in various forms all over the world. Among the simplest are gourds filled with pebbles, castanets, cymbals, and tubular chimes (often made of bamboo). Drums form perhaps the most widespread class of percussion instruments; see the separate article DRUM.

Percussion instruments form the third section of an orchestra, after the string and wind sections. Some produce distinct musical notes, while others have no definite pitch but add to the rhythm and feeling of the music.

The instruments making distinct musical notes are played either from a keyboard or with sticks. The keyboard percussion instruments include the piano and the celesta, which looks like a little piano. It has only four octaves and its bell-like notes are obtained from steel plates, which are struck by hammers mechanically linked to the keys.

Those without keyboards are the tubular bells, which are hung in a wooden frame and played with a stick; the glockenspiel, giving bell-like notes when its steel plates are hit with small hammers; the xylophone, whose hardwood bars of different lengths sound different notes when struck with sticks called beaters; the marimba, a large instrument of the same type popular in Mexico and South America; and the vibraphone, another xylophone-like instrument with metal bars instead of wooden ones, whose sounds can be made to "waver" by means of electrically operated equipment. (See XYLOPHONE.) The most important of these percussion instruments in

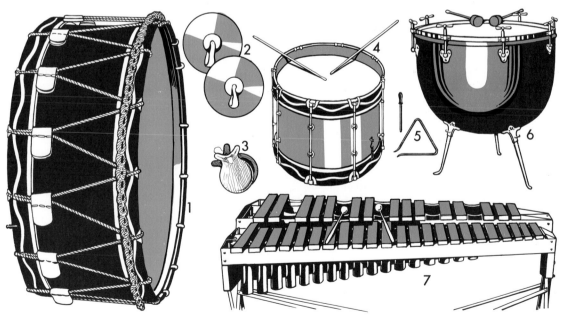

Some instruments of the percussion family: **1** bass drum; **2** cymbals; **3** castanets; **4** snare drum; **5** triangle; **6** kettledrum; **7** xylophone. (Kettledrums are also often referred to as timpani.)

orchestral music are the kettle drums, or timpani (see DRUM).

Percussion instruments that give rhythm without a distinct note include the bass drum and the snare drum. Both these are used in military bands and in orchestras. The tenor drum, which is between them in size, is seldom used in orchestras. The tambourine, cymbals, castanets, and triangle are others in this group, along with the gong, or tam-tam, the rattle, and the anvil, an instrument used by Richard Wagner in his music drama *The Rhinegold*.

Among the above-named instruments, the tambourine, castanets, and triangle have become popular in school orchestras. The tambourine, a very ancient instrument, is made of parchment stretched over a wooden hoop with little bells or metal plates set into the hoop. It is played by striking the parchment with the knuckles or rubbing it with the thumb, as well as by shaking the whole instrument. The castanets, popular in Spanish music, consist of two small, hollow pieces of wood attached to the finger and thumb of each hand and are played by being "clacked" together. The triangle is a steel rod bent into a three-cornered shape with one corner left open to allow it to vibrate freely. It hangs from a loop of gut or nylon by which the player holds it and strikes it with a metal stick to make a high, jangly sound. Other percussion instruments found in school bands include the claves and several items used in West Indian steel bands and jazz groups. (See JAZZ; POPULAR MUSIC.)

See also BELL; CYMBAL; PIANO; XYLOPHONE.

PERFUME.

PERFUME. The word "perfume" comes from the Latin words *per*, meaning "through" and *fumus*, meaning "smoke". This suggests that one early way of creating a sweet smell was by burning fragrant woods, gums, and leaves. Perfumes have certainly been used for thousands of years. Vases containing scented ointments were found in the tomb of King Tutankhamun of Egypt, who died in about 1350 BC, and in the Bible there are directions for making perfume from spices and gum (Book of Exodus, chapter 30).

Fritzsche Brothers, Inc.

Top: In Malaysia sun filters through slender bamboo trees to shrubs below which yield oil of patchouli.
Above: In Sri Lanka bark from cinnamon sticks will be crushed and distilled to produce fragrant oil.

Early perfumes were made chiefly from scented resins, balsams, leaves, spices, and the woods of some kinds of trees. The oils which contain the scents of these vegetable substances are usually called essential oils, but are sometimes called volatile oils because they are easily evaporated, or changed into vapor. They occur in flowers (jasmine, orange-flower, rose); in leaves (geranium, patchouli, cypress); in barks (cinnamon, cassia); in woods (sandal, cedar); in roots (angelica, ginger, orris); in fruits (lemon, lime, orange); and in seeds (bitter almond, caraway, nutmeg). (See also OIL.)

Manufacture of Perfume

There are several methods by which the essential oils are extracted from vegetable substances. The first, *distillation*, was known to the Arabs, who were the first to prepare rose water by distilling the petals of roses with water. (See DISTILLATION.) Arab perfumes were introduced to Europe by the Crusaders, who brought them home as presents. Otto or attar of rose is a perfume made in Bulgaria, Turkey, and Morocco by distilling rose petals. One hectare (2.5 acres) of roses yields about 2 tonnes (2.2 US tons) of petals, from which only about 1 kilogram (2.2 pounds) of otto is distilled.

Another method of extracting essential oils is by *expression*, or squeezing. The peel of the lemon, orange, and bergamot (a greenish-yellow citrus fruit widely used in perfumes and toilet waters) is rasped and pressed, formerly by hand but nowadays by machine. In this way 450 kilograms (1,000 pounds) of fruit may give up to 2 kilograms (4.4 pounds) of oil, as well as juice and pulp.

The method of *enfleurage*, used chiefly for jasmine and tuberose (a type of lily), depends on the absorption of perfume by fats. Sheets of glass set in wooden frames coated with a mixture of pure beef tallow and purified lard are covered with flower petals and piled one above the other. In some hours the fat absorbs all the perfume and fresh petals are applied until the "pomade", as the fat is

G. Mestrallet/Rapho Guillumette

In Provence, southern France, oil is distilled from lavender by boiling plants and distilling the vapor.

Squibb's Studios

The monks of Caldey Island off the coast of Dyfed, Wales, make perfume from flowers such as gorse.

called, is fully charged with perfume. In *maceration*, a process used with most other flowers, the petals are put in fat or oil heated to about 65°C (150°F). A more modern way of extracting vegetable perfumes is by using a *volatile solvent*, such as petroleum ether and benzene. The plants or flowers are put in sealed containers and the solvent is allowed to run through them slowly, dissolving their essential oils. The solvent is then distilled for use again, leaving behind the essential oils which are purified with alcohol.

When the essential oils have been obtained, the final product is prepared. The perfumer chooses a basic scent and builds on it by mixing, blending, and adding essential oils and fixatives. Fixatives fix, or hold, the perfume together, making the fragrance lasting. They are obtained from animals, mosses, and resins. The most important of them used to be musk, which is obtained from a gland in the body of the male musk deer found in central Asia. Most of the musks used nowadays, for their delicate and long-lasting sweetness, are made artificially. Other fixatives of animal origin are civet, obtained from the Abyssinian civet cat; castoreum, from the Canadian and Russian beaver; and ambergris, a rare waxy substance that comes from the inside of the sperm whale.

To complete a perfume, the natural oils and

Sampling perfume at Grasse, France, the center of the perfume industry. Customers can choose a blend of fragrances from those on the counter.

Robert Harding Picture Library

fixatives must be diluted in alcohol. The mixture is then allowed to age. A properly aged perfume has a more mellow and subtle fragrance than one that has not aged.

Uses of Perfume

Perfumes became popular in Europe in the 16th century, although only rich people could afford them. The main reason why people used perfume was to hide their smell, for in those days baths were rare. Queen Elizabeth I was thought to be exceptionally clean because she had a bath every three months. Gradually people became cleaner in their habits and the use of such violently strong perfumes as valerian and undiluted civet went out of fashion.

During the 20th century progress in chemistry has led to the introduction of many perfumery chemicals that occur naturally in essential oils and many that do not. It is possible, in fact, to produce almost exact copies of flower oils with chemicals which come from such materials as coal tar and petroleum.

Perfume comes in many different forms. A fine perfume may contain as many as three hundred elements—a blend of natural essential oils, synthetics, and fixatives. The amount of alcohol added determines the strength of the fragrance. Next in strength is toilet water, which is lighter and more subtle. Cologne is the lightest form of all and

is usually a diluted form of perfume. It is also possible to buy perfume in solid form, sometimes known as sachet.

Perfume is also used to scent powder, creams, bath and shower preparations, soap, and lotions. Candles can also be scented, and some people like to burn sticks of incense in their homes, which was the original form of perfume.

PERICLES (*c.*495–429 BC). In the city of Athens during the 5th century BC lived one of the greatest of ancient Greek statesmen: Pericles. He began his career in Athens at an exciting time. In those days Greece was divided into separate parts known as city states, of which Athens and Sparta were two of the most important. These states had recently banded together against their common enemy Persia, and had driven the Persians from Greece. This victory filled the hearts of the Athenians not only with thanksgiving but with tremendous pride. These were the people who, in about 460 BC, elected Pericles as their leader.

His chief aim was to build up the power of Athens on both land and sea. Sometimes he did it by conquest, but when this was not altogether successful he saw that Athens could best establish its empire by peaceful means. Athens, said Pericles, must be the center of the civilized world.

The main achievement the Athenians

prided themselves on was their way of government, a democracy (or "government by the people") in which every free Athenian citizen had a share in making state decisions and an equal chance of holding public office. Pericles strengthened the democracy by arranging for citizens to be paid for their public services, which meant that every free citizen, rich or poor, could take part in the city's affairs. Pericles wanted every Athenian to care about his city and to understand its laws and business; and also to be able to enjoy the finest drama and music that the great writers and artists of the time could provide.

Michael Holford

A bust of Pericles, the elected leader of ancient Athens for 30 years.

Some of the greatest works of Greek art and literature were created in Pericles' time. One of the finest of Greek playwrights, Sophocles, was his friend, and among other writers who knew and admired him was the famous writer of history, Thucydides. Pericles encouraged sculptors and architects to make Athens beautiful by their works, and it was largely due to him that the group of buildings on the hill known as the Acropolis was erected (see ACROPOLIS), the chief of which was the Parthenon, the temple to the goddess Athena.

The last years of Pericles' life were troubled by wars between Athens and other states which were jealous of its growing power and influence, and the high hopes for the city's peace and prosperity began to disappear. In 431 BC the Peloponnesian War began (see PELOPONNESIAN WAR). The Athenians were at first confident that their strongly walled city could withstand siege and that their naval raids on enemy coasts would eventually bring them victory. But in 430 a plague in Athens itself killed thousands of citizens, including two of Pericles' sons, and one year later he himself died, after 30 years of leadership.

PERIODIC TABLE. The periodic table is a list of all the known chemical elements arranged in order of increasing *atomic number* (now sometimes called proton number—see PROTON). The list is organized so that elements with similar properties fall together.

In 1869, the Russian chemist Dmitri Mendeleyev made a list of all the chemical elements that were known at that time, in order of increasing atomic mass. He already knew from the research of the British chemist John Newlands that there was a repetition of similar chemical and physical properties at more or less regular intervals throughout his list and he drew up a table so that elements of similar properties lay above and below one another. There were many gaps in the table, and Mendeleyev correctly foretold that elements would be found to fill them. A German called Lothar Meyer made the same discovery as Mendeleyev at about the same time.

Mendeleyev's original table had 17 columns but was later revised to only 8. It has since been altered many times as new elements have been discovered. A satisfactory way of arranging the periodic table is shown in the diagram. Each square shows the chemical symbol of the element. In the case of beryllium (at the top left of the table) this is Be. You car

The Periodic Table

Groups	I	IIa												IIb	III	IV	V	VI	VII	0
Periods																					
1	1 H																				2 He
2	3 Li	4 Be													5 B	6 C	7 N	8 O	9 F	10 Ne
3	11 Na	12 Mg	←			TRANSITION ELEMENTS			→						13 Al	14 Si	15 P	16 S	17 Cl	18 Ar
4	19 K	20 Ca	21 Sc	22 Ti	23 V	24 Cr	25 Mn	26 Fe	27 Co	28 Ni	29 Cu	30 Zn	31 Ga	32 Ge	33 As	34 Se	35 Br	36 Kr
5	37 Rb	38 Sr	39 Y	40 Zr	41 Nb	42 Mo	43 Tc	44 Ru	45 Rh	46 Pd	47 Ag	48 Cd	49 In	50 Sn	51 Sb	52 Te	53 I	54 Xe
6	55 Cs	56 Ba	57 La	72 Hf	73 Ta	74 W	75 Re	76 Os	77 Ir	78 Pt	79 Au	80 Hg	81 Tl	82 Pb	83 Bi	84 Po	85 At	86 Rn
7	87 Fr	88 Ra	89 Ac	104 Unq	105 Unp	106 Unh	107 Uns		109 Une									

Lanthanides	58 Ce	59 Pr	60 Nd	61 Pm	62 Sm	63 Eu	64 Gd	65 Tb	66 Dy	67 Ho	68 Er	69 Tm	70 Yb	71 Lu
Actinides	90 Th	91 Pa	92 U	93 Np	94 Pu	95 Am	96 Cm	97 Bk	98 Cf	99 Es	100 Fm	101 Md	102 No	103 Lr

find out the chemical symbols for most elements by looking up the table with the article CHEMICAL ELEMENT. As well as showing the element's symbol, each square in the periodic table also shows its atomic number. For beryllium this is 4, indicating that beryllium has four protons in its nucleus. There are 18 vertical columns, known as *groups*. The elements contained in each group possess similar properties because they have similar arrangements of electrons in their outer electron shells (see ELECTRON). These similarities are repeated at regular intervals (periodically) in the horizontal rows, which make up the seven *periods*.

Electrons are added to shells of atoms in going across a period from left to right. Usually electrons are added only to the outer shell, but in th᷾ center block of the table so-called *transition* ᷾nts are built up by adding electrons to ᷾ inner shells. Two inner transition series ᷾ts are seen at the foot of the table. The ᷾c *lanthanide* or *rare-earth* elements are chemically very similar. They exist only in chemical combinations with other elements, and are difficult to separate from the compounds in which they occur. Some are very scarce, but one called cerium is more plentiful than either gold, silver, or tin. The *actinide* series of elements are radioactive elements. Only four are found in nature, of which one is uranium. The rest, including plutonium, are laboratory made by bombardment of other nuclei with high-energy particles (see NEUTRON; PARTICLE ACCELERATOR). Uranium and plutonium are used in the generation of atomic energy (see NUCLEAR ENERGY). Elements with atomic numbers greater than 92 are called *transuranic elements*. The newest transuranic elements are named according to their atomic number; thus element 106 is unnilhexium (from *un*, meaning "one", *nil*, "zero", and *hexium*, "six"). It has the symbol Unh. Unniloctium (Uno), or element 108, has yet to be discovered. Element 109, Unnilennium (Une), was discovered by West German scientists in 1982.

There are at present only 109 known elements, whereas compound substances are extremely numerous. It is therefore very useful for scientists to have a table which shows the relationship between the elements. For example, the inert gases are all difficult to condense. The alkali metals in group 1A are soft, metallic solids with low melting points; and so on.

See also ATOM; CHEMISTRY; ELEMENT.

PERISCOPE. To see objects where there is no direct line of sight from them to the eye, an instrument called a periscope is used. The simplest kind of periscope consists of a tube or frame carrying two mirrors. The mirrors are arranged at each end of the tube so that their silvered surfaces are opposite one another and so that when the periscope is in use the mirrors are at an angle of 45° to the

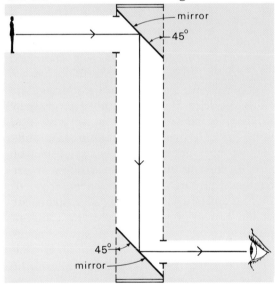

A periscope's angled mirrors change the direction of light rays from an object being observed. This diagram shows how the angled mirrors of a periscope reflect light from a figure being observed (top left) to the eye of the observer (bottom right).

horizontal. Light travels in straight lines, but is reflected by certain substances (such as a mirror). In the periscope, light reaching the top mirror is reflected on to the bottom mirror, and from there into the eye of the observer. So the eye sees whatever is in line with the top mirror. (See LIGHT; REFLECTION

AND REFRACTION for more about light.)

Simple periscopes were used by the soldiers in World War I (1914–18), when much of the fighting was done from trenches. A soldier with a periscope could see what was going on outside the trench without exposing his head to the enemy's bullets. A simple periscope is also useful for seeing over the heads of other people in a crowd. More complicated periscopes, containing a system of lenses and prisms and sometimes 12 meters (39 feet) tall, are used in submarines to see what is happening on the surface while the submarine itself remains under water. In industry periscopes are used when direct viewing would be difficult or dangerous, for example, inside furnaces, wind tunnels, or nuclear reactors. In medicine special periscopes called cystoscopes and endoscopes enable a doctor to examine organs inside a patient's body.

PERIWINKLE is any of various trailing or erect plants of the dogbane family. There are three common species. One (*Vinca minor*) is known by several names: lesser, creeping, running, or grave myrtle. It has small, glossy, oval leaves that remain on the plant all winter. Lesser periwinkle creeps on the

John H. Gerrard

The periwinkle has violet-blue flowers and is grown in gardens as a ground-cover plant. In North America it is also called running myrtle.

soil's surface, forming mats. In early spring, blue flowers appear. It is frequently used, therefore, in cemeteries as a grave covering. In fact it gets its name from the Russian *pervinka*, derived from *pervi* meaning first, as it is one of the first spring flowers. Greater periwinkle (*Vinca major*) is a long vine with blue flowers and roundish leaves, often edged with white. It is grown by florists for window boxes. Madagascar periwinkle (*Vinca rosea*) is an erect plant, grown as an annual. It is usually less than 45 centimeters (18 inches) high and looks somewhat like a small bush. Red, pink, or white flowers cover the plant during the summer and autumn. Extracts of the plant are used as a treatment for the blood disease leukemia.

Vincas, as periwinkles are also called, grow well in shady places. The vine species are grown from cuttings of the stem. The annual is grown from seeds. The vines frequently root along the stems where they touch the soil. These may be dug up and cut off to be planted elsewhere. This is called layering.

PERMAFROST see TUNDRA.

PERON, Juan and Eva. Juan Domingo Peron (1895–1974) was the president of Argentina from 1946 to 1955 and 1973 to 1974. His wife Maria Eva Duarte (1919–52), better known as Evita, was his active partner and a prominent politician herself.

Peron was born near Lobos in Buenos Aires province. He moved with his parents to Patagonia, then to Buenos Aires, where in 1913 he graduated from the Military College. By 1936 he had advanced to the rank of colonel in the Argentine army. During the next few years he was sent on special missions for the army to Chile and Italy.

Eva Duarte was born in Los Toldos, Buenos Aires province. A prominent radio and film actress, her interest in public affairs led to meetings with well-known leaders, including Juan Peron. They were married in 1945.

With a group of young army officers, Juan Peron took control of the government in June 1943. He rose rapidly as a leader in the new government. As secretary of labor and social welfare, he laid the groundwork for his future Peronista party. He brought labor unions under government control and did a great deal to help the under-privileged workers who were known as the "shirtless ones". He soon took over the positions of minister of war and vice-president. By 1946 he had built up enough power to be elected president for a six-year term.

BBC Hulton Picture Library

Juan Peron ruled Argentina as dictator, with his wife Eva. They did much for the poor but made many enemies, too.

As president, Peron set up a military dictatorship. (See also DICTATOR.) He increased government control of both social and economic life. He won public approval of his changes by increasing wages and welfare benefits for the workers. An armament program and pay raises kept the army loyal. To prevent opposition he closed newspapers, controlled education, and packed the Congress and Supreme Court with members of his party. To make sure he would remain in office, Peron changed the constitution to permit his re-election in 1951.

Eva Peron encouraged the Argentines to support her husband. She helped organize labor unions. She promoted the women's right to vote in 1947. She gave food, money, and medicine to the needy and helped to promote better hospitals and housing. She owned many radio stations and severely censored the press, closing down many newspapers and magazines. In 1952 she died of cancer.

By 1955 Peron had made many enemies. His

attacks on the Roman Catholic Church resulted in his excommunication (expulsion from the Church). In September of that year, he was overthrown by a military coup and fled into exile in Spain.

Peron's followers kept his party active during his absence. In 1973 they formed a coalition which allowed Peron's return. In September 1973 Peron was again elected president of Argentina. When he died in 1974, his third wife Isabel succeeded him as president but she was replaced in 1976 by a military government.

See also ARGENTINA.

PERSEUS. A famous legend of the ancient Greeks told the story of Perseus. It began when Acrisius, King of Argos in Greece, heard a prophecy that he would be killed by the son of his own daughter Danae. Accordingly Acrisius imprisoned Danae in a bronze tower so that no man should marry her; but Zeus, the king of the gods, turned himself into a shower of gold and visited her. In time Danae gave birth to a son, whom she named Perseus. Acrisius shut them both up in a chest and flung it into the sea.

However, the chest was washed up on the island of Seriphus, and Danae and her son were rescued by the king of the island, Polydectes. Years passed, and when Perseus grew up Polydectes wanted to marry Danae. He determined to get rid of Perseus and sent him off to seek the head of the monster Medusa, one of the Gorgons, a quest from which he was not expected to return. (See GORGON.)

But the gods favored Perseus. They gave him wonderful shoes to fly with, a sword and shield, and the Cap of Darkness which made him invisible. Thus he was able to approach the Gorgons unseen and cut off Medusa's head, guiding his sword by her reflection in his bright shield, for anyone who looked directly at her was turned to stone. Now that Perseus had Medusa's head he possessed a terrible weapon. With its help he rescued a maiden named Andromeda from a sea monster, turning it to stone, and eventually destroyed Polydectes and his followers, who were persecuting

Danae. Then he returned to Argos, and by accident killed Acrisius with a discus which he threw during an athletics contest. So the prophecy was fulfilled.

PERSIA, ANCIENT, was one of the great empires of the ancient world. It reached its height during the reigns of Cyrus, Cambyses, and Darius in the 6th century BC. But people lived in Persia long before that. We know that about 2000 BC a people called the Elamites, in southwest Persia, had developed their own version of the earlier cuneiform ("wedge-shaped") way of writing on clay tablets, and that they enjoyed an advanced civilization with cities, armies, and religious systems. The name *Persia* comes from the Greek name for the tribes living in the southwest of the country. Today Persia is known as Iran, from the Aryan or Irani tribes who moved into Persia from India and the Near East about 1500 BC. Among these Aryan tribes were the Medes, Parthians, and Scythians.

In 553 BC Cyrus led the Persians in a rebellion against the Medes. He founded the Achaemenid dynasty, under whose rule Persia became great. Cyrus was a skillful general and led his armies to victories against the Lydians and Babylonians. He ruled the conquered peoples sensibly and well. His son Cambyses, however, was a harsh ruler. He conquered Egypt but then went mad and killed himself. Darius, who became king of Persia in 522 BC, failed to conquer Greece, being defeated at the Battle of Marathon (see MARATHON, BATTLE OF). But Darius was a great king. It was he who built the magnificent capital city of Persepolis. He divided the empire into 20 provinces, each governed by a *satrap*. Each satrap led his own army, but the king maintained a large army of his own, including a special bodyguard known as the "Immortals". Good roads, with inns and a postal system, enabled Darius to govern his empire, which stretched from Asia Minor to India—the largest empire the world had yet known.

Its official religion was Zoroastrianism. Little is known about the prophet Zoroaster (or Zarathustra) who is thought to have lived

The remains of the city of Persepolis, the capital of ancient Persia chosen about 520 BC by Darius I (the Great). Situated in a remote mountain region of southwest Iran, it was overrun by Alexander the Great in 330 and taken into the Macedonian empire. The once great city declined into ruins during the time of the Seleucid rulers. This picture emphasizes the bleak isolation of Persepolis.

Barnaby's

in the late 7th and early 6th centuries BC. He taught his followers to believe in one god, called Ahura Mazda or Ormazd, the god of light and truth. Zoroastrianism became the royal religion, but the Persians allowed people throughout their empire to follow their own religions. (See ZOROASTER.)

After Darius, his son Xerxes struggled to overcome the rising power of Greece. The Persians won victories at Thermopylae and Artemisium but were defeated heavily at Salamis (see SALAMIS, BATTLE OF) and Plataea. After these setbacks, the Persian might began to crumble. Less able kings tried vainly to hold the empire together, but in 333 BC it fell to the Greeks under Alexander the Great (see ALEXANDER THE GREAT). From the middle of the 2nd century BC until the beginning of the 3rd century AD Persia was ruled by the Parthians, a people from the steppes east of the Caspian Sea, who were fine horsemen and fought with bows and arrows.

Weakened by wars with the Romans, the Parthian rulers were replaced by the Sassanians, who governed Persia until the Arab Conquest, which was complete by AD 650. Persia accepted the Muslim religion and became prosperous, but in the 11th century it was invaded and conquered by the Turks. Then in the 13th century Persia was overrun by the Mongols, who destroyed most of the cities and

whose rule lasted until the end of the 15th century. Power passed into the hands of the Safavids, a line of Persian sovereigns who took the title of shah (ruler). With them began the modern history of the country that we call Iran (see IRAN).

Persian Art

Persia has an old and fine literature. Two great poets of the 11th century were Omar Khayyam and Firdousi. The beauties of medieval Persian art are also famous. This art found its most perfect expression in books, handwritten in wonderful script and illustrated with richly colored miniature paintings. The best-known painter was Behzad,

Barnaby's

The ruined palace of Darius I at Persepolis, viewed from the Audience Hall, or Apadana.

who worked at the end of the 15th century and had many pupils and imitators. In pottery and porcelain Persia ranks with China. Persian architects showed great skill in building arches and domes and they used colored glazed tiles, especially blue ones, for decoration on walls and floors both inside and outside.

PERSIAN GULF. The great rivers of the Middle East, the Euphrates and Tigris, reach the sea at the head of a large and fairly shallow inlet called the Persian Gulf. It is known as the "Arabian Gulf", or just simply as the Gulf. Nowhere is it more than 90 meters (300 feet) deep. The gulf is 990 kilometers (615 miles) long and 340 kilometers (210 miles) wide at its widest point, narrowing to 55 kilometers (35 miles) at the Strait of Hormuz, where it connects with the Indian Ocean.

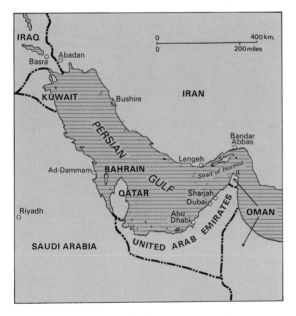

The waters have high salinity (salt content) because only a small quantity of fresh water flows into the Gulf, mostly from the Tigris and Euphrates rivers. Because of this many species of plants and animals found in the Indian Ocean cannot live in the Persian Gulf.

The larger countries around the Persian Gulf are Iran on the north side, Saudi Arabia on the west, and Iraq at the head of the gulf.

Much of the Arabian coast is made up of small states, each with its own hereditary ruler. The most imprtant of these states are Bahrain, Kuwait, and Qatar. To the east of Qatar are the United Arab Emirates, which until 1971 were under British protection. Northeast of the United Arab Emirates the land comes to a point at Ru'us al-Jibal, which is in Oman and overlooks the Strait of Hormuz.

The chief product of the Persian Gulf is oil. The Gulf and neighboring countries produce about 30 per cent of the world's oil. Offshore exploration has shown that there are large reserves of oil and gas below the Gulf itself. Huge tankers carry oil from the terminals at Khark Island, Dhahran, and other locations to all parts of the world. Many traditional industries, such as pearl fishing, have declined as the production of oil has grown in importance. Dates are grown on the few fertile strips of land along the coast, and camels are bred for transportation. Fishing is a highly organized industry and great catches of prawns are exported from the region. The climate is one of the hottest in the world and there are few wild animals except gazelles, hares, and wild goats.

There are separate articles on the countries mentioned and also an article ARABIA.

PERSIMMON is any tree of the genus *Diospyros* of the ebony family. The trees are well known for their fruits, called persimmons, which have an edible pulp. When ripe the fruit is deep orange-red, wrinkled, soft, and sweet. The persimmon frequently sold in markets is the Japanese persimmon (*Diospyros kaki*). Though native to eastern Asia, it is now grown in many warm parts of the world, including Hawaii, California, and the southeastern United States. The fruits, 7 to 10 centimeters (3 to 4 inches) long and about 7 centimeters (3 inches) in diameter, somewhat resemble tomatoes in shape. Persimmons are usually eaten fresh, although puddings, jellies, pies, and ice cream may be made from them. Until fully ripe and soft, the fruit has a bitter taste.

The native American persimmon (*Diospyros virginiana*) grows wild from central Pennsyl-

John Regensburg/National Audubon Society

Persimmon fruits are only edible when fully ripe. This is the Oriental persimmon from China and Japan.

vania and central Illinois southward to the Gulf States. The tree may be 12 meters (40 feet) tall, but it is usually smaller or even shrubby. The fruits are about 2.5 to 5 centimeters (1 to 2 inches) long. Their color is orange-yellow, dark red, or sometimes blue-purple. They do not ship well, and so they are seldom seen in northern markets. The Texas persimmon (*Diospyros texana*), which grows in Texas and northern Mexico, is also a native American plant and has a black fruit about 2.5 centimeters (1 inch) long. Both of these North American native persimmons are important food for wildlife.

PERTH is the capital of Western Australia and the fifth largest city in Australia. It lies chiefly on the north bank of the Swan River about 19 kilometers (12 miles) from the port of Fremantle at the mouth. The metropolitan area stretches some 65 kilometers (40 miles) north to south, and 40 kilometers (25 miles) east to west.

Perth has hot summers with temperatures of 29°C (84°F) and mild winters down to 17°C (62°F). It has many parks and gardens, the finest being King's Park which looks over the city from the west and which has many beautiful Australian trees and wild flowers. There are rows of attractive houses along the banks of the broad river and bathing and sailing are favorite sports. The city has many modern public buildings, office buildings, hotels, and shopping arcades. Hay Street Mall is one of the busiest. As with many other Australian waterfront cities, tall skyscrapers dominate the shoreline. There are two universities at Perth: the University of Western Australia and Murdoch University. There are also several technical colleges and many schools. Mining and truck farming are the main industries of the area, and a great many city dwellers work in manufacturing, building, and transportation.

Perth and Fremantle which, with the metropolitan area surrounding them, have a combined population of 948,800 (1983), 75 per cent of the state's population. They are important commercial centers. Perth is the western terminal of the trans-Australian railroad. The city's airport provides direct links with the rest of the world, and Fremantle is the first Australian port of call for ships which have crossed the Indian Ocean.

History

The area was first sighted by the Dutch navigator, de Vlamingh, in 1697. He named the Swan River after the black swans he saw there. The British were wary of French and

Promotion Australia

Like other Australian coastal cities, Perth offers a wealth of water-sports, including sailing.

United States interest in Australia's west coast in the early 19th century and so dispatched Captain James Stirling to set up a settlement, in 1827. Two years later Sir Charles Fremantle took over the site which was declared a colony. In the 1850s convicts were sent there and built many of the public buildings. Perth was proclaimed a city by Queen Victoria in 1856. In the 1890s the goldrush helped its development, as did the opening of Fremantle as a deep-sea port.

PERU is a republic on the west coast of South America. It is the third largest country of the continent, and is bounded by Ecuador and Colombia to the north, by Brazil and Bolivia to the east, and by Chile to the south. To the west is the Pacific Ocean.

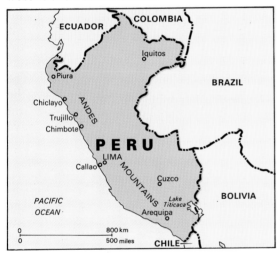

The main feature of Peru's geography is the mighty range of the Andes (see ANDES MOUNTAINS) running parallel to the coast, with several peaks more than 6,000 meters (19,500 feet) high. Running parallel between the mountains and the sea is a coastal belt between 15 and 150 kilometers (9 and 90 miles) wide, much of it a desert of drifting sand. The Atacama Desert, which lies to the south and stretches into Argentina, is one of the driest places on Earth. About 50 rivers and streams cross the coastal belt but, because of the lack of rain, only a few of them reach the sea all the year round. These river valleys are fertile when irrigated, grow valuable crops, and are thickly populated. The *sierra*, or mountain, region is more than 300 kilometers (185 miles) wide and consists of steep ridges with high tablelands and valleys between them. The eastern slopes of the mountains form a belt called the *montana* which falls away gradually to the forested plains of the upper Amazon River. On the borders of Peru and Bolivia is Lake Titicaca, which is the largest lake in South America and, at 3,809 meters (12,496 feet) above sea-level, is the world's highest navigable lake.

FACTS ABOUT PERU

AREA: 1,285,216 square kilometers (496,225 square miles).
POPULATION: 22,332,000 (1990).
GOVERNMENT: Republic.
CAPITAL: Lima, 5,493,900.
GEOGRAPHICAL FEATURES: Two chains of the Andes Mountains, running parallel to the Pacific coast, divide the country into three very different regions: (1) a coastal zone; (2) mountainous areas consisting of chains of high peaks, known as the cordilleras. high plateaus, or tablelands, and deep valleys; (3) heavily forested slopes east of the mountains, leading to the low-lying Amazonian plain.
CITIES: Arequipa, 591,700; Callao, 560,000; Trujillo, 491,000; Chiclayo, 394,800; Piura, 297,200.
ECONOMY: Products and exports.
  Agriculture: Sugar-cane, potatoes, rice, corn, cassava, plantains, cotton, coffee, sheep, pigs, chickens, wood, fish.
  Mining: Iron ore, zinc, copper, lead, silver.
  Manufacturing: Cement, wheat flour, animal feed, refined sugar, sulfuric acid, cooking oil, urea, motor vehicles.
  Exports: Copper, petroleum derivatives, lead, zinc, fish, flour, textiles, coffee.
EDUCATION: Children should attend school between the ages of 6 and 15.

Climate and Wildlife

The climate of Peru varies between its three major regions. The western coastlands have little rain, but on the montana there is heavy rainfall brought by winds from the east blowing across the damp Amazon forests. The rainfall is carried by swollen streams which link up to form one of the world's great river systems (see AMAZON RIVER). The climate of the Amazon lowlands is hot and damp, with aver-

Tony Morrison/South American Pictures

Indian fishermen maneuver their reed boats on the world's highest navigable lake – Lake Titicaca.

age monthly temperatures of 27°C (80°F), and annual rainfall between 2,030–2,540 millimeters (80–100 inches).

There is not much natural vegetation in the coastal belt or on the seaward slope of the Andes except shrubs, cactuses, and short hardy grasses. The *montana*, on the other hand, is thickly forested with many kinds of trees, creeping plants, and tree-ferns.

The cold Peru Current flowing north along the coast is rich in fish, which provide one of Peru's main natural resources. Peru is one of the world's chief fishing nations, and fishmeal, used for animal feed and fertilizer, is an important export. The fish are preyed upon by millions of sea-birds, whose droppings form a thick coating on the small islands off the coast of southern Peru. This substance, called *guano*, is collected for fertilizing crops. In the Andes live the llama, the alpaca, and the vicuna (members of the camel family) as well as the chinchilla, a fur-bearing rodent. Overhead soars the mighty condor, a type of vulture and one of the world's largest flying birds. On the *montana* and the Amazonian plains live monkeys, pumas, jaguars, tapirs, and many kinds of parrot and snake.

Peoples and Cities

About one-eighth of the Peruvian people are of European, mainly Spanish, descent. They live in the coastal region. A far larger group are *mestizos*, that is, people of mixed Spanish and Indian ancestry. There are also a number of Peruvians of Chinese and Japanese descent whose ancestors came to Peru during the last century. The largest group, however, are the Indians, the original inhabitants of Peru. Most speak Quecha or Aymara, which are the main Indian languages, but many also speak Spanish. Both Spanish and Quecha are official languages. The official religion is Roman Catholicism, but some of the Indians still retain their traditional religions.

The country has a very high birth rate. Two-fifths of the population are under 15. Many people have migrated to the towns along the coast in search of work, but there is high unemployment. Despite efforts by the government, housing, sanitation, and health care are inadequate. Many people suffer from malnutrition and infectious diseases such as typhoid, tuberculosis, and whooping cough.

Children between the ages of 6 and 15 are

Paul Conklin/Pix from Publix

Indians sell their wares on market day in Pisac.

David M. Fretz

Cattle being loaded for market near the northern border of the country with Ecuador.

altitudes. Cattle and sheep are raised. Llamas are used as beasts of burden, while alpacas provide wool. Many Indian women weave their own cloth and sell wool and hair in the markets, as well as pottery and wood carvings. Cotton and sugar are the chief crops grown in the river valleys of the coastal belt, together with rice, vegetables, and fruits. Coffee, tobacco, and quinine (used as a medicine) are grown in the eastern lowlands.

Minerals form a large part of Peru's wealth. Petroleum (oil) is obtained at Talara and Lobitos in the coastal region near the northern boundary. Important mineral discoveries are being made in the Amazon region. Peru in colonial times was famous for its gold and silver, and these are still mined. Copper, lead, and zinc are also mined, the chief mines being in the high *sierra*. Vanadium (used for hardening steel) and bismuth, a metal valuable because it melts at a low temperature, are also mined. Factories in Peru make goods such as clothing, paper, and cement, but most machinery has to be obtained from abroad.

Transportation in Peru is very difficult, chiefly because of the high mountains. The main ports are Callao, Chimbote, Ilo, and Salaverry. A coastal road through the country forms part of the Pan-American Highway (see PAN-AMERICAN HIGHWAY), and there is an important road running eastwards from Lima across the mountains to the Amazonian port of Pucallpa. There are several railroads, a number of them built to

supposed to attend school but this is not always possible in remote areas. There are two large universities at Lima, and others at Arequipa, Cuzco, and Trujillo. In the days of Spanish rule, Lima was a center of South American culture and a number of writers reached fame both before Peruvian independence and afterwards. Perhaps the best-known Peruvian writer today is the novelist Mario Vargas Llosa whose work has been translated into many languages (see LATIN AMERICAN LITERATURE).

Peru has many ancient buildings left from earlier civilizations. Cuzco was the capital of the Inca Empire, and has many Inca and pre-Inca ruins. The ancient fortress city of Machu Picchu lies about 80 kilometers (50 miles) southwest of Cuzco. It was rediscovered in 1911 (see INCAS).

The capital is Lima (see LIMA), which is a few kilometers inland from Callao, its port. Other important cities are Arequipa in the south, the coastal city of Trujillo, and Cuzco, which is more than 3,300 meters (10,826 feet) above sea-level.

Agriculture and Industry

Most of the Indians living in villages and towns in the high *sierra* grow crops of corn, potatoes, beans, and a variety of grain called *gaina* which is suitable for growing at high

Hutchison Library

Boats lie waiting to transport bananas at the port of Pucallpa on the Ucayali River.

join inland towns with the nearest port. In a country where ground travel is so difficult, air transportation is widely used.

History

Peru has been inhabited for at least 10,000 years. Many different Indian societies reached high levels of civilization, cultivating crops still grown today, building cities, and making pottery and textiles. The Inca empire was built up in a series of conquests, beginning in 1438. (There is a separate article on the INCAS.) Less than 100 years later it stretched from what is now southern Colombia to northwestern Argentina and Chile.

In 1532 the Spanish conqueror Francisco Pizarro, on whom there is a separate article, met the Inca emperor Atahualpa at Cajamarca. Atahualpa gave him a friendly welcome, but in spite of this Pizarro treacherously seized him. Atahualpa's people brought gold and silver to ransom him until there was enough gold to fill a whole room and enough silver to fill an even larger one. Instead of freeing Atahualpa, Pizarro had him put to death in 1533 and later in the same year entered the capital, Cuzco.

Spain took control of Peru, which remained under Spanish domination for nearly 300 years. During this time the Spanish tried to convert the Indian peoples to Roman Catholicism and to the Spanish way of life. Until 1739 the viceroyalty of Peru, as it was known, included all of South America except what is now Venezuela.

During the early part of the 19th century there were several revolts in the South American colonies against Spanish rule. Chile and Buenos Aires (Argentina) were the first to declare their independence. They sent a force by sea under the command of General José de San Martin to overcome the Spaniards at Lima in 1820. The Spanish viceroy (ruler) withdrew with his army inland and the independence of Peru was proclaimed in 1821. The last Spanish resistance was not beaten until Simon Bolivar's armies came to Peru after freeing the northern port of South America. (See BOLIVAR, SIMON.)

ZEFA

Cuzco dates from the 11th century. It was capital of the Inca Empire and sacked by the Spanish in 1533.

The years after independence were difficult ones for Peru. Governments constantly changed as different generals seized power. There were conflicts with Bolivia and later Chile. In 1895, however, a democratic government was elected. Law and order were restored and Peru became more prosperous. Production of cotton and sugar increased and the nation's copper and oil resources were developed. But nothing was done to protect the rights of the Indians whose lands were being seized and sold by white settlers.

A series of unstable governments followed, but despite this the development of Peru's natural resources continued and the economy expanded. In 1969 the army took control of the country.

The new military government brought in changes, breaking up the old estates into small farms to help the Indian communities and improving education for both children and adults. It also seized industries owned by foreign companies.

In 1980 Peru returned to civilian rule, under President Ferdinand Belaunde Terry. In 1985 he handed over power to a democratically elected successor, Alan Garcia Perez, who in 1990 was succeeded by Alberto Fujimori, a Peruvian of Japanese descent. Fujimori inherited severe economic problems and opposition from several groups of guerrilla fighters, the largest of which is called the "Shining Path". Fighting between guerrillas and the army has made the Andes region dangerous. The great majority of the people remain very poor, and Peru has many problems to overcome, but its vast mineral wealth and other natural resources offer hope for the future.

PESTS. The word pest, which comes from the Latin for "plague", is applied to creatures that destroy such things as crops, food, furniture, clothes, and the wooden parts of houses. Most pests are insects of some kind, but some rodents, such as rats and mice are important pests, as are many species of birds that raid crops, and carry disease.

The most dreaded of all insect pests is the locust. With its powerful jaws it chews up and then swallows the leaves and fruit of any plant it settles on. Locusts collect in swarms so great that they darken the sky, and in Africa, India, Australia, and many other hot parts of the world, they leave the country bare of green plants for miles around.

In gardens and orchards the pests include the larvae of various types of insects. Caterpillars, the larvae of moths and butterflies, feed on leaves and some kinds are especially fond of cabbages. The larvae of various insects, including moths, attack fruits and seeds such as apples, plums, and peas. Leatherjackets, the larvae of the cranefly, and wire-worms, the larvae of click beetles, live in the soil and attack the roots of plants such as grasses.

Houseflies have always been a nuisance. They spoil food and spread several serious diseases by carrying germs on their feet and mouthparts.

An animal which is introduced into a new country, where it may have no natural enemies, can swiftly increase in numbers and therefore become a pest. When rabbits were taken from Europe to Australia, they spread so rapidly that they quickly became the country's worst pest. Similarly, the gray squirrel, which was taken to Britain from North America, soon became a very common pest, as well as displacing most of the native red squirrels.

Rats and mice eat large quantities of stored food and may also spread the germs which they carry around with them. Grain, flour, nuts, and dried fruit are among the foods which are attacked by the larvae of beetles and moths. Some weevils, which are kinds of beetles, are very destructive, and in the days of sailing ships the ships' biscuits were frequently full of them. Mites, which are eight-legged arachnids, not insects, often get into stored flour and grain.

Among the pests that destroy wood is the deathwatch beetle, which has a grub that bores into wooden beams in old buildings. Sometimes this and the larvae of other wood-boring beetles burrow into the wood to such an extent that whole buildings may become unsafe. In the tropics the termites are the worst wood pests.

Controlling Pests

Many pests have to be killed by poison. Since the 1930s chemical insecticides such as DDT have proved very effective in destroying disease-carrying insects. But by the 1970s many insect species had developed immunity to these poisons. In addition, it was found that insecticides such as DDT not only were polluting the soil and rivers but also were poisoning other creatures such as birds and fish.

Scientists are always looking for safer chemicals to use against pests, and for other ways of controlling their numbers. It is important that animals which naturally prey on

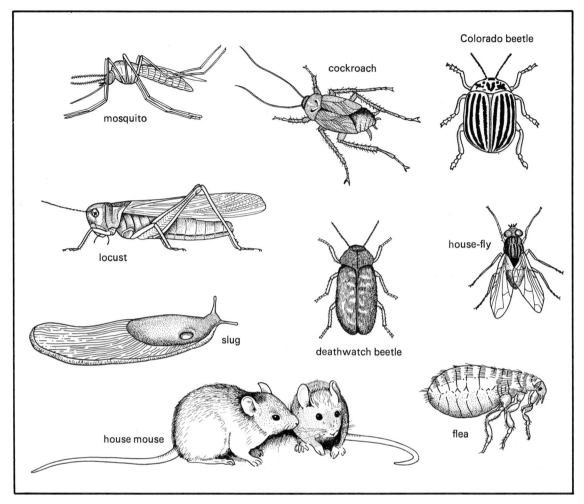

mosquito

cockroach

Colorado beetle

locust

deathwatch beetle

house-fly

slug

house mouse

flea

pests be left undisturbed to carry out this useful task. Hawks and owls, for instance, eat rats and mice and so are helpful in controlling these pests. However, large numbers of birds of prey are still being killed by the build-up of pesticides in their bodies from the small birds and mammals that they have eaten.

There are many examples of biological control of pests, where one or more animals have been introduced into an area to control a pest. Unfortunately, many of these have "backfired" and not done what they were intended to do. For example, foxes were taken to Australia when it was found that the rabbit was becoming a serious pest, in the hope that they would keep the number of rabbits down. But they preyed on many of the native animals and birds rather than the rabbits. However, rab-

bits were controlled in Australia in the 1950s by introducing the myxomatosis virus which causes a fatal disease in rabbits.

Another successful case of biological control was the destruction of a mealybug, a pest of citrus trees in California, by the introduction of two small wasp species.

Some pests can be controlled by constructing buildings which keep them out, or by keeping buildings clean and tidy. Rats, for instance, often enter food stores through damaged drains, or through holes in walls where water pipes go in. Insects may be able to lay their eggs or to live during the winter in cracks in walls or floors, or in piles of rubbish. In general, the more dirt there is the more chance there is of pests breeding in large numbers.

See also BIRD; HOUSEFLY; INSECT; LOCUST;

Mite; Moth; Mouse; Rabbit; Rat; Termite; Weevil.

PETER, Saint. The story of St. Peter is told in the New Testament of the Bible. Peter and his brother Andrew, both fishermen, were the first two disciples, or apostles, whom Jesus Christ called to follow him. Peter's original name was Simon but Jesus changed it to Peter, which comes from a Greek word meaning rock. This was intended as a sign that, whatever his weaknesses at the time when he became a disciple, Peter would eventually turn into the rock-like and fearless character around whom the Church could be built up.

In all lists of the Twelve Apostles, Peter is always put first and it is clear that the writers of the Gospels regarded him as the chief apostle. He was one of three—the others were James and John—whom Jesus allowed to be present on very important occasions. For example, it was these three who were present at the Transfiguration (see John, Saint), and who were with Jesus while he prayed in the Garden of Gethsemane just before he was arrested and crucified (see Jesus Christ). Again, Peter was the first to realize that Jesus was more than a prophet and that he was the long-awaited Messiah, or savior (see Prophet). The Gospel of St. Matthew (chapter 16) describes how, after Peter had said, "Thou art the Christ, the Son of the living God", Jesus replied, "Thou art Peter, and upon this rock I will build my church".

Peter plays an important part in many of the Gospel stories and in the early part of the Acts of the Apostles. The Gospels show him as full of energy, determined to strive in the service of Jesus, but sometimes he loses courage, as when he denied that he knew Jesus after Jesus had been arrested. St. Matthew (chapter 26) describes how Jesus prophesied to Peter "that this night, before the cock crow, thou shalt deny me thrice", and how this was exactly what happened. In the Acts, however, after Peter has seen Christ come back to life after the crucifixion, he fears nobody. With Paul, he was largely responsible for spreading the Christian faith after Christ's death.

Peter is believed to have met his death during the anti-Christian persecutions of the Emperor Nero (see Nero), probably in AD 64 and probably in Rome. Roman Catholics regard Peter as the first pope, or "father of the Church". (See Pope.)

PETER PAN, the boy who never grew up, became known to the world in the play *Peter Pan* by the Scottish writer Sir James Barrie. The play was first acted in 1904 and is nowadays put on the stage in Britain nearly every year at Christmas. One of Sir James Barrie's friends had five small sons, and the story of Peter Pan's adventures grew out of the long series of make-believe games that the author and the boys played together.

According to the play, all children when they are little would like never to have to grow up, but to be children for ever in a wonderful imaginary land of adventure. This was just what Peter Pan was able to do, for he had escaped from ordinary life and lived in the Never Never Land, a country of fairies and other story-book creatures. There Peter had endless adventures with redskins and wolves, and with the pirates commanded by the terrifying Captain Hook. Sometimes Peter would come to the real world and take real children back with him to the Never Never Land, and in the play it was the Darling family—Wendy, John, and Michael—who went with him and shared his adventures. With Peter too were a number of Lost Boys who had no mothers and could not get back to the ordinary world. During her visit Wendy Darling looked after them and became a mother to them.

Peter was very sure of himself and very brave in danger. When he thought in one adventure that he was going to be drowned, he did not let himself be afraid, but just said, "To die will be an awfully big adventure". He was saved, however, and together with the children managed to destroy Captain Hook. The Darling family went back to their home and their parents, but Peter returned to the Never Never Land to live as a boy for ever.

In Kensington Gardens in London there is a statue of Peter Pan playing a pipe, standing on a pedestal round which are carved figures of children and animals. Barrie himself arranged for it to be put up. He gave the profits from all performances of the play, and from the book made from it, to the Hospital for Sick Children, in Great Ormond Street, London.

PETER THE GREAT (1672–1725). Peter I, tsar (emperor) of Russia, transformed Russia from a backward, isolated country into a major Western power, but at great cost in terms of his people's lives and sufferings. He was born in Moscow, the son of Tsar Alexis. Peter was a gifted and hard-working child who learned carpentry, printing, blacksmithing, and science, as well as doing army training.

Michael Holford

Peter the Great worked in disguise in different parts of Europe to learn modern techniques for use in Russia.

Peter's sole reign began in 1694 and in 1695 he embarked on a war against the Ottoman (Turkish) Empire. He set out with his ships to attack the Turkish port of Azov, near the present-day Black Sea port of Rostov. He was completely defeated, and on his return set his workmen to building a navy. Peter himself worked with his men, and in 1696 the new Russian navy blockaded and captured Azov.

Between 1697–98, Peter toured the capitals of Europe, in disguise, to learn Western techniques, which would help make Russia a powerful nation. He studied guns in Germany, shipbuilding at Deptford, in England, and engraving in Amsterdam. All this showed him that Russia was a backward country and needed the technical knowledge and efficiency of the West.

While Peter was away, the *streltsy*, or musketeer regiments, rebelled. The tsar hurried back to Russia and suppressed the rebellion with great cruelty. He then set to work to impose Western customs, beginning by ordering the Russian nobles to cut off their beards and to wear Western dress.

In 1700 Peter made peace with Turkey and turned against Sweden, which then controlled the Baltic Sea. His army was destroyed by Charles XII of Sweden during a terrible snowstorm in the same year, but Peter was able to raise and train a new army to go on fighting the Northern War, as this struggle was called. To do this he changed the old methods by which Russia had been governed until then. Peter also founded the new city of St. Petersburg, which became the Russian capital in 1712. Thousands of peasants, drafted in to build the city on the unhealthy marshes where it was founded, died. St. Petersburg has also been called Petrograd (1914–1924), and Leningrad (1924–1991). It still retains many of the imposing Western-style buildings, fortresses, public square, bridges, and palaces of Peter's reign. (See ST. PETERSBURG.)

In 1709 Peter defeated Charles XII at the Battle of Poltava, but he next began a disastrous campaign against Turkey, which lost him all the advantages he had previously gained. Not until 1721 was the Northern War finally ended with the Treaty of Nystad, which gave Russia some Baltic lands.

Peter had fought Turkey for trading ports in the south and in 1722 he attacked Persia for the same reason, conquering lands by the Caspian Sea. He even sent expeditions into the Pacific Ocean to look for gold and to found trading stations.

Besides founding the Russian navy, Peter

also began the iron industry in the Ural Mountains, driving miners, manufacturers, and traders to increase production. He sent Russians to study in the West, tried to educate the boyars, or land-owning aristocracy, and punished those who failed to carry out his policies. Because the Russian Orthodox Church opposed most of his reforms, he got rid of the patriarch at its head and made it support his government in all ways. In 1721 he was proclaimed Peter the Great, Emperor of All the Russias. He was unpopular because of his violent changes and the severe taxes he imposed. The people were also shocked when he had his second wife Catherine crowned empress in 1724, with a crown of 2,564 precious stones. (His first wife had been exiled to a convent.) Catherine was a peasant who could neither read nor write, but Peter was devoted to her.

Peter the Great was a good ruler in the sense that he realized what his country needed. His aim was to make Russia great through contact with the more advanced countries of the West. He was, however, capable of terrible rages and cruelty, one of his worst deeds being the killing of his son Alexis in 1718. Peter was only 52 when he died, worn out by his campaigns. He was succeeded by his wife Catherine I.

PETRARCH (1304–74). Francesco Petrarca, who is usually known as Petrarch, was an Italian poet and thinker whose work marked the beginning of the Renaissance. He is best known today for the beautiful poems he wrote to a woman named Laura. But when he was alive he was known throughout Europe as a scholar, a fiery orator, and a brilliant writer.

Petrarch encouraged people to use their minds and talents. He urged the wealthy to sponsor artists, writers, and musicians. He was one of the founders of the movement called "humanism," which was one of the most important elements of the Renaissance, the so-called revival of learning. (See HUMANISM; RENAISSANCE.)

Petrarch was born in Arezzo, Italy, after his father had been banished from Florence for his political beliefs. The family then moved to Avignon in France where Petrarch started school. He loved poetry more than all his other studies. There is a story that his father once threw his poetry books into the fire, hoping to make him study other things. Petrarch did study law for several years. But after his father died, the poet began to work at the subject he liked.

In 1327 Petrarch saw Laura for the first time in a church in Avignon. No one knows who she really was, but for 40 years he wrote about her beauty and his love for her.

Petrarch set out on the first of his many long journeys in 1333. He visited France, Belgium, and Germany. Wherever he went he talked with educated people, searched for manuscripts of works by ancient authors, and walked miles through the countryside.

In 1337 Petrarch went to live in Vaucluse, France, in the service of Cardinal Colonna. He lived alone, wrote *Canzaniere* (poems to Laura), began a history of Rome, and an epic poem, "Africa", about the Punic Wars in North Africa. In 1340 he was invited to teach at the University of Paris. At the same time King Robert of Naples invited him to his court. Petrarch went to Naples in southern Italy. His poems were becoming famous, and in 1341 he went to Rome where he was given the title of poet laureate and received a laurel crown from a Roman senator.

Invitations to visit rich and powerful men began to pour in. Pertrarch loved fame and fashionable living. Throughout his life, he felt torn between material things and the spiritual life, and his essay, "Petrarch's Secret", is about this conflict.

The next few years were sad ones for Petrarch. His old friends, Cardinal Colonna and King Robert, died. His brother entered a monastery and shut himself away from the world. Many friends died of the terrible plague which was sweeping through Europe and finally, in 1348, Laura herself died of the plague. Boccaccio, the poet, and Petrarch's lifelong friend, gave him great encouragement during this time.

Petrarch gave his many books to the Republic of St. Mark, Venice, in 1363, and in 1369 he retired to the quiet village of Arqua. Five years later he was found dead among his beloved books and papers.

STORM PETREL · LEACH'S PETREL · CAPE PIGEON · STORM PETREL · SOOTY SHEARWATER · FULMAR · FULMAR

PETREL. The petrels (which include the shearwaters and the fulmar) are sea-birds related to the albatrosses. Many kinds skim the tops of the waves and paddle or patter with their feet as though they are walking, and it is said that they are named after Saint Peter, who walked on the water of the Sea of Galilee. There are many kinds, from the giant petrel (*Macronectes giganteus*) of the southern seas which is about the size of a goose, to the storm petrels (family Hydrobatidae) which are no larger than house-martins. Petrels and albatrosses are distinguished from other birds by having their nostrils in tubes on top of their beaks.

Some petrels have such short, weak legs that they are hardly able to walk. They fly for miles over the surface of the sea and only come to land to breed. The Bermuda petrel (*Pterodroma cahow*), indeed, went unrecognized for hundreds of years because it enters and leaves its nest burrow only by night. It was thought to have died out in the 17th century, but in 1951 a few pairs were discovered on an islet off Bermuda.

Most petrels can squirt bad-smelling liquid at anyone who goes too close to their nests. Their eggs are white.

PETROLEUM is a word that comes from the Latin words *petra*, meaning "rock" and *oleum*, meaning "oil". Petroleum and its products are of great importance to modern life. These products include motor fuels, kerosine gasoline and diesel oil, fuel oil, lubricants, bitumen, and wax. Gasoline, of course, is used in automobiles. Kerosine is used in oil lamps, farm tractors, and jet-engined aircraft. Diesel oil is used in the diesel engines

for buses, trucks, and ships. Fuel oil is burned to make steam in the boilers of steamships and in furnaces to obtain heat for processes of many kinds, such as the manufacture of steel, glass, and pottery and for warming buildings. Lubricants are the oils and greases needed to make machinery of any kind run smoothly and easily. Bitumen is used in asphalt and for waterproofing. Separate articles on oils and fuels and their uses are ASPHALT; BOILER; DIESEL ENGINE; FUEL; GAS; INTERNAL COMBUSTION ENGINE; JET PROPULSION.

Petroleum has been used in simple ways for thousands of years. The Babylonians used bitumen for paving and cementing, and the Romans used asphalt from Sicily for their roads. The ancient Chinese evaporated brine over fires of natural gas to obtain salt. In Italy, Germany, North America, and in Burma crude petroleum was believed to have medicinal properties.

Kerosine and Paraffin

In 1850 the Scottish scientist James Young invented a method of obtaining kerosine from the rock called shale. He used it for lamps instead of vegetable or whale oil.

The two main types of kerosine are burning oil and vaporizing oil. Burning oil is used in lamps, stoves, and heaters. Vaporizing oil is used as the fuel for the engines of many farm tractors and small fishing vessels. The fuel used in aircraft jet engines is similar to vaporizing oil.

Kerosine is known as paraffin in Great Britain. The word paraffin is also used to mean paraffin wax, which is obtained from petroleum and used for making candles, tapers, and polishes, and also for waterproofing cardboard and paper. The clear, heavy oil called "petroleum jelly" and used as a medicine is yet another petroleum product.

Discovery of Oil

Until the middle of the 19th century crude oil was collected where it seeped naturally from the earth. Often oil was regarded as a nuisance as it seeped into streams where animals were watered and into wells sunk for brine. In about 1850 in the United States, Colonel A. C. Ferris and later S. M. Kier started pioneer work on petroleum as a source of lamp oil. Then George Bissell and Jonathan Eveleth, two New York lawyers, formed a company to prospect for oil in Pennsylvania. They secured the services of Colonel E. L. Drake, a retired railroad contractor, and set him drilling near the little town of Titusville, Pennsylvania.

On 27 August 1859, at 21 meters (70 feet), Drake struck oil. Soon he was pumping 8 barrels a day, then 20. The petroleum found a ready market, as it was a cheaper and a surer source of lamp oil than the risky business of hunting whales. The oil rush was on and the age of petroleum had come.

How Petroleum is Formed and Found

Petroleum was probably formed from dead plant and animal life of the seas. The dead remains decayed on the seabed until only fatty and oily substances were left. These substances became buried under mud and as time went on the mud was squeezed into a layer of rock, while the oily substances were changed into petroleum and gas. Sometimes upheavals of the Earth's crust replaced the sea by dry land and buried the oil-bearing rock thousands of meters deep.

The oil seldom remained in the rock where it was formed. Sometimes it traveled many kilometers or miles through pores (tiny holes) in the rock until it reached the surface, where it evaporated (changed into gas) and left a pool of bitumen, or pitch. Often it met hard, non-porous rock which it could not get through. Here, securely trapped beneath a domed cap of non-porous rock, the oil is to be found contained in porous rock like water in a sponge. Usually there is a layer of natural gas above the petroleum and often lying beneath it there is salt water from the ancient sea.

Only drilling can prove that oil exists in a particular place, but geologists, who study the Earth and its rocks, can usually suggest likely places. Often maps are made from aerial photographs and the geologists choose promising areas which are then explored on foot. The rocks and vegetation are studied and samples of underground rock obtained by drilling are brought up for examination. There are a number of scientific methods depending on special instruments by means of which geologists can discover the position, depth, hardness, and even the kind of rock which exists beneath the surface. Even then it is by no means certain that oil will be struck when a well is drilled.

Oilwells, Pipelines, and Tankers

Most modern oilwells are made by boring with a revolving bit like that used by a carpenter when drilling a hole, only much bigger. The bit is fixed to lengths of drill-pipe slung by wire cables from a tall tower called a derrick. The drill-pipe passes through a turntable in the derrick floor. The drill-pipe is rotated by machinery driven, usually, by a diesel engine, although in very modern "turbo-drilling" electricity is sometimes used. As the hole deepens, fresh lengths of drill-pipe are added. An artificial mud is pumped down the drill-pipe and circulated continuously through holes in the bit and back up the sides of the hole. This mud is a very important material indeed, for not only does it clear away chips of rock from the bit, but also lubricates and cools the bit while its fluid pressure keeps the exposed walls from falling in. Later the hole is lined with steel casing and cemented. A very deep hole has several sets of casing, the width decreasing from about 45 centimeters (18 inches) at the top to about 10 centimeters (4 inches) at the bottom.

Unless care is taken, the oil may spurt

The Search for Petroleum

The remains of tiny plants and animals that once lived in the seas have been changed over millions of years into petroleum (oil). Today the petroleum lies deep beneath the surface of the Earth.

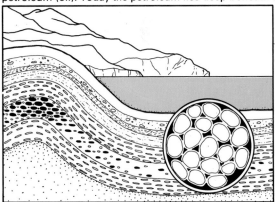

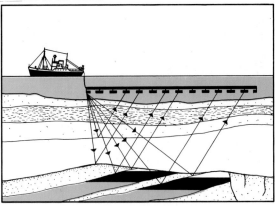

Oil can seep through certain types of rock, but not through others. When it meets a layer of hard, non-porous rock, it is trapped.

A survey ship uses echo-soundings to build up a picture of the rock structures under the sea. Scientists then decide where to make test drillings.

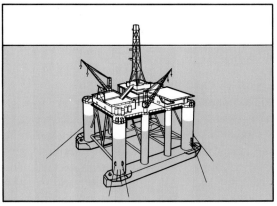

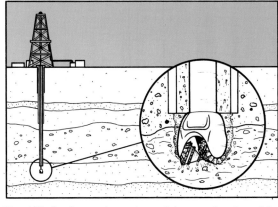

In difficult weather conditions, in the North Sea for instance, semi-submersible rigs are used for test drillings. They can be moved from place to place.

The drill-pipe bores down through layers of rock until it strikes oil. Drilling on land is much easier than offshore drilling.

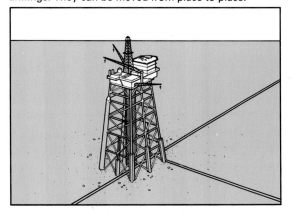

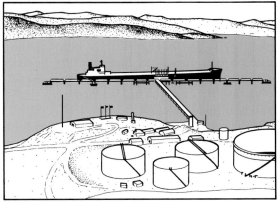

If the test is successful, the mobile rig is replaced by a fixed production platform. These huge structures are built on land and towed out to sea.

Oil is piped from the production platform to an onshore terminal. From there it is loaded on to tankers and shipped all round the world.

Courtesy, Standard Oil Company (N.J.)   *Courtesy, Standard Oil Company (N.J.)*

Left: Welding lengths of pipeline, used to carry oil overland. **Right:** Drilling for oil. When the drill bit becomes dull (blunt) it is brought out of the hole and the bit is replaced.

violently out of the hole when the drill reaches it, creating a "gusher" which wastes oil and risks fire. To prevent this, heavy drilling mud is used to weigh down the oil and a system of valves and pipes is arranged so that the pressure can be released slowly. When the natural pressure is unable to force the oil out of the well, it may either be pumped out or "repressured" by injecting gas at high pressure. This is called a "gas lift".

To carry large quantities of oil overland, pipelines are used. The pipes are made of steel and may be from 15 centimeters (6 inches) to 2 meters (6 feet) wide. The pipelines cross ravines, climb mountains, and burrow beneath rivers (see PIPELINE).

For carrying oil overseas, ships called tankers are used. They are specially designed with the engines at the stern, or rear end, most of the hull being divided into oil compartments. Large tankers carry oil more cheaply than smaller ones. As tankers of 550,000 tonnes (600,000 US tons) are now being built, the problem of finding suitable berths for them arises. Instead of using harbors, the tankers moor alongside floating buoys in deep water, unloading and loading through pipelines linked to storage tanks ashore.

Oil Refining

Crude oil is separated at a refinery into "fractions" such as gasoline and kerosine. These different fractions boil to form vapor (gas) at different temperatures and can therefore be separated by fractional distillation (see DISTILLATION). The crude oil is heated and pumped as a mixture of liquid and vapor into a tall steel tower called a fractionating column. The liquid flows out at the bottom, becoming heavy products such as fuel oil and bitumen. The vapors flow up the tower, cooling as they rise. The heavier oils such as diesel oil become liquid first and are drawn off from trays fixed at different levels. Gasoline vapor leaves the top of the tower and is then condensed to liquid.

Distillation is only the first stage in refining. The refiner must be able to treat crude oil to meet changing needs in various parts of the world. "Cracking", a high-temperature treatment, breaks heavy fractions into lighter ones and so increases the amount of gasoline. All substances are made of molecules which in turn are made up of atoms (see ATOM; MOLECULE). Petroleum molecules are hydrocarbons, which means they are formed of atoms of the two elements, carbon and hydrogen, but not all the molecules contain the same number of atoms. The molecules of fuel oil contain more atoms of hydrogen and carbon and are heavier than the molecules of kerosine. In the cracking process, heat and pressure are used to crack some of the heavier molecules into lighter molecules, almost as large stones might be cracked into gravel.

"Reforming" is the most important process in refining. It is a high-temperature, high-pressure treatment which changes the *shapes* rather than the sizes of the molecules. Hydrocarbon chains are "reformed" into ring or "aromatic" compounds, giving gasoline of superior quality.

Rosskam

Part of an alkylation plant. It produces a blending agent for high-octane fuels from waste refinery gases.

In the United States, for instance, a barrel of crude oil may well give 63 liters (16.6 US gallons) of gasoline and 22 liters (5.8 US gallons) of heavy fuel oil, but in the Middle East a barrel would give only 31 liters (8 US gallons) of gasoline but 63 liters (16.6 US gallons) of fuel oil. Petroleum is measured either by the barrel of 159 liters (42 US gallons) or, particularly when transported by sea, by the long ton (2,240 pounds, 1,016 kilograms) or the metric tonne (2,204.6 pounds, 1,000 kilograms.)

Some of the lesser known petroleum products have surprising uses. (See CHEMICAL INDUSTRY.) Candles and polishes contain petroleum waxes, and scents, cosmetics, and a substance to prevent cheese going bad are made out of the oils. Other petroleum oils are contained in the liquids used in sprays for killing insects. Gases obtained from refining operations are the source of products such as ethylene—used for artificially ripening tomatoes—and acetone, which is used in making artificial silk and nail polish. Other petroleum chemicals are the source of artificial rubber, plastics, and washing-up liquids. Many medicines, paints, and even substances such as chewing gum and high explosives, may contain petroleum products. Petroleum gases can be liquefied by cooling and compressing them, and bottled gases of this kind such as propane and butane are often used for lighting and cooking.

Natural Gas

In many countries natural gas obtained from oilwells on land or under the sea is piped to the towns and used for heating and lighting in factories and homes. The gas is separated from the oil and treated to remove the most inflammable vapors. Most of the natural gas is methane, sometimes known as marsh gas. It is found with petroleum and with coal but sometimes occurs by itself. Natural gas wells discovered in the United States in the early 19th century were referred to as "burning springs". Oil prospectors at first ignored the gas, the pressure of which served to drive the oil to the surface. The gas liberated from the oil at the surface was piped to a flare and burned as a gigantic torch. Wells that gave gas only were flared and allowed to burn themselves out over the years. The first use of natural gas was not made until the 1870s in the United States when experiments were made in piping it into houses.

The sources of domestic gas for many years have been the traditional gas-making processes using coal and naphtha, a light mineral oil, as raw material.

Natural gas is usually found thousands of meters below the surface, trapped in a layer of porous rock, such as sandstone, which is covered by a layer of impermeable rock. This layer prevents the gas from escaping. The search for the gas is conducted in the same way as the search for oil. Britain first began prospecting for natural gas in the 1930s, after it had been shown in the United States that it was possible to drill and tap the underground gas reservoirs and pipe the gas to the consumers in the towns. In the 1950s small deposits were found in Yorkshire, England, and near Edinburgh in Scotland.

Courtesy, British Gas

The drilling rig *Orion* operating in the North Sea.

In 1964 the first licenses were issued for exploration in the North Sea. Oil companies sent giant drilling rigs to prospect for gas and rich supplies were discovered off the eastern coast of England. The gas fields were large enough to supply Britain's demands for gas. Pipelines were laid under the sea to bring the gas ashore from the wells and into the new feeder mains running across the country. The North Sea operations are often made dangerous by bad weather and drilling rigs have been lost.

The greatest producers of natural gas are the United States and Russia. In Russia, a pipeline begun in 1967 now carries gas from western Siberia to the Urals and the countries of the western part of the Commonwealth of Independent States (CIS). The Netherlands exports gas to Germany, Belgium, and France from offshore fields in the North Sea. Australia also obtains gas from natural supplies.

In the late 1980s companies in several countries successfully began using the energy produced from methane gas found in decaying garbage heaps to drive turbines for making electricity.

Oil Supplies

Petroleum in large quantities is found in comparatively few areas. Russia and the United States, followed by Saudi Arabia, are the world's largest producers. The largest known reserves are in Saudi Arabia and Russia, in the Western part of northern Siberia. The United States is the largest consumer.

The Middle East is the region of the Earth with the largest known oil reserves. Apart from Saudi Arabia, Iran, Iraq, Kuwait, Qatar, and Abu Dhabi also have large quantities. These countries, along with Nigeria, Libya, Algeria, Indonesia, Ecuador, Gabon, and Venezuela, form the Organization of Petroleum Exporting Countries (OPEC) which negotiates the selling price of the oil.

Offshore drilling on the continental shelves around countries also takes place, for example in the British and Norwegian parts of the North Sea.

The world's proved reserves of oil are about 900,000 million barrels, over half of which is in the Middle East. This is oil which it is known can be taken out of the ground. More oil awaits discovery, especially offshore. As technology improves, it will be possible to recover oil from beneath very deep water, to release oil locked in shale deposits in the United States and in tar sands in western Canada, and maybe to tap more oil from existing fields. Present methods have to leave much of the oil in the ground.

Oil in a Changing World

In the 1970s experts warned that alternative sources of energy should be found quickly because the world's deposits of oil were being used up too rapidly. Between 1973 and 1974 the price of oil increased fourfold. People tried to save energy and use less oil; more oil fields were opened up. As a result oil became less scarce.

In the 1980s and 1990s scientists were giving a different reason for finding alternative sources of energy. When oil and other fossil fuels are burned, they produce carbon dioxide which contributes to the warming of the Earth's atmosphere. The possible consequences of this phenomenon, known as the "greenhouse effect", are discussed in the article CARBON DIOXIDE AND CARBON MONOXIDE.

PETS. People have kept animals as pets since earliest times. It is probable that the first domesticated, or tame, animals were kept as pets, perhaps by Stone Age children.

Courtesy, RSPCA

Children feel close to animals and have a natural curiosity about them. This is a white rat, an animal kept as a pet and also bred for medical experiments.

Animals kept as pets cannot go and find food, drink, and shelter, as their wild ancestors did. They must be cared for by their owners. There are a few general rules for the care of nearly all pets. First, animals should be given enough food of the right kind. It must contain the carbohydrates, fats, proteins, minerals, and vitamins essential for the animal's well-being. Next, enough clean drinking water should be provided. Third, the living quarters must not be cramped or wet and must be kept clean. The fourth rule is that animals needing exercise must be given regular opportunity to take it. Lastly, the animal itself must be kept clean and if it is sick must be attended to by a vet. (See VETERINARY MEDICINE.)

There are separate articles about some of the animals kept as pets. Use the Index volume to find them quickly. The following sections contain advice about the care of pets commonly kept.

Dogs

Puppies must be accustomed gradually to solid food before they are weaned from their mother. Very young puppies need five meals a day, but the number is gradually reduced as they grow bigger. A puppy should be fed canned puppy food or soaked puppy meal. These contain a formula to replace the mother's milk. It is best to avoid cow's milk, since this sometimes gives puppies an upset stomach. Adult dogs need only two meals a day – a light breakfast of dry or soaked dog meal and a main meal of meat (from a can of commercial dog food or freshly cooked) and dog meal. Most dogs enjoy fish: several canned varieties of dog food contain fish, but fresh cooked fish can also be given provided the bones are removed. Green vegetables should be added to fresh meat or fish to avoid vitamin deficiencies.

Small dogs can sleep in a box or basket, while large dogs should have a blanket or bean bag which is regularly brushed and washed. If the dog has a kennel it must be dry and should have a bed of clean straw. Dogs should be given plenty of exercise each day. Puppies should be taken to the vet to be vaccinated. Advice on house-training and local dog-training classes is available at the veterinarian's office. The dog's coat should be brushed daily and a long-haired dog needs combing. A bath with

Courtesy, R.S.P.C.A.

A girl grooms her pet dog by gently but firmly brushing its coat in the direction in which the hairs lie.

warm water and dog soap should be given as often as recommended for the breed. Long-haired dogs need particular attention to remove burrs, grass, and other objects picked up on the coat while running in the country. The owner's name and address must be on the dog's collar in case the dog should get lost.

Cats

Cats should be given two meals a day and should have a mixed diet. Chopped raw meat is best (for long-haired cats, lean meat) but cooked fish may be given instead. Cats tend to be more choosy than dogs. But most will happily eat canned foods. Starchy foods such as potatoes are not good for cats, and chicken bones or fish bones are dangerous. Mix green vegetables in the food occasionally. A saucer of clean water should always be available. Not all cats like milk. Kittens need to be accustomed gradually to solid food when they leave their mother at the age of five or six weeks. At first they need three or four meals a day.

The cat's sleeping place should be warm and out of a draft. A stout basket or lidless wooden box turned on its side makes a good bed. It should be raised from the floor, and should contain an old cushion covered with washable material and laid on thicknesses of newspaper. Cats are naturally clean animals and if they are given a pan of cat litter or clean dry earth or sand, they rarely make a mess indoors. A long-haired cat should be regularly brushed and combed.

Rabbits

Two meals a day keep rabbits healthy and the diet should be varied from among the following foods: cooked potatoes, hay, clover, waste bread, meal, leaves of cauliflower, broccoli, lettuce and dandelion, fresh grass, cow parsley, celery tops, carrots, and other roots, such as turnips. Mashes should be in a crumbly state, nearly dry. Never give a rabbit onions, potato stalks, raw potatoes, rhubarb, foxglove, geranium or chrysanthemum, or clippings of privet, yew or evergreen shrubs. Ask your local pet store for advice on packaged foods ready-made for rabbits.

Divide the rabbit hutch into a sleeping compartment and a day compartment with a round hole in the separating wall. The sleeping compartment should be dark and the day compartment open to the light, and fronted with wire netting. The floor in both compartments must be regularly and thoroughly cleaned. The hutch should be at least four times the length of the rabbit and three times its height. Drafts are harmful, so see that the hutch is well sheltered, and keep it off the ground. Cover the floor with wood chips, sawdust, or other suitable litter and over this spread straw or chaff. Hay should be used for bedding. Rabbits need exercise and an open-air run should be provided.

Guinea-Pigs

For guinea-pigs, a morning meal of bread and milk, not too moist, should be followed by a midday meal of greenstuff. The greenstuff may be leaves of broccoli or cauliflower, or groundsel, plantains, dandelions, parsley, watercress or chickweed. It must be fresh and clean. In the evening, give bran with a little meal, either dry or moistened to a crumbly state. Give cooked rice sometimes for a change. Guinea-pigs lose their appetites if they do not drink, so see that they have fresh water.

The hutch should be airy but without drafts. Close in the front with small-mesh wire netting and make a good big door so that the hutch can be cleaned easily. The bedding should be of dry straw, hay, or soft wood shavings and must be changed at least weekly. If possible, there should be an exercise run.

A long-haired guinea-pig needs regular brushing with a small hair-brush but should not be combed. If the sow (female) is going to have babies, she should be separated from the boar (male) shortly before the young are born, and kept apart from him until they are weaned; that is, until they are old enough to give up feeding from their mother's milk.

Mice

A pet mouse should have oats, coarse oatmeal, or bird seed, or a mixture of these, in the morning. It likes green food such as dandelion leaves or lettuce in the middle of the day and bread and milk at night. Occasionally a pet mouse can be given a small piece of carrot or apple.

A roomy cage is advisable and is ideally much like a rabbit hutch. Allow room for ladders and swings to be fixed so that the mice can take exercise and amuse themselves. A removable zinc tray at the bottom of the cage makes cleaning easier. Give the mice a clean bed of hay every week and strew litter on the tray after cleaning the cage.

Birds

Cage birds need to be fed on good seed and a little grit or sand to help them digest their food. For variety, they like millet, hemp, lettuce, apple, seeding grass, and groundsel. Sweet rape seed is good for canaries in winter. Every day, change the drinking water and fill the seed pan after blowing away the empty husks.

Most pet birds thrive best in an aviary (a room-sized cage). The aviary may be in the open, provided that the birds have a covered refuge for protection against cold and wet. The wire netting of the aviary must keep out cats, rats, and other predators. Perches should be made of rough branches, as aviary birds usually kill off living shrubs. The floor should be covered with sand or grass. The perches should not be round but oval and should be made of soft wood. Oval perches are more comfortable for the bird's claws to grip.

A bird cage should not be hung so that it is in the direct rays of the sun or in a draft; so do not hang it in the window. Fresh air is better for the birds than an overheated room. Parakeets like to fly about the room, but before letting them out see that doors and windows are closed.

Birds like to take a bath in a shallow bowl of water in the cage. Canaries may nest either in a nest-box or in a nest-pan, which is like a small hollow dish with a soft lining. The birds should also be given some extra soft material for nest-making. Parakeets must have a nest-box in which to lay their eggs. The nest-box contains a hollowed-out block of wood for the eggs. The hen parakeet lays about five eggs on each occasion of nesting and should not be allowed to nest more often than twice a year. (See also BUDGERIGAR; CANARY.)

Other Pets

Advice on the care of tortoises is given in the article TORTOISE. Goldfish should be kept not in a round glass bowl but in an aquarium, which is also necessary for tropical fish. There are separate articles AQUARIUM; GOLDFISH. There is a section on stables and the care of ponies in the article RIDING. See also the separate articles GERBIL and HAMSTER.

There are many books about the care of pets of different kinds. Whatever your pet, it is a good idea to consult a specialist book, or ask a friendly expert for advice. There are magazines for lovers of horses, dogs, cats, fish, and cage birds, while useful advice can also be had from the local pet store. To look after pets properly, the owner must know what they need. Mistakes made through ignorance are just as unkind to the pets as careless treatment. It is also wrong to keep wild or rare animals as pets. The best pet is a happy animal, well cared for and contented.

PETUNIA. The home of the petunia flower (*Petunia*) is South America, and it is especially common in Argentina and Brazil, so that its name has been taken from a Brazilian word. This word, *petun*, means "tobacco" and was given to the petunia because it belongs to the same family as the tobacco plant (Solanaceae). It is also related to the nightshade and the potato.

Petunias grow about 30 centimeters (12 inches) high and have rather small leaves. The big flowers grow singly and are funnel-shaped, with the petals spreading out at the top. They may be white, pink, puce (a brilliant bluish-pink) or purple, and sometimes they are striped. There are about 12 different species, or kinds, of petunias, some with sticky hairs all over the plants.

They are grown in greenhouses and in warm corners of gardens, where they flower freely in the late summer and autumn. They are widely used as summer bedding plants and are also very suitable flowers for growing in pots and hanging baskets.

NHPA/George Bernard

The garden petunia has many colorful varieties.

PEWTER is a silver-gray metal, usually made by alloying (mixing) tin with lead or copper. It began to be used instead of wood for plates and bowls in the Middle Ages. English pewter made in London, York, and Newcastle soon became known all over Europe for its high quality. The tin came from the county of Cornwall and much pewter was exported to the American colonies. Articles such as plates, jugs, trays, and salt cellars were made of "fine pewter" consisting of tin and copper, but the coarser articles such as pots, bowls, and candlesticks were of common pewter, containing lead instead of copper. Pewter went out of general use in the 19th century when crockery made from earthenware became

Barnaby's

English pewter beer mugs in pint and half-pint sizes.

cheap, but pewter beer-tankards are still made. Pewter is easily cast, or melted and poured into a mold having the shape of the article required. Tankards are first cast and then finished by hammering.

Pewter articles had the advantage of being unbreakable and fairly cheap, but they were easily bent or dented because of the softness of the metal. Traveling pewterers went around the country to recast damaged articles. That is why, although pewter candlesticks and mugs are often seen as ornaments in people's houses, really old pewter is rare.

PHALAROPE. Phalaropes are nicknamed "little swimming sandpipers". They belong to the order of shore birds, which includes such larger species as gulls and auks. They are among the smallest of the group, ranging in size from 20 to 25 centimeters (8 to 10 inches). As they inhabit the marshes and wide open spaces, it is not surprising that the birds are unknown to most persons.

The phalaropes somewhat resemble tiny ducks in appearance. They have a heavy, duck-like plumage which protects them from the icy waters. Their feet are partly webbed, and they are expert swimmers. Their food is insects such as mosquitos, and small marine life.

Unlike most birds, the female phalarope is more brightly colored than the male. It is she who does the courting of the shy male. The male builds the nest and hatches the eggs, completely reversing the accepted order of bird life. For example, in the red phalarope (*Phalaropus fulicarius*), which nests in the far north, the male's plumage is dull cinnamon, with a reddish breast. He does all the work. The female has an upper coat of rich brown, and underparts wine red.

Phalaropes have lobed toes for swimming. The females are more brightly colored than the males.

Both have white patches on the cheeks, but the female's are more pronounced. They nest in hollows in the ground, with a poor lining of moss or grass.

The northern phalarope (*Lobipes lobatus*) is found in both the northern parts of the Old World and the New. It is abundant in Greenland and Alaska. In summer, flocks of these birds may be seen along the New England coast in the United States. They are so small that they can not be seen from any great distance. The female is richly dressed in gray and white, streaked with yellowish brown. There are patches of red and of white on the throat. The male has a dull brown back and white underparts. Both the red phalarope and northern phalarope change their plumage according to the seasons. In winter their plumage is a white and pale-brown mixture that blends with the winter landscape. Their summer shades are bright.

PHARAOH is the Hebrew form of the Egyptian word *per-'o* and is the name used in the Bible for the kings of ancient Egypt. At first *per'o*, "the great house", meant the royal palace but it later came to be another name for the king. For descriptions of famous pharaohs see EGYPT, ANCIENT, and TUTANKHAMUN.

The kings of ancient Egypt began to be known also as pharaohs during the New Kingdom, which started about 1570 BC. Pharaoh was a term of respect but never a formal title. The pharaoh was the chief patron of arts and sciences and he was the high priest of all the many gods worshipped in Egypt. More importantly, the people worshipped the pharaoh as a god himself. They identified him with the sky-god Horus and with the sun-gods Amon, Aton, and Re. On his death they believed he was changed into Osiris, the god of the dead. The pharaoh had supreme power and his decisions and laws were regarded as divine decrees. The pyramids, the enormous tombs built for the pharaohs in the desert near Memphis, are symbols of the vastness of the royal power and of the pharaoh's divine role as a mediator between gods and men.

PHARISEES. Between 200 BC and AD 200 the Pharisees were a major Jewish religious group. The word Pharisee in the Aramaic language means "separated one" and this explains what the party stood for. They were very strict in their religious behavior and regarded their fellow-countrymen as far too easy-going in religious matters. Hence they were looked on as separated from the rest of the Jews. In particular they stood for the strict observance of all the rules laid down in the Law of Moses in the Old Testament.

This led them into conflict with Jesus Christ who believed that these laws, though important, sometimes had to be interpreted according to the spirit rather than the letter. For example, the Pharisees thought that in order to keep the Sabbath holy, no one should lift a finger to do any work at all. Jesus also believed in this fourth commandment, but at the same time he believed that if someone was ill, then it was acceptable to break the commandment in order to help him.

Some of the Pharisees were very good people, but as a religious party they opposed Jesus Christ and their leaders played a big part in the events leading to his trial and crucifixion. They were so intent on keeping all the rules of their religion that they lost its heart and spirit, and so could not accept Jesus as what he claimed to be, the Messiah (savior) for whom all Jews had been waiting so long. They thought Jesus was guilty of blasphemy when he claimed to be the Messiah, and it was this that made them demand his death.

PHEASANT. There are some 50 species of pheasant, long-tailed birds that feed on seeds, berries, and insects in fields and open woodlands. Although they roost in trees, they feed on the ground. Unlike grouse, pheasants have bare nostrils and legs. Male pheasants usually have beautiful plumage, and spurs at the base of their legs used for fighting for their mates during the breeding season. Pheasants have a noisy, whirring flight and the cock birds have a loud, crowing call.

NHPA/E. A. Janes

A male common pheasant feeding. The cock's plumage is much more colorful than the hen's.

Pheasants are popular game birds ("game" means they are shot for sport and food) and their flesh is good to eat. Many kinds have been introduced round the world from their native Asia. The common pheasant (*Phasianus colchicus*) is found right across Asia from the Caucasus mountains to Japan. There are many different races of this bird including the ring-necked pheasant that was introduced into Europe in the 18th century and to Australia and North America during the latter part of the 19th century.

The male common pheasant mates with two or three females. The nest is a simple hollow scraped in the ground under cover of brambles or grasses. It is lined with leaves and grass and the hen lays 8 to 15 olive-brown eggs.

Some pheasants have truly spectacular coloring and are very popular in wildfowl collections; they include Lady Amherst's pheasant (*Chrysolophus amherstiae*) and the golden pheasant (*Chrysolophus pictus*). Among the most brightly colored pheasants are the monals of southern Central Asia, for example, the male Himalayan impeyan (*Lophophorus impejanus*) with a metallic green head and throat, coppery nape and neck, purplish wings, white back, orange tail, and black under parts. Tragopons, or horned pheasants, are also among the world's most brightly colored birds.

PHILADELPHIA is the largest city in the state of Pennsylvania and the fifth largest in the United States. It is located in the southeastern corner on the Delaware River, where the Schuylkill River flows into the Delaware. The city lies in part on the upland Piedmont Plateau and partly on the low Atlantic coastal plain. About 150 kilometers (95 miles) northeast of Philadelphia is New York City, and 140 kilometers (88 miles) down the Delaware River lies the Atlantic Ocean.

The city has witnessed some of the key events of American history, and its historic buildings attract thousands of tourists annually. It was at the hub of the 19th-century industrial revolution and is now a major industrial center.

Industry, Trade, and Transportation

Philadelphia's growth was made possible by its nearness to coal, petroleum, water power, and other natural resources, and by its location on the north and south trade routes of the Delaware River and Atlantic Ocean. Leading industries include manufacture of textiles, carpets, clothing, paper, chemicals, glassware, and railroad cars, oil refining, shipbuilding, metalworking, shipbuilding, sugar refining, and printing and publishing. Its oil refineries are among the oldest on the Atlantic seaboard.

ZEFA

Philadelphia lies on the Delaware River. The Franklin Bridge crosses the river in the background.

The Philadelphia industrial area, stretching from Boston to Virginia, accounts for a large amount of the United States' output of finished wool textiles, lamp shades, carpets and rugs, children's dresses, refined petroleum and refined sugar. It is also a center for radio and television manufacturing.

The city is one of the largest freshwater ports in the world and handles more shipping than any other in the United States except New York City. About half of this traffic is accounted for by movement between Philadelphia and other United States ports. Imports of petroleum, sugar, sulfur, nitrates, iron, and manganese ore come into Philadelphia through a deep channel to the Atlantic. Petroleum products, coal, grain, flour, textiles, lumber, railroad equipment, and other manufactured goods are shipped out.

Philadelphia has two airports and good railroad connections. A large transportation system operates inside the city. There are buses, a subway, and streetcars. Several bridges cross the Delaware River, including the Benjamin Franklin Bridge, span the Delaware.

An Historic City

The criss-cross pattern of Philadelphia's streets follows the original plan of the city's founder, William Penn (on whom there is a separate article). He named the city from the Greek word meaning "city of brotherly love". The heart of the city is Penn Square, which

has the City Hall. Its tower, rising to a height of more than 150 meters (500 feet) is topped by an 11-meter (37-foot) statue of William Penn. Around the City Hall is the main business district of banks, office buildings, department stores, shops, and railroad terminals. The oldest stock exchange in the United States was founded (1790) in the city. East of Broad Street to the Delaware River is the old city—the Philadelphia of William Penn and Benjamin Franklin. Here are Independence Hall, Congress Hall, Carpenters' Hall, Christ Church, and other notable buildings.

Independence Hall, which stands on Chestnut Street, was completed in 1756 as the Pennsylvania State House. It was the meeting place of the Continental Congress when the Declaration of Independence was signed. It was the scene of George Washington's appointment to the command of the Continental Army, and was the place where the Articles of Confederation were signed. The Constitutional Convention framed the Constitution of the United States at Independence Hall in 1787.

The Liberty Bell, rung when the Declaration of Independence was signed, is preserved in a special pavilion near Independence Hall. The bell was made in England in 1751, but had to be remade twice before it was hung in the State House. The bell cracked in 1835 while tolling the death of John Marshall, chief justice of the Supreme Court.

To the west of Independence Hall stands Congress Hall. This was the capitol of the United States from 1790 to 1800. At the other end of the block is the old City Hall. It was the home of the Supreme Court of of the United States from 1791 to 1800. Near by is Carpenters' Hall, where the first Continental Congress met in 1774. It lies on Elfeth's Alley, the oldest continuously inhabited street in the United States.

Other historic buildings in the old part of Philadelphia are the First Bank of the United States and the Second Bank of the United States. The Second Bank building was long used as the Custom House and now is a national historic shrine. Other historic places in Philadelphia include Old Swedes' Church, now Gloria Dei Episcopal Church, built 1698–1700, the oldest of the city's more than 1,000 churches. St. George's Methodist Church is said to be the oldest Methodist church in the world, dating from 1769. Benjamin Franklin's tomb is at Fifth and Arch streets.

Near Independence Hall is the Hall of the Philosophical Society, begun by Franklin in 1743. The University of Pennsylvania, dating from 1740, established the first school of medicine in the American colonies. Its campus occupies a large section of West Philadelphia.

Among other educational institutions is the Penn Charter School, which operates under a charter dating from 1701. Philadelphia has many other schools, colleges, and institutes of education.

Philadelphia has always been a musical center. The Philadelphia Orchestra, founded in 1900, is known throughout the world. The Philadelphia Museum of Art is one of the largest buildings in the city and one of the greatest art museums in the world.

In 1876, the Centennial Exhibition, which was the country's first international exposition, was held in Philadelphia to celebrate the 100th anniversary of the Declaration of Independence.

PHILIP II of Macedon (382–336 BC) gained control of the whole of Greece, laying the foundation of the empire of his son Alexander the Great. In 367 BC he was given as a hostage to the Thebans. He spent three years in Thebes, where he learned the use of the phalanx formation of infantry in war from its inventor Epaminondas. Philip's brother Perdiccas had inherited the kingdom of Macedon, or Macedonia as it is better known, but in 359 BC he was killed during a revolt of the hill tribes. Philip seized the throne and began to create a Macedonian national army. He conquered the hill tribes and then turned his eyes to Greece.

In 358 BC he took the Athenian colony Amphipolis which gave access to the gold

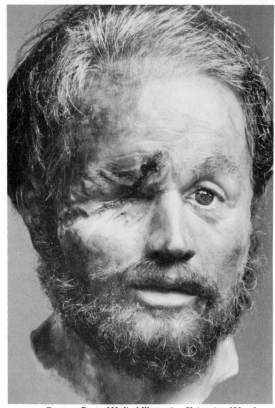

Courtesy, Dept. of Medical Illustration, University of Manchester
A wax reconstruction of the head of Philip II, showing the arrow wound that scarred his face.

mines of Mount Pangaeus, and later he founded the city of Philippi at the mines. Then two other cities fell to him. He was able to calm the suspicions of the Greeks by promising to return Amphipolis to Athens and by handing over the newly taken cities to the Olynthian Confederation. In 352 BC he suddenly advanced into Thessaly and Magnesia and occupied them, and in 347 captured Olynthus. The following year Philip allied himself with the city of Thebes, and crushed the Phocians.

Philip was a brilliant diplomat. By costly bribes and promises he had kept Athens from offering resistance while he made himself master of Greece. His victory over the Phocians allowed him to pose as the deliverer of Greece, for the Phocians had scandalized everyone by occupying the holy city of Delphi. In 346 BC he held the Pythian Games at Delphi and presided over them, thereby showing that

PHILIP II of Spain

Professor M. Andronicos

This miniature ivory head is thought to be a portrait of Philip II. Compare it with the modern reconstruction on page 315.

PHILIP II of Spain (1527–98) was the son of the Holy Roman Emperor Charles V, who was at the same time king of Spain. Philip was brought up as a Spaniard. In 1555 he was entrusted by his father with the government of the Netherlands. In 1556 Charles V abdicated. His son Ferdinand took the empire, while to Philip were left Spain, Spanish America, the Spanish possessions in Italy, and the Netherlands. Philip's kingdom was a threat to France. England was Spain's ally by Philip's marriage with Queen Mary I. Flanders on the north and Spain on the south aided in encircling France.

The Bridgeman Art Library

A satirical painting of Philip II, whose painstaking involvement in every branch of government was famous.

he considered himself a Greek and not a foreign conqueror. In Athens, Demosthenes, ever his enemy, accused him of destroying the liberties of Greece (see DEMOSTHENES). But a strong party, led by Isocrates, saw him as a leader who would end the petty quarrels of the Greek cities and lead them all in a crusade against Persia.

For the next few years Philip was engaged in extending his power to the north. Although Philip was recognized as captain general of the Greeks, he was assassinated before he could complete his plans. Alexander the Great, Philip's son by his queen Olympias, succeeded him.

In AD 1977–78, archeologists working at Verginia, northern Greece, unearthed three royal tombs, in one of which they found the partly burned remains of a man. The man is thought to be Philip II.

But the whole scene changed when Elizabeth I came to the throne of England. Both England and the Netherlands adopted the Protestant religion. Philip was a devout Catholic and nothing could shake his belief that he was the person chosen by God to punish the Protestants. Moreover, the English under Elizabeth were raiding Spanish ships, and France was a political enemy. Philip only added to his difficulties when he tried to enforce Catholicism in the Netherlands by war. Grave and self-possessed, he was disliked by all but the Spaniards. He was no soldier, but a fanatically keen administrator. He made all the decisions that affected his kingdom, and worked day and night reading and drafting messages. But his industry and thriftiness were his ruin. He would not trust his generals and admirals, and he would not provide them with enough money. The Netherlands won its independence, and England shattered the armada that was sent against it in 1588 (see ARMADA, SPANISH). Three later armadas were unsuccessful because they were ill equipped and led by admirals whom Philip had chosen without regard to naval ability. Towards the end of his life he was tortured by dreadful skin diseases, but he never ceased working. For 50 days and nights before his death he lay in the chapel of the Escorial monastery, surrounded by chanting monks and priests.

PHILIPPINES. Some 800 kilometers (500 miles) off the coast of southeast Asia between Taiwan and Indonesia, is a large group of islands called the Philippines. Together they form the republic of the Philippines, which has been an independent country since 1946. It was formerly ruled by the United States and, until 1898, by Spain. The capital is Manila.

ZEFA

Wonderfully sculptured terraces high up in the north of Luzon. Rice is the staple crop of the Philippines.

Palawan, Panay, Mindoro, Leyte, Cebu, Bohol, and Masbate. Among the smaller islands is the chain known as the Sulu Archipelago.

Land and Climate

Most of the Philippine islands are mountainous, with the main ranges and river valleys generally running north and south. The highest mountain is Mount Apo, at 2,954 meters (9,692 feet) in Mindanao. Like some other mountains in the Philippines, it is an active volcano. Another is Mayon at 2,410 meters (7,907 feet) in southern Luzon, which is crowned at night with a fiery glow.

The rainfall is heavy, and in the lowlands temperatures are warm to hot throughout the year. Violent winds called typhoons, accompanied by torrential rains, sometimes strike the northern islands and do great damage. Earthquakes occur, but they are seldom severe. The Philippine forests cover more than two-fifths of the total land area. Although they have been depleted by illegal cutting of trees they still contain some of the finest timber in the world. It includes hardwoods such as mahogany, as well as many softwoods, including pine. There are also 800 species of orchid.

There are few large wild animals, the main

Altogether, there are more than 7,000 islands, though many are only small rocky islets. The area of the islands measures about 1,770 kilometers (1,100 miles) north to south and 1,050 kilometers (650 miles) east to west. The largest islands are Luzon in the north of the group and Mindanao in the south. The other chief islands are Samar, Negros,

A stilted-village on Mindanao inhabited by sea gypsies and pearl fishermen.

ZEFA

ones being crocodiles, pythons, and buffaloes. More numerous are the smaller animals, among which are deer, mongooses, otters, wildcats, monkeys, rats, and poisonous snakes. Large fruit-eating bats are common and there are more than 750 kinds of bird. The waters surrounding the Philippines are rich in marine life. The pearls obtained from oysters in the Sulu Archipelago are famous, and so are the many beautiful varieties of Philippine seashells.

Peoples and Towns

The people of the Philippines are known as Filipinos. Most are brown-skinned Malays, who came to the Philippines from other Pacific islands and from southeast Asia. The vast majority are Roman Catholic, although the Moros of Palawan and the southern islands are Muslim. The population also includes people of Indian and Chinese descent. The *mestizos*, people of mixed descent, are usually Malay on one side and Spanish or Chinese on the other. There are scores of languages and dialects, of which Tagalog, a Malay language, is the most common. Although Spanish influence is still strong, English is widely spoken and is the language used most in government and business.

In the country districts, most Filipinos live in bamboo or other wooden houses that have steep thatched roofs and sliding shutters of woven matting. The houses are often raised off the ground on stilts, and the cattle and pigs shelter underneath. The people wear light cotton clothing of Western type, and their chief foods are rice, corn, vegetables, and fish. The typical town or village is built round a *plaza*, or square, with a Roman Catholic church built in Spanish style. The people are fond of their local, Spanish-flavored music and nearly every village has its traditional band. Baseball and basketball are popular sports. The education system is one of the best in southeast Asia.

The capital and largest city of the Philip-

FACTS ABOUT THE PHILIPPINES

AREA: 300,000 square kilometers (115,800 square miles).
POPULATION: 59,906,000 (1989).
GOVERNMENT: Independent republic.
CAPITAL: Manila, 1,728,400.
CITIES: Quezon City, 1,165,865; Davao, 610,375; Cebu, 490,281; Caloocan, 467,816.
ECONOMY. Products and exports.
    Agriculture: Sugar-cane, coconuts, rice, corn, bananas and plantains, copra, cassava, pineapples, timber, fish.
    Minerals: Coal, petroleum, natural gas, limestone, copper, chromite, silver, gold.
    Manufacturing: Food items, beverages, chemicals, electrical machinery, petroleum products, iron and steel products, textiles and clothes.
    Exports: Electrical machinery, coconut oil, clothing, ores and metals, cork and wood, bananas, sugar, canned pineapples.
EDUCATION: All children go to school between the ages of 7 and 13.

pines is Manila in central Luzon (see MANILA). From 1948 to 1976 Quezon City, just outside Manila, was the national capital. The other cities are much smaller than Manila; they include Davao, on Mindanao, and Cebu, on Cebu island.

Fishing and Farming

Although most Filipinos live in villages and work as farmers or fishermen, the country has to import food. The growing of crops is not easy in the mountainous regions. In the highlands of northern Luzon, for example, there are people called the Ifugao who grow rice on irrigated terraces built up on steep mountainsides. Fish are bred in ponds of fresh water. Besides rice, corn, bananas, and coconuts grown as food for the people, the main crops are sugar, copra (dried coconut kernel), and abaca, a plant which is used to make rope and cord. To assist them in their farm work the Filipinos use carabao (water buffalo) more than horses, oxen or machinery. Timber is exported and used locally in the making of furniture. Oil, dyes, and other chemicals are also produced from Philippine trees. Minerals including gold, copper, manganese, chromium, and iron ores are exported.

ZEFA

Children ride a water buffalo – an indispensable beast of burden, particularly in the rice paddies.

The people make baskets, hats, mats, and woven fabrics in their homes. There are few large factories, but the government has encouraged light industries, such as the assembly of electrical and electronic goods. Other industries include processed foods, chemicals, textiles, rubber, and wood products. Most of the factories are near Manila.

A railroad runs most of the length of Luzon, and there are short lines in Panay and Cebu. Land travel is chiefly by road, but most of the roads are unpaved, and a good network for commercial traffic is lacking. Although the islands are linked by air services, most passengers and goods travel between them in launches and small coastal vessels.

History

The ancestors of the people of the Philippines came from Asia in migrations spread over many thousands of years, long before the arrival of Europeans. It was from Borneo, in the 15th century, that the Muslim religion was introduced into the southern Philippines. Christianity was introduced by the Spanish soon afterwards.

The European discovery of the Philippines occurred in 1521, when Ferdinand Magellan's Spanish expedition reached the island of Cebu, in the course of the first ever voyage round the world. Magellan was later killed by islanders on Maran, but other members of his party survived and managed to get home again. Spain sent out more expeditions and laid claim to the islands, naming them Philippines after Prince Philip of Asturias, (a province in northwest Spain). Philip later became king Philip II of Spain. However, there was no permanent Spanish settlement in the Philippines until 1565, when General Miguel Lopez de Legazpi started one on Cebu. A few years later he established Manila as the capital.

By 1600 most of the tribes had recognized Spanish rule and had been converted to Roman Catholicism. The only important tribe successfully to resist the Spaniards were the fierce and well organized Muslims of Mindanao, Palawan, and the Sulu Archipelago. The Spaniards called these people Moros (in English, Moors), after the Arab Muslims who had once conquered Spain.

The Chinese, Japanese, Portuguese, Dutch, and British were also all opposed to the Spanish occupation of the Philippines, chiefly because they too wanted the islands' gold and other riches.

To hold on to its power in the Philippines, Spain had to make greater use of force. Finally, in 1851, the chief Moro stronghold at Jolo was captured and the Manila government claimed control of the whole group of islands. Later, however, the Moros began to be rebellious again, while other Filipinos demanded big social and government reforms. Spain rejected the most important of these demands and executed Dr. José Rizal, the greatest of the Filipino leaders. Then the spirit of rebellion grew among the people.

In 1896–97 there occurred in Luzon the first revolution aimed at national independence. The revolution was put down but Spain needed a large army to do it. The outbreak of the Spanish-American War in 1898 was the signal for Filipino nationalists, under General Emilio Aguinaldo, to seize power; and when the war ended in American victory, the nationalists controlled most of Luzon. However, the peace treaty gave the Philippines to the United States. In 1899 the islanders rebelled again and fought for three years before being defeated by American troops.

American rule brought better schools and other improvements to the Philippines. As a first step towards independence, the islands became a commonwealth under American control, with an elected president and parliament, in 1934. During World War II Japan conquered the Philippines and ruled them harshly until driven out by the Americans in 1945.

From Independence in 1946

In 1946 the Philippines became independent. The United States helped to repair the damage done by the fighting. Much of Manila had been destroyed, and agriculture, mining, and other industries had been crippled. Also the Hukbalahaps, a Communist-led group who had fought against the Japanese, were in rebellion against the government. But President Ramon Magsaysay (in office from 1953 to 1957) brought in reforms to give the peasants more land and the army put down the rebellion.

In 1965 Ferdinand Marcos became President. He ruled the country under martial (military) law from 1972 to 1981 and was re-elected President after lifting martial law. Muslim unrest, poverty, corrupt government, and a fast-growing population were major problems in the 1980s. After a disputed election in 1986, Marcos was succeeded by Corazon Aquino, the wife of the country's main opposition leader, who was murdered in 1983. In 1989 an attempted coup against Mrs Aquino was put down by government forces helped by the United States Air Force.

PHILISTINES. The Philistines were a people who settled in a strip of country along the southern coast of Palestine in the 12th century BC. This area was known as Philistia, and the Philistines also gave their name to the whole country of Palestine, in a slightly different form.

The Philistines were the traditional enemies of the Hebrews. It is thought that they came originally from the coast of Asia Minor (now part of Turkey), and the Aegean Islands. In the days of Abraham, their capital was Gerar, and Abimelech was their king. By the time of Joshua they had come to possess more territory – the fertile land of western Palestine – and had the five strong cities of Gaza, Ashdod, Ascalon, Gath, and Ekron.

Joshua fought the Philistines but did not manage to drive them out, although for a time he held Gaza, Ascalon, and Ekron. By the time of the Judges, Israel was constantly being attacked, and sometimes enslaved, by the Philistines. Samuel fought a great battle against them at Mizpeh and defeated them, but they grew strong again and continued to trouble Israel. Saul fought against them and David killed their champion Goliath (see DAVID). Solomon was strong and held them in check, but whenever Israel was weak they reappeared, often with other non-Jewish tribes living in the lands bordering Palestine.

The term "Philistine" is still used today to describe someone who is indifferent or hostile to culture. The Israelites were contemptuous of their enemies' lack of learning.